CAMBRIDGE STUDIES IN AMERICAN LITERATURE AND CULTURE

The American T. S. Eliot

Cambridge Studies in American Literature and Culture

Editor
Albert Gelpi, Stanford University

Advisory board
Nina Baym, *University of Illinois, Champaign-Urbana*
Sacvan Bercovitch, *Harvard University*
Richard Bridgman, *University of California, Berkeley*
David Levin, *University of Virginia*
Joel Porte, *Cornell University*
Eric Sundquist, *University of California, Berkeley*
Mike Weaver, *Oxford University*

The American T. S. Eliot
A Study of the Early Writings

ERIC SIGG

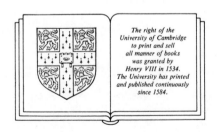

The right of the
University of Cambridge
to print and sell
all manner of books
was granted by
Henry VIII in 1534.
The University has printed
and published continuously
since 1584.

CAMBRIDGE UNIVERSITY PRESS

Cambridge
New York   Port Chester   Melbourne   Sydney

Published by the Press Syndicate of the University of Cambridge
The Pitt Building, Trumpington Street, Cambridge CB2 1RP
32 East 57th Street, New York, NY 10022, USA
10 Stamford Road, Oakleigh, Melbourne 3166, Australia

First published 1989

Printed in the United States of America

Library of Congress Cataloging-in-Publication Data
Sigg, Eric Whitman.
The American T. S. Eliot : a study of the early writings / Eric
W. Sigg.
p.   cm. – (Cambridge studies in American literature and
culture)
Bibliography: p.
Includes index.
ISBN 0-521-36561-9
1. Eliot, T. S. (Thomas Stearns), 1888–1965 – Criticism and
interpretation.   I. Title.   II. Series.
PS3509.L43Z8653 1989   88-24040
821'.912 – dc 19   CIP

British Library Cataloguing in Publication Data
Sigg, Eric W.
The American T. S. Eliot : a study of the
early writings. – (Cambridge studies in
American literature and culture).
1. Poetry in English. Eliot, T. S. (Thomas
Stearns), 1888–1965
I. Title
821'.912

ISBN 0-521-36561-9 hard covers

Contents

Preface

Having written keeping certain assumptions in mind, I should like to acknowledge them before proceeding. Though discussing Eliot's poetry published after 1927 only briefly, and mentioning his plays hardly at all, I have drawn from Eliot's critical writing throughout his career. I have supposed that as is often true of modern poets (Pound, Williams, and Stevens come to mind), Eliot's critical prose offers the best avenue into his poetry. And I have assumed that Eliot's deep American past, extending far back in time before his birth, influenced his interests, his problems, and his poetry. I affirm these conclusions even though some of Eliot's formulations, notably his statements about the poet's impersonality, have tended to mislead readers and critics, at least as that theory has been commonly applied. Fortunately, ever since Randall Jarrell's famous apostrophe on this topic in "Fifty Years of American Poetry," Eliot's audience has been less reluctant to bring the poet and his poems into more accurate relation, a relation Eliot's own subsequent comments authorized in any event.

To few poets have biographical considerations, especially in the senses in which I have applied them, been so relevant yet so curiously ignored. Every sort of writing Eliot did has a root in his personal past, especially insofar as it involves the historical past. Examining Eliot's life pattern, St. Louis to Boston to Europe to England, we trace everywhere his tense, complicated relation to New England, to his extraordinary family, to their religion, and to his native land. In Eliot's case, his family's moral and historical consciousness translates somehow – and though most of my remarks reflect on this operation sooner or later, I should be happier to have articulated precisely *how* it takes place – into aesthetic and stylistic self-consciousness. In that translation rest the riddles and divisions of Eliot's consciousness, as well as significant sources of his literary achievement.

Ignoring the links between Eliot's writing in various forms means that a good deal of the poetry may be misread, that it and much of Eliot's prose will make less sense than they might, and that sometimes it might make little sense at all. The various writings Eliot published form a set of parallel texts, and they should be read to discover their connections with one another. Regrettably, by far the greater part of Eliot's prose, because it has never been collected and published in an accessible format, never appears in critical discussions of his poetry. Though this is changing, Eliot's critics, by allowing him to establish the canon of his own criticism, have largely permitted him to define the ambit of the discussion, as it were, from the grave. The fugitive literature reveals how productive, wide ranging, and complex a thinker and writer Eliot was apart from his poetry, even when, as is often true, the poetry supplies this prose with what interest it may contain. Leaving such a huge body of Eliot's prose unexplored means that significant dimensions not only of the man but of his poetry will remain hidden.

To reiterate, my remarks assume about Eliot, his career, and his writing what ought to be obvious about them but which has received insufficient attention despite Eliot's own acknowledgments on this score. I refer to his American – distinctly, self-consciously, irrevocably American – heritage. The ambivalence pervading his writing, his surprising and sometimes bizarre opinions on diverse subjects, his theoretical inconsistencies, and the relations – both continuities and gaps – between his critical dicta and poetic practice: these troublesome matters, and perhaps less demonstrably many of the beautiful and striking qualities of his poetry, partake of American facts and traditions insofar as Eliot preserved or overthrew them.

If religious conversion shaped his later years, Eliot's early life turned on his expatriation. This fact, which places Eliot in the tradition of those Americans who have found life – especially a literary or artistic life – insupportable in the United States, counts as not the least of the live issues Eliot's example raises. Such exiles represent the casualties of the country's nervously experimental nature, of its sense of social incompletion, of its unexamined sense of what it is. As Eliot wrote in "The Social Function of Poetry," "no art is more stubbornly national than poetry." That extremes of ideology, religion, race, manners, and habits of thinking and living exist within American borders, that such extremes remain at odds with one another and with constitutional, democratic, and other civil dogma, and that the ambiguities produced by these extremes place some individuals and perhaps the entire society under chronic pressure are truths that seem self-evident. That it rebels against its own past and against its own identity, wishing to keep its future open-ended, makes American culture unique, but also uniquely vulnerable and perhaps uniquely ill at ease. Into this permanently paradoxical society Eliot matured, and out of it his ambivalences grew.

My remarks do not, however, explore only narrowly national matters. Each chapter focuses upon a particular issue or set of issues, qualify-
ing or elaborating others as they proceed. The sequence is simply chronological: Chapter 1 explores Eliot's early life and the lives of his family
before him, later chapters move sequentially through the major literary
and other texts of his early writing, and Chapter 6 concludes by discussing *The Waste Land*. Because Eliot's thought contains innumerable cir-
clings and switchbacks, however, when it is relevant to do so the discussion abandons both chronology and the time restraint imposed by Eliot's
"early" writing.

Both halves of the title, that is, are equally important. Along with its
American focus, this study also examines the early writing as an entity
with its own themes and shape, and as a stage in the progress of Eliot's
entire career. To pursue both the movement and the stability of Eliot's
thought and imagination, using evidence throughout his writing, the
discussion freely refers to developments after 1927. The events of that
year, though clearly changing Eliot's life and point of view, also cast
another light on what had come before. Confining a book of this sort to
the first half of Eliot's life and poetic career may make it manageable; it
need not make it arbitrary.

A thematic sequence parallels the chronological one. My remarks seek
to show how Eliot's interests and problems originated in American life.
But they propose to demonstrate as well how his imagination resorted to
three systems – philosophy, poetry, and religion – which at various
times but in roughly that order seemed progressively to mediate difficulties of self, art, and spirit. Eliot's career produced a sequence of attempts
to unite extremes, resolve ambivalences, and harmonize the dissonance
between and within the self and society. It is this progression that the
following remarks, likewise sequentially, endeavor to set forth.

I am pleased to have this chance to thank my parents, Robert and Patricia
Sigg, and my grandmother, Marion Day Davies, for their help and
encouragement; to acknowledge the personal and scholarly inspiration of
my teachers, Richard Lanham and Edward Tayler; to recognize the critical and editorial acuity of Albert Gelpi and Robert Byrnes; and to thank
Elizabeth Maguire and Andrew Brown at Cambridge for their dedicated
efforts on behalf of this book. The notes provide details of quotations
used by permission.

Los Angeles, California
August 1988

1

The Souls of the Devout

In New England, where education and liberty spring from morality and religion and where an already old and long-settled society has been able to shape its own maxims and habits, the people, though rid of all forms of superiority ever created by wealth or birth among men, are accustomed to respect intellectual and moral superiority and to submit thereto without displeasure; and so we find New England democracy making choices better than those made elsewhere. . . . But [in] the new states of the Southwest, where the body of society, formed yesterday, is nothing but an agglomeration of speculators and adventurers, one is appalled to see into what hands public authority has been entrusted, and one wonders by what power, independent of legislation and of men, the state has been able to grow and society to prosper.

De Tocqueville, *Democracy in America*

The essential idea of humanity is not derived from weakness and sin, but from that mysterious connection of the soul and body, – the immortal spirit with the corruptible flesh, – by which the soul is made subject to earthly influence. Our spiritual nature is probably the same, in its elements, with that of the most exalted archangel.

Rev. William Greenleaf Eliot, *Discourses on the Doctrines of Christianity*

Too much pudding choked the dog.

Henry Ware Eliot, Sr., on why he chose not to become a Unitarian minister

FAMILY, NATION, AND RELIGION

The primary channel of transmission of culture is the family: no man wholly escapes from the kind, or wholly surpasses the degree, of culture which he acquired from his early environment.[1]

1

T. S. Eliot's distinctly uncontroversial definition of culture begins where human life and consciousness begin, in the family. He published it in 1948, however, as a man who had tried to succeed in youth at the very thing he calls impossible in maturity. As the phrases unfold, the absolute "no man" precedes the less confident "wholly," which in turn qualifies the vivid predicates "escapes" and "surpasses," suggesting freedom and aspiration. No man, that is, not even Eliot; yet if he cannot do so "wholly," he may nonetheless try, and may even partly succeed. Although this unexceptionable dictum verges on platitude, to escape the kind, if not the degree, of culture that surrounded his youth was just what Eliot himself once set out to do.

He had not earlier regarded culture and family with such conspicuous equanimity. In 1919, at age thirty, he declared: "The Arts insist that a man shall dispose of all that he has, even of his family tree, and follow art alone. For they require that a man be not a member of a family or of a caste or of a party or of a coterie, but simply and solely himself."[2] The record of Eliot's family helps us measure its influence upon him and suggests in turn some motives behind his repudiation. The family's remarkable past; its involvement with American history; its high "degree" of culture – religious, intellectual, and literary; and most important, its self-consciousness of these things and of its own unusual position: Having issued from the same source, the benefits and privileges of this background merged with its burdens and responsibilities. If Eliot late in life spoke affectionately about his early years, he nonetheless altered his middle ones decisively to escape their influence. We shall later explore the extent to which Eliot would "follow art alone." But so far as we can determine his motives, the nature and negativity of Eliot's reaction suggest flight at least as much as pursuit. If such pursuit could require someone to "dispose" of his own family history, it makes possible the inference that Eliot's responses to his origins affected not only his sense of self, but his writing as well.

Such inference relies partly upon family history. The Eliots had lived in North America since the 1670s; Eliot's maternal ancestors arrived even earlier. They and their descendants engaged in education (including two presidents of Harvard), law enforcement (including sheriffs and judges, one of whom sat at the Salem witch trials), politics (including revolutionary figures and elected officials), and other public service. Many, including Eliot's grandparents, were pioneers.[3] Forebears proliferate quickly, their numbers doubling every generation, and the tiny New England population in the seventeenth and even the eighteenth centuries made consanguinity almost inevitable. It is difficult nevertheless not to be struck by how frequently Eliot's ancestors attained prominence, often becoming historical personages. Their past blended with the history of New England, which in turn fused with its religions. Most notably, Eliots became preachers and ministers.

Even excluding collateral lines, the Eliots left an enviable and consistent record of achievement. Generation after generation, the Eliots and the elite tended to coincide. Of course, under these circumstances the simple term "family" may designate a complex network of blood and emotion extending in many directions. We must also remember how far modernity has impoverished the wealth of family associations – to morality, myth, nationality, class, religion, region, and tradition – frequently leaving the nuclear family little more than a not particularly durable arrangement of convenience.

His flight from home took Eliot farther than it does most people, but the distance he put between himself and his early life may give a clue to its intensity. In the Eliot home, intensity meant the Unitarian religion, in the person of the patriarch, Rev. William Greenleaf Eliot. In 1904, the year before T. S. Eliot left St. Louis for Massachusetts, his mother published a lengthy biography of her father-in-law. She dedicated it: "Written for my children, 'Lest They Forget.'"

Rev. Eliot's almost dynastic presence, and the values it authorized, pervaded the family even after his death. Although T. S. Eliot never knew his grandfather, who died a year before his birth, he testified convincingly to the influence exerted from the grave. Having been brought up to be very much aware of his grandfather, T. S. Eliot thought of him as the head of the family, for whom Eliot's grandmother acted as "vicegerent." Rev. Eliot's standard of conduct governed his grandchildren's "moral judgments, our decisions between duty and self-indulgence." That standard bore a virtually Mosaic authority, "any deviation from which would be sinful."[4] If Rev. Eliot bore the posthumous image of a stern, Old Testament lawgiver, while alive he wore a public face of energy, cheer, light, and liberalism. He was, in short, a typical Unitarian, except for the lengths to which he was prepared to go in spreading his faith. He was the first Unitarian minister west of the Mississippi, and "Philanthropy," the first sermon he delivered in his Cambridge Divinity School course, presaged an exhausting commitment to benevolence.[5] His dedication still seems prodigious: an indefatigable, successful fund-raiser; minister and church builder; helper of the sick during St. Louis's "year of pestilence"; member of the Western Sanitary Commission; reformer of the public schools and founder of two private ones; during the Civil War, abolitionist, friend to slaves, adviser to Union generals and President Lincoln, and an advocate of keeping Missouri in the Northern camp; prison reformer; founder and third chancellor of Washington University; unpaid professor of metaphysics; and author. (Grief also must have overflowed at times; only five of Rev. Eliot's fourteen children survived to maturity.)

Contemporary testimony considered his character to be as virtuous as his achievements were legion; Emerson called him the "Saint of the West."[6] And Rev. Eliot did not doubt; he acted. According to a memorial tribute from the Washington University Board of Directors: "The great and marked characteristic of the Chancellor was his unaltering faith in the ultimate success of all honest endeavor in harmony with the divine purpose; and whatever obstacles seemed to retard, or difficulties to oppose, they never seemed to disturb his confidence, to cloud his hopes or discourage his efforts towards a beneficent result."[7] For men like Rev. Eliot, Unitarianism meant certitude; Henry Adams wrote a classic paragraph about it:

> Nothing quieted doubt so completely as the mental calm of the Unitarian clergy. In uniform excellence of life and character, moral and intellectual, the score of Unitarian clergymen about Boston, who controlled society and Harvard College, were never excelled. They proclaimed as their merit that they insisted on no doctrine, but taught, or tried to teach, the means of leading a virtuous, useful, unselfish life, which they held to be sufficient for salvation. For them, difficulties might be ignored; doubts were waste of thought; nothing exacted solution. Boston had solved the universe; or had offered and realized the best solution yet tried. The problem was worked out.[8]

The solutions of the fathers, however, may be visited upon their sons, and the Unitarian ones did not satisfy T. S. Eliot (or Henry Adams, either). Reviewing *The Education,* Eliot described the wholly American species to which Adams – and Eliot himself – belonged, products of the "Boston doubt," which worked against conscience. Conceding the difficulty of explaining this sort of skepticism to those who were not born to it, Eliot nonetheless called it "a product, or a cause, or a concomitant, of Unitarianism; it is not destructive, but it is dissolvent. . . . Wherever this man stepped, the ground did not simply give way, it flew into particles."[9] Eliot writes of both the skepticism and the conscience in a particularly knowing way, and they mark two poles of his intellectual life. (Indeed, he would later claim, paradoxically, that skepticism gave him the method by which he regained his religious conscience.) In Part II of *After Strange Gods,* Eliot proposed that classifying individual writers by the kind of Protestantism in which they were raised and by the state of decay it had reached offered the "chief clue" to understanding them and assorted defects he assigned to their work. This generalization from his own experience supplies only one instance of Eliot's frequent irritation with liberal Protestantism and with Unitarianism in particular. It contributed, for instance, to the reaction against gentility appearing throughout his early poetry. Moreover, it influenced his temperament, his attitude toward society and the individual, and even perhaps his eventual Anglo-Catholicism. (Typically, those fleeing Unitarianism headed for Canterbury; the especially persistent pushed on to Rome.)[10]

Daniel Walker Howe's *The Unitarian Conscience* and the denomination's most famous apology, William Ellery Channing's "Unitarian Christianity," help demonstrate how Unitarianism affected Eliot's life and thought, both positively and negatively.[11] First, however, to give a context to Eliot's reaction, F. O. Matthiessen summarized how nineteenth-century religious liberalism inverted traditional theology by altering the object of belief from God-Man to Man-God, shifting the emphasis from Incarnation to Deification, and exchanging belief in human salvation through a sovereign God's mercy and grace for belief in every individual's potential divinity:

> That alteration centered around the Crucifixion . . . especially in protestant, democratic America, the emphasis was no longer on God become Man, on the unique birth and Divinity of Christ, who was killed and died back into eternal life; but on the rebel killed by an unworthy society, on Man become the Messiah, become God. That celebration of Man's triumph involved also the loss of several important attitudes: that there was anything more important than the individual; that he might find his completion in something greater than himself; that the real basis for human brotherhood was not in humanitarianism but in men's common aspiration and fallibility, in their humility before God.[12]

Unitarians enthusiastically participated in this adjustment. It animates Emerson's "Divinity School Address," for instance, and this peculiarly Protestant reversal has otherwise influenced American thought and letters incalculably. In particular it sustained the Unitarian denominational identity. As anti-Trinitarians, they denied Christ's complex divinity, claiming instead that he simply represented a more completely spiritual, consistent, or sincere version of principles to which everyone should aspire, and from which everyone could profit.

Eliot professed an early skepticism about religion, at least before an audience of academic philosophers in 1917: "Might it not be maintained that religion, however poor our lives would be without it, is only one form of satisfaction among others, rather than the culminating satisfaction of all satisfactions?"[13] He had nevertheless already framed the issue upon which faith or doubt turned. Eliot invited philosophy to show the meaning of the statement that Jesus was God's son. But a "unique fact" formed the basis of orthodox Christianity: Jesus was born of a virgin. That proposition, Eliot argued, "is either true or false, its terms having a fixed meaning." He therefore concluded that simply claiming that Jesus

was a historical person seemed insufficient.[14] In this way Eliot responded
to the liberal emphasis upon Christ's humanity in time by urging another
"fact" – parthenogenesis – which could have arisen only from His divinity in eternity. This conflict, between liberal and orthodox theology,
Deification and Incarnation (humanity ascending to God's spirituality
versus God's descent to human flesh), reason and dogma, and human
perfectability and Original Sin, divides Eliot from Unitarianism and
liberal Protestantism. It is, moreover, a conflict from which, once resolved, a host of literary, political, and psychological consequences
follow.

For Eliot, Original Sin remained a fundamental doctrine. Channing
had regarded it as one of the most pernicious tenets of the Calvinism that
Unitarianism intended to overthrow; indeed, rational opposition to
Original Sin amounted to Unitarian dogma. A passage from "Unitarian
Christianity" illustrates the doctrine's central status and how sure Eliot
was to seize upon it:

> We farther agree in rejecting, as unscriptural and absurd, the explana-
> tion given by the popular system, of the manner in which Christ's death
> procures forgiveness for men. This system used to teach as its funda-
> mental principle, that man, having sinned against an infinite Being, has
> contracted infinite guilt, and is consequently exposed to an infinite
> penalty. We believe, however, that this reasoning, if reasoning it may
> be called, which overlooks the obvious maxim, that the guilt of a being
> must be proportioned to his nature and powers, has fallen into disuse.
> Still the system teaches, that sin, of whatever degree, exposes to endless
> punishment, and that the whole human race, being infallibly involved
> by their nature in sin, owe this awful penalty to the justice of their
> Creator.[15]

Original Sin offended the sense of justice among Unitarians, who refused
to consider themselves bound by punishment for acts they did not perform. Without Original Sin, the idea that God should dispatch His son to
suffer and die appeared to Unitarians either purposeless or repulsive.
They further recoiled from any suggestion of a fleshly divinity for scrip-
tural, theological, and historical reasons.[16]

Most important, Original Sin clashed with the Unitarian self. A suffering, incarnate Christ despiritualized devotion, detracted from worship, and, perhaps most tellingly, offended Unitarian intellectual and
aesthetic sensibilities as unseemly:

> That Jesus Christ, if exalted into the infinite Divinity, should be more
> interesting than the Father, is precisely what might be expected from
> history, and from the principles of human nature. Men want an object
> of worship like themselves, and the great secret of idolatry lies in this
> propensity. A god, clothed in our form, and feeling our wants and

sorrows, speaks to our weak nature more strongly, than a Father in heaven, a pure spirit, invisible and unapproachable, save by the reflecting and purified mind. . . . We do believe, that the worship of a bleeding, suffering God, tends strongly to absorb the mind, and to draw it from other objects, just as the human tenderness of the Virgin Mary has given her so conspicuous a place in the devotions of the Church of Rome. We believe, too, that this worship, though attractive, is not most fitted to spiritualize the mind, that it awakens human transport, rather than that deep veneration of the moral perfections of God, which is the essence of piety.[17]

In short, the Incarnation interfered with primary Unitarian desiderata: rationalism, spiritualization, and, most crucially, the necessity of conscious self-cultivation. Howe writes that the theme of spirit triumphing over matter fascinated the Unitarians. For individuals, that theme meant believing in the "perfectability of the human personality," preferring ethics and common sense philosophy to dogma and theology, emphasizing human progress from animal to spirit, and assuming a parental and pedagogical rather than a judicial, punitive God.[18]

At their root, the ideas that human nature was basically moral, that a person's task lay in cultivating the conscience, and that virtue consisted in conforming deeds to moral criteria contradicted Calvinist notions of Original Sin and predestination. In the Unitarian scheme the individual, not God, claimed responsibility – and credit – for his elevation. Christ simply offered an example – however stirring and paradigmatic – of someone who had realized his own moral nature perfectly and completely. As Channing phrased it:

> We believe that all virtue has its foundation in the moral nature of man, that is, in conscience, or his sense of duty, and in the power of forming his temper and life according to conscience. We believe that these moral faculties are the grounds of responsibility, and the highest distinctions of human nature, and that no act is praiseworthy, any farther than it springs from their exertion. We believe, that no dispositions infused into us without our own moral activity, are of the nature of virtue, and therefore, we reject the doctrine of irresistible divine influence on the human mind, moulding it into goodness, as marble is hewn into a statue.[19]

Instead of being arbitrary and mysterious, virtue became a matter of conscious effort and common sense. The individual had principally to incline toward the moral and spiritual, and away from his lower nature. This imperative also applied to history, which a famous liberal clergyman interpreted as recording the evolution of divinity out of humanity, a continuous progressive change, from lower to higher, and from simpler to more complex. . . . The church, Christian society, the individual, are all a strange intermixture of paganism and Christianity, in which Christianity is steadily, but surely, gaining the victory over paganism. . . . Society is partly pagan selfishness and partly Christian love; but Christian love is steadily displacing pagan selfishness. Theology is partly Christian truth and partly pagan superstition; but truth is steadily displacing superstition. The individual man is partly the animal from which he has come, and partly the God who is coming into him; but God is steadily displacing the animal. . . . Under the inspirational power of the divine spirit [men's] spiritual nature is growing stronger and their animal and earthly nature more subjugated.[20]

Eliot repudiated each of these notions in their turn. He observed a passage not from lower and simpler to higher and more complex, but just the reverse, and questioned whether Christianity inevitably supplanted paganism. Eliot proposed that Christian brotherhood and love had for some time given ground to pagan selfishness and superstition; *Poems, 1920* argued that modern life tended to reinforce humankind's animal nature and foreclose whatever divinity it contained. Eliot substituted pessimism for optimism, decay for progress, de-evolution into sensuality for evolution to spirituality. In short, against Unitarian reason and humanitarianism, he opposed dogma, the Incarnation, and Original Sin.

Eliot's fugitive essays and reviews frequently impugn Unitarianism and related ideas. Of Aldous Huxley and Middleton Murry, he wrote: "Perhaps if I had been brought up in the shadowy Protestant underworld within which they all seem gracefully to move, I might have more sympathy and understanding; I was brought up outside the Christian Fold, in Unitarianism; and in the form of Unitarianism in which I was instructed, things were either black or white."[21] "Underworld" is sly, with its shady pairing of Dante and Dillinger, gargoyle and gangster, Hades and hoodlum. So is the hint that Unitarians are not properly Christian, resembling lupine predators upon the "Christian Fold." This drawing-room Manichaeism may partly explain the attention Eliot paid to epistemological ambiguity, or his images of mysterious half-light, dusk and dawn. It is not idle to wonder whether Eliot's early exposure to rigid moral categories might have prompted both intellectual and sensory inquiry into the the zone where the extremes mix, where black and white blend in shades of gray. As Chapters 4 and 5 explore, when inflexible moral judgments clothe social valuations, as genteel valuations tended to do, a change in the relation of social classes creates moral and metaphysical ambiguity.

Eliot's own moralism asserted an anti-Unitarianism, brandishing a

Calvinist rigor if not that stricter system's theology. In 1916 Eliot archly dismissed efforts to palliate Christian teachings by reference to a "principle of development" that denied or "boiled away" whatever was anarchic, unsafe, or disconcerting in what Christ did and said. "Certain saints," Eliot concluded, "found the following of Christ very hard, but modern methods have facilitated everything."[22] As this quotation implies, Eliot drew upon orthodox doctrine long before he officially professed Christianity. In the same year, Eliot defined classicism as "essentially a belief in Original Sin – the necessity for austere discipline," and its opposite, humanitarianism, as the "belief in the fundamental goodness of human nature."[23] These antinomies reflect the underlying unity of Eliot's thought, and he used them to express his views both in early prose and in late poetry (e.g., in Section IV of "East Coker"). The attraction Original Sin exerted may have had other sources, but one was surely that it contradicted the Unitarian humanitarianism of his youth.

It is not always clear how precisely he used the phrase or the extent to which he wished to revive its more severe doctrinal corollaries.[24] Original Sin, however, represented many things to Eliot. In art, its presence conferred aesthetic realism. Once Original Sin and the notion of intense moral struggle disappeared, Eliot argued that characters in contemporary literature "tend to become less and less real."[25] A sense of sin seems, moreover, to have formed part of the civilizing principle. If the horror of sin were to disappear, Eliot wrote to a correspondent, it would be so much the worse for human beings, because sin would persist even should people regard it as a delusion for a generation or two. "Psychology may help us to distinguish between disease and sin, but does not abolish either. To do away with a sense of sin is to do away with civilisation."[26]

Eliot's distinction rejects the notion that sin can be "cured" or "healed," but it also criticizes the theology out of which that therapeutic idea arose. If liberal theology held that civilization, as presently conceived, makes sin inevitable, Eliot answered that sin, as immutably present, makes civilization necessary. The argument that theology had abandoned Original Sin helped Eliot diagnose the errors that led civilization into what he considered its contemporary trouble. Eliot eventually labeled those errors Romanticism, democracy, and Protestantism – each linked to "humanitarianism," to the United States, and to "that deceitful goddess of Reason" born in the Enlightenment.[27] These errors became heretical insofar as they forsook the doctrine of Original Sin, to which we will return after examining one way in which Eliot remained faithful to his Unitarian heritage.

Notwithstanding his misgivings about Unitarian theology, Eliot's two efforts to describe an ideal society, *The Idea of a Christian Society* and *Notes Towards a Definition of Culture,* resemble nineteenth-century American Unitarian social thought. His family's Unitarianism taught a prescriptive, morally evaluative attitude toward society and history. This culture's members, predisposed to see themselves as leaders and civilizers, almost reflexively assumed wide-ranging social responsibilities. Upon his ordination in 1834 and frequently thereafter, for example, Rev. William Eliot declined offers to speak from a prestigious Boston pulpit. He accepted instead an infant church in a crude, undeveloped, and even unsafe city at the fringe of settlement. He gave up the friendship of Channing, Henry Ware (after whom he would name his second son, T. S. Eliot's father), Ticknor, Margaret Fuller, and other Boston and Cambridge luminaries to establish a Unitarian beachhead and civilize the frontier.[28] His choices typify how the nineteenth-century Protestant clergy in general, and Unitarians in particular, conceived of themselves as the instruments of rectitude and reform.

Having banished doubt in favor of what they imagined to be common sense, the Unitarians earned deserved fame for their fervor. They aimed to sensitize wealthy people to moral action. Their customary links to wealth by birth or marriage made it especially clear in their eastern Massachusetts bailiwick how snugly their peculiar morality fit that region's mercantile elite. As Howe relates, the Harvard moral philosophers negotiated an "implicit bargain" with the merchants: If the moralists could justify commercial enterprise and the accumulation of property, as consideration the merchants would acquiesce in their cultural and moral leadership.[29] As if the primary means of legitimating the acquisition of wealth was to give it away, the bargain provoked philanthropic endeavor that reached grand proportions in Boston, and Rev. Eliot made it work even in the provinces. Before a St. Louis audience, he bluntly distinguished civilizing ideals from their enemy:

> The motives . . . which chiefly actuate this better class of our community in locating themselves here, are such as to divert their minds from the best interests of society, namely purity of public morals and feeling and the general diffusion of knowledge.
>
> The first settlers of some of the Eastern states . . . came to this country with the express object of intellectual and religious freedom, and therefore their first thought was of religion and education. . . . But with the West . . . the grand motive which actuates all who come here is . . . to make money. The motive which has brought the vast majority of us here is not liberty of conscience, not intellectual improvement, not the desire to do good, but to better our own condition, to make ourselves rich and influential members of society. . . . And in the universality of this motive . . . I discern the greatest danger which threatens our ultimate prosperity . . . to which the West is peculiarly exposed; that religion and learning and morality and education, and

everything which makes a people truly prosperous, shall all be forgotten, all made to bow to one god, mammon.[30]

Consider how closely "religion, learning, morality, and education," not to mention the passage's implicit historical pattern, describe his poet grandson's values. Rev. Eliot's words also confirm Howe's conclusion about the Unitarians' self-conception as civilizers. Possessing and cultivating the conscience of society, Unitarians felt, entitled them to direct society's purposes. As conscience should never yield to a lower faculty, so the Unitarian moral elite resisted encroachment upon their jurisdiction as arbiters of social morality.[31]

In eastern Massachusetts, for a time, the Unitarians realized their social ideal of well-placed moral magistrates presiding over society. That neighborhood, however, had the incalculable and untranslatable advantage of being conservative socially, as well as descended from a religiously (and ethnically) homogeneous society founded upon ironclad axioms of moral elitism. Eventually, however, Jacksonian democracy, the Civil War, the settlement of the West, immigration, and the postbellum industrial plutocracy jointly dislodged this moral judiciary. That displacement and the values it overthrew – the moral attitude toward society, history, and education, a suspicion of social mobility, the upholding of a deferential and stratified society, the antagonism between civilization and mammon, and an emphasis on impersonality, self-restraint, civility, and the cultivation of belles-lettres[32] – formed the background of Eliot's life. He inherited a loyalty to an obsolete system of ideals he could not easily accept insofar as he found it to be at odds with social facts he could not afford to ignore. If the way Eliot resolved this conflict was different from the way earlier Unitarians had, his options nevertheless largely resembled theirs. As Howe indicates, for example, the difficulty in reconciling moral leadership and conservative apologetics, and elitism and democracy, posed a third problem for New England Unitarians. The tension between nationalism and cosmopolitanism meant that even though they wished to consolidate an American national culture, Unitarian literary thinkers looked to Europe for clues about how to realize that goal.[33] Eliot, that is, chose differently than traditional Unitarians, but from the alternatives they presented to him.

Howe also reveals how congruently Unitarian ethical theory arranged society and psychology to correspond. It ranked the faculties vertically, the moral sense supervising prudence, which in turn monitored the appetites and emotions. The Unitarian good society would thus distribute influence hierarchically, valuing moral above prudent individuals, who would nevertheless retain more influence than passionate ones. Not surprisingly, in practice their abstractions positioned the moral philosophers

– clerical and academic men – as the morally powerful elite. Next came men of wealth and commerce, and those who derived their values and professions from that group. The lowest classes, with neither knowledge nor wealth, fared least well morally; when it did not ignore them altogether, the Unitarian scheme dismissed them as irresponsible or dissolute.[34]

Eliot's portrayals of lower-class characters take the Unitarian attitude toward them; Sweeney, Doris, and the young man carbuncular seem distinguished primarily by their appetites and emotions. Social evaluation in literary disguise appears in the essays as well, such as the railway compartment in "The Function of Criticism" which Eliot crowded with Swansea-bound football fans festively auditing the "inner voice." Eliot differed from his forebears mainly by crediting these passionate characters with typifying their times and with greater influence than the Unitarians would have admitted. Of course, Eliot's personal descent from a high social and intellectual level (having ended his philosophical career) to one somewhat lower (a bank clerk in a basement office) remains relevant in evaluating his views. Eliot nonetheless agreed with the Unitarians that a society permitting such influence cannot be a very good one, morally speaking.

Important as these negative attitudes may be in illuminating the mood of some poems and other writing, Eliot's two volumes of social criticism reflect several facets of the positive Unitarian social ideal. Owing perhaps to their metaphysical roots in Scottish common sense philosophy, like the Scottish thinkers (who viewed the state as reproducing many qualities of the kinship group) the Harvard Unitarians tended to see both the church and the state as extended families.[35] Such notions might also have descended from colonial American circumstances. In seventeenth-century Massachusetts, church members formed a distinct minority possessing special rights and privileges, considered themselves morally elect, and could bequeath a form of church membership to their descendants. A degree of tribalism thus characterized that social ethos.[36] Eliot reflected these influences when he called the parish "an example of community unit," small enough to permit "direct personal relationships, in which all iniquities and turpitudes will take the simple and easily appreciable form of wrong relations between one person and another."[37]

Eliot criticized the secular, democratic state for having inverted the social hierarchy and frustrated its moral effect upon individuals. Both he and his Unitarian forebears considered local society's influence natural and positive. In his view, electoral power should concentrate at the village level, where voters were most competent to make decisions. Contradicting the modern hierarchy of nation before district, followed by local community, Eliot espoused a Unitarian view – though not solely that – when asserting that "we are only capable of understanding the nation through its relation to the family."[38] Eliot conceded that society would not likely reform itself into this idealized Christian *Gemeinschaft*. Like his Unitarian antecedents, he emphasized changes to foster social harmony. Unlike them, however, Eliot's writing admitted the danger and conflict that politeness or the cushion of class had prevented earlier Unitarians from dwelling upon, as if those negative images made realizing positive community, however chimerical, the more imperative.

Paradoxically, Eliot's social ideal depended upon the conscious cultivation by social leaders of unconscious behavior among the mass of citizens. (Eliot's work on Bradley, his criticism, and such poems as "Prufrock" and "Gerontion" betrayed a similar mistrust of conscious knowledge and behavior.) Viewing consciousness as a burden greater than most people could bear led Eliot to render an ideal Christian society that seems no less extraordinary for having descended immediately from Unitarianism, and ultimately from Plato. At the highest social level, only a small number of "conscious human beings" would bear the moral and spiritual burden of a "conscious Christian life." Men of state, from whom was required only "conscious conformity of behaviour," governed those in the Christian community whose "largely unconscious behaviour" realized an "ingrained faith" in customary religious observance and traditional ethical conduct in daily life, with religious and social life forming a "natural whole." That life remained whole and natural because undisturbed by the effort required to think about the objects of faith or about the gap between conduct and Christian ideals. Thus ordinary people ideally would lead lives free of the "intolerable strain" of behaving as Christians, which burden, by implication, Eliot's small, conscious, thinking Community of Christians shouldered.[39]

Growing up amid Unitarian striving for ethical and spiritual perfection undoubtedly acquainted Eliot firsthand with this intolerable strain. Eliot developed amid a regime that made consciousness the highest value, which indeed mistook consciousness for spirituality. But Eliot's thought and values, "consciously" antithetical to those of his development yet consistent with them in other ways, thrust forward another value, that of unconsciousness. Unitarians held the harmonious congruence of Christian ideals and ordinary behavior to be not only possible in every conscious moment but life's principal discipline and purpose. Eliot warned that the burden of conscious Christianity should properly fall only upon an elite whose intellectual, moral, and social constituents resembled the Unitarian model.

As a morally superior, socially secure class, Eliot's Community of Christians would instruct, guide, and challenge the rest of society. Distinct from the institutional church, it would function by being intellectually and spiritually conscious of what people usually let remain un-conscious, by being theologically sophisticated, and by upholding orthodoxy. It would comprise both clergy and laity, but include only those whose high spiritual and intellectual development, similar beliefs, and shared educational and cultural background permitted them collec-tively to form the nation's conscience and its conscious mind.[40] Eliot's scheme recalls how nineteenth-century Unitarians regarded themselves, seeking to preside over society like a conscience supervises individual behavior. As compensation for accepting ideals too onerous for most people, they expected to receive deference and exert influence upon deci-sions involving national policy. (It is worth noting how the incorpora-tion of unconscious habits of thinking and living likewise characterized Eliot's political philosophy. Seeking not a party program, but a way of life, he defined a political philosophy as not merely the conscious for-mulation of a people's ideal aims, but the "substratum of collective temperament, ways of behaviour and unconscious values which provides the material for the formulation.")[41]

The Unitarians tried to conceive of a modern function for a traditional social elite. *Notes Towards a Definition of Culture* takes up that project, seeking to fit traditional ideas about family, class, education, and religion to modern, post–World War II conditions. Less overtly Christian than *The Idea of a Christian Society,* and far more dynamic, it actually recom-mends a positive social friction among various classes and social in-terests, whose heat will keep culture alive. Among other issues, the later volume asks, What does an elite do, how should it behave, and of whom will it be constituted?

These questions reflect Eliot's response to having grown up feeling himself a member of the elite in a society too often anxious to observe the conspicuous forms, but less often the moral responsibility, thought to be incumbent upon those who occupy the social pinnacle. Eliot's inquiry aims at little less than dealienating a class that modern society seemed anxious to ignore. He insisted that he had not advanced a "defence of aristocracy," but instead set forth a "plea on behalf of a form of society in which an aristocracy should have a peculiar and essential function, as peculiar and essential as the function of any other part of society."[42] It might appear an odd sort of "plea" in a time when power and privilege seem to have encountered little difficulty in finding something with which to occupy themselves. But Eliot refers to an informal, loosely organized group not necessarily exercising political or economic power, but exerting instead a moral, restraining influence on others who do. Crucially, Eliot structures his conceptions with mechanisms to admit new members as well as to ensure continuity, so that this elite may both produce new culture and transmit established culture.

However different its cultural content, Eliot's ideal shared many goals pursued by Rev. William Eliot and the nineteenth-century Unitarians. They likewise intended the moral and intellectual elite to maintain tradition, culture, religion, public ethics, and national life. In short, they considered themselves to have assumed responsibility for civilization, even if that word's connotations, harnessed to progress and reform, resonated rather differently for T. S. Eliot. The twentieth century's economic and managerial elites, by contrast, made only the most narrow moral claims, when they bothered to make them at all. Academic, professional, and even religious elites frequently predicated their moral legitimacy upon talismanic abstractions such as equality, social change, or personal freedom, or whatever label (e.g., "doing as one likes") these phrases carried in Eliot's time. Eliot considered these solutions to be the problem, urging instead the restraints of personal morality and well-defined social responsibility. "It may be argued that complete equality means universal irresponsibility," he wrote, for example. "A democracy in which everybody had an equal responsibility in everything would be oppressive for the conscientious and licentious for the rest."[43]

Eliot, like his grandfather and the Harvard Unitarians, pointed to mammon as one of civilization's chief threats. In September 1939, Eliot asked some hard questions about the state of British civilization. These questions, which his poems ask on one level or another as well, are ones he had learned growing up in turn-of-the-century St. Louis. Confessing to feelings of humiliation and responsibility, Eliot turned from politics to values, suggesting that commercial practice and institutions had overtaken supposedly more permanent ideals and had replaced them with chattels, to be bought and sold. Success in the economic marketplace had led to vulnerability in the marketplace of ideas and had weakened the force of faith. Without convictions or ideas that could prevail over those that opposed them, Eliot asked, "was our society, which had always been so assured of its superiority and rectitude, so confident of its unexamined premises, assembled round anything more permanent than a congeries of banks, insurance companies and industries, and had it any beliefs more essential than a belief in compound interest and the maintenance of dividends?"[44]

Eliot's inquiry arose from the same sentiment his grandfather had voiced in St. Louis nearly a century earlier when he opposed intellectual and religious values to commercial ones. His primary questions addressed not specific social defects, but the abstract purpose of social organization; not means, but ends. "What – if any – is the 'idea' of the society in which we live? to what end is it arranged?"[45] For Eliot, society's inability to agree upon an answer to this question remained at once the cruelest fact of modern life and the most telling index of its dissolution, requiring, in the terrible circumstances of 1939, personal contrition. Disagreement about basic, constitutive values produces communal deterioration, individual confusion, and cultural mediocrity. This central attitude, or mood, from which much of Eliot's social commentary proceeds, often frames his poetry as well. Though he took many false steps and otherwise erred along the way, Eliot's teleological ambition vigorously endures after succeeding decades have produced no answer to these questions that is both clear and satisfactory. The case for Eliot's social critique rests on his claim that modern society suffers from its inability to find and apply a principle of selection – an ideal – to guide, organize, and give it meaning. To perceive a vacuum at the center of belief exposes its insubstantiality and weakness. It further suggests that the surrounding society lacks an identity, which among other problems may render it the victim rather than the product of change transpiring more or less out of control.

Eliot tended to resist a liberalism he connected to a series of negations. On one hand, he blamed it for impoverishing the social dimension, destroying traditional habits and dispersing collective identity into its individual parts. His indictment extended in several directions, but concluded that "by fostering a notion of *getting on* to which the alternative is a hopeless apathy, Liberalism can prepare the way for that which is its own negation: the artificial, mechanised or brutalised control which is a desperate remedy for its chaos." Its religious manifestation, he proposed, involved removing not only abuses and legitimately objectionable practices, but also apparently superfluous elements of historical Christianity whose value, it can be inferred, Eliot considered far less dubious. He concluded that the movement's negative procedure limited its survival. "As its movement is controlled rather by its origin than by any goal, it loses force after a series of rejections, and with nothing to destroy is left with nothing to uphold and with nowhere to go."[46] Though this passage suggests one reason for Prufrock's "hopeless apathy," it is more important to notice how it manifests Eliot's own ambivalence toward his family's values and religion. Eliot's targets often coincided with his relatives' ideas. President Charles William Eliot of Harvard, for one example, a third cousin once removed of Eliot's grandfather, modernized Harvard, increased its size and endowment, made its curriculum more pragmatic, introduced the elective system, proposed the "religion of the future," and, symbolical of his thought and influence, created the "five-foot shelf of books."

Though it had numerous sources, Eliot's rejection of liberal education and theology appeared first at Harvard. As an undergraduate, he gravitated toward teachers like Santayana, Barrett Wendell, and Irving Babbitt, who opposed President Eliot. Herbert Howarth's *Notes on Some*

Figures Behind T. S. Eliot explores their influence and President Eliot's innovations. His young cousin disdained the seven propositions of President Eliot's religion of the future, a kind of twilit Unitarianism heralding religious, cultural, and social progressivism, yet composed almost entirely of negations:

> (1) "the religion of the future will not be based on authority, either spiritual or temporal . . . "; (2) "no personifications of the primitive forces of nature"; (3) "no worship, express or implied, of dead ancestors, teachers, or rulers"; (4) "the primary object will not be the personal welfare or safety of the individual in this world or the other . . . but . . . service to others, and . . . contributions to the common good"; (5) It "will not be propitiatory, sacrificial, or expiatory"; (6) It "will not perpetuate the Hebrew anthropomorphic representations of God"; (7) It "will not be gloomy, ascetic, or maledictory."[47]

Much of T. S. Eliot's effort went toward negating these negations; on most points, in both substance and mood, he tended toward the very things the "religion of the future" wanted to replace.

Eliot later reproached President Eliot's elective system as well, censuring a curriculum comprising only subjects that interest students[48] and warning against the harmful cultural effects of the specialization fostered by the elective system. "Cultural disintegration may ensue upon cultural specialisation," Eliot wrote, calling it "the most radical disintegration that a society can suffer."[49] He traced this disintegration to a flawed educational philosophy, which could not agree upon the body of knowledge an educated person would necessarily have acquired. The social consequences – the disappearance of wisdom and its replacement intellectually by "sporadic and unrelated experimentation" – led Eliot to consider a society's educational system far more important than its system of government, because only a proper educational system could unify the active and contemplative life, action and speculation, politics and the arts.[50] In his revaluation of tradition, his preference for educational quality over mere size, his religious orthodoxy, his mistrust of utilitarianism and liberalism, and his pessimism, Eliot reacted against his famous and powerful cousin's philosophy. Influenced by Irving Babbitt, Eliot probably acquired his views on education at Harvard, but twenty years later he still referred to "Five Foot Shelf Culture" dismissively.[51]

Eliot's relation to his family complicated his thought in less obvious ways. The seventeenth century had proved critical in family history, which may have contributed to Eliot's interest in the period, or explain why his literary judgments concerning it frequently clothe historical ones. The "dissociation of sensibility," for example, alleged that a "unified sensibility" existed before the English Civil War, in circumstances that included a monarchical government, religious orthodoxy, and a flourishing literature. Culturally, religiously, and politically (or so at least it might have appeared to someone avid to find these things), the sixteenth and seventeenth centuries had produced reticulated, authoritative, civilized traditions that Puritanism destroyed, closing the theaters, "purifying" the liturgy and hierarchy, and killing the king. Eliot's ancestors had belonged to that denomination and party, and if their Unitarianism departed from Calvinist theology, its progressivism otherwise extended the Puritan legacy.

As Van Wyck Brooks acutely observed, by embracing European and English tradition, Eliot abandoned the American one.[52] He could bully Milton, the Puritan poet par excellence, with apparent insouciance: "Is anyone seriously interested in Milton's view of good and evil?" If timid American readers shunned Baudelaire as *outré* or obscene, Eliot upended their judgment by praising him as a moralist.[53] He admired Machiavelli particularly for his rare "impersonality and innocence" and his noble, statesman-like attitude.[54] Five months before becoming a British subject, Eliot appeared to derogate American dogma: "Liberty is good; but more important is order; and the maintenance of order justifies every means."[55] Such statements seem calculated to make excitable patriots see not only red, but white and blue as well.

This iconoclasm occasionally sank into gratuitous insult, as when Eliot called the poet Rufus Dawes, his great-great-uncle and imitator of Byron, a "pest."[56] But Eliot did not limit deliberate provocation to literature; in his criticism he embedded prickly asides on political and national matters. For instance, Eliot's staunchly New England family had supported the Union in the War between the States, with Rev. Eliot advising President Lincoln and organizing pro-Unionist sentiment in Missouri. Charlotte Eliot called the Civil War "a struggle whose moral grandeur has never been equaled."[57] Her son, however, more than once pursued a provocative regionalism. A few months after returning from his first trip to America in seventeen years, he expressed little hope for the future of the United States until it "falls apart into its natural components, divisions which would not be simply those of the old North and South and still less those of the forty-eight states."[58]

During that trip, Eliot had delivered lectures at the University of Virginia that became the notorious, never reprinted *After Strange Gods*. Aside from its other sins (the gratuitous exclusion of "free-thinking" Jews from the ideal commonwealth being the most serious), the book's opening pages, viewed from a family perspective, seem calculated to offend. They proclaim that "your country – I speak as a New Englander" retains "some recollection of a 'tradition,' such as the influx of foreign populations has almost effaced in some parts of the North, and such as never established itself in the West," and call the Civil War

"certainly the greatest disaster in the whole of American history."[59] That judgment launches an extended lamentation on New England's return to its unsubdued state, a thinly veiled meditation on the decline of a tradition, a region, and a people – Eliot's people, both in New England and in "the West," which arguably included St. Louis. It recites a litany of those forces and values Eliot blamed for displacing his family and past: foreign immigration; industrial expansion; "economic determinism"; the Civil War; and the besetting Unitarian, Liberal vice, a "spirit of excessive tolerance."

To these destructive forces Eliot opposes stability; a homogeneous population; a common religious background; loyalty to the local and family community as opposed to the "periphery of humanity entire"; a "balance between urban and rural, industrial and agricultural"; "habitual actions, habits and customs"; and "a good deal which can be called *taboo*." Insofar as he pronounces a historical verdict on his own family and people like them, Eliot judges that they failed to preserve these values and that their breach met with a just but no less bitter reward. He concludes by severing himself from that history (as he already had done by expatriation and renouncing American citizenship) with a negative affirmation: "It is only a law of nature, that local patriotism, when it represents a distinct tradition and culture, takes precedence over a more abstract national patriotism. This remark should carry more weight for being uttered by a Yankee."[60] Thus we observe the spectacle of a descendant of ten generations of New England city folk – Eliot once characterized his urban habits as "pre-natal" – declaring his sympathies with agrarian views of the sort expressed in *I'll Take My Stand*. (It should also be noted that Eliot's views on these subjects resemble those of another of his teachers, Josiah Royce.)[61]

These curious episodes had in a sense followed from Eliot's preface to *For Lancelot Andrewes: Essays on Style and Order* in 1928, which announced him a "classicist in literature, royalist in politics, and anglo-catholic in religion." My discussion should have partly illuminated the elements of this triumvirate, but they evoke several further responses. First, each owes something to the doctrine of Original Sin. Second, their relation had cohered in Eliot's mind much earlier. Though he later qualified this view, a dozen years before he had argued, concerning modern French literature and the "French mind," a return to the "ideals of classicism," which he defined as

> *form* and *restraint* in art, *discipline* and *authority* in religion, *centralization* in government (either as socialism or monarchy). The classicist point of view has been defined as essentially a belief in Original Sin – the necessity for austere discipline. . . . No theory ever remains merely a theory of art, or a theory of religion, or a theory of politics. Any theory which

> commences in one of these spheres inevitably extends to the others. . . .
> The present-day movement is partly a return to the ideals of the seven-
> teenth century. A classicist in art and literature will therefore be likely to
> adhere to a monarchical form of government, and to the Catholic
> Church.[62]

In 1923, in "The Function of Criticism," the same three categories illustrated Eliot's analysis of how those supporting "Classicism" believed in
the necessity of giving allegiance to something outside themselves.[63]

Finally, the force of Eliot's declaration depends upon a trans-Atlantic
context. Whatever Eliot did tended to rub someone the wrong way; even
his peculiarly studied blandness could provoke intense reaction in some
quarters. This particular avowal might have seemed worth making partly because he knew Americans would be listening. Eliot's acquired view
offered him ideas not available in America, whose literary, psychological, and social traditions were Romantic, whose initially republican politics later subsided into democracy, and whose cardinal principles included disestablishment and religious freedom. These ideas, objects of
secular faith, were what America claimed for itself, and believed itself to
mean. For Eliot, however, they meant diverse – though not unrelated –
varieties of inchoate, negative formlessness. To this extent, Eliot's royalism, Anglo-Catholicism, and classicism proclaimed not simply a trinity
of antiquarian abstractions, but a poignant disavowal of a national way of
thinking and feeling.

Related to so many actors in the American historical drama, Eliot
would have had little difficulty in linking abstract national dogma to
people in family history. Unitarianism fueled American Romanticism,
which in turn inspired the westward movement Eliot's grandfather had
joined. (His wife, whom T. S. Eliot not without some pride referred to
as a pioneer, "shot her own wild turkeys for dinner.")[64] President Eliot's
educational reforms and "religion of the future" extended the Romantic
excursion. Ancestral revolutionaries had secured independence, after
which family history and national myth coincided to sacralize the Revolutionary War. Eliot's Unitarian forebears had permitted, and even assisted, the disestablishment of their own denomination in 1833, Massachusetts being the last state to take this step.[65] Such facts, with nation,
family, and religion linked together and awarded their proper weight,
give Eliot's career and his apparently disparate pronouncements a unity
purely literary or philosophical explanations cannot.

This analysis urges us toward psychology, because family, religion,
and nationality affect the growth, and hence the nature, of the self. The
facts, however, merit one further twist. This chapter began by comparing two of Eliot's evaluations concerning the family. Although his later
view affirmed the family's influence, formerly Eliot had appeared to

reject everything related to it, or to any social ties, in favor of aestheticism. Eliot did make a rejection, but not out of an entirely negative
motive. Rather, he migrated to England to pursue a positive tradition,
another way of politics, and eventually another religion. He might have
wished to escape, but he desired also, in Henry James's apt phrase, to
remount "the stream of time to the head-waters of his own loyalties."[66]
Certainly in London he also sought a more vital literary climate, a greater
respect for intellectual endeavor, and a social complication and density he
thought he could not find in America.

    Yet if he deliberately tried to distance himself from his family, Eliot
did so neither mindlessly nor completely. *In Notes Towards the Definition
of Culture,* after calling it the primary channel of civilization, Eliot defines
"family" to comprise more than its living members. As he speaks of the
family bond, the values attached to this broadened definition – "a piety
towards the dead, however obscure, and a solicitude for the unborn,
however remote" – shed some light on Eliot's own life. That interest in
previous generations differed from the "vanities and pretensions of genealogy; such a responsibility for the future is different from that of the
builder of social programmes."[67] Whatever measure of self-justification
these sentences may contain, they nonetheless tend to dispel some of the
invidious inference to which other facts might give rise. What could have
appeared as Eliot's rejection of family, for instance, may seem instead to
be a kind of loyalty. Viewed trans-Atlantically, Eliot may deliberately
have chosen the English, original branch of the Eliot family instead of its
American one. Lest the scion seem more like a sport, Eliot grafted his
future onto his English family heritage as best he could.

    Some unusual circumstances made that choice possible. Eliot inherited
a legacy of achievement and social prominence that recent American
history had jeopardized. The Eliots had preserved their family connections, history, and identity with self-conscious thoroughness. They had
remembered themselves as a family for as long as eight centuries, only
just more than two of which had been spent in America. Even William
de Aliot, a Norman invader to whom some family members (though
not, it must be noted, Eliot himself) imagined they could trace descent,
had migrated to England from France, where ancestors had presumably
come from Scandinavia. From this perspective, two centuries in North
America represented only one part of a family history of considerable
antiquity.

    To take the most concrete example of the use Eliot made of this
heritage, he found it appropriate to quote Sir Thomas Elyot's *The Boke
Named the Governour* in a poem named for the Somerset village Andrew
Eliot left for America, a neighborhood where Eliots had lived for two
centuries.[68] His Tudor ancestor's life and words gave Eliot a positive

image of primitive but natural harmony that the New England Eliots had not known or had deliberately eschewed. Little more need be said on this point, except to note that Eliot arranged for placement of his remains in the parish church of those Somerset ancestors. A visit to East Coker reveals that he was not the only American Eliot to acknowledge ancestry in this way.

The need for roots and his discovery of a greater affinity for his English than for his American past illuminate Eliot's life and art alike. The greater, or at least more recognizably traditional, reticulation of European society apparently yielded greater art; this fact strikes with peculiar force Americans who are pleased to call their own social organization superior. How could Americans loyal to the European intellectual and aesthetic traditions reconcile themselves to the relatively meager state of these things in their own land? This gap between national loyalty and cultural inferiority has recurred in most generations, but for some it assumes an enlarged and complicating importance. As Chapter 4 supposes, such cultural awareness forces a few Americans to choose between aesthetic tradition and nationality. Such polarities provoke a self-consciousness about either choice that only delays their reconciliation and alienates or impoverishes the minds of those who suffer acutely from the conflict. Such divisions produce or revive historical and social polarities, but they also create ambiguities that severely strain the self. To that subject we now turn.

SELF

> The crucial problem of personality development in its earliest stages is not how to get commitment to the "right" values, but how to get commitment to *any* values. . . . The process of building up a personality structure is one in which preparation of the "soil" for the growth of value-commitments must take precedence over concern with the content of those commitments. The basis of this view is the conviction of how very precarious a truly human level of personality development in any sense is.[1]

Eliot once called "a kind of emotional reserve and intellectual integrity" the best aspect of Unitarianism.[2] It is not difficult, for instance, to see these values surviving to be transmuted into Eliot's theory of poetic impersonality, religious becoming aesthetic. And if Eliot sometimes wrote with confessional bluntness, inbred reserve ordinarily reigned in any errant impulses to emotional candor. In the latter respect, he was surely of his origins. Yet the intensity of Eliot's emotions – that something existed which *needed* subjection to some form of reserve – tends to suggest that family, religion, and history remained problematical. History and autobiography in Eliot's case seem to coincide with significant and inextricable relation. That relation implied Eliot's negation of some American principles, on one hand, and his pursuit of some positive English qualities, on the other. If Eliot refused certain immediate family influences, he could do so in the name of more distant ancestors, whose values presumably conferred superior prestige and authority. Thus pushed and pulled, he waged a conservative iconoclasm, espousing stiffer principles than those his immediate family supposedly had held. In this way Eliot managed to keep his rebellion in the family: a most elegant strategy.

That project, however, remains a psychically expensive one insofar as denying parental and family values costs more than imitating them. It further tends to leave the self in disarray, without an orientation. And it risks remaining wastefully engaged in psychological sciamachy – a struggle with shadows or imaginary enemies. Much of Eliot's criticism reveals his search for objective values that, by grounding the intellect, may discipline the self and emotions. (His poetry likewise, if less explicitly, reflects the hardships that search involved.) Eliot's classicism, as we have observed, involved the belief "that men cannot get on without giving allegiance to something outside themselves."[3] At a public level, this led to tradition, royalism, and an established, orthodox church. Privately, philosophy, then art, and finally religion came forward as candidates for the "something outside."

Each of these allegiances, however, demands a certain "surrender," the agony of assertion and abnegation an unruly, inchoate self wants most yet least easily secures. In Eliot's case, the "something outside" may be literary tradition, to which the artist must "surrender and sacrifice himself" to acquire his unique status. It may also be history, to which the poet must surrender himself in a progress of "continual self-sacrifice, a continual extinction of personality." But not only poets or artists need this "something outside"; Eliot argued that it is also a part of religious sensibility. Because the object of his contemplation evoked a purely impersonal contemplation, Lancelot Andrewes responded with the "adequate emotion." Oddly, a Renaissance figure whose name has become a synonym for ruthlessness signified for Eliot a similar approach to politics. He described Machiavelli as "wholly *devoted*" to the task of his own place and time, and by "surrendering himself" to his political causes, he achieved "impersonality and detachment."

After trying several paths to order, Eliot himself decided upon religion, though his fondness for dogma would surely have been anathema to his Unitarian family, living and dead. Eliot's Christianity supplied the "discipline and training of emotion" through a dogmatic approach that neither the intellectual training of philosophy or science, humanist wisdom, or the "negative instruction of psychology" had otherwise offered. Before Eliot took that step to faith, however, poetry imposed this necessary restraint. He wrote, for example, that like all of Valéry's poetry, *Le Serpent* was "impersonal" inasmuch as it extended personal emotion and experience and completed it in something impersonal. Impersonality, Eliot warned, should not connote poetry divorced from personal experience and passion. When Lucretius "annihilates himself in a system and unites himself with it, gaining something greater than himself," he performs a passionate act, a "surrender" requiring great concentration.[4]

Forging the shield of impersonality into a sword, "Tradition and the Individual Talent" states these matters definitively. When Eliot's powerful feeling temporarily disperses his reserve, oblique candor mixes exposure and concealment. "Poetry is not a turning loose of emotion, but an escape from emotion; it is not the expression of personality, but an escape from personality. But, of course, only those who have personality and emotions know what it means to want to escape from these things."[5] Just so. With their competing themes of discipline and devotion, allegiance and detachment, expression and annihilation, surrender and escape, Eliot's views on tradition, history, religion, politics, dogmatic training, and poetic creation suggest that his thought proceeds from emotional as much as from intellectual sources. His career represents a series of efforts to locate an object worthy of his redemptive ambition in philosophy, art, or faith, which might organize the self and give or add value to life. By defining life as a thing to be redeemed – insufficient, in itself, to justify its own existence – Unitarianism by turns aroused that aspiration and frustrated its satisfaction. Its ingathering – or truncation – of the Trinity into a unitary, abstract, and rational monotheism affirmed the redemptive imperative, yet denied the means to achieve it. As the source of values that affected Eliot's thought and feeling, Unitarianism deserves some further scrutiny.

In the hard-edged Unitarianism Eliot knew, "things were either black or white."[6] He recalled being brought up in an environment resembling the "intellectual and puritanical rationalism which is found in the novels of George Eliot. . . . Herbert Spencer's generalized theory of evolution was in my childhood environment regarded as the key to the mystery of the universe."[7] Commenting on his mother's verse drama, *Savonarola,* Eliot disclosed further clues to his attitude toward his origins. He traced the play's documentary value to the way it rendered a state of mind contemporary with its author, portraying not a historical Savonarola but a disciple of Schleiermacher, Emerson, Channing, and Herbert Spencer.[8] Eliot further observed that the tacit moral assumptions he remembered from youth promised that thrift, enterprise, intelligence, practicality, and prudence in not violating social conventions would lead to a "happy and 'successful' life. Failure was due to some weakness or perversity peculiar to the individual; but the decent man need have no nightmares."[9] In one sense this inventory recalls the precepts of Horatio Alger, Jr., who left the Unitarian ministry to broadcast those values by means of American popular culture. But Eliot's list of virtues also reveals a high-minded, intellectualized climate of arid gentility – the elevation of social convention to an absolute, to be scrutinized in others and propitiated oneself. The domestic atmosphere buzzed ominously with a moral charge, as Eliot remembered his grandfather's posthumous surveillance of "our decisions between duty and self-indulgence." The phrase leaves little doubt as to which pole carried the positive charge and which the negative. Such melodramatized Manichaeism, however, tends to divide and desiccate the self, as well as the sense of actuality.

Nor can the peculiar distance liberal Protestant parents often cultivate between themselves and their children be altogether overlooked.[10] Philip Greven's *The Protestant Temperament: Patterns of Child-Rearing, Religious Experience, and the Self in Early America* can help complete a pattern the evidence describes only in part. Greven examines the preoccupation of Protestant "moderate" parents with the conscience, the faculty diverting the child from "selfishness" to "duty." Overlooking nice distinctions between moral development and convenience, such parents place responsibility for development and control on the child as early as possible. Left to an abstract standard of good and evil allowing neither appeasement nor escape, and offering no reward save dull virtue, a child may, instead of a "conscience," develop a censorious, self-observing faculty that impedes enselfment and encourages social isolation. Such severity purchases moral awareness at the price of emotional strength.

Eliot's background conformed in significant respects to Greven's "moderate" temperament (as distinguished from "evangelical" and the misleadingly named "genteel"). Moderates cultivated rootedness, loyalty to place, and awareness of extended family ties, welcoming grandparents into the family and involving them in child raising. They taught children the variety and complexity of human relations, leaving them aware of their own social position and the status of those around them. They emphasized mutuality – the reciprocal obligations of both superior and inferior in social, familial, and theological relations – as summarized in the concept of duty. They praised hierarchy and the great chain of being in their social thought and arranged their churches on the parish model to include all who lived in a certain territory. Not surprisingly, they recommended moderation in all aspects of a person's outward life.[11]

Although devoted to Unitarianism, whose theology epitomized nineteenth-century Protestant liberalism, Rev. William Eliot himself spoke for social conservatism. Although a liberal and a reformer, he was in no discernible sense left wing. His liberalism was more precisely anti-Calvinism; he disbelieved, for instance, in sudden regeneration and in the doctrines of "Original Sin and Total Depravity":

> The Calvinistic doctrine of original sin is, that in the fall of Adam the whole human race were made sinners; that in consequence thereof, sin is *imputed* to every human being at his birth, in such a sense that he is under the wrath of God and is subject to eternal damnation; that his nature, being essentially corrupt, is capable of no good thing, not even to wish or pray for good. Its best actions therefore are hateful in the sight of God, and absolute, total depravity is the necessary result of its development. For a nature such as this, there is but one hope of salvation, which is in the miraculous and irresistible grace of God. The change of heart is therefore . . . an absolute change of nature, it comes not because of a man's own seeking, but irrespectively thereof. [12]

What seemed especially to stick in the Unitarian craw was the unearned increment of Calvinist grace. Unitarians objected to the fast redemptive buck, to the idea that people had no control over their own salvation, and to any claim that sudden regeneration produced the same result as the sort requiring a diligent lifetime. T. S. Eliot once objected to the "verbalism" of liberal sermons, claiming they corrupted language by unilateral alteration of what words meant. Using this very method, Rev. Eliot preferred to redefine the Calvinist vocabulary:

> In this sense, we believe in original sin. We are certainly born imperfect, with many tendencies to evil. These tendencies are also, to some extent, inherited. . . . But if, on the one side, there are evil tendencies, there are, on the other, equally strong tendencies to good; amiable dispositions and a natural love of truth and purity. These also come to us in part as our birthright. [13]

Rev. Eliot's views on human nature fit Greven's "moderate" pattern closely. Even though they recognized worldly evil, the moderates did not reduce human nature to sinfulness. They admitted good into humanity, emphasizing its hopeful promise rather than its utter depravity. [14] A "mixed" nature implied that people could influence their own salvation and control their own regeneration, slowly and with effort rather than instantly and dramatically. By removing the theological gamble from salvation, Unitarianism "rationalized" the process, placing it on something like a contractual footing, with performance or breach causing a predictable result. The soul governed its own progress rather than impotently relying on an all-powerful God to dispense salvation. Furthermore, a mixed self meant that moderates did not indulge in battling the self's desires or violently denying its existence, as evangelicals seemed compelled to do. [15] Instead, they guided and developed it upward, first toward the intellectual and finally the moral nature, steering it away from the lower, physical ones.

Rev. Eliot's mixed, hierarchical psychology remained typically Unitarian and "moderate," negotiating obstacles of dissonance and conflict, yet optimistic about a spiritually happy ending:

> We are born with a mixed constitution, physical, intellectual, and moral. . . . The moral nature is the highest, that is the soul, and to this the physical and intellectual, the body and the mind, should minister. . . . Our first wants . . . are purely physical. The first exercise of the faculty of thought takes that direction. Self-love, which is needful for self-preservation, is thus early developed. Self-indulgence in what is pleasant, and angry resistance to what is unpleasant, are the natural consequences. All this is not sinful, it is simply of the earth, earthy. It is our physical nature. Gradually the higher nature begins to appear. The sweet affections of the child, pure and truthful, begin to expand. A sense of right, of justice, and of truth, gradually shows itself. . . . The period when moral responsibility begins is hard to determine . . . but whenever it begins, the child is conscious of difficulties. His first exercise, as a moral being, is a struggle, a conflict. There is an enemy to be conquered, a victory to be won.[16]

Rev. Eliot and other moderates defined sin as self-indulgence and Christian virtue as self-denial, but they did not confuse self-control with self-annihilation.[17] Regeneration for Unitarians meant that the intellect endeavored, slowly and consciously, to control the physical nature and cultivate the moral one. As Rev. Eliot phrased it, "The change must be accomplished from the earthly to the spiritual, from the worldly to the religious, from the selfish to the self-denying character, after we have come to the years of conscious self-direction."[18] Translating religious into aesthetic, "Tradition and the Individual Talent" prescribed very nearly the same regimen for the artist, surrendering himself in a continual self-sacrifice and extinction of personality.

"Years of conscious self-direction": the phrase foreshadows T. S. Eliot's view of the need for spiritual discipline, both before and after adopting Christianity. The similarity between Rev. Eliot's progress of the soul and that of his grandson, however, raises a question. If they agreed upon the goal, and on the procedure, why did T. S. Eliot disclaim liberal Unitarianism in favor of a self-consciously orthodox, theologically dogmatic Anglo-Catholicism? Eliot, after all, ultimately embraced the very Trinitarianism his grandfather had condemned as unscriptural, a mere extrabiblical doctrine of inference.[19]

The answer may lie in the atmosphere of Eliot's childhood, which, to use Rev. Eliot's terms, likely provided too stiff a dose of altruism, self-control, and self-denial and too little "self-love, which is needful for self-preservation." It is a commonplace that nineteenth-century American Protestantism discarded Calvinist theology but preserved Puritanical conventions, ethics, and manners. The psychological effect of these changes, a kind of delayed reaction, has been explored less frequently. As moderate views in general and Rev. Eliot's writings in particular demonstrate, gradual, self-directed, autotelic regeneration demanded great effort and sacrifice but withheld any spiritual compensation, such as election or grace.

This imbalance hastened what Eliot later called the decay of Protestantism. Eliot had many quarrels with Protestantism, but criticized especially its negativity: Once the objects to be negated had been overthrown, what remained had little positive content, its existence having depended upon the thing it had argued against. In an almost Nietzschean manner, for example, Eliot discussed the emotional ramifications of historical change by arguing that Massinger's corrupt, decadent morals did not imply that contemporary morals had changed or diminished. Instead, the real, personal emotions, which that morality had formerly supported and set in order, had simply disappeared. Their disappearance made the morality giving order to the emotions appear "hideous." "Puritanism itself," Eliot concluded, "became repulsive only when it appeared as the survival of a restraint after the feelings which it restrained had gone."[20] By analogy, the final sentence suggests Eliot's attitude toward Unitarianism once it had discredited Calvinism, the thing it had reacted against, and after personal, inner restraint had ossified into external convention. Eliot sensed the difficulty posed by morals that rely on negation once the objects of negation no longer exist. By the late nineteenth century, having effaced Calvinist theology, Unitarianism remained only the negation of a negation, prompting Eliot's indifference and hostility.

Self-denial, on the one hand, and altruism, on the other, may produce literal selflessness: not self-restraint, but an absence of self. Eliot appears to have felt, or at lest understood, this sort of absence and the vulnerability it inserted into human relations. In an introduction to Djuna Barnes's *Nightwood,* Eliot's remarks about Doctor O'Connor's monologues might apply equally well to Prufrock. O'Connor's brilliant, witty monologues arose not from his indifference to others, but instead from a "hypersensitive awareness of them." What sent the doctor raving at the end, Eliot concluded, was "his revulsion against the strain of squeezing himself dry for other people, and getting no sustenance in return."[21] Issues of a problematic self inform Eliot's philosophical writing, his aestheticism, his theological interests and eventual conversion, and, of course, his poetry. The Unitarian emphasis on public duty at the expense of the private self, although coming into question by the time Eliot matured, still pervaded American culture – for example, in the academic world and in America's distinctive civil religion.[22] That it so easily declines into conventional observance, and that its ethic can harm an emerging self, suggest why Unitarianism and liberal Protestantism bear so importantly upon Eliot's origins and writing and why he so anxiously sought things "outside" to which the self might "surrender."

Eliot frequently reacted to Unitarian precepts. Writing of Pascal, Eliot contrasts the Pelagian heresy (which Rev. Eliot at least approximated and may have espoused unequivocally) to Calvinist predestination, against which Rev. Eliot had argued. Traces of liberal Protestantism survived in T. S. Eliot's theological exposition: "Heresies are never antiquated, because they forever assume new forms. For instance, the insistence upon good works and 'service' which is preached from many quarters, or the simple faith that anyone who lives a good and useful life need have no 'morbid' anxieties about salvation, is a form of Pelagianism."[23] Good works and "service" were the values Unitarianism preached and Eliot's family practiced. Concerns about salvation were precisely the "morbid" anxieties – one senses Eliot's quotation marks again holding a discredited term at arm's length – they felt their theology entitled them to dismiss.

Dwelling on the defects of a liberal theology, Eliot continued by criticizing the view that the loss of traditional religious sanctions upon moral behavior would not matter. The supposed rationale for this false notion was that "those who are born and bred to be nice people will always prefer to behave nicely, and those who are not will behave otherwise in any case: and this is surely a form of predestination – for the hazard of being born a nice person or not is as uncertain as the gift of grace."[24] Having doubtless mastered anti-Calvinist weaponry at an early age, Eliot here deploys it to demolish a salient of liberal theology, accusing it of being a variant of that despised Calvinist doctrine, predestination. More literary is his insinuating use of "hazard." In one sense, the word can take its innocent meaning of arbitrary "chance." But Eliot also has in mind the ironic meaning of "danger" to describe the Unitarian regime. The ambiguity's arch vigor expresses Eliot's distaste for this element in his background.

While Rev. Eliot's opinion on salvation and grace resembled Pelagianism, his view of Trinitarianism restated the Socinian heresy. "The Unity of God" in *Discourses on the Doctrines of Christianity,* in refuting Trinitarianism, reiterates many Socinian dicta: "The doctrine of the Trinity is nowhere plainly taught in Scripture, nor can it be stated in Scripture words; it is a *doctrine of inference,* built up by arguments, and depending upon distinctions so nice and difficult that it requires a good deal of metaphysical acuteness to perceive them."[25] T. S. Eliot acquired this acuteness through his philosophical studies, and his eventual conversion to orthodoxy completed its acquisition. It involved acknowledging not only theology's extrabiblical substance, but also the corollary that the Bible remains insufficient without theological supplement.

Eliot's views appear in less religious contexts, as when he speaks about Dante's *Paradiso:* "Cheerfulness, optimism, and hopefulness . . . stood for a great deal of what one hated in the nineteenth century."[26] These words, however, recall Rev. Eliot's values:

> Cheerfulness of heart is often promoted by lessening the outward sources of delight, and compelling the heart to be a source of cheerfulness to itself. If we were required to name, among all whom we have known, those who have retained the most perfect cheerfulness and sweetness of temper, we should probably name some whose lives have been the continued experience of pain and suffering. Let there be Christian faith as the foundation, and in almost any given case, if our object were to train a human soul to habitual contentment and cheerfulness, and therefore to the enjoyment of life, the better course would be to place it under the discipline, not of unvaried prosperity, but of frequent pain and loss, and sometimes of severe suffering and bereavement.[27]

One can hardly blame someone who refuses such demoralizing "cheerfulness." Observing in such instances Rev. Eliot's influence upon his grandson, however indirect, suggests how T. S. Eliot in some ways extended those ideas, but in others deliberately undid them.

Rev. Eliot's writings typify advice adopted by moderate Protestant parents, especially in arguing how a child's relation to his parents foreshadows the adult's relation to God. Rev. Eliot frequently expounded this psychotheology, insisting on teaching children

> *obedience.* . . . the only foundation on which the religious character of the young can be established. . . . It is an easy transition from filial respect to religious awe. Children who have been early taught the lesson of obedience to their parents, can easily learn the higher lesson of obedience to God. . . . By the early and judicious exercise of such authority, children are taught those lessons of self-denial and self-control, of reverence and trust, which are so good a preparation for their willing self-consecration to God.[28]

The instances from Eliot's writing that seem to issue from an ambivalent relation to family might by analogy suggest that a related ambivalence to God presented the obstacle he had to overcome before his religious conversion, and apparently after it as well. The crux of Eliot's Christianity, what made it unusual, interesting, and so distinct from Unitarianism, was that it incorporated so much doubt. He could affirm that "doubt and uncertainty are merely a variety of belief" or propose, with complete seriousness, that "Christianity will probably continue to modify itself, as in the past, into something that can be believed in." Like Pascal, Eliot knew the "demon of doubt which is inseparable from the spirit of belief."[29]

Another phrase from Eliot's essay on Pascal recalls the darker extremities of the "moderate" regime. Eliot seemingly described himself when he wrote that Pascal's "intellectual passion for truth was reinforced by his passionate dissatisfaction with human life unless a spiritual explanation could be found."[30] In Eliot's case, Unitarianism seems a primary source of an ennui that passes understanding. The malaise pervades Eliot's early writing and seems to have arisen as a byproduct of the moral and ethical idealism surrounding his youth. In *Early Religious Education,* Rev. Eliot wrote, "The child must be taught to feel that he is living in a spiritual world, and that the highest relations of life are not with a world of sense, but with things unseen and eternal."[31] As a Christian, Eliot would come to echo these sentiments, having by then founded them upon dogmatic orthodoxy.* But without that hard theological rock, Rev. Eliot's Unitarianism offered only an ethic and, at least where children are concerned, a particularly obstinate one at that:

> It makes the will of God our law, instead of our own changing desires, or the customs of the world. Instead of selfishness and self-seeking, whatever form they may take, it teaches self-denial, and, it may be, self-sacrifice. It requires us to live for others, not only by separate acts of kindness, but by going about to do good, and by making the ordinary occupations of life the means of usefulness.[32]

Black-letter imperatives against selfishness and self-seeking, however, seem just the sort that parents should beware, lest in obeying them children deny or sacrifice their selves. In children with intelligence but without some other frame of reference, living by these rules may produce what Eliot diagnosed in himself as an "aboulie and emotional derangement which has been a lifelong affliction." From "Prufrock" to "The Hollow Men," his early poems express the tension of someone analyzing and overcoming the effects of having been rigorously detached from the self's desires and fastened instead to the needs of others. If some part of Eliot's self was sacrificed to the ideals of those around him, it could explain how he might preserve strong continuities with that upbringing and its values, yet exhibit strong reactions against them.

Nor would it be surprising that Eliot early began efforts to repair the sacrificial damage or that his efforts originated in the intellect. His self-

---

* Speaking to an audience of Unitarian clergymen in Boston, Eliot proposed that belief in the supernatural did not mean that after death successful, virtuous people could expect to "continue to exist in the best-possible substitute for this world." Nor did it mean that in eternal life one could expect to receive as compensation all the good things one lacked on earth. Instead, Eliot affirmed, to believe in the supernatural is "to believe that the supernatural is the greatest reality here and now. We have to make it our source of values and the pattern of our life" ("The Modern Dilemma," *Christian Register,* October 19, 1933, p. 676).

diagnosis continued, "Nothing wrong with my mind. . . ."[33] There is considerable pathos in the report that Eliot's mother and sisters left him alone when he was reading.[34] Some lines from "Animula" poignantly render the atmosphere:

> The heavy burden of the growing soul
> Perplexes and offends more, day by day;
> Week by week, offends and perplexes more
> With the imperatives of 'is and seems'
> And may and may not, desire and control.
> The pain of living and the drug of dreams
> Curl up the small soul in the window seat
> Behind the *Encyclopaedia Britannica*.

Thus the poet's own analysis of his childhood, with the (to a child) incomprehensible connection between ethics and a supernatural world; the estrangement wrought by the prematurely introduced "moderate," Unitarian antinomies ("desire and control"); and the effect of these antinomies, which render life painful and even the recompense of dreams a drug, to be suspected and restrained. Not the child but its soul therefore curls up, withering and dying instead of growing and blooming, shielded by intellectual, encyclopedic (and Britannic?) barriers. What shrivels the child cripples the adult, who becomes "selfish," "misshapen," and "lame," a "spectre in its own gloom."

For twenty years or more before "Animula," however, Eliot had undergone a process that left the literary evidence the remainder of this book will explore. A later anecdote reveals the circumstances of Eliot's vocation. At age sixteen years, he composed some verse that impressed an English master at school. The master asked if he had received an older person's help; Eliot, surprised, answered that he had not. Although Eliot's school paper published the poems, he did not tell his family about them. After the issue was shown to Eliot's mother, however, "she remarked (we were walking along Beaumont Street in St. Louis) that she thought them better than anything in verse she had ever written. I knew what her verse meant to her. We did not discuss the matter further."[35] The master's impertinent inquiry as to the verse's originality, the vividness of the remembered conversation (to the extent of recalling the St. Louis street near the Eliot home in which it occurred, fifty or more years earlier), his mother's devotion to her verse and her acknowledgment of his talent – confirmed, typically, by subsequent silence on the subject – all add to the anecdote's rich texture.

Most crucially, however, it reveals that Eliot had withheld mention of the verses or their publication from his family. Apparently he had already pursued a literary path to enselfment; already poetry had given him an essentially private form of self-assertion and discovery. That it involved the imaginative faculty and aesthetic emotions, which occupied a distinctly secondary place in his family's estimation, must only have increased poetry's attractions. Eliot once wrote that Paul Elmer More's "Marginalia" contained the suggestion of a spiritual autobiography "oddly, even grotesquely more like my own" than that of anyone Eliot had ever known. More had wondered how he might have developed had he been raised in a liturgy that did not so ruthlessly evict "the office of the imagination and aesthetic emotions." Eliot wrote, "I have made the same speculation."[36] Available ecclesiastical offerings having proved spiritually deficient, Eliot and More looked to aesthetics and the imagination for sustenance. Even though it expanded beyond poetry, impelling him toward writing about social policy, on the one hand, and toward religious conversion, on the other, Eliot's aesthetic development originated in emotional necessity.

It is possible to trace Eliot's positive literary models (Dante, Jacobean dramatists, the French Symbolists) and his negative ones as well (Milton, certain English Romantic poets) to the intense effort he devoted to enselfment.[37] Eliot may partly have had his own development in mind when speculating that experiences which mix sensuous and intellectual elements cause men to ripen best. The keenest ideas, he said, may arrive like sense perception, and sensuous experiences may take place "as if the body thought."[38] Indeed, Eliot carefully recorded his own dramatic experience of such corporeal cognition. Late in his life, Eliot acknowledged his debt to Laforgue, saying he owed more to him than to any poet, in any language.[39] Much earlier – about ten years after the events actually occurred – Eliot recounted the profound psychological and spiritual change his exposure to Laforgue provoked, drawing an analogy between the experience that develops a man and one that develops a writer:

> Experience in living may leave the literary embryo still dormant, and the progress of literary development may to a considerable extent take place in a soul left immature in living. . . . There is a kind of stimulus for a writer which is more important than the stimulus of admiring another writer. . . . This relation is a feeling of profound kinship, or rather of a peculiar personal intimacy, with another, probably a dead author. It may overcome us suddenly, on first or after long acquaintance; it is certainly a crisis; and when a young writer is seized with his first passion of this sort he may be changed, metamorphosed almost, within a few weeks even, from a bundle of second-hand sentiments into a person. The imperative intimacy arouses for the first time a real, an unshakeable confidence. That you possess this secret knowledge, this intimacy, with the dead man, that after few or many years or centuries you should have appeared, with this indubitable claim to distinction; who can penetrate at once the thick and dusty circumlocutions about his reputation, can call yourself alone his friend; it is something more than *encouragement* to you. It is a cause of

> development, like personal relations in life. Like personal intimacies in
> life, it may and probably will pass, but it will be ineffaceable. . . . We do
> not imitate, we are changed; and our work is the work of the changed
> man; we have not borrowed, we have been quickened, and we become
> bearers of a tradition.[40]

A self-consciously confessional quality, as well as the carefully crafted
tone of awe before the events it renders, make this autobiographical
passage an extraordinarily rich one. The general theme concerns how
poems and poets supplied crucial objects of imitation to Eliot, enabling
him to discover those aspects of the private self that are publicly – in his
case, poetically – negotiable.[41] Enselfment ordinarily finds human agents
– usually family members, if all goes well – to participate in the "kinship"
and "personal intimacy" that after the crisis results in a "person." Here,
however, literature – a dead author – becomes its agent, supplying both a
means of self-discovery and the substance of the new, vital self that
emerges. For Eliot, the process partly involved acquiring technique or
point of view. It also extended to his obsessive quotation of other writers,
as if he had scavenged hungrily for analogues to persistent but neglected or
inchoate experiences and feelings.[42] The practice reveals him strengthen-
ing poems and the self piecemeal, but simultaneously.

   Eliot's startling account, however, most importantly records dramatic
personal change, variously maturation, "stimulus," "profound kinship,"
"a peculiar personal intimacy," and "passion." "It is certainly a crisis"
that may "overcome us suddenly" and that roughly "seizes" a "bundle of
second-hand sentiments" and "metamorphoses" it "into a person." It
produces an unshakable "confidence," doubly comprising not only intimacy and trust between two writers, but also a belief in one's own powers
and abilities. It offers "secret knowledge" that is "something more than
encouragement." Eliot's organizing metaphor tells the story best. A passionately apprehended author (undoubtedly Laforgue, though Eliot described F. H. Bradley in similar language)[43] takes the dormant literary
"embryo" and "*quickens*" it "into a person," transforming something
inertly fetal and merely potential into something alive, kicking, and
anxious to be born.

   Nothing else in Eliot's writing so vividly records dramatic, violent
personal change. This is the event so often sought in Eliot's poems and so
seldom found. Yet here it is, tucked away in a corner, where Eliot was
content to leave it. Eliot's poetry has its moments of mysticism, but this
is not one of them. The moments in the garden with the hyacinth girl or
in the rose garden in "Burnt Norton," though remaining with the poet
indelibly, seem to affect the self only temporarily and persist primarily as
a memory. Those transitory glimpses realize something hitherto intangi-
ble in the external world. Here, by contrast, Eliot gains access to what

already exists within but that until now has remained out of reach. In Eliot's later mystical moments, it would seem, the consciousness of self, and of the division between that self and others and the world, disappears. In his early crisis of literary enselfment, however, the self exults in the consciousness of itself and of its freedom. The change is permanent, producing an enduring, "ineffaceable" source of power.

Poetry, in short, gave Eliot what his life had so far withheld: the means to discover or invent a self, which in his case involved fusing the parts in the same way his poems fused disparate elements of experience, emotion, and lines analogically borrowed from other writers. The literary and psychological processes, in Eliot's case, paralleled one another, and perhaps for a time became indistinguishable. Some ramifications of this parallel will follow, as will the conclusion that Eliot's literary enselfment remained intermediate, for twenty years or so, until it finally yielded neither a self nor a quickened literary embryo, but spiritual accession.

When it came, religious consummation required a new, though not wholly dissimilar, metaphor. At the religious moment, Eliot wrote, "a kind of crystallisation occurs, in which appears an element of *faith* not strictly definable [*sic*] from any reason or combination of reasons."[44] (Significantly, on another occasion, Eliot used the same word – "crystallisation" – to refer to the poem-making moment.)[45] Eliot's decades-long "enselfment" produced a large body of poetry and criticism, involved expatriation and emotional upheaval, and eventually reached a religious conclusion. Before saying more about these matters, however, I shall discuss two early and revealing examples of the process: "Preludes," one of Eliot's most intimate early poems, and Eliot's dissertation on F. H. Bradley. I shall then explore how they relate to the similar "crystallisations" of poem making and soul making. Marking the first stage of Eliot's long transit, these two early writings suggest the extent to which his beginning predicted, and in a sense contained, his conclusion.

2

Divisions and Precisions:
Ambivalence and Ambiguity

It is a sad fact, but there is no doubt that the poor are completely unconscious of their own picturesqueness.

Oscar Wilde, "London Models"

Light and Darknes, Life and Death, Contraries one opposed to another. How in an History, in a Theatre do we take the greatest pleasure to have afflicting passions of pity, fear, grief raised in us even unto sighs, a real melancholy, and tears, while we know, that this is only a *part* in the *whole;* a Scene, which adorns and heighthens the beauty of the whole, and then loseth the melancholy of its shade, and discord in the universal lustre and sweetness?

In the last place, that which makes the *Variety* full, is the *return* of the *whole* thorow the *Contrariety* by a sweet and full close into its *Unity;* the return by the Contrariety from its low estate, to its first and most perfect heighth.

The Lord Jesus in his Mediatory Person, is the fairest, the richest Draught or Portrait of the Divine Design and Work, as it lies in the Divine Mind; animated and heightened by the most immediate, intimate, mutual Union with the Divine Mind. Here therefore is to be expected the most ample Variety.

Peter Sterry, A Discourse of the Freedom of the Will

"PRELUDES"

Many themes associated with Eliot's poetry initially appeared in "Preludes," which Wyndham Lewis's experimental modernist journal, *Blast,* first published in 1914. Forward looking, inclined to spleen, and bent on social and aesthetic iconoclasm, *Blast* survived only long enough to prophesy a strident, chaotic postwar scene. The Great War silenced *Blast,* but not before the second and final issue delivered "Preludes" to a distracted world.

Lewis's edgy Vorticist drawings and Pound's ham-fisted polemic at a minimum reflect their talent to alarm. The pages of *Blast* still make

36

unlikely company for Eliot's tentative cameos of urban languor. "Preludes" may nevertheless typify the modernist claim that poetry can draw beautiful art from ugly material. Eliot had already learned how to refine what crude matter lay about him. Composed four to five years earlier as one result of his expeditions through the South Boston slums (with echoes of Paris and St. Louis), "Preludes" foreshadows much of Eliot's later writing. Besides offering a window upon his sensibility as a very young man, it raises some more purely intellectual issues that would concern Eliot for several years as a graduate student in philosophy. For these reasons, and because of its quality and charm, "Preludes" merits some scrutiny as it peers into the lives of busy desperation the mass of men quietly lead.

Both the method and the mood of "Preludes" rely more upon feeling than intellect, nuance rather than discursiveness, and suggestion instead of paraphrasable content. In short, it asks a reader to wear its sensibility, to read with the same sympathy the poem extends to its characters. Understanding a poem this oblique most particularly requires us to make backward inferences, to imagine opposites of what is presented, to keep in mind how that which exists contains clues about, and may in some sense depend upon, that which does not. The poet, and the knowing reader, remember and anticipate other times, people, places, and incidents. They add those memories and expectations, which no longer or do not yet exist, to the present, which does.

They also know the multiple meanings of words, which meanings, though they may add to the poem's reality, may also complicate it. Eliot's presence, his voice and diction, his relation to the poem's characters, places, events, and even the extent to which "Preludes" offers a psychological and philosophical portrait: All these vantage points give rise to ambiguity. The poem presents a world unconscious of what lies outside it. That is one kind of poetry. As the poem ends, a more conscious, outside world negates the unconscious one within it. That is another. Thinking about "Preludes" involves beholding something that is not there as well as the something that is.[1]

The first way to explore these complications involves examining the medium: the poem's words, their method, and the patterns they form. In so doing we may learn how "Preludes" supports its author's later claim that "genuine poetry can communicate before it is understood."[2] "Preludes" communicates most urgently a voice and a set of images. The voice tenders both intimacy and reserve, blending an awareness of ugliness, loneliness, and routine with an apparently nonevaluative, almost journalistic acceptance of the immutable facts of life, or at least of this sort of life. The voice seems to accept despair nearly as compliantly as do the characters themselves. Even more oddly, the poem's "sordid" images seem carefully selected from a narrow, deliberately unpoetic range. As Eliot once proposed, the artist's contemplation of the horrid, sordid, or disgusting is the "necessary and negative aspect of the impulse toward the pursuit of beauty. But not all succeed as did Dante in expressing the complete scale from negative to positive. The negative is the more importunate."[3]

Eliot's candid statement reveals an essential fact. It allows that he might have wished to pursue beauty, but admits that his own sensibility, inconveniently, declined to cooperate. And by placing ugliness and negativity on a continuum, Eliot links them to their opposites, beauty and positivity. Verbally, imaginatively, and philosophically, "Preludes" depends on that implication of opposites, the one suggesting the other when either appears. Understanding "Preludes" requires a habit of irony and a willing resort to ambiguity, imagining what the poem implies, and constructing the poem by constant comparison to what it is not. That "Preludes" ultimately contains its own negation confirms this approach.

How can a poem paradoxically render ugly things beautiful, or beautifully? It can do so insofar as it can perform the tricky balancing act of using both disjunctions and identities between word and thing, exploiting natural relations as well as purely verbal ones. Like most of Eliot's early poetry, "Preludes" relies on repetition, though not of a strictly rhetorical or conscious kind. As brief, lightly punctuated sentences and phrases slowly accumulate, they subtly disguise and undercut the poem's metrical norm, iambic tetrameter. In Section I, for instance, two of the three dimeter lines preserve the iambic rhythm and rhyme with lines nearby, thus maintaining rhythmic and aural consistency even though deviating from the tetrameter. Likewise, when Eliot abandons the iambic norm, except for the third line he still uses four feet. Furthermore, while poets often vary the rhythm to emphasize a syllable inconsistent with the expected ictus, Eliot drops the stress altogether. Instead of varying the beat, he skips it: "And newspapers from vacant lots . . ." The metrical contract between poet and reader entices us to expect a stressed fourth syllable, but this line has none, and neither has the third or fifth. This broken metrical promise suspends our satisfaction until the sixth and eighth syllables make it good once more. (The same thing happens in the sixth syllable, the word "of," in line eleven.)

Rhyme behaves similarly. In Section I, every line save two has a corresponding rhyme, but only twice do they rhyme consecutively. The contrast between this drawling, relaxed diffusion and the predictable satisfactions of, for example, heroic couplets should be clear to all but the most metallic ears. In Section II, for instance, the initial rhyming words – "consciousness," "stands," "masquerades," and "resumes" – hang in aural suspension for three lines before they find their complements. Section IV pushes this auditory gamble to its extreme: The reader must twice endure five intervening lines before rhyme returns to keep a promise an impatient reader might have forgotten was ever made.

Thus to the aural pleasure of rhyme Eliot adds the dramatic delight of surprise. The technique requires restraint, since it adds frustration and suspension to poetic pleasure, by this means emphasizing a property of poetry of which we ordinarily remain unconscious. In other words, because "Preludes" contains both regularity and variation, it introduces an element of uncertainty and uneasiness. Yet when it does so, it compensates for any disruption of rhythm, line length, or rhyme by observing regularity in the other two of these three formal elements. This "constant evasion and recognition of regularity," Eliot wrote in an early essay, "this contrast between fixity and flux, this unperceived evasion of monotony . . . is the very life of verse."[4] The tactic creates a formal tension that in turn recapitulates the poem's themes. Like these rhythms, rhymes, and lines, its people exist suspended between poles of order and awkwardness, desire and frustration, beauty and ugliness. The surface of their lives nonetheless remains composed, even routine. There is subliminal dissonance, yet no outright disturbance.

Even if these structural clues did not point the thematic way, the poem's repeated words and images would do so; the search for its intrinsic interpretation can begin as well from its image patterns as from its form.[5] Words, for instance, recur: "street," "hands," "world," and "feet" appear several times, and "vacant lots," "smell," "images," "showers," "curled," "newspapers," and "trampled" appear twice. The poem also has consistent connotative patterns, as in the motif of decay, predicated either by images of remnants ("the burnt-out ends of smoky days"; "withered leaves"; "newspapers from vacant lots"; "broken blinds"; "stale smells of beer"; and "sawdust") or by images of filth ("grimy scraps"; "muddy feet"; "dingy shades"; "sordid images"; "the yellow soles of feet"; "the palms of both soiled hands"; "a blackened street"). Such patterns provide a key to the poem's cosmos, another law that governs it, inviting us to apply the qualities of their circumstances to the people themselves. The connotative shift from inanimate to human subjects constitutes the poem's psychological method.

Light supplies yet another pattern. Images of half-light – day turning into night, night becoming morning – define the poem's chronology, a temporal structure that has been called a "diurnal round" and a "chiasmic subject arrangement."[6] The poem starts and stops at six o'clock in the evening; the second and third sections witness night dissolving into morning. Significantly, the poem moves in a circle; it "revolves." Half-light, however, whether dawn or dusk, remains the salient detail, hinting that the urban routine may conceal unsuspected drama. Though circles may be images of perfection, as in Donne or Marvell, they also imply predictability, from which Eliot's stage lighting affords a measure of relief.

An explicitly dramaturgical image, in exaggerating the passage from darkness to daylight confirms both its routine and its unreality:

> With the other masquerades
> That time resumes,
> One thinks of all the hands
> That are raising dingy shades
> In a thousand furnished rooms.

Here Eliot doubles time's nature: Though impersonal, predictable, and regular, it also has volition, "resumes" at daylight a "masquerade" (one, apparently, of many others). The latter word, too, unites opposites: It denotes a masked ball, replete with mystery, sophisticated adventure, and suspended identities, but may also refer to deceit and disguise, with overtones of futility. Signifying both illusion and disillusion, seductive drama and reality unmasked, it points two ways at once, permitting us to regard time playfully, or to consider it an insidious, confining convention. Moreover, the aristocratic sense of "masquerade" amid the bedsitters' proletarian anonymity emits a semantic friction that subtly charges the word's surroundings. The stanza as a whole reverses ordinary signifiers even while uniting them. To time, ordinarily featureless and abstract, Eliot awards a will, yet his image of people connotes incompletion, uniformity, and mechanism. In brief, he personifies time, and depersonalizes people.

Other images reinforce impressions of painful loneliness, as do Eliot's familiar dismemberments – fingers, feet, eyes, and the palms of hands. These figures imply that urban life mutilates its citizens, rending limb from self. Antisynecdoche, or synecdoche as mere mimesis – part eloquent not of the whole, but strictly of the part – applies as well to their disconnected inner lives, composed of a kaleidoscopic "thousand sordid images." City life places all souls under pressure, depleting them ethically and spiritually. Such souls may find themselves overextended, as in the painful, membranous "stretched tight across the skies," or victimized, "trampled by insistent feet." From the heavens to the pavement, the poem's atmosphere renders pathos stranded amid indifference, and emphasized by it.

Another impulse works against this sorrow, however, and by mitigating it, complicates the poem's mood. Consider, for example, the moment when the final couplet disturbs the tranquility of Section I. Empty of people save for the poet and reader (Eliot creates poetic privity by seeming to exclude others while privileging us with these quiet confidences),

Section I ends with a commonplace event that here seems almost momentous, bearing a dramatic or emotional weight greater than lighting-up time might ordinarily be expected to yield. That it is a couplet formally distinguishes it from earlier lines. Rhyme contributes one element of surprise; so do the alliterative stresses of "steams and stamps" and "lighting of the lamps." And isolating the last line from the stanza encourages the reader to pause and catch an anticipatory breath.

The lighting of the lamps ends the suspense, but the question remains how Eliot elevates an ordinary event to a not altogether explicable significance. Form supplies one clue: The last line reads more quickly than its companion, because although both have eight syllables, the final line has one fewer stress. It has lost a beat, which "lightens" the line, compared with the tetrameter norm. Moreover, the quantities of the stresses – "lonely," "cab-horse," and especially the st and m consonants in "steams and stamps" – freight and retard the penultimate line. The fragment "and then the lighting of the lamps" becomes, by contrast to the previous complete sentence, a "lighter," more rapid line, rhythmically, aurally, and syntactically speaking, than its slower, heavier companion.

Nor can these formal quantities be separated from the qualities the images themselves possess. The penultimate line, for instance, glances down; it is earthbound and has great "presence," with its complex, sense-laden images of a lathered horse's breath steaming in cold, dusk air and the sound of a great, shod hoof thudding impatiently on the cobble. Like everyone else, the horse is "lonely," and his steaming and stamping add an ingredient of impatience or even protest, however reigned in. By contrast, the last line seems altogether less material: A more simply visual image, it lights the air, glances upward, and depicts the magical split second as if the curtain were suddenly about to rise upon some unexpected drama.

The couplet at the end of Section I inaugurates another pattern throughout "Preludes," that of lightening and upward movement. It parallels phrases like "the morning comes to consciousness," "the light crept up between the shutters," and perhaps even "the conscience of a blackened street impatient to assume the world." Pound called such images generic to Eliot's early verse, referring to "his wholly unrealizable, always apt, half ironic suggestion."[7] These "unrealizable" (because impossible to picture) images – the awakening morning, the myriad-imaged soul, the vision that the street cannot understand – link the abstract and the concrete to produce an emotional charge. Were this not the case, "Preludes" might easily be dismissed as merely painterly, an urban version of Paterian twilight, or pretty, picturesque clutter, in which words existed mainly to be combined with other words "poetically" but irresponsibly in a way Eliot would condemn in "Swinburne as Poet." Though Eliot did not emerge entirely unscathed from contact with Paterian values, "Preludes" at least places the Paterian sensorium amid dirty, urban surroundings and endeavors to incorporate the contemporary world, even if the effect verges on surrealism. This remains true even if we cannot always distill a precise, paraphrasable meaning from "You had such a vision of the street as the street hardly understands," or if we cannot concretely envision someone's soul "stretched tight across the skies."

Connotation helps account for part of the poem's indefinable effect, which both results from and increases the feeling that its literal level remains more or less unhelpful. Combining an abstraction – the conscience – with something concrete – a blackened street – reveals that these characters' inner world shares something with their external circumstances. (This is especially true insofar as a number of these abstractions and other words – "soul," "vision," "conscience," "revealing," and the entire penultimate stanza – come from a religious and ethical vocabulary, hinting at a numinous presence suffusing the profane metropolis.) Their inner lives have adapted to the city by taking on its sordid qualities, yet "Preludes" attributes to them an inchoate, residual spirituality. That a soul is stretched tight, trampled, or revealed at night to be composed of a thousand sordid images suggests that "Preludes" really concerns the self, the inner being, and the pain city life inflicts upon it. If atomistic urban existence reduces people to anonymous, uniform insignificance; if their souls must submit to unrelenting, deforming pressure; and if such people can do little more than cope submissively and automatically with burdens as trivial as they are insistent – then perhaps the poet has not misplaced his sympathy.

But why would Eliot have chosen such material in the first place? Why would someone leave the Cambridge Gold Coast and seek out instead drab, down-at-the-heels precincts across the tracks? Why set poetry amid such unpromising surroundings? The answer partly involves the joining of aesthetic opposites. "Preludes," for instance, deliberately incorporates stubbornly unpoetic matter, such as litter and decay. At the time this task animated many writers, and artists as well: The Ashcan school, for instance, formed just about the time Eliot wrote "Preludes." William Dean Howells's *A Hazard of New Fortunes,* whose Basil March tours the urban landscape in a detached, "aesthetic" manner similar to that in "Preludes," offers a fictional precedent. Though the poem's melancholy ennui at times nearly verges on comedy, "Preludes" illustrates how a sense of latent drama may at moments break, and thereby transform, an otherwise enervating routine.

In Eliot's case, his sense of aesthetic opposites doubtless also involved some moral and social opposites embedded in his background. People and places at the lower end of the social scale had traditionally absorbed the attention of other Eliots. Eliot's mother devoted herself to social reforms at the local level, such as a juvenile house of detention, and numerous sisters and cousins embarked upon public-spirited careers addressed to people in need.[8] It is hardly inconsistent with his moral and social origins that such a class might preoccupy Eliot as well; it is only unusual that he would employ poetry as his vehicle. The travail of those beneath him had absorbed Rev. Eliot too, who had constantly urged personal salvation through righteous, self-controlled behavior. He issued a pamphlet on how controlling prostitution depended not on better hygiene or police vigilance but on individual spiritual reform. His grandson, by contrast, published "Preludes," "Rhapsody on a Windy Night," and "Morning at the Window." Substantively equivocal, these poems rendered the pathos of the demimonde, borrowing images from Charles-Louis Philippe's low-life French novel *Bubu de Montparnasse,* but scrupulously avoided religious or reformist exhortation.[9]

Like his grandfather, and like Bubu's creator, Eliot felt "pity for the humble and oppressed." Unlike Rev. Eliot, the poet of "Preludes" adopted Philippe's dispassion. Eliot wrote that Philippe had a "pathos which . . . trembles on the edge of the maudlin" and noted his lack of religious or humanitarian zeal to change things. Like *Bubu,* "Preludes" involves people who are underfed, inarticulate, and "too depressed to be rebellious."[10] One might almost say that Eliot's social and moral cultivation "naturally" inclined him to take an interest in such people, toward whom his own family had customarily addressed its moral concern. But his refusal to adopt their didactic, humanitarian approach may have caused him to assume what he termed Philippe's self-consciously distant, detached attitude, more concerned in reporting than reforming the silent, bored masses. The "passer-by with muddy skirts," "the epileptic on the bed," "the typist home at teatime," and the crowd that twice daily flowed over London bridge testify to Eliot's predisposition toward this material.

This brief reprise of family influence and the persistence of such subject matter throughout Eliot's early poems suggest the likelihood that Eliot felt the moral claims of social opposites, the familiar tendency of some well-off elites to tether their moral fortunes to poverty, redeeming guilty leisure through good works. At this stage, however, Eliot appears to have declined that method, with all its potential for misunderstanding and hypocrisy, in the same way he excused himself from other impositions of his background. "Preludes" simply presents a more catholic, inclusive consciousness observing and trying to inject itself into a more parochial, limited one. In essence, the poem and its method portray urban crudeness with sophisticated urbanity. The nether world lured Eliot with a range of experience from which gentility and righteousness had otherwise barred him. This social and experiential gap, which parallels a gap in consciousness, "Preludes" experimentally endeavors to close.

The poem's verbal doubleness confirms these experiential opposites, frequently expressing two widely disparate viewpoints, taking on multiple, ambiguous meanings, instead of single, fixed ones. On the one hand, this may produce vagueness: Has "masquerade" positive, festive connotations or insidious, disillusioned ones? Does "assume" in its context mean "to seize or ascend to," "to suppose or take for granted," or "to put on a role or mask"? Deciding which of these meanings applies, or how they all do, will doubtless affect how a reader views the poem. Perhaps the reverse is true as well.

More important, only ambiguous diction and ironic, multiple meanings can express the gap between the depicting consciousness and the consciousness depicted. In the phrase "eyes assured of certain certainties," for example, the speaker considers a quality of assurance he notices in someone else or in the eyes of many city people he observes. This assurance and these certainties may well reflect a bold simplicity – or simple-mindedness – toward which the hesitant, complex speaker feels something like envy. Yet the diverging meanings of "certain" – "unquestionable" and "undoubted," on the one hand, and "particular, but unspecified or indefinite," on the other – enable the speaker also to question these certainties as facile or wholly mistaken, and in any case not nearly so certain in light of *his* knowledge. The ambiguity contains both sympathy and condescension, an approach and a retreat. The speaker observes the unknowable eyes, yet keeps his distance: seeing them, but not being seen.

This sort of irony, balancing alternative responses without affirmatively adopting either one, reflects Eliot's effort to enter imaginatively a world whose surface attracts him but whose inhabitants' hearts and minds remain opaque. The poem raises the possibility that their surroundings furnish, and can be equated with, their consciousness. That equation puts them at the mercy of their environment, which amounts to calling them as seedy and deteriorated as their dismal circumstances. The soul's thousand images are "sordid"; somehow the blackened street comes to have, or to resemble, a conscience. "Preludes" shows people suffering because the mind cannot detach itself from what it perceives, a kind of mental weakness that implies a concurrent spiritual vulnerability.[11] It expresses the same tendency in the author's mind. Different as the poem's characters and their author are, they share this psychic or sensible permeability. The difference is that while the poem's characters come to resemble aspects of their environment because they have no other choice, Eliot's mind fastens itself to them and their cramped universe through a – more or less – conscious act.

How necessary sympathy is to civilized, social life, and to the life of the mind as well. Yet how frequently objects, ideas, and people unworthy of sympathetic attention abound, especially in the city, with its carefree ugliness, anomic manners, and indigestible crowds. So "Preludes" seems to suggest when its speaker, in the concluding lines, laughs at the sympathetic attitude, rejecting it as so much misplaced sentiment.

We shall return to the poem's conclusion, but only after exploring Eliot's treatment of Bradleyan philosophy, which pertains to the way "Preludes" treats consciousness and materiality, personal identity and social reality. Eliot's emotional ambivalence, of which "Preludes" is an instance, created epistemological ambiguity; his work on F. H. Bradley addresses this latter, philosophical problem. Too much, or too automatic, sympathy – stated the opposite way, too little distance – left Eliot preoccupied with things of which many people remain blissfully innocent: of how insufficient ideals are when detached from the social facts that cushion them; of how chaotic the terms of reality are without a point of view to organize them; of how easily ugliness, rudeness, and insensibility violate receptivity; of how supposed moral absolutes in fact remain matters of social convention, in need of constant tending. Like "Preludes," Eliot's work on Bradley reveals his early conclusions, which had so much to do with the first half of his career: that the self was permeable and unformed, time (and perhaps the material world) unreal, and reality radically ambiguous.

BRADLEY

Many signposts in Eliot's early work point to his dissertation, written for a Harvard doctorate that, in the event, he never actually received. Between 1910 and 1916 Eliot's life followed a circuitous, international course, influenced by many accidents, both public and private. By the end of 1916, in any case, he had moved to London, met and married his first wife, befriended Ezra Pound, finished his education, and abandoned his philosophical career. He had also written his dissertation, published forty-eight years later as *Knowledge and Experience in the Philosophy of F. H. Bradley*. The least known book of Eliot's prolific, lengthy career, it alludes, in another genre and vocabulary, to several themes bearing upon his early writing and reveals some problematical aspects of his sensibility that his religious orientation ultimately resolves.

Eliot often praised Bradley's prose and once wrote to Lytton Strachey that Bradley was the "finest philosopher in English," calling *Appearance and Reality* the "Education Sentimentale of abstract thought."[1] Though

Bradley's influence resembled Laforgue's in its extent, it was gradual and cumulative rather than abrupt and intense. Bradley supplied a philosophical system and a vocabulary compatible with Eliot's ideas and tending to validate and sharpen those ideas rather than replace them with something substantively new. As Laforgue had done poetically, Bradley extended "encouragement" of another, intellectual sort.

Yet Bradley's ideas, and philosophical endeavor itself, proved inadequate. Having completed and filed his thesis, Eliot determined not to return to Harvard to make his required oral defense. Eliot in this fashion refused his degree, deliberately burning professional bridges that lay in front of him, or perhaps making a grand, even ostentatious, gesture of intellectual aloofness.[2] In the dissertation itself Eliot does not pursue Bradley as a mere acolyte. Even if, as he later claimed, Bradley mainly influenced his prose style, Eliot applied his own ideas to Bradley's philosophy, which they partly affirmed but also partly criticized.

These qualifications aside, Bradley's epistemology, ontology, and metaphysic remain inseparable from his style, so to admit its influence is in the end to say quite a lot. Eliot called the blend of wit and gently corrosive irony in Bradley's prose "solemn banter"[3] and often tried to imitate it, although with only occasional success. When it fails, Eliot's prose overshoots the mark with an unseemly shrillness or unnecessary pugnacity. While dozens of Eliot's near epigrams and terse formulas have earned a deserved currency, his less careful sentences can be ungainly, turgid, or downright clumsy. Rarely do they equal Bradley's syntactic poise or his enviable simplicity of diction, qualities that not infrequently combine to create an effect both authoritative and playful. That Bradley can sustain these qualities throughout even the most abstract discussion marks only one of the excellences of his prose, but it adds literary merit to whatever philosophical matter it recommends.

As for his own philosophical language, Eliot commented that forty-six years after his philosophical career had ended, he found himself unable to think in his dissertation's terminology and claimed he did not pretend to understand it.[4] Despite its distracting textual problems, its relentless style, and the unfamiliarity of turn-of-the-century English, American, and Austrian philosophy, the dissertation introduces certain of Eliot's preoccupations for the first time in his prose. These bear on his poetic themes, clarify some of Eliot's criticism, and occasionally even echo or anticipate his poetry. In an oblique way, they also foreshadow Eliot's religiosity.

Bradley's system, and Eliot's treatment of it, begin with "immediate experience," also called "feeling." Either term refers to

> the general condition before distinctions and relations have been developed, and where as yet neither any subject nor object exists. And it

means . . . anything which is present at any stage of mental life, in so far as that is only present and simply is. In this latter sense we may say that everything actual, no matter what, must be felt; but we do not call it feeling except so far as we take it as failing to be more.[5]

This stage exists before any act the mind might perform upon it, preceding any interpretation, placement of the feeling into relation with something else, or application of abstractions, universals, or other intellectual categories to it. It occurs before being connected to memory and before being isolated or distinguished in a way that might compromise its immediacy or (most especially) interpose a division between subject and object. Should any of these events take place, "feeling" disintegrates from an undistinguished, un-self-conscious monad to a distinct component in a relational, pluralistic field.

Although the next stage, "thought," into which feeling develops but does not entirely disappear, corresponds to the mind's effort to increase the reality of a feeling, thought nevertheless remains appearance. Feeling exists before thought analyzes its aspects, "sides," or parts, places it in relation to something else, or discovers it to be the identical object of a perceiving subject. It is the raw thing, uncut, uncooked, and un-self-conscious, before the ground is broken and the (mental) construction gets underway. Thought, by contrast, attempts "to complete our object by relational addition from without and by relational distinction from within."[6] Thought, that is, equals "relational consciousness," adding to feeling's reality by placing it in relation. By dividing its unity and provoking its self-consciousness, thought's addition inevitably alters feeling; to establish objectivity by relation and distinction also calls forth a perceiver's subjectivity. A perceiving, intellectual subject necessarily augments its knowledge of the object, but just as surely destroys the unity, what we may almost call the naiveté, of feeling. Though some aspects of feeling never disappear entirely, persisting as the base upon which thought and eventually the "Absolute" develop, nevertheless once thought intervenes, it reveals feeling as incomplete appearance.

Neither, however, can thought stake any definitive claim to reality. Thought's elaboration, construction, and objectification, while enhancing the object for the perceiving subject, have no effect whatever on the object itself. Its identity, as distinct from its objectivity, remains impervious to such extraneous intellectual, relational, and subjective business. Thought may dirempt feeling's unity for the perceiver, but it leaves the object's essence, and its identity, serenely undisturbed. Relations, though they may heighten the object's apparent reality by adding to the subject's knowledge of it, nonetheless remain purely ideal:

The reality, as thought of or as perceived, in itself simply is. It may be given, or again sought for, discovered or reflected on, but all this –

however much there may be of it – is nothing to *it*. For the object only stands in relation, and emphatically in no sense is the relation in which it stands.

This is the vital inconsistency of the real as perception or thought.[7]

Eliot's dissertation concerns itself principally with thought and relational consciousness, the middle level of Bradley's system. Although Eliot's attitude toward Bradley's highest level, the Absolute, remains clear, curiously his dissertation says next to nothing about it. To this topic we shall return, after exploring some other uses, criticisms, and qualifications Eliot makes of Bradley's scheme.

Though grounding his system in feeling, Bradley readily admits its fragility, transience, and instability, instructing us to expect the quick demise of immediate experience as inevitable and a thing not to be lamented unduly: While the lowest stage may provide intimations of the highest, feeling is not the Absolute, which Bradley defines as "immediate like feeling, but not, like feeling, immediate at a level below distinction and relation."[8] After perception undergoes a transit from preliminary feeling (or immediate experience) and through relational and distinguished thought (or practical reality), it reaches the Absolute, which crowns Bradley's three-tiered metaphysic. Bradley's Absolute subsumes both lower tiers, containing feeling's immediacy yet retaining thought's distinctions and relations. Thought initially disintegrates feeling, but may also redintegrate itself into the Absolute.[9]

Though it is not invariably present, one must always pause to inquire how much of Bradley's technical meaning Eliot preserves when using the terms "feeling" and "thought." The dissociation of sensibility theory, for example, seems to retain something of Bradley's scheme and vocabulary. There Eliot purports to tell what happens when fluency between feeling and thought breaks down, isolating the two from one another. In a unified sensibility, thought and feeling achieve a symbiosis, with thought making feeling self-conscious, illuminating its latent distinctions, and placing aspects it distinguishes in feelings into relation with other things: "Jonson and Chapman . . . were notably erudite, and were notably men who incorporated their erudition into their sensibility: their mode of feeling was directly and freshly altered by their reading and thought. In Chapman especially there is a direct sensuous apprehension of thought, or a recreation of thought into feeling."[10] Illustrating a unified sensibility, Eliot suggests that poets – at least metaphysical ones – had a special ability. They apparently could *reverse,* for their own purposes, the Bradleyan process in which feeling became thought, transform or "recreate" thought into feeling, and express that transformation verbally. After the dissociation, so goes the exposition, the fluency congealed, or mechanized. After the sentimental age began in the early eighteenth century, having revolted against the descriptive and "ratiocinative," poets "thought and felt by fits, unbalanced; they reflected."[11] In these poets, feeling had dispersed into related and distinguished object and contemplating subject; thought had abandoned its links to feeling, not to meet again, according to Eliot, until modern times. His account in Bradleyan vocabulary suggests that Eliot's familiar theory might profitably be interpreted by at least partial reference to Bradley's less well known system.

Eliot diverges most clearly from Bradley at the middle level – thought, relational consciousness, practical reality – between immediate experience and the Absolute. In essence, although he carefully accords immediate experience "independent reality," Eliot resoundingly affirms its shortcomings and, somewhat less definitely, those of the Absolute as well. He first argues that we possess time, space, and selves only in the world of objects. "Lack of harmony and cohesion," that is, permits no experience to remain "merely immediate"; intermediate thought, so to speak, must necessarily infringe upon immediate experience. Hence, Eliot reasons, we discover ourselves as "conscious souls in a world of objects." That discovery pushes us further to conceive of an "all-inclusive experience outside of which nothing shall fall." Having thus defined the highest or ultimate stage of his own scheme, however, Eliot at once descends from this philosophical altitude, carefully distinguishing his definition from Bradley's Absolute and drawing the ambit – between mere experience at the beginning and complete experience at the end – within which his remarks will proceed. After conceding that immediate experience at either extreme remains "annihilation and utter night," Eliot states that he does not presume that Bradley himself would accept this interpretation of his "positive non-distinguished non-relational whole." Nor do Eliot's remarks require Bradley's acceptance, since they concern not the ultimate nature of the Absolute, but only some intermediate steps that precede it.[12]

Having staked out this middle ground, Eliot's Chapters 2, 4, and 5 contend that psychology and epistemology proceed from false assumptions and cannot solve or even address the problems of this middle state. That metaphysics reduces the reality of this intermediate level to mere appearance only complicates the problem and remains in a sense so much the worse for metaphysics. It is finally in ordinary, quotidian, or – Eliot's favorite term, arising almost automatically when he raises this issue – "practical" reality that metaphysical, ideal construction will cohere or crumble, stand or fall. The situation creates a paradox: Metaphysically this practical world remains chaotically contradictory, yet the effort to unify it by using a practical perspective yields a metaphysically real, if still perspectival, orderliness.

Having ruled Bradley's Absolute out of court, Eliot explores the middle level of thought and practice, where placing things into relation and articulating distinctions, similarities, and differences organize the world. This effort involves discovering patterns – of physical sensation, memory, history and time, ideas, or one's own self and private experience. Epistemology's false assumption – against which Eliot repeatedly warns – remains that a single, complete, and consistent world of external reality exists. Eliot dismissed that assumption as "not only ungrounded but in some sense certainly false. Reality contains irreducible contradictions and irreconcilable points of view."[13] Not a single, objective reality to which we can expect to conform, that is, but rather a reality that relies upon our position – our perspective, our point of view – within it: Such is the metaphysically unsatisfactory but practically real procedure.

This double-edged metaphysic inevitably cuts two ways. Certainly relational consciousness is indispensable; try to live without it. To dwell solely upon the isolate thing sooner or later impoverishes, and may even destroy, its reality. Bereft of all relation, a thing may cease to have objectivity – to a perceiver at least – and so may relinquish existence. Not only does a thing alter what it is placed in relation to, but it also may be said – practically speaking – to constitute that other thing. That is, insofar as a thing has relations to other things, its reality increases, at least from the point of view of anyone who can perceive, receive, or conceive of those relations. This disconcerting possibility holds within it a means by which to reverse the conventional relation between practical appearance and ideal reality. The Absolute may be nothing, and appearance may remain only what we, as perceivers and creators of relations (ranging from opposites through the gradations of dissimilarity, similarity, resemblance, and equality, even unto the magic threshold of identity), are capable of constructing it to be.

Yet while relational consciousness creates patterns that order the world, these relations contain an instability in their very nature. That is because, for better or worse, such relations can be altered simply by a change in their terms. If we see ourselves as empowered to make those changes, this metaphysic may appear liberating indeed, as it was for Wallace Stevens, whose perspective it strongly resembles. But if we perceive metaphysical (here not to be distinguished from practical) change as transpiring unmindful and regardless of our position (which is only tenuously and even arbitrarily fixed to begin with) in it, such ontological insouciance may suffuse reality and freight the self with joylessness and dread. Thus Eliot bravely analyzed the process of developing a "real world" as working in two directions. We neither add "our imaginings" *to* a real world, nor "select" an individualized world, real to us, *from* a real world. Instead, "the real and the unreal develop side by side."

The problem stems from a notion of "reality" itself, which falls short insofar as it excludes what is illusory instead of admitting it. Rather than regarding the world as "ready made," Eliot urges us to think of the world of meaning for us "as constructed, or constructing itself . . . at every moment, and never more than an approximate construction, a construction essentially practical in its nature." Only then, Eliot concludes, do the difficulties of unreal and real cease. The dual process of developing a real world runs along a track comprising parallel rails of epistemological certitude and practical ambiguity. Arguing that the contrast of unreal and real cannot survive translation from epistemological theory to the point of view of practice, Eliot can conclude that "while the real world of epistemology is hard and fast . . . the real world of practice is essentially vague, unprecise, swarming with what are, from a metaphysical point of view, insoluble contradictions."[14]

Eliot's perspective, then, remains metaphysically sophisticated and self-conscious, but insistently practical. It admits all manner of skepticism and qualification, but does so to suggest that theoretical and practical world views ultimately only coexist. To put it bluntly, they remain both incompatible and inseparable, the theoretical viewpoint inevitably growing out of the practical one, with theory full of practical motives and consequences, and practice based largely upon speculation. "We can never . . . wholly explain the practical world from a theoretical point of view, because this world is what it is by reason of the practical point of view and the world which we try to explain is a world spread out upon a table – simply *there!*"[15] Eliot had earlier clarified the metaphysicality of practicality by dismissing a doctrine dear to metaphysicians, that of degrees of reality. His discussion partially disarms metaphysicians, but licenses ordinary people, who he says effectively resemble them insofar as both preserve some sense of "real" and "unreal," however crude or refined. That is because without the concept of the "unreal," there can be no world of finite experience; all experience would necessarily be "infinite." Eliot points out that the world of finite experience involves emphasis and selection, just as interest and valuation support the world of practice. To the objection that our interests and values vary from moment to moment, Eliot answers, "So does the real world, according to that fragment of it which happens to be the focus of our attention."[16] Further paradoxes, then: Insofar as we have a point of view – interests and values – we can create, or at least assume, a real world. But since those interests and values change, so do our viewpoints. So, therefore, does the real world – whose mutability thereby gives us all the more reason to regard it as all the less real.

Hence the epistemologist's all-purpose crux between subject and object can hardly supply reliable information about reality. Yet our "interests and values" can give us a criterion against which to measure reality, because by intending a world we extend a personal point of view that pretends to an impersonal, objective reality. Although lacking metaphysical objectivity, this intended world nonetheless retains practical validity. "The reality of the object does not lie in the object itself, but in the extent of the relations which the object possesses without significant falsification of itself."[17] Thus the justification for allowing reality, which establishes our point of view, as it were, independently of us, to establish likewise the reality of the object. Reality gives us a point of view upon the object. From that point of view – determined by the "extent of the relations which the object possesses without significant falsification of itself" – the object appears real.

Here we might well ask how felicitously, by this account, things turn out for the object. Real as the object might be practically, its ideal reality – subordinated to practicality's fickle uses – becomes temporary and mutable. Objects in a relational ontology remain exposed to unceasing variation. As such they, and that ontology, offer little help in assuaging the metaphysical hunger for a true, unchanging reality. At times it seems that Eliot's dissertation intends covertly to starve that appetite, since the subject – the self – provides no sustenance either. Bradley's problematical "finite centre," though related to the self, soul, ego, spirit, and identity, nonetheless differs from all these things. But it too *pursues* immediate experience, out of which it is itself constructed ideally. Recall that in immediate experience, subject and object remain indiscernible. Creatures of "thought," they simply do not yet exist. Once immediate experience undergoes contemplation, however, its nature changes: It becomes an object itself.

Similarly, since a self or finite centre can contemplate itself, it too relinquishes its reality to that extent. Even though it may retain a commonsensical, practical reality, it nonetheless becomes "appearance." "We have no right, except in the most provisional way, to speak of *my* experience, since the I is a construction out of experience, an abstraction from it."[18] This "I," whose genesis resembles relational reality insofar as both arise from feeling, is similarly ideal, and appearance: "The world . . . exists only as it is found in the experiences of finite centres, experiences so mad and strange that they will be boiled away before you boil them down to one homogeneous mass."[19] Here, then, reappear "the thousand sordid images of which your soul was constituted."

If the world "swarms" with contradictions; if finite centres consist of ideal constructions of and upon that world, which "boil away" precipitously; and if objects have only a partial, practical objectivity, where then do individuals locate coherence? Point of view remains an insufficient answer, and not only because it changes. Point of view is also multiple: There exist, as even cursory notice must admit, other people in the world. This practically infinite number of finite centres all about us poses the crucial stumbling block of Eliot's thesis, and not coincidentally of his poetry as well. Since no single consistent world exists, the life of the soul consists of contemplating difference and diversity. As we shall see, its "painful task" was to unify their incompatibility by passing from them to a "higher" viewpoint. In Bradley's scheme, this involved the discovery of "relations," which when sufficiently inclusive, encompassed the philosophical Absolute. For Eliot, of course, this passage ultimately involved a religious solution. It is in any case significant how his philosophical inquiry posed the problem that would preoccupy him throughout so much of his early life.[20]

An inquirer who pursues Eliot's scheme long enough to grasp it even sketchily may encounter a certain grim quality. Occasionally the tone suggests that only gritted teeth kept it unswervingly on course, and assorted despairing gestures part, at intervals, the curtain of strict philosophical detachment. But despite the practical insufficiency of metaphysics, and the metaphysical unreality of practice, as ontological bedrock; despite a relational epistemology; and despite an unstable, private self that verges on solipsism, Eliot nonetheless left himself an escape hatch from all this uncertainty, even if some would sidestep it as rather more like a trap door. In organizing the world and the self – and "the real is the organized" in a relational epistemology – we have the assistance first of Nature and then of other selves, which severally contain a principle of identity:

> A point of view . . . need not be considered as identical with one human consciousness; so that we may be said to move from one point of view to another when we determine an object by another relation. If this be true, then the movement between one "finite centre" and another will not differ in kind from that inside of one consciousness, and will consist in the constitution of a real world by ideal references of many aspects.[21]

This is the sort of language that makes Eliot's dissertation at times so trying. If I understand it and can paraphrase it, the passage argues that as different people may share a single point of view, so may consciousness move from one point of view to another insofar as it may regard even a single thing in many relations. Therefore, a single consciousness may contain within it many points of view. And just as a single thing may be regarded in different relations by many "finite centres," so may a single consciousness regard many aspects of a thing in relation to many other things. In this manner it may not only construct a world, but do so in a way that both imitates and dovetails with the constructions of other finite centres.

So much for paraphrase. Fortunately, the doctrine flowing from Eliot's analysis is easier to follow. As distinguished from the "Reality" of metaphysics, Eliot maintains, the real world of epistemology will be an "essentially idefinite world of identical references of an indefinite number of points of view, particularly those of other civilized adults with whom we come in contact, but quite possibly extending to all finite centres with which we can establish an identical reference."[22] Eliot's penultimate chapter, "Solipsism," concerns just how such "identical reference" comes to be. Practically speaking, as Eliot carefully notes, the social world forms the basis of both public and private reality. Instead of thrashing about in a swampy solipsism, we acquire a social self related to but distinguishable from our private (what Chapter 3 of this volume will call a "central") self. Chapter 3 will explore how Eliot's writing extends the homo duplex idea briefly mentioned here. For now, let us observe that perhaps only the social world of public behavior broadly construed contains any sufficient reality-conferring, much less identity-conferring, principle. "The self depends as well upon other selves; it is not given as a direct experience, but is an interpretation of experience by interaction with other selves."[23]

And what of this "interaction"? What enables it and the "interpretation of experience" to proceed? What medium permits a disparate (though surely not random) set of finite centres cooperatively to intend an identical world at once subjectively credible and objectively sufficient? What, in short, supplies the means of social life? Eliot awards this organizing, reality-conferring power to language. Not coincidentally, in so doing he marks off a privileged territory for poets, the masters and guardians of language. To authorize an epistemologically real world, we may through language cooperate with the points of view "of other civilized adults with whom we come in contact, but quite possibly extending to all finite centres with which we can establish an identical reference."[24]

One hopes the finite centres with which one establishes such reference are "civilized adults," though they may turn out not to be, as the bitterness in Eliot's poetry not infrequently exhibits. His impatience with the world's Sweeneys and Bleisteins merges with this precept. It acknowledges both the psychological fact that other selves irrevocably influence one's own and the social fact that we do not always exercise unfettered choice in determining the selves with which we have contact. Though Eliot's hostility might have had something to do with his philosophical conclusion, it undoubtedly arose from a more personal source. "Identical reference" with civilized adults of one's own choosing is one thing. But when it arises (as it inevitably does, given the theory, which is undoubtedly correct) with whomever one has contact, it comes to resemble a kind of coercion, rather like handing over one's self to whomever one meets. Here is a source for the vulnerability of the characters in "Preludes," and it suggests why Prufrock must defend himself emotionally by preparing a social mask.

Even testing one's own interpretation against those of others, however, cannot pretend to metaphysical objectivity, since it reflects the decay of immediate experience. This process, the socialization of Bradleyan feeling, though necessary if we are to avoid solipsism, nonetheless does no little bit of violence to metaphysics. An individual's state of Bradleyan feeling may persist indefinitely, without giving that perceiver any sense of subjectivity or objectivity. Only when the world of practice, and in particular other people, bump up against feeling does feeling diverge from the thing that elicits it and (for the perceiver) subject divide from object. In feeling, the whole world is subjective, because it cannot be contrasted with anything else objective; objectification has not yet occurred, and there is no reason it should so long as the one feeling lasts and pervades consciousness. But how long will "the one feeling" persist? "It is only in social behaviour, in the conflict and readjustment of finite centres, that feelings and things are torn apart. And after this separation they leave dim and drifting edges, and tend to coalesce."[25] An almost Prufrockian melancholy circulates about this remark, which laments in miniature the fall of man, the acquisition of self-consciousness (ever the byproduct of social behavior), and the dissolution of the childlike (even if false) sense of unity between self and world. Such conclusions occasioned Eliot's fall into radical ambiguity. Combined with a sense of distance and indifference – social and personal, as well as metaphysical – its uncertainties fueled his early poetry.

If this unity – mythic, childlike, undifferentiated, and much like Bradleyan immediate experience – fails, language compensates the loss. Unity of reference creates unity of intention, or at least a unity of an intended world; words with shared meaning hold us, and our world, together. Here appears a link between Eliot the poet and Eliot the social critic, tirelessly comparing the state of the language to that of society, at times seeming even to advocate social reorganization as a means of producing better literature. Word and world march, in this conception, more or less in step. Eliot's use of the word to resolve, or at least allay, metaphysical confusion invites us to notice how it parallels his aesthetic – uniting fragments into a poem; his psychology – uniting the disparities of the self; and his sociology – trying to discover a principle of unity in society.

In discussing the relation between a symbol and that which it symbolizes, Eliot calls the two continuous. He asserts that properly speaking, no relation exists between them, since relation implies a difference between its two terms that can be described in a way distinct from either one. "The reality without the symbol would never be known, and we cannot say that it would even exist (or subsist); but on the other hand the symbol furnishes proof of the reality, inasmuch as without the reality it would not be that symbol: i.e. there would be an identity left which would for our purposes be irrelevant."[26] Moving from symbol to sign, Eliot then argues that besides linking the finite centre to the objects of its thought and perception, a word is continuous with meaning. Even more boldly, he contends that in some sense an identity – as distinct from a mere relation – exists between the symbol and that which it symbolizes, and between the word and its meaning. Elsewhere he explains how essential it is to his argument that the symbol or sign not be "arbitrarily amputated from the object which it symbolizes, as for practical purposes, it is isolated. . . . No symbol, I maintain, is ever a mere symbol, but is continuous with that which it symbolizes. Without words, no objects."[27] This doctrine confers some obvious benefits upon someone about to switch from philosophy to poetry. Among other advantages, it endows the poet with the power not simply to legislate for the world, but indeed to create it.

It furthermore suggests a means by which to organize reality, since words exert epistemological authority. During immediate experience, before the object is named or indeed can even be called an object, it remains "only a bundle of particular perceptions; in order to be an object it must present identity in difference throughout a span of time." Only when we pass from immediate experience and, Eliot argues, through the agency of speech and words can we distinguish our mental attention – "thought" – from the object to which it attends. "Our only way of showing that we are attending to an object is to show that it and ourself are independent entities, and to do this we must have names."[28] Words gather reality into objects, and shape it by distinguishing objects from perceiving subjects.[29]

Should words be accused of being mere abstractions, Eliot would respond with equanimity: "Every perception involves some degree of recognition and the operation of a universal."[30] Abstractions, after all, mean convenience – and on this theory, perhaps even reality itself – in a relational, practical world. They rescue us from inchoate sense perception and dumbness alike. And they do more than that; even though objects are known independently of the words that refer to them, "the object *qua* object would not exist without this bundle of experiences, but the bundle would not be a bundle unless it were held together by the moment of objectivity which is realized in the name."[31] Mental life, on this theory, presupposes naming and words, which, by designating, design reality. Insofar as someone can recognize, much less use, his surroundings, he must rely upon words. To name is to organize reality, for oneself and by implication for the community. Even though the name differs from the object, it remains nevertheless a category through which to grasp an object. "Try to think of what anything would be if you refrained from naming it altogether, and it will dissolve into sensations which are not objects; and it will not be that particular object which it is, until you have found the right name for it."[32]

Eliot lingers on this topic, and though philosophically his discussion of this "mystic marriage" between name and object can hardly have concluded the issue, practically speaking (which is how Eliot writes following this discussion), we can recognize the necessity of words given the presuppositions of Bradleyan metaphysics, especially as Eliot has truncated them. Eliot's system is even more severe than Bradley's, because it lacks an Absolute, contending that the middle ground of relation and practice is more or less all we have. Given that stark axiom, words as Eliot describes them functioning assume prime importance. Verbal abstraction may involve artifice, mediation, and even distortion, but properly so, since it serves to discipline perception lest we remain infantile or animal, and organizes reality into something coherent, beautiful possibly, or, at the very least, bearable.

Perhaps one tries to make a verbal reality, a poem, as a last resort: "You quite underestimate the closeness with which particular words are woven into our reality." Bradley's work did not alone render self, society, and metaphysics problematic for Eliot. Instead, it gave him a philosophical vocabulary with which to think and write about these things. Discovering the job words had to do for Eliot, and why they had to do it, will occupy the remainder of this chapter and to a degree the chapters that follow it. "Preludes," for instance, describes the progress of a Bradleyan finite centre through a grotesque city in which aspects of the physical and social surroundings encroach upon the self – and in which aspects of the soul and consciousness extend into these surroundings – so that, momentarily, they merge. The characters seem marooned in Bradleyan feeling, or immediate experience. The pity and horror with which the poet responds to them issue from that entrapment, at once an immersion in the city and an isolation from one another and from any other, higher consciousness. As summarized by Bradley's student: "The soul only differs from the finite centre in being considered as something not identical with its states. The finite centre, so far as I can pretend to understand it, *is* immediate experience."[33]

Eliot here defines the soul as – roughly – that state in which consciousness does not differ from what it is conscious of, when no boundary – such as words and language, the creatures and agents of thought – intervenes between the self and the external world, and the perceiver finds himself chained to what he perceives.[34] It is not the way Eliot would have defined the soul twenty years hence, but it helps us understand his starting point. This aspect of Eliot's personality is inseparable from his literary interests; it provided him with his problem and with a perspective on that problem, and gave him a source of poetic raw material as well. Eliot did not simply quote fragments culled from literary sources. He also quoted fragments from his surroundings. Perhaps he found there some analogy to his own consciousness and found poetic viability, and poetic value, in that analogy. In any case, Eliot once acknowledged that his poetry showed traces of every environment in which he had lived.[35] Much earlier, he also affirmed that "a writer's art . . . must be based on the accumulated sensations of the first twenty-one years."[36]

RELATION, POETRY, AND INCARNATION

By introducing a first-person, lyric voice and by responding discursively instead of through ironic verbal nuance, the final seven lines of "Preludes" mercifully release us from the tough philosophical sledding of Bradleyan metaphysics. What we have observed about how important "relations" are to Bradley and to Eliot, however, can shed some light on how "Preludes" fits into Eliot's poetry as a whole. If the final two stanzas differ enough from earlier ones to constitute a fifth part, the poem offers an early instance of a pentamerous structure, which Eliot used in *The Waste Land,* "The Hollow Men," and in each of the *Four Quartets.* "Preludes," however, anticipates not merely the construction but more significantly the matter of later poems. Dirty, ugly, urban images, for instance, permeate Eliot's verse from start – "a broken spring in a factory yard" – to finish, with dead leaves rattling on like tin. "Preludes" also employs Eliot's main themes: the ambiguous nature of the self, its ambivalent relation to what lies beyond, and an unresolved inquiry about whether the self should seek engagement or detachment, commitment or aloofness. This early poem tries to decide between sympathy and distance, assertion and withdrawal, desire and control. To some people, such decisions might remain automatic and unconscious. Eliot, however, confronts them at the conscious level and, characteristically, takes a double attitude toward a single set of facts.

In this respect above all, "Preludes" sets the pattern for Eliot's career: It shows how opposite attitudes toward the same stimulus may exist in a poem and how such conflicting responses may prove equally genuine. Through the poem's first four parts, the speaker feels hopeless because he faces so much helplessness. The helpful, interventionist ethics of the Gospels were never meant for cities, where the objects of sympathy exceed any single person's capacity to remedy the suffering of multitudes. This may simply state the obvious, but just as obviously it tends to transform urban life into a quotidian tragedy, in which disparities of fortune sharply reproach us at every ethical turn. "Preludes" incorporates this disturbed relation, yet the poem's conclusion denies the moral prestige that suffering and sympathy conventionally enjoy. The poem's ambivalence expresses Eliot's wish to free himself from the encroachments of an ideal whose claims he felt acutely but from which he withheld assent. Essentially, he laughs at his own acutely felt, "sincere" response, which is a way of distancing himself from it.

On one level this derision instances Eliot's need to establish a similar distance from his familial, religious, and perhaps even national heritage. Moral sensitivity, optimistic meliorism, and the individual's willingness to seek out social responsibility – the indicia of the Eliot family's liberal, Protestant America[1] – fail before modern facts, which reward the regard of traditional ethics with countless instances of arguably irremediable degradation. Psychologically and practically speaking, such examples may condemn moral sympathy to morbidity. Some people discover they must avoid them lest sympathizer and victim merge indistinguishably. Self-preservation may demand this capitulation, but if self-esteem depends upon loyalty to these ethical ideals, one is left complicated, doubled, suspended between irreconcilable opposites. Twenty years later, Eliot prayed, "Teach us to care and not to care."

"Preludes," in short, concludes by predicting the matter Eliot would expend considerable effort resolving:

> I am moved by fancies that are curled
> Around these images, and cling:
> The notion of some infinitely gentle
> Infinitely suffering thing.

Though possibly a Bradleyan "Absolute," this quatrain seems less philosophical than religious, referring on some level to the Crucifixion.[2] Given Eliot's habit of regarding things from opposed viewpoints, "Preludes" further illustrates how verbal ambiguity may spring from emotional ambivalence. Ambiguity may thus come to involve a word, a relation, an idea, or a deity occupying the middle ground between opposites: not a mere vagueness, but a *tertium quid,* partaking of two complementary, related extremes or opposites, yet distinct from either; a syzygy; a *coincidentia oppositorum.*[3] It is this theme, and its verbal, philosophical, and religious implications in Eliot's career, that my remarks will pursue.

Notwithstanding its philosophical relation to Bradley and Hegel,[4] the "infinitely gentle, infinitely suffering thing" suggests a religious source for Eliot's negative emotional ambivalence and its resolution in positive,

religious ambiguity. Christ's sufferings realize Christianity's most ambiguous moment, the "Mittelpunkt,"[5] when in extremis, Christ's latent
ambiguities become patent. Although divine, He suffers human pain.
Although immortal, His earthly life nears its conclusion. Though He
advocates faith and represents its proof, He doubts His father and God.
He loves and suffers for others, yet in His moment of maximum sympathy, others torture, revile, and betray Him. Son of God and son of man,
the word made flesh, emblem of spiritual fortitude overcoming physical
suffering, "the point of intersection of the timeless with time," *kairos* and
chronos, heaven and earth, in His person and His personage Christ unites
these great opposites.

The occasion contains countless such complexities. The commission
of a sin more grave even than the original one – then man disobeyed
God; here he kills Him – this new transgression paradoxically supplies
the means by which to efface the results of Adam's sin and redeem the
souls of his descendants. The attitudes the Crucifixion elicits are likewise
complex. Sadness at the torture and at Christ's departure mixes with joy
for the fulfillment of the divine design and the possibility of hitherto
unavailable salvation. Gratitude to God for dispatching Christ on this
merciful errand qualifies the shame provoked by this renewed proof of
human capacity for sin. Mortal beings can identify the pain Christ suffers, but cannot identify with it: Christ's fleshly humanity authorizes His
suffering, yet His endurance before it elevates Him above the merely
human. The Crucifixion proves Him both man and god, of the same
flesh as humanity but alien in essence. The greater one's sympathy with
His passion, the wider is the distance that yawns between the observer of
Christ's trial and the divine creature who transcends it.

It would be difficult to argue that "Preludes" portrays Christian faith.
More likely it renders that awkward if not uncommon state, a Christian
sensibility without Christian belief. "Preludes" expresses this residuum
by acknowledging the sufferings of the lowly and anonymous; by alluding to a supernatural, spiritual, or ideal presence suffusing the material
world; by preferring ambiguity and irony; and most crucially by referring to infinite suffering as the favored representation of seriousness. It
might be worth noting that the name for Christ's agony, the Passion,
and the attitude Christianity takes toward it, sympathy, spring from the
same etymological root, the Greek *pathos.* Christianity, at least one
strand of it, has so bound the two together that they perhaps cannot be
teased apart. The two attitudes can come to verge on identity: to suffer is
to feel, to feel is to suffer. This chiastic conflation describes Eliot's sensibility – in his way of regarding self, body, word, and world – even
when he evidently lacked Christian belief. His feeling was mixed, his
sufferings never simply painful, and his pleasures rarely simple.[6]

It seems neither inappropriate nor accidental that Eliot chose laughter to attack this seriousness or that when Christianity circumscribed Eliot least his verse displayed the most humor. Although the religion authorizes diverse emotions – joy, awe, wonder, and gratitude as well as sadness – the Christian emotions remain exclusively serious, and lack humor entirely. Even though, for instance, the Gospel stories teem with irony, which is so close to humor in other contexts, their irony remains serious, often bitterly so. This may explain why "Preludes" rejects seriousness and sympathy with a laugh:

> Wipe your hand across your mouth, and laugh;
> The worlds revolve like ancient women
> Gathering fuel in vacant lots.

The poet rids himself of the ethically and emotionally refined words that had come out of his mouth, in favor of a less articulate, preverbal, even primitive gesture. The purgative laugh signals a change of attitude, from sympathy to derision, almost as a matter of self-protection.[7]

The poem's chronology is circular, and even the vacant lots signify that phase of the development cycle when investment avoids a declining district. The final two lines seem to say that ancient women have always gathered fuel in vacant lots, and always will. Moreover, the planets have always revolved and will continue to do so despite the tender feelings of poets (and, by implication, of those – such as the Eliots – who take to heart the suffering of others). Equating old women with revolving planets implies that since these sad but inevitable patterns cannot be changed, it is futile and perhaps juvenile or self-indulgent to become overwrought about them: an attitude strikingly opposed to the one in the preceding stanza. The poet is "moved," but the world is not. Instead of progressing, things only revolve. This conclusion may not be very attractive ethically. As an exposition of the ordinary, daily responses to suffering, however, it is neither logically nor empirically far off the mark; such is the tense moral ambivalence built into city life. Eliot later wrote, "One is not very loving between seventeen and twenty-four." Surely that perception is as significant with regard to "Preludes" – written during that span in his life – as is Eliot's deletion of this confessional phrase from later versions of the essay in which it first appeared.[8]

The mood of these final lines points well beyond "Preludes." Eliot's desire for belief competed with skepticism about its possibility, and this ambivalence led him to philosophy and aestheticism. In his dissertation, Eliot admitted that "there is no absolute point of view from which real and ideal can be finally separated and labelled."[9] Rational, relational consciousness led only to a more systematized, explicit awareness of how much that consciousness excluded. Speaking of the various types of object and their relations, Eliot asserted that "every transformation of type involves a leap which science cannot take, and which metaphysics must take. It involves an *interpretation,* a transmigration from one world to another, and such a pilgrimage involves an act of faith." From this assertion he concluded that the notion of literal truth had little direct application to philosophy. "A philosophy can and must be worked out with the greatest rigour and discipline in the details, but can ultimately be founded on nothing but faith."[10] In 1916, Eliot argued that because rationally based metaphysics relies upon faith, it cannot pretend to truth. He thus used an essentially religious notion to discredit a rational scheme.

By 1927, the year of his conversion, Eliot had reversed himself, both on the specific issue – the possibility of objective, literal truth – and on how far such truth may or must rely on faith. His argument partly resembles fideism, exposing the shortcomings of reason so as to leave faith, if only by default, as the basis of truth. His faith, he said, did not make truth a function of the will, but instead fixed truth as an object toward which to direct the will:

> If truth is always changing, then there is nothing to do but to sit down and watch the pictures. Any distinctions one makes are more or less arbitrary. I should say that it was at any rate essential for Religion that we should have the conception of an immutable object or Reality the knowledge of which shall be the final object of that will; and there can be no permanent reality if there is no permanent truth. I am of course quite ready to admit that human apprehension of truth varies changes and perhaps develops, but that is a property of human imperfection rather than of truth. You cannot conceive of truth at all, the word has no meaning, except by conceiving of it as something permanent. And that is really assumed even by those who deny it. For you cannot even say it changes except in reference to something which does not change; the idea of change is impossible without the idea of permanence.[11]

His argument, a definition by semantic antithesis, seems born of his philosophical skepticism. As we shall see, this method, incorporating as it did the unity of opposites, became a key element of his religious imagination. Here, by resorting to the antonym "change," Eliot fixes the meaning of "truth" by insisting upon "permanence" as one of its indispensable qualities. Though rational metaphysics claimed not to rely on faith, Eliot argued that it had to do so, and hence on its own terms could not pretend to Truth. Religion, by contrast, required the faith of believers in an objective reality and a permanent Truth as an (albeit supernatural) axiom. Hence, paradoxically, it could withstand skeptical attack. Eliot thus used a rational argument to render a religious scheme credible.

The final two stanzas of "Preludes" treat similar issues. Eliot first advances serious, religious emotion, only to undercut it summarily in favor of a more or less naturalistic or mechanistic metaphor, effectively rendering the prior humane emotion irrelevant. Besides whatever religious elements it contains, Eliot's penultimate stanza also tries to unify the poem's images in a Bradleyan fashion. On the one hand, "Preludes" contains images of violence and conflict: "beat," "broken," "stamps," "trampled," and "press." On the other, quite opposite images suggest intimacy and fusion: "settles down," "wraps," "curled," and "cling." "The notion of some infinitely gentle, infinitely suffering thing" unites these two themes. Out of these divergent particulars, the poet tries to abstract a single point of view or a "relation" between the poem's diverse facts that will transcend, harmonize, and unify them, thereby coming that much nearer to the Bradleyan Absolute. The soul, Eliot wrote in his dissertation, does not contemplate a single, consistent world. Instead, it engages in the "painful task of unifying . . . jarring and incompatible ones, and passing, when possible, from two or more discordant viewpoints to a higher which shall somehow include and transmute them."[12] On a philosophical level, this "inclusion" and "transmutation" of diversity into a more elevated viewpoint involves the triadic logic of Bradley and Bosanquet, and Eliot's own theory of the "half-object." Eliot's assertion, moreover, implies that the ordinary mental or spiritual life pursues this "painful" but unifying task. Most particularly, however, the process Eliot sets forth describes the poet's task quite precisely. The passage from diverse, lower, discordant viewpoints to a single, higher, inclusive one restates the process of poetic metaphor in philosophical (and psychological) terms. It is that metaphoric process in which the penultimate stanza of "Preludes" engages.

As the final stanza indicates, however, the poem's speaker does not succeed. In this sense "Preludes" poetically foreshadows Eliot's later philosophical rejection of rational metaphysics. Eliot the metaphysician concluded that these efforts foreseeably fail, creating something only marginally valid, and barely even real:

> The soul is so far from being a monad that we have not only to interpret other souls to ourself but to interpret ourself to ourself. Wherever a point of view may be distinguished, I say, there a point of view is. And whereas we may change our point of view, it is better not to say that the point of view has changed. For if there is a noticeable change, you have no identity of which to predicate the change. The point of view, we may say, is as such purely ideal; it can hardly be said to possess existence.[13]

The soul, Eliot implies, responds to the activity of thought more completely than it resembles feeling or the Absolute. And this is why, in brief, the poem's unifying effort collapses. If an interpretation of other souls, or of one's own, must have real existence and especially permanence, either, it would seem, must necessarily dissolve at the interpreter's will, or whim. This is just what happens when without warning or explanation, the last stanza of "Preludes" ridicules its fragile, unstable predecessor.

However anachronistic it may be to compare the two, Eliot's reaction in this early poem anticipates his disillusion with Bradley's areligious, purely philosophical Absolute, which Eliot dismissed as unified only by an act of faith:

> Upon inspection, it falls away into the isolated finite experiences out of which it is put together. . . . The Absolute responds only to an imaginary demand of thought, and satisfies only an imaginary demand of feeling. Pretending to be something which makes finite centres cohere, it turns out to be merely the assertion that they do. And this assertion is only true so far as we here and now find it to be so.[14]

Eliot's dissatisfaction proceeded from a familiar complaint: Confronted by skepticism and by the withdrawal of faith in the conclusion's coherence, the Absolute fell apart, split into its isolate sides or components. The conviction that such dissociation pervades all thought not adequately grounded had awakened Eliot's craving for an Absolute in the first place. When self and actuality fail to cohere, a metaphysic that merely imitates that confusion instead of resolving it may possess a certain consonance, but it remains worse than useless in terms of the basic problem. For these reasons, the leap of faith the Bradleyan Absolute required apparently dissuaded Eliot from a metaphysic predicated on practice and persuaded him to one dedicated to dogma.

The truth of such an assertion, however, turns out to be not so very remote from the religious method Eliot later adopted to address similar issues. Heresy, Eliot argued, arose when one-half of a truth split or floated free from its corresponding, corrective other half, which dogmatic, orthodox theology had held together. Without the covalent dogma, divergent principles had nothing to balance one another. This imbalance set loose heretical half-truths, like free molecules, to roam about doing mischief. Eliot defined heresy "taken philosophically as the overemphasis of part of the truth."[15] He used this theory to stalk the bête noire of secularism, for example, when describing Descartes as an ancestor of such characteristically modern antinomies as faith and reason or absolute idealism and materialism. Hence Cartesian philosophy, with its two-sided quality, bore the "marks of important heresy." Eliot argued that despite individual aberrations of narrowness or ignorance, Plato and Aristotle had restrained the medieval philosophers by guiding them toward "balanced wisdom," a governing principle that had prevented thought from "flying to peripheral extremes." Descartes, by contrast, "released" these antithetical elements, leading Eliot to assert that "you need only to press one aspect of his philosophy or another to produce the extremes of materialism and idealism, rationalism and blind faith."[16] Eliot focused on what he considered a dissociative, centrifugal habit in secular philosophy, which lacked the theological means to combine principles not easily reconciled logically or rationally.

How did theology redress this secular shortcoming? Setting out to define the characteristics of "philosophies without revelation," Eliot listed two – "instability" and "recurrence" – which led to a third: "*the tendency* of each extreme philosophy *to evoke an opposite,*" rationalism thus oscillating with intuitivism, for example, and creating the possibility that immoderate humanism could give rise to cruelty and tyranny. Eliot carefully noted that his discussion of philosophies without revelation presupposed that "revelation in the complete sense is the Incarnation."[17] Presumably reconciling opposites in a concrete and incarnate (as opposed to exclusively rational and logical) fashion provided the pattern both for reconciling theological and philosophical contrariety and for establishing the purpose of doing so: both means and end, and hence "revelation in the complete sense."

We can trace Eliot's dissatisfaction with professional, secular philosophy, and some part of his later espousal of orthodox Christianity, to this analysis. He asserted, for instance, that the "divorce of philosophy from theology" not only created the vagaries of modern philosophy, but also caused his own dissatisfaction with philosophy as a profession.[18] Eliot hinted that this divorce influenced his own religious moment, tracing conversion to Christianity to a "latent dissatisfaction with all secular philosophy, becoming, perhaps, with apparent suddenness, explicit and coherent." (He noted, however, that his remarks were "deliberately disregarding the operation of grace in order to keep it to the secular plane.")[19]

Another description of Eliot's progress toward conversion similarly reports how a necessary dissatisfaction may assume a status almost like that of agency. Eliot admitted the impossibility of saying to what degree self-discovery, or observing the outside world, caused a particular Christian conversion. He nevertheless expressed certainty that for himself, "the strongest outside influences were negative. Observation of the futility of non-Christian lives has its part; and also realization of the incredibility of every alternative to Christianity that offers itself. One may become a Christian partly by pursuing scepticism to the utmost limit."[20] The final sentence unearths the buried link between the Unitarian skepticism Eliot had learned in youth and sophisticated as a philosophy student and his ultimate, quite unforeseeable use of it to lead himself to faith. Moreover, the quotation contains a particularly important parallel to another comment concerning his own aesthetic emotion and the sources of his poetry. Recall Eliot's statement that an artist's contemplation of ugliness is a necessary, negative aspect of his impulse to pursue beauty. Not all artists, however, succeed in expressing the complete scale from negative to positive. "The negative is the more importunate."[21] As in poetry, so in religion: "I am sure that for me the strongest outside influences were negative."

Where did this negative observation lead? Explaining the sequence culminating in faith, Eliot described how skepticism, having pursued various alternatives to their unsatisfactory conclusion, prepared him to accept the Incarnation:

> The Christian thinker . . . proceeds by rejection and elimination. He finds the world to be so and so; he finds its character inexplicable by any non-religious theory: among religions he finds Christianity, and Catholic Christianity, to account most satisfactorily for the world and especially for the moral world within; and thus, by what Newman calls "powerful and concurrent" reasons, he finds himself inexorably committed to the dogma of the Incarnation.[22]

Negative means – "rejection and elimination" – permitted Eliot to understand the Incarnation's fundamental status. As these disparate quotations reveal, the Incarnation, understood conceptually, assisted Eliot in providing the intellectual unity that philosophy could not. Yet it also supplied a moral foundation, as he implied by stating that if he did not believe in something so fundamental as the Incarnation, he should have found it difficult to defend the morality he tried to practice.[23] Christian revelation sprang from the same source. Eliot took it for granted that all Christian revelation was to be understood in relation to the "essential fact of the Incarnation," the element that made Christian revelation the only full revelation.[24]

However useful it might have been to Eliot intellectually, morally, and religiously, the Incarnation also exerted considerable power imaginatively, as an event to which poetic creation could be analogized. Focusing on its process rather than its truth, Eliot applied the pattern of Incarnation to poetry:

> Poetry . . . is not the assertion that something is true, but the making that truth more fully real to us; it is the creation of a sensuous embodiment. It is the making the Word Flesh, if we remember that for poetry there are various qualities of Word and various qualities of Flesh. . . . What we find when we read Lucretius or Dante is that the poet has effected a fusion between that philosophy and his natural feelings, so that the philosophy becomes real, and the feelings become elevated,

> intensified and dignified. . . . Poetry cannot prove that anything is *true;* it can only create a variety of wholes composed of intellectual and emotional constituents, justifying the emotion by the thought and the thought by the emotion: it proves successively, or fails to prove, that certain worlds of thought and feeling are *possible.* It provides intellectual sanction for feeling, and esthetic sanction for thought.[25]

Written in 1930, this passage illustrates how durable certain issues that interested Eliot in his philosophical phase proved to be. Though it seems initially to contrast thought and emotion in the usual way, the final two sentences suddenly translate "emotion" into "feeling." By pairing "feeling" with "thought," the conclusion abruptly recasts the entire discussion into Bradley's categories. Eliot here argues, moreover, that poetry neither gives us truth nor leads us to it. Not truth, but reality; poetry makes certain states of thought and feeling possible by giving them a body made out of words (the "verbal equivalent for states of mind and feeling," as Eliot wrote in "The Metaphysical Poets"). It acts as a Bradleyan "relation," joining two things that ordinary psychology and everyday discourse suppose to be discrete and even opposite. And although his vocabulary hints at the conclusion much earlier, the word he uses twice in the final sentence also reveals Eliot's mature view of poetic uniqueness. Some of this vocabulary, with words such as "fusion" and "intensity," Eliot used again and again when pointing out the special quality of poetic language. Listen carefully, however, to the religious overtone in "sanction"; poetry provides a sanction not simply by authorizing, legitimizing, or ratifying in the secular sense, but by implying a holy act of religious sanctity. If after acquiring religion Eliot no longer looked to poetry for substantive truth, his Christianity enabled him to acknowledge that poetry had functioned in a religious way. Its procedure, endowing feeling with reason and thought with beauty, held a nearly miraculous significance so far as it imitated the essential Christian miracle of Incarnation, making divine possibility real and concrete.

In biographical terms, orthodox theology may have appealed to Eliot insofar as his upbringing had deliberately suppressed key parts of that system. The Incarnation particularly might have supplied what had been hitherto a "missing element." It was, after all, the single most important concept, theologically speaking, with which Unitarianism had dispensed. Anyone arguing anti-Trinitarianism must first discredit the Incarnation, which among its practical results places God on earth in a human form. Secondarily, the Incarnation also sophisticates (or from a Unitarian viewpoint, corrupts) monotheism into Trinitarianism.

Aside from a supposed autobiographical appeal, the Incarnation gave Eliot a way to unify his spiritual and aesthetic needs and to harmonize emotional and intellectual dissonance. As I have suggested, Eliot's poetry

and its favored techniques and effects prefigured this catalysis. I refer to a
cluster of effects that arise when verbal ambiguity mediates intellectual or
sensible opposites. Of the various types of ambiguity, the one I have in
mind resembles Empson's seventh: a *tertium quid,* occupying a middle
ground between two opposites, distinct from either yet partaking of
both. Empson's seventh type of ambiguity, the most ambiguous that can
be conceived, occurs when a word's two meanings, "the two values of
the ambiguity, are the two opposite meanings defined by the context, so
that the total effect is to show a fundamental division in the writer's
mind." Empson compared it to the symbol of the Cross, at once an
indecision and a structure.[26] This sort of "literary ambiguity" approxi-
mates Eliot's use of irony, a figure likewise incorporating opposites.
I. A. Richards, for instance, called irony the "bringing in of the opposite, the complementary impulses."[27] Other ironies exist – Socratic,
dramatic, Christian – but among the most characteristic in Eliot's poems
was a kind of social irony, verbally established. Fowler defines this irony
as utterance that "postulates a double audience, consisting of one party
that hearing shall hear and shall not understand, and another party that,
when more is meant than meets the ear, is aware both of that more and of
the outsiders' incomprehension."[28] In the quatrain poems and *The Waste
Land,* this "social" irony permits Eliot to "establish identical reference"
deliberately with some, yet to avoid doing so with others, conquering
his audience by dividing it.*

Since Eliot's ironies arise from his sense of both social and metaphysical divisions, it is not surprising to find that these two ironic impulses have something to do with one another. Eliot's background
taught him to interpret reality with the ideal in mind. Social complication, however, tended to disrupt a world view that held its ideals to be
self-evident. What hostile critics label Eliot's sarcasm and scabrous irony
often indicates their failure to see or imagine the positive pole upon
which such negativity relies as a countervailing, if silent, partner. Henry
James defined this aspect of the ironic temperament:

> The strength of applied irony [is] surely in the sincerities, the lucidities,
> the utilities that stand behind it. When it's not a campaign, of a sort, on
> behalf of the something better (better than the obnoxious, the provok-
> ing object) that blessedly, as is assumed, *might* be, it's not worth speak-
> ing of. But this is exactly what we mean by operative irony. It implies

---

* In *Sweeney Agonistes,* for instance, Eliot admitted he intended to have one character
speaking not only to the play's other characters, who were literal-minded and without
vision, but also to the audience's most sensitive and intelligent members, who would
"overhear" his remarks. "There was to be an understanding between this protagonist
and a small number of the audience, while the rest of the audience would share the
responses of the other characters in the play" ("Conclusion," *U.P.U.C.,* p. 153).

and projects the possible other case, the case rich and edifying where the actuality is pretentious and vain.[29]

This "possible other case," not necessarily stated expressly but present nonetheless as an implied term, remains crucial to detecting the positive pole underlying the negatives, ironies, and ambiguities of Eliot's early poetry. Biographically, these positive values originated in the liberal, Unitarian idealism of Eliot's youth. Discovering how remote this idealism was from actuality compromised the ideals, and so, on one hand, Eliot's poetry endeavors to discredit them. But on the other, their moral residue left a stronghold from which Eliot could criticize a patently imperfect actuality. Instead of having it both ways, Eliot chose for a while to have it neither, using the real and the ideal to disparage one another in his early poems.

"Literary ambiguity" – mediating the conflict of opposites that, unresolved, remains "irony" – reflects in Eliot's case a sensibility deeply influenced by a truncated Christianity which the incarnate Christ ultimately resolves and completes. In "Preludes" and elsewhere, emotional ambivalence balanced sympathy toward suffering with detached derision. Although liberal religion helped produce these divisions, it could not bind them up again. Philosophy also failed, leading Eliot to orthodox religion. The thing that created Eliot's paralyzing consciousness of opposites, and his appetite for a secure, "metaphysical middle," eventually rescued him from them – or so it is pleasing to think.

Until that resolution, however, Eliot pursued an intermediate strategy for treating his divisions in art: that is, using the word to acknowledge opposite emotions. As Peter Sterry's epigraph to this chapter suggests, for example, an emotional or perceptual – and perhaps even a neurological or anthropological[30] – similarity joins the contemplation of tragic and Christian drama. (Consider how the New Testament trains ironic perception. Though Eliot's are quite unlike the Gospels' peculiarly rancid, ferrous ironies, they may have a similar source: the gap between a religion's demanding ideals and the world's disreputable practice.)[31] Important similarities exist between dramatic and religious tragedy, particularly that of the Crucifixion, the opposite or complementary aspect of the Incarnation. Tragic catharsis and the Crucifixion represent the supremely serious moments of their respective aesthetic and religious systems. Both sorts of seriousness issue from a similar core of ambivalence; each involves, emotionally, a *coincidentia oppositorum*. Each inspires pity and terror; the urge to approach competes with the desire to flee, and sympathy collides with fear.

Does part of the attraction of high tragedy and of Christianity lie in their capacity to trigger simultaneously opposite emotions that usually occur apart? As Peter Sterry saw, the most serious moments and the highest emotions of religion and drama converge:

> A Poetical History . . . hath this, as a chief rule. . . . That persons and things be carried to the *utmost extremity,* into a state where they seem altogether uncapable of any return to Beauty or Bliss: That then by just degrees of harmonious proportions, they be raised again to a state of highest Joy and Glory. . . . excellent Poets in the heighths of their fancies and spirits, were touched and warmed with a Divine Ray, through which the supream Wisdom formed upon them, and so upon their work, some weak impression and obscure Image of it self. Thus it seemeth to be altogether *Divine,* That that work shineth in our eyes with the greatest Beauties, infuseth into our Spirits the sweetest delights, transporteth us most out of our selves unto the kindest and most ravishing touches and senses of the Divinity, which diffusing it self through the amplest Variety, and so to the remotest Distances, and most opposed Contrarieties, bindeth up all with an harmonious Order into an *exact Unity;* which conveyeth things down by a gradual descent to the lowest Depths, and deepest Darknesses; then bringeth them up again to the highest point of all most flourishing Felicities, opening the *beginning in the end,* espousing the end to the beginning. This is that which *Aristotle* in his Discourse of Poetry, commendeth to us as the most artful and surprising *untying of the knot,* Διὰ ἀνάγνωσιν, or by a *discovery*. This is that which *Jesus Christ* pointeth at in himself, who is the Wisdom of God.[32]

Similarity of emotional response, then, defines the temperament that sees tragedy and religion as versions of one another. The similarity may partly explain why two systems of high seriousness – Christianity and drama – might appear compatible when in so many other respects they remain at odds.

If we accept – at least for the sake of the argument – the orthodox notion that Christ joins opposites, representing a unity in diversity that the Incarnation inaugurates and the Crucifixion makes manifest, and if this conception attracted Eliot to Christian faith, we should also recall how the innovations of nineteenth-century American Protestantism affected these ideas. By diminishing Christ's divinity and emphasizing his humanity, theological liberalism split apart his mediatory, dual being. Essentially, it refused the complication inherent in the traditional figure. The new theology surely intended to bring Christ and Christians closer, elevating the believer, if demoting the Christ. For some, however, this simplification and approximation impoverished the religion, leaving it not only less interesting, but daunting and desultory.

Liberal theology left Christ less a god and more a man. So to alter His nature, however, is to alter the effect and image of His suffering, and to alter His suffering is to alter one's own position in relation to it. Taken to its logical extreme, it may transform a god-man into a madman and make a compelling event, for some, a repellent one. This alteration furthermore divorces religious from aesthetic seriousness; it elevates art and demotes religion. Hence some nineteenth-century aestheticism: art as an ethical repository, identity conferring and value defining. Art, not religion, for a time and for a certain group, became the vehicle of the highest and most complex emotional seriousness. Cut off from religious orthodoxy and social reality alike, it produced the hothouse, bizarre eccentricity that Eliot by turns exemplified and criticized.

In this as in so much else, Eliot took a double attitude, seeing both sides of the question, wishing to allow room for opposite responses in his sensibility to preserve its unity – and perhaps also to keep the empirical faith with truth. Eliot's sensibility points to complication, doubleness, and the need to reconcile extremes. Nowhere is this more clear than in his rhetoric, and nowhere is his debt to Christianity more apparent. Doubleness finds rhetorical expression in figures like antimetabole, oxymoron, irony, bathos, paradox, catachresis, and perhaps non sequitur, but most concretely, since it comes from the Greek for "crossing," in chiasmus. "He that findeth his life shall lose it: and he that loseth his life for my sake shall find it," "but many that are first shall be last; and the last shall be first," we read in Matthew, and in Luke that "he hath filled the hungry with good things; and the rich he hath sent empty away." Besides these and other aphorisms of reversal, the most prominent example must be the chiasmus that called forth a Christian civilization: the Golden Rule. Such typically Christian figures repeat Christian sensibility and emotions rhetorically; hence the irony and bathos early in Eliot's work, and the paradox, oxymoron, and chiasmus that pervade his religious poetry. "In my beginning is my end" and "In my end is my beginning" refer not only to the course of Eliot's life, but also to the course of his spirit, and of his art.

I have omitted from the above list the most important figure, the one I have used in a restricted and, it is hoped, precise way: "literary ambiguity." This ambiguity harmonizes opposites that the rhetorical terms merely express. Moreover, it prefigures in a *poetic* word what Eliot would come to see as the *incarnated* Word. Eliot ultimately held this quality of "literary ambiguity" to be the religious function his poetry, and more especially his drama, should try to imitate. Significantly, Bradleyan idealism, itself descended from Hegel, remains philosophically compatible with this notion of ambiguous word and mediatory Christ. A logical "third side," or *tertium quid,* analogizes Eliot's poetic language and his eventual religiosity.[33] As early as the 1920s, Eliot discerned the pattern, the Word, to which his poetic words led when, in 1926, he called real irony an "expression of suffering." He made these ideas explicit elsewhere in his Clark Lectures; just as Christ incarnates an ethical system and a concept of God, Eliot argued, the poetic image in its highest form becomes a kind of knowledge that "clothes the abstract, for a moment, with all the painful delight of flesh."[34]

Eliot linked verbal aesthetics and Incarnation most strikingly in "The Aims of Poetic Drama." Its most remarkable passage once more uses the Incarnation to illustrate the ideal of poetic drama and describe how it should penetrate the hearts and minds of an audience. In one of his last and most considered meditations on the social function of poetry, Eliot urged a conception that would reach out to a broad audience with the goal of elevating each one of its members:

> The people on the stage should seem to the audience so like themselves that they would find themselves thinking: "*I* could talk in poetry too!" Then they are not transported into an unaccustomed, artificial world; but their ordinary, sordid, dreary world is suddenly illuminated and transfigured. And if poetry cannot do that for people, then it is merely a superfluous decoration. What poetry should do in the theatre is a kind of humble shadow or analogy of the Incarnation, whereby the human is taken up into the divine.[35]

That the world, in 1949, still seemed to Eliot ordinary and dreary indicates how little that part of his vision had changed since writing "Preludes" nearly forty years earlier. And not unlike what takes place in "Preludes," with its "lighting of the lamps," Eliot still looks to poetry to take simple language and "illuminate" that "sordid" world. This fusion of art and life, a harmonization of opposites like that of the Incarnation, "transfigures" daily living into a species of *theatrum mundi,* as indeed the "masquerade" in "Preludes" had done much earlier. One feels this is so despite the "artificial" and "superfluous decoration" of facile poetry, the antithesis against which Eliot measures the religious, even supernatural, transfiguration offered by the sort of poetry he favors. Arguing that the poetic act resembles, or is a dimension of, the religious process implies that the one led Eliot to the other. Eliot's early writing does seem frequently to foreshadow Eliot's later religiosity, addressing the same conflicts, dissonances, and divisions that Christianity eventually mediated.[36]

Here the analogy between poetic and religious incarnation emerges. For Eliot, poetic words performed the reconciliation that philosophy had failed to achieve and religion had not yet done. Like philosophy studied "as a human discipline," poetry did not establish truth. It acted instrumentally, as a stage preliminary to achieving belief, yet was only incidentally the thing believed in. Significantly, poetry unified the Bradleyan opposites of thought and feeling. And like religion, poetry composed of irony and "literary ambiguity," in which a single word might connote multiple and even opposite meanings, could satisfy an appetite for ambivalence, greedy to hold onto extremes or reluctant to choose between them. Later, Christianity offered the incarnated Christ as a means to this satisfaction. A poem bonds feeling and thought; the ambiguous word keeps opposite meanings in suspension; Christ personally and corporeally reconciles things that theology, no less than common sense, insists remain divided.

Eliot's most explicit statement of this theory links the Incarnation to semantic complexity, occurring when words perform the multiple functions characteristic of poetic language. The following passage not only summarizes Eliot's view of how poetic language differs from ordinary language, but sets forth the similarity between poetry and his religious imagination:

> Symbolism is that to which the word tends both in religion and in poetry; the incarnation of meaning in fact; and in poetry it is the tendency of the word to mean as much as possible. To find the word and give it the utmost meaning, in its place; to mean as many things as possible, to make it both exact and comprehensive, and really to *unite* the disparate and remote, to give them a fusion and a pattern with the word, surely this is the mastery at which the poet aims; and the poet is distinguished by making the word do more *work* than it does for other writers. Of course one can "go too far" and except in directions in which we can go too far there is no interest in going at all; and only those who will risk going too far can possibly find out how far one can go. . . . no extravagance of a genuine poet can go so far over the borderline of ordinary intellect as the Creeds of the Church.[37]

The symbol, it would seem, unites opposites the way the poet and the saint use the word. Moreover, Eliot here makes the church a kind of poet, or more likely, a kind of poem. The poet's essentially experimental efforts aspire to, but fall short of, the breadth the church incorporates unto itself, reaching beyond mere poetic "extravagance" and beyond "ordinary intellect." Maximum ambiguity as the joining of extremes corresponds to the divine reconciliation of these things. Both operate by injecting a third thing – the word, the incarnated Christ – to be suspended between them.

Eliot's imagination, at various stages of his development, incorporates related senses of this word: suspense – the dramatic emotion; and suspension – the Christian one. This resemblance, especially given the genesis of secular drama from the Catholic mass, suggests a few further speculations about the identity of religious and dramatic satisfactions. As we have seen, aesthetic and religious extremity must balance, in a single moment, the opposite responses of pity and fear, sympathy and distance that they elicit. Doubt and skepticism, moreover, pose a crucial problem that faith and the theater share: how to achieve the suspension of disbelief. And moral, religious sensitivity often seems to overflow into aesthetic sensibility, especially when religious faith evaporates. By a curious reversal, the lives of aesthetes also provide many examples of a return to faith.

Both religious and aesthetic forms of high seriousness, then, may share causes and effects, which I have characterized as suspension between extremes or opposites. Eliot represents a Protestant, American version of the type, which tries to read the tangible world as a moral text and a sign of divine intent. Though close to allegory, the device is not literary, but rather ontological. To assume that the tangible world only leads us to moral reality or acts as a providential signifier means constantly to suspend one's own interpretation of things and events, on the assumption that providential involvement implies hermeneutic consistency. Events cannot, given this assumption, contradict one another. Should they seem to do so, we must reject our interpretation as faulty and await another event that will reveal or clarify the pattern.

A Bradleyan passage from "East Coker" typifies this habit of mind when Eliot speaks of the limited value of knowledge derived from experience. Such knowledge, he writes, both imposes a pattern and falsifies. In every moment the pattern is new, making a valuation of experience that is likewise new, and shocking. Although the passage does not specify whether "knowledge" derives its pattern only from personal experience, the falsification that the pattern's constant novelty reveals extends to experience broadly conceived. In terms of Christian history, time remains a matter of marking time until the end of time, which will efface mundane discontinuities between self and society, heaven and earth, immortality and death. Human life, according to Christian history, has to it more than a little unreality. Time, except at moments when it becomes "full" – for example, the birth, crucifixion, and resurrection of Christ – resumes a masquerade. It constitutes a waiting, a suspension, until the world's salvation or the individual's death and resurrection. Soul and world alike hang in suspension, stretched tight across the skies, always subliminally conscious that final form lies beyond, somewhere in the future, always later, never now.[38]

Liberal Protestantism takes this deferral to the extreme, denying the satisfactions of the mass and the theater – both spheres in which time may, even if only temporarily, be made "full," hinting concretely at what will one day come. It may partly explain why Eliot termed Protestantism a form of decay, why he pursued his art across the ocean, and why he eventually turned to Anglo-Catholicism. In a letter to Paul Elmer More, Eliot confessed his amazement at the existence of people who found religion unnecessary. Although such people could be happy, or good, they seemed to be unaware of a void that Eliot said he found "in the middle of all human happiness and all human relations, and which there is only one thing to fill. I am one whom this sense of void tends to drive towards asceticism or sensuality, and only Christianity helps to reconcile me to life, which is otherwise disgusting."[39] Eliot's admission, on one hand, illustrates the theme: Christianity, of the "incarnational" sort, mediates the personal qualities of temperament, "asceticism," and "sensuality." On the other hand, these opposite qualities eerily recall Eliot's primordial Unitarian categories, desire and control, self-indulgence and self-effacement. That there existed a "middle" in human relations and human happiness that remained empty for Eliot presents the emotional difficulty his resort to philosophy, poetry, and finally religion might ease. The single "void" makes it possible to line up the intellectual similarities among these three quite disparate areas. And it makes it possible to show how, and why, Eliot might have sought the same satisfaction from Bradleyan "relation," through poetic language as he specially defined it, and finally in Christian incarnation.

What makes "Preludes" so intriguing, despite its ultimate withdrawal from ambiguity and suspension, is that it raises many issues – metaphysical, psychological, social, temporal, religious, and even political and national – that Eliot spent much of his life and writing working out. Its ambiguities; its blend of intimacy and aloofness, sympathy and distance; its allusion to intense yet fragile emotion in homely diction, fantastical images, and playful rhythms; its sad response to irremediable everyday suffering; and the way it miraculously extorts beauty and mystery from the most meager surroundings: These things will, I hope, compensate the labor expended upon "Preludes," for its words perform an incarnation, transfiguring a thousand sordid images into utterance at once poignant, disturbing, and magical.

3

A Gesture and a Pose: Homo Duplex

One *must* not eye oneself while having an experience; else the eye becomes "an evil eye."

Nietzsche, *Twilight of the Idols*

Man is least himself when he talks in his own person. Give him a mask, and he will tell you the truth.

Oscar Wilde, "The Critic as Artist"

Qui nescit dissimulare, nescit vivere.

SELF-DIVISIONS

If Eliot's study of Bradley argues that things possess identity only in relation to other things; that identity depends on such relation, which leaves it a transitory state; and that things therefore remain, at best, only indeterminate metaphysically, "The Love Song of J. Alfred Prufrock" endows these propositions with poetical flesh. Philosophical ambiguity, in this case, corresponds to psychic ambivalence, and most theories explaining Prufrock's problems share the concept of doubleness or division.

On one hand, Prufrock recalls a characteristic strain of American Puritanism, the tendency to "auto-machia." In such "self civil war," humility and self-denial fuse awkwardly but firmly with personal assertion. The habit flourished long after the theology withered, and Prufrock, straitened by everyday social circumstance yet unbuttoned – even unhinged – in his imagination, tries to master the world by rejecting it.[1] However futile such dominion might seem, Prufrock's vaccinal retreat into the self, refusing infectious social contact, dovetails with a tendency in American literature – and American life – extending back to their earliest Puritan origins.

On the other hand, Prufrock's difficulties stem from the familiar Romantic alienation between frustrated subject and unresponsive object, and from an even more traditional estrangement between spirit and flesh.

76

No single term among this array of polar opposites offers him any satisfaction, since he lacks the strength to force either the mystical or the
erotic, the religious or the sexual moment to its crisis. Prufrock is no
prophet, and no philanderer either.

So he withdraws into a feeble dream of lassitude, self-division, and
Weltschmerz. Although hardly the first instance of this sort of insinuating
melancholia, Eliot's poem perfects indifference into a rarefied, an elitist,
the intelligent reaction to importunate yet predictable circumstance. Prufrock's indifference to social trivia maps out not only a style of response,
but a form of resistance. If modern life has forfeited the blessings of ritual
for the burden of routine, Prufrock sponsors a kind of polite subversion
through what Eliot called the use of irony "to express a *dédoublement* of
the personality against which the subject struggles."[2] Though Prufrock's
critics have not overlooked this *"dédoublement,"* neither have they cared
to press it much further than the familiar subject–object or mind–body
polarities. A few have framed the issue by referring to schizophrenia,
which, despite its frequent but incorrect employment as a synonym for a
split personality, at least notices a significant element in the poem.

Another model, contemporary with Eliot but having a long history of
its own, helps explain the self-divisions and self-consciousness, the ironies and satire of Eliot's early poems. In *Varieties of Religious Experience,*
William James introduced a chapter, "The Divided Self," with a paradigmatic quotation:

> "Homo duplex, homo duplex!" writes Alphonse Daudet. "The first
> time I perceived that I was two was at the death of my brother Henri,
> when my father cried out so dramatically, 'He is dead, he is dead!'
> While my first self wept, my second self thought, 'How truly given was
> that cry, how fine it would be at the theater.' I was then fourteen years
> old."

While James applied this passage to the "psychological basis of the twice-
born character," homo duplex extends to contexts distant from religion
and remote in time from the late nineteenth century.

Indeed, Plato's *Symposium, Phaedrus,* and *Gorgias* define the two homo
duplex selves: a stable, serious, spiritually ambitious self competes with
one immersed in dramatic, role-playing, social enterprise. The paradigm
distinguishes between a Socratic, ideal privacy of timeless beauty and
eternal truth, on one hand, and the Sophistic, worldly activities of theater
and politics, on the other. Even as Daudet weeps, he may also muse with
satisfaction upon how convincingly utter histrionic sorrow might appear
before an audience. Sincerity – the identity between feeling and its presentation – maintains such religious, cultural, and ethical prestige that it
pretends not only to describe the soul, but also to prescribe behavior. For
that reason, recognizing sincerity itself as a dramatic construct remains a

favorite Sophistic paradox, the reef upon which waves of Socratic and adolescent emotion cruelly, if routinely, break.

Besides their philosophical, political, and educational differences,[3] the Sophists and Socratics sharply disagreed about the self. If someone defines his identity through relations with others, he will likely interpret reality socially and dramatically. He will thus conceive of it, and of his personality, in terms of performer and audience, responding eagerly to circumstance and occasion and perfecting a sense of what decorum will suit an audience or situation. He will become expert at knowing what will be accepted and what will succeed. Although language will become the primary social medium, it will hardly exhaust the repertoire of social gesture.[4] And with attention turned to presentation, a society valuing performance, rhetoric, and civic occasion will likely be prepared to sacrifice ideals somewhat to achieve a pragmatic harmony. Instead of insisting upon political absolutes, the Sophist "liberal temperament" will prefer harmony based on compromise to stalemate on behalf of intransigent principle.[5]

If, however, someone locates his identity in a soul, psyche, or spirit, he may define reality more as ideal, absolute, and metaphysical than social, dramatic, or political. He will regard an actor or rhetorician suspiciously, as Socrates does in *Gorgias,* and may devote considerable effort to regretting the difference between appearance and reality. Dismayed by the Sophist's comfortably multiple selves, the Socratic, inner orientation tries to fix, limit, and refine an entity able to present itself singly in any circumstance. Rather than manipulating language, the Socratic personality aims to transcend it, likewise holding the rough-and-ready world of politics and compromise at arm's length. Insofar as it approaches practical politics, the Socratic view offers, oxymoronically, a kind of nostalgic utopianism. Ideally, such a philosophy forestalls discordant argument, composing a consensus automatically instead of having to hammer it out moment by moment, issue by issue. Loyal to a preconception, the Socratics work to discover what they allege already exists. The Sophists make it up as they go along.

"For what is a man profited, if he shall gain the whole world, and lose his own soul?" the Socratic might have asked. Reversing the equation, the Sophist would wryly respond, "For what is a man profited, if he shall gain his soul, and lose the whole world?" These fundamental strategies remind us how conflict between the two selves – and between the two views of which they form a part – tends to recur.[6] Each era has adjusted the homo duplex problem differently – or in the post-Romantic, modernist era, indifferently. Daudet continued: "I have often meditated on this dread duality. Oh! the terrible second *I,* always still while the other is up, acts, lives, strives, suffers! – this second *I,* that can not be intoxicated, nor made to shed tears, nor put to sleep! And how it sees! and how it mocks!"[7] Upon encountering this sober, dry-eyed, mocking self, we enter Prufrock's neighborhood.

Eliot wrote when the two selves did not cohere; writers and thinkers struggled to know whether to embrace homo duplex or to try to simplify it out of existence. Eliot's early poems frequently reflect a conflict between the two selves that causes a failure of the personality to cohere meaningfully. The problem may come from the inability to set up a psychic economy: Which self will take responsibility for which tasks? If the eighteenth century answered that question satisfactorily, the nineteenth did not, an indecision its commercial, technologized, and urban nature doubtless had something to do with. These forces and the embourgeoisement of culture seem to have upset the balance between the two selves, or to have so blurred the distinction between them that the criterion of sincerity became rigidly applied to social contacts between relative strangers.[8] Perhaps instead of acting in public, the modern citizen could only transact, a simplification that deceived the unwary about the innate singleness of their character. The dissonant nineteenth-century self, to be sure, had many sources, and commerce, in any case, was hardly a Victorian invention. But in Great Britain, many late-nineteenth-century writers and thinkers responded to Romantic values by questioning the premium placed upon sincerity and by dividing the self that society formerly presumed it had unified.[9] Eliot and the modernists joined a project – already underway for several decades – that aimed to criticize Romantic sincerity, reexamine the self's unity, and redefine rhetoric.[10]

In "My Station and Its Duties," for instance, F. H. Bradley called the individual, considered to be something distinct from the community, an unreal abstraction:

> I am myself by sharing with others, by including in my essence relations to them, the relations of the social state. If I wish to realize my true being, I must therefore realize something beyond my being as a mere this or that. . . . In short, man is a social being; he is real only because he is social, and can realize himself only because it is as social that he realizes himself. The mere individual is a delusion of theory; and the attempt to realize it in practice is the starvation and mutilation of human nature, with total sterility or the production of monstrosities.[11]

Written several years after "Prufrock," Eliot's dissertation preserves something of this view, though avoiding Bradley's almost contemptuous dismissal of individual identity outside a social context. Bradleyan thought, an activity inevitably private yet intensively involved in objectification, in finding and creating relations between objects in the external, social world, leads Eliot to propose a theory of the "half-object."

The presence of other finite centres – that is, other people, encountered in society – divides reality, and the self, but also remedies that division:

> The first objects, we may say, with which we come into contact are half-objects, they are other finite centres, not attended to directly as objects, but are interpretations of recognized resistances and felt divergences. We come to interpret our own experience as the attention to a world of objects, as we feel obscurely an identity between the experiences of other centres and our own. And it is this identity which gradually shapes itself into the external world. There are two (or more) worlds each continuous with a self, and yet running in the other direction – *somehow* – into an identity. Thus in adjusting our behaviour to that of others and in co-operating with them we come to intend an identical world.[12]

"Somehow," indeed. Though in a sense implicit in the Bradleyan metaphysics, Eliot's theory restates homo duplex. The part of the self having contact with experience requires another part to make an interpretation, and so objectify that part of other finite centres presenting "resistances" and "divergences." The interpretation alters the interpreter's immediate experience by objectifying it, but that objectification extends only to that part of another finite centre that is public and social. Hence the objectification produces only a half-object. The interpreting self – the central self – abstracts a point of view from those half-objects it encounters. It also shares the result – the social self – with other interpreting selves. That sharing compares and adjusts the diverse interpretations until they overlap sufficiently to create an "identical world." Out of half-objects, that is, the world – an instance of "identity in diversity," as Eliot calls it – comes to appear whole. As far as concerns the participants, who become part of a community of intention, it *is* whole. This identity, as Eliot concludes, remains no less real for being ideal.

As discussed in Chapter 2, Eliot completed his theory by interposing language as the medium by which the private and public selves could mediate the "resistances" and "divergences" between the two worlds to which the selves had reference. The poet could balance craft, art, and rhetoric against Romantic sincerity and the private self. Fusing the two selves by disallowing the claims society made upon an individual, Romantic values judged behavior against a sincere, consistent presentation of self or "conscience." That someone might present various selves, or clothe himself in a role temporarily, seemed the root of social and psychological evil, promising a mischievous, cynical poisoning of human relations. Romantic values viewed eighteenth-century poetic diction, the verbal correlative of a ritualized, public culture, the same way, perceiving it as empty ornament that estranged art from nature, and both from readers. These judgments assumed that rhetoric imperiled psychological and social health; words somehow mediated between poet and audience incompletely or dishonestly.

At least officially, Romanticism rewarded fidelity to emotion rather than the employment of verbal variety or skill. Yet suppressing form, rhetoric, and role in art and life tended to narrow literary choice. To reach an audience, a poet must render actions, feelings, or thoughts verbally. In so doing, the poet must adopt a voice and a role or, if writing drama, many voices and roles, which necessarily remain distinct from his "sincere" self. Romantic sincerity, though initially a revolutionary anti-style, thus harbored its own contradiction. If Romanticism unified or simplified the self, writers in the late nineteenth century divided and complicated it. Consider, for example, how Clough's aptly titled "Dipsychus" anticipates Prufrock:

> Yet I could think, indeed, the perfect call
> Should force the perfect answer. If the voice
> Ought to receive its echo from the soul,
> Wherefore this silence? If it *should* rouse my being,
> Why this reluctance? Have not I thought o'ermuch
> Of other men, and of the ways of the world?
> But what they are, or have been, matters not.
> To thine own self be true, the wise man says.
> Are then my fears myself? O double self!
> And I untrue to both.

As if to contradict the notion that the human personality innately lacked the potential for evil as well as for good, Robert Louis Stevenson created Dr. Jekyll and Mr. Hyde, competing halves of a split moral personality. Shaw's *Pygmalion,* raising issues of such poignancy that at times it only barely preserves its generic pretense to comedy, concerns the damage the identity may sustain upon losing the social cues (dress, grooming, occupation, social class, and, most crucially, language and pronunciation) that prop it up. To change the social aspects of the personality alters the inner self they express; the surface affects the essence. A slighter but more optimistic version of this paradox, involving the nineties' favorite device, the mask, appears in Max Beerbohm's "The Happy Hypocrite." In that story, a saintly mask encourages a virtuous life and eventually converts a dissolute soul to innocence. When the mask is torn off, it reveals that the former roué underneath now appears indistinguishable from the mask's innocent features.

That fable, however, puts the very best face on things. For all its incidental triviality, Oscar Wilde invented the most sophisticated critique of the single self. Wilde reintroduced style and role playing as primary elements of art. He went further, translating their importance from art into life, an extension suggesting why Wilde was so revolutionary and perhaps also accounting for his persecutors' ruthlessness. *The Picture of Dorian Gray*, implying how the nineteenth century ignored the self's double nature, proposed that the canons of good society should be the same as those of art, form being essential to both:

> Is insincerity such a terrible thing? I think not. It is merely a method by which we can multiply our personalities.
>
> Such, at any rate, was Dorian Gray's opinion. He used to wonder at the shallow psychology of those who conceive the Ego in man as a thing simple, permanent, reliable, and of one essence. To him, man was a being with myriad lives and myriad sensations, a complex multiform creature.[13]

Daring to prefer style to truth and manners to morality, as Wilde redivided the self he redoubled its energies. He likewise elevated rhetoric above feeling, contradicting what privileges self-expression or sincerity might claim: "All bad poetry springs from genuine feeling. To be natural is to be obvious, and to be obvious is to be inartistic."[14] Most epigrammatically, Wilde lampooned the artless self, simply composed and sincerely presented: "To be natural . . . is such a very difficult pose to keep up."[15] So it would seem that sincerity can be faked in a way hypocrisy, for example, cannot. Is sincerity potentially the most artificial pose of all? To constrain presentation, sacrificing occasion, audience, and context to consistency, may impose the most – not the least – manipulation and control of the self.

Wilde had the courage of Pater's convictions, and his reversal of Victorian categories took this particular paradox perhaps as far as it can be taken. His solution nevertheless could scarcely conclude the argument the two selves created, and not only because it had such disastrous personal consequences for him. The man of a hundred roles seems as tedious as the man of only one; automatic dissemblance subverts human relations as surely as unrelenting sincerity; and a life of pure play proves as barren as one reduced to pure principle. If Wilde showed how masks could liberate, Prufrock proved they could also superintend a kind of pathological withdrawal. Within Prufrock's divided character, two selves cancel one another instead of adding up to a whole person.

Such developments framed the English literary moment just before Eliot's first poems. It is also possible, however, to observe nineteenth-century American writers treating these issues. Their attachment to a sincere, inner self and related values meant that an undertone of dissatisfaction with those constraints would inevitably appear in nineteenth-century American literature. Precedents in several major American writers foreshadow the homo duplex themes in "Prufrock," "Portrait of a Lady," and "La Figlia Che Piange." Far from being exotic borrowings,

Eliot's poems portraying a self at cross-purposes with society, and at odds with itself, come from somewhere quite close to home.

Emerson's "Self-Reliance," for instance, inheriting as it does the suspicious Puritan scrutiny of social behavior, makes a declaration of independence in favor of the individual conscience. As we enter into the world, Emerson writes, voices heard in solitude grow faint and inaudible, drowned out by the social conspiracy. "Society is a joint-stock company, in which the members agree, for the better securing of his bread to each shareholder, to surrender the liberty and culture of the eater. The virtue in most request is conformity. Self-reliance is its aversion. It loves not realities and creators, but names and customs. Whoso would be a man, must be a nonconformist." Emerson's figure expresses a typically American objection to social claims because they arise from nothing more worthy of moral deference than economic convenience. But his doubts went further, encompassing charity itself, which Emerson deprecates as "glittering" and as a "spectacle" and "parade." Though the target is somewhat extreme, the accusations typify how, to preserve its purity, inner absolutism indicts the social world. The spiritual and, in Emerson's case, self-reliant consciousness reserves that accusatory vocabulary to associate social behavior with fleshpots and other iniquitous dens:

> Men do what is called a good action, as some piece of courage or charity, much as they would pay a fine in expiation of daily non-appearance on parade. . . . Their virtues are penances. I do not wish to expiate, but to live. My life is for itself and not for a spectacle. I much prefer that it should be of a lower strain, so it be genuine and equal, than that it should be glittering and unsteady. . . .
>
> What I must do is all that concerns me, not what the people think. . . . It is easy in the world to live after the world's opinion; it is easy in solitude to live after our own; but the great man is he who in the midst of the crowd keeps with perfect sweetness the independence of solitude.

Emerson's final sentence wisely withdraws from an absolute commitment to abandon society for a privileged, isolate self. Having admitted worldly, social claims, Emerson acknowledges the individual's difficulty in balancing the claims of both solitude and society, which is simply to recognize the existence of moral complexity. Such moments, however, are rare, and Emerson often yielded when tempted to condemn social considerations. It is striking how frequently his disdain equates society with money, incorporating economics into his moral vocabulary. A passage from "The Divinity School Address," however, also contains the usual, shopworn abuse of social claims as superficial glitter, cheap theater, deceitful rhetoric, and an inconstant, painted harlot:

Can we not leave, to such as love it, the virtue that glitters for the commendation of society, and ourselves pierce the deep solitudes of absolute ability and worth? We easily come up to the standard of goodness in society. Society's praise can be cheaply secured, and almost all men are content with those easy merits; but the instant effect of conversing with God will be to put them away. There are persons who are not actors, not speakers, but influences; persons too great for fame, for display; who disdain eloquence; to whom all we call art and artist, seems too nearly allied to show and by-ends, to the exaggeration of the finite and selfish, and loss of the universal. The orators, the poets, the commanders encroach on us only as fair women do, by our allowance and homage. Slight them by preoccupation of mind, slight them, as you can well afford to do, by high and universal aims, and they instantly feel that you have right, and that it is in lower places that they must shine.*

Herman Melville focused even more sharply on the way commerce poisoned social life, which in turn contaminated the inner self. Though Melville recognized the positive possibilities of social theatricality, like Emerson he could not sustain this amiable view. *The Confidence Man: His Masquerade* explores the *theatrum mundi* half of the homo duplex paradigm with special reference to economic and commercial life, and weighs decisively against the promise of theatrical regeneration Melville presented so convincingly in "The Two Temples."[16] Far from reasserting the social bond and personal good faith, the confidence man's ability to assume a role that does not betray his true intention ruptures society and contaminates personal integrity. Throughout the novel, Melville remains hypersensitive to the way sincerity may be dissembled, as when the confidence man makes his debut as a mute stranger of "singularly innocent" aspect, scratching charitable maxims on a slate. Later, a cosmopolitan "philanthropist" advises a "misanthrope" to become more sociable. "Life is a pic-nic *en costume;* one must take a part, assume a character, stand ready in a sensible way to play the fool. To come in plain clothes, with a long face, as a wiseacre, only makes one a discomfort to himself, and a blot upon the scene." By placing arguments favoring theatricality in the confidence man's mouth, Melville manages to discredit both the cosmopolitan (who offers the advice only to deceive) and

---

* Although interested mainly in traditionally religious self-division, Rev. William G. Eliot occasionally echoed Emerson's treatment of the homo duplex theme: "The great fault of the young . . . is the want of a fixed aim, and of resolution in keeping it. There is a want also of self-reliance. They too readily yield their own principles and purposes to those around them, and instead of forming themselves after the model which they held before them at first, they suffer themselves to be formed by others. It is here that the importance of self-education is seen" (*Lectures to Young Men* [Boston, American Unitarian Assoc., 1882], pp. 31–2).

the solitaire (whose sullen refusal to follow these precepts confirms their relevance).

The Confidence Man teems with references to the theater and role playing, and with synonyms for confidence – trust, credit, belief – and its opposite – skepticism, cynicism, mistrust. Several authorial asides suggest how literary fiction corresponds to fiction in everyday life. In Chapter 14, for example, Melville judges readers who cannot suspend disbelief as harshly as he does the con man who unfailingly demands credit:

> Is it not a fact, that, in real life, a consistent character is a *rara avis?* . . . That fiction, where every character can, by reason of its consistency, be comprehended at a glance, either exhibits but sections of character, making them appear for wholes, or else is very untrue to reality; while, on the other hand, that author who draws a character, even though to common view incongruous in its parts, as the flying-squirrel, and, at different periods, as much at variance with itself as the caterpillar is with the butterfly into which it changes, may yet, in so doing, be not false but faithful to facts.

Such authorial faith, however, contrasts with social disbelief. If the author may portray multiple roles and social multability, the "facts" nonetheless seem to warrant his characters' Emersonian suspicions.

In the chapter "Very Charming," the philanthropist's "magical" persuasive powers convince the skeptical barber to agree to take down his "no trust" sign for the rest of the trip, in return for the philanthropist's promise to indemnify him for any resulting loss. Not surprisingly, the transaction ends when the philanthropist, arguing that immediate payment would "violate the inmost spirit" of their contract, stiffs the barber for the price of a shave. As they negotiate, however, the philanthropist inquires, "How does the mere handling of the outside of men's heads lead you to distrust the inside of their hearts?" The barber replies that professional intimacy with macassar oil, false moustaches, and other tricks of the tonsorial trade protects barbers from believing in cosmetic appearance.

> What think you, sir, are a thoughtful barber's reflections, when, behind a careful curtain, he shaves the thin, dead stubble off a head, and then dismisses it to the world, radiant in curling auburn? To contrast the shamefaced air behind the curtain, the fearful looking forward to being possibly discovered there by a prying acquaintance, with the cheerful assurance and challenging pride with which the same man steps forth again, a gay deception, into the street, while some honest, shock-headed fellow humbly gives him the wall. Ah, sir, they may talk of the courage of truth, but my trade teaches me that truth sometimes is sheepish. Lies, lies, sir, brave lies are the lions!

Just before deceiving the barber, the confidence man finds himself beaten at his own role-playing game by a youth who successfully withstands all arguments in favor of extending credit. The confidence man's inability to prevail so enrages him that he forgets his role and merges with it. As he stomps offstage, the loser's anger reminds the young man of the famous Shakespearian "All the world's a stage" rendering of *theatrum mundi*. This metaphor underpins Melville's tale, whose very title, *The Confidence Man: A Masquerade,* alludes to society's theatricality. The novel, however, evaluates the "arts of impression management" mainly by discrediting them. By placing these arts solely in an economic context, Melville presumes their sole use to be squeezing money out of the gullible. Having confidence means being conned. *The Confidence Man* equates role playing with deceit, theatricality with imposture, and multiple selves with fraud. Emerson would not have disapproved.

Melville, however, goes further, dismissing innocence as naiveté, gullibility, or misanthropy. Like "The Two Temples," the novel contains a few hints of more benign possibilities were life to be theatrically conceived. But the divided self – with an attenuated conscience and a sinister, corrupted theatricality – dominates *The Confidence Man* as the product and cause of social strain and personal breakdown. While Melville thus anticipates such later riverine charlatans as the Duke of Bridgewater and the French Pretender, Twain could treat his shysters comically. In *The Confidence Man,* however, no force comparable to Huck and Jim's inner moral strength and resilient innocence ballasts Melville's grim, faithless ship of fakers and fools.

These examples have so far assumed a clear division between the outer society and the inner being, a tension between an immutable self and changeable roles. There also exists, however, a precise "difference between the observer and the spectacle," as Emerson theorized in "Nature." In a state of motion or in an unaccustomed perspective, "a low degree of the sublime is felt, from the fact, probably, that man is hereby apprized that whilst the world is a spectacle, something in himself is stable." What happens, however, when the self becomes the spectacle? Emerson's distinction between the stable self and the worldly spectacle may then no longer seem so sharp. Another theme runs through American writers who notice the self observe itself in the world, becoming divided into actor and critic, role and spectator. In *Walden,* for instance, "Solitude" shows Thoreau to be fully conscious of these inner difficulties, precipitated by his experiment of living without neighbors and "gossips":

> With thinking we may be beside ourselves in a sane sense. By a conscious effort of the mind we can stand aloof from actions and their consequences; and all things, good and bad, go by us like a torrent. We

are not wholly involved in Nature. I may be either the driftwood in the stream, or Indra in the sky looking down on it. I *may* be affected by a theatrical exhibition; on the other hand, I *may not be* affected by an actual event which appears to concern me much more. I only know myself as a human entity; the scene, so to speak, of thoughts and affections; and am sensible of a certain doubleness by which I can stand as remote from myself as from another. However intense my experience, I am conscious of the presence and criticism of a part of me, which, as it were, is not a part of me, but a spectator, sharing no experience, but taking note of it, and that is no more I than it is you. When the play, it may be the tragedy, of life is over, the spectator goes his way. It was a kind of fiction, a work of the imagination only, so far as he was concerned. This doubleness may easily make us poor neighbors and friends sometimes.

Sophistication, it would appear, is no stranger to a woodland, pondside retreat. It is a relief to observe Thoreau feeling no compulsion to simplify his perceptions by pressing them through a moralistic filter. He relates his remarkably complex response as if it were the most natural thing in the world, occurring as it does in simple surroundings. Miles from a theater, it was possible to be surrounded by performances and scenery and to experience the impersonality of the critic and spectator toward the drama of one's inner life.

Thoreau's theater took place out-of-doors, but also within; feeling one with nature did not preclude being of two minds about the experience, or about oneself. Whitman, expressing similar sentiments, also demonstrates an ability to accept them instead of subjecting them to agonized moral artifice. Far busier than Thoreau, Whitman also tended to organize his experience by dispersing it intellectually, perhaps to keep up with his life's more rapid tempo. Whitman thus treats the issue cerebrally, dryly balancing the various alternatives in an almost algebraic way. The fourth section of "Song of Myself," both a catalogue of social engagement and a categorization of two selves, concludes with a splendid perception and a sense of self-acceptance, not unlike Thoreau's:

> Trippers and askers surround me,
> People I meet, the effect upon me of my early life or the ward
>   and city I live in, or the nation,
> The latest dates, discoveries, inventions, societies, authors
>   old and new,
> My dinner, dress, associates, looks, compliments, dues,
> The real or fancied indifference of some man or woman I love,
> The sickness of one of my folks or of myself, or ill-doing or
>   loss or lack of money, or depressions or exaltations,
> Battles, the horrors of fratricidal war, the fever of doubtful
>   news, the fitful events;

These come to me days and nights and go from me again,
But they are not the Me myself.

Apart from the pulling and hauling stands what I am,
Stands amused, complacent, compassionating, idle, unitary,
Looks down, is erect, or bends an arm on an impalpable
     certain rest,
Looking with side-curved head curious what will come next,
Both in and out of the game and watching and wondering at it.

Henry Adams, while feeling himself to be composed of multiple
selves, remained less capable of acknowledging their existence with
equanimity. Like Thoreau and Whitman, however, Adams sought a
superior (if not transcendent) point of view from which he could survey
the two selves and the two worlds to which they were connected. In
1895, Adams's need for such a superior perspective posed a spiritual
problem in "Buddha and Brahma," though making only a somewhat
muted appearance:

Gautama's way is best, but all are good.
He breaks a path at once to what he seeks.
By silence and absorption he unites
His soul with the great soul from which it started.
But we, who cannot fly the world, must seek
To live two separate lives; one, in the world
Which we must ever seem to treat as real;
The other in ourselves, behind a veil
Not to be raised without disturbing both.

This was not the first time Adams felt the separateness of the two
worlds, and of the two selves. Much earlier, in 1862, in a letter to his
brother written from London, Adams acknowledged a perception identical to that of Thoreau and Whitman. In so doing, he linked the dual self,
actor and critic, to a sense of humbug and failure. Out of that diagnosis
he would ultimately develop his third-person narrative persona in *The
Education of Henry Adams:*

You find fault with my desponding tone of mind. So do I. But the evil
is one that probably lies where I can't get at it. I've disappointed myself,
and experience the curious sensation of discovering myself to be a
humbug. How is this possible? Do you understand how, without a
double personality, *I* can feel that *I* am a failure? One would think that
the *I* which could feel that, must be a different *ego* from the *I* of which it
is felt.[17]

From Adams it is a short step to Prufrock, by way of a sentence from
Eliot's dissertation rendering the inner drama of actor and critic that
Thoreau, Whitman, and Adams recorded: "To say that one part of the

mind suffers and another part reflects upon the suffering is perhaps to talk in fictions. But we know that those highly-organized beings who are able to objectify their passions, and as passive spectators to contemplate their joys and torments, are also those who suffer and enjoy the most keenly."[18] This "objectification" and "contemplation," so prominent in Eliot's early poetry, survive to reappear in "Little Gidding." There, catching the look of a dead master, the poet sees a "familiar compound ghost" and assumes a "double part" in which he speaks of "knowing myself yet being someone other."

Homo duplex goes by various names and has a diverse history, but it was a part of the culture in which Eliot matured. The study of multiple, disintegrating or insubstantial personalities had attained some prominence in Boston and Harvard circles when Eliot arrived to live in the city and began writing. In 1906, for instance, the Boston neurologist Morton Prince had published a study of "Miss Beauchamp," *The Dissociation of a Personality;* and other contemporary books, essays, and reviews on this theme inform the atmosphere surrounding Eliot's early poems. Whether commentators blamed idleness, remoteness from nature, skepticism and cynicism, or their favorite, "over-civilization," for such as "Miss Beauchamp," a supposed increase in these personality-related problems evidently alarmed more than a few of them. In this sense "Prufrock" and the other poems in Eliot's first volume warn against overrefinement by satirizing products of such a tendency.[19]

As we have noted, William James participated in these investigations, so it is appropriate to mention James's discussion of the "central" and "social" selves in Chapter 10 of *Principles of Psychology*. It described the "social self" as

> the recognition which he gets from his mates. . . . Properly speaking, *a man has as many social selves as there are individuals who recognize him* and carry an image of him in their mind. . . . he has as many different social selves as there are distinct *groups* of persons about whose opinion he cares. He generally shows a different side of himself to each of these different groups. . . . From this there results what practically is a division of the man into several selves; and this may be a discordant splitting, as where one is afraid to let one set of his acquaintances know him as he is elsewhere; or it may be a perfectly harmonious division of labor, as where one tender to his children is stern to the soldiers or prisoners under his command.[20]

This social self responds primarily to the audience, the surroundings, and the occasion, changing as they change; it potentially ramifies into as many selves as there are people, groups, or situations it confronts. A poet uses this self when adopting distinct personae; in drama, an author's several characters adopt diverse styles of behavior, dress, and manner.

Similarly, conceiving of the self as social means constructing a new self, or some variation of it, to address each new audience, at which point the self becomes dramatic and theatrical.

By contrast, James describes the spiritual, "central active self," a person's "inner or subjective being," as the "most enduring and intimate part of the self."

> We take a purer self-satisfaction when we think of our ability to argue and discriminate, of our moral sensibility and conscience, of our indomitable will, than when we survey any of our other possessions. Only when these are altered is a man said to be *alienatus a se*.
>
> What is this self of all the other selves? . . . Whatever qualities a man's feelings may possess, or whatever content his thought may include, there is a spiritual something in him which seems to *go out* to meet these qualities and contents, whilst they seem to *come in* to be received by it. It is what welcomes or rejects. . . . It is the home of interest. . . . It is the source of effort and attention, and the place from which appear to emanate the fiats of the will. . . . Being more incessantly there than any other single element of the mental life, the other elements end by seeming to accrete round it and to belong to it. It becomes opposed to them as the permanent is opposed to the changing and inconstant.[21]

The central self exists independent of audience, circumstance, and occasion; instead of adapting to change, the central self aspires to fixity. Refusing multiple selves, it clings to singleness, simplicity, and permanence. A poet would reflect this self by writing a lyric, the form most amenable to self-expression, and especially a confessional lyric, in which words supposedly mediate the poet's "true" feelings as little as possible.

Eliot's poems arrive late in the sequence my remarks have described, which may account for the extremities of psychological stalemate they contain. To "Prufrock," "Portrait of a Lady," "Gerontion," *The Waste Land,* and "The Hollow Men" we may apply a political analysis; in each, the balance of power shifts away from the speaker. What he speaks about leaves him acutely aware of his own inability to change, or to resist social and hence emotional pressure. The dissonance between inner and outer selves precipitates an intense self-consciousness in Eliot's earliest poems. The term, of course, is more than a little misleading: Self-consciousness never arises without an audience. To put it another way, self-consciousness means an awareness of someone else reacting to the self one presents. When the audience reacts negatively, with derision or hostility, self-consciousness may appear as something best avoided; this sort of self-consciousness darkens some of Eliot's early poems as an ominous, uncontrollable presence. By contrast, an audience's approval enhances one's ability to choose a self to present. Having a choice makes the ability to manipulate that self and that audience at least manifest, if not necessarily easily achieved: One may control one's self, and hence one's audience.

In short, one becomes an actor, and human relations become dramatic. Self-divided, self-critical, and self-observing, Eliot's earliest characters cannot take this step. The next section will explore why.

PRUFROCK AND OTHER OBSERVATIONS

Prufrock epitomizes a man *alienatus a se,* a man who has lost the "self-satisfactions" James refers to. He can neither commit nor express himself, argue or discriminate:

> In a minute there is time
> For decisions and revisions which a minute will reverse.*

Lacking any principle of selection, Prufrock cannot find either the words or the determination to speak his feelings. "It is impossible to say just what I mean!" Prufrock has neither a functioning moral sensibility, nor a conscience that applies itself to real or significant circumstance. He asks if he dares disturb the universe, but his question reveals that even if he had the power, he lacks the courage to do so. Having passed through various crises – saintly weeping, fasting, and praying, but also suffering the eternal Footman's snickers – he confesses why he does not dare: He is afraid. Given this self-criticism, nobody would accuse J. Alfred Prufrock, whose name connotes a starchy, refined prude, of possessing an "indomitable will." A sugary, refined diet of tea, cakes, and ices connotes both physical and inner weakness, and his self-doubting question makes a kind of acknowledgment that in fact he lacks the strength to force the moment to its crisis.

Without interest, will, concentration, or energy, Prufrock suffers from an infected central self. Conversely, Prufrock's painstaking attention to his social self illustrates how uneasily his two selves coexist. Two of Eliot's most famous lines allude to self-division:

> There will be time, there will be time
> To prepare a face to meet the faces that you meet;

Prufrock touches up his social mask listlessly, resigned to the way it serves him and everyone else so falsely. He resents the artifice of his own mask, which permits him to imply the falseness of everyone else's. Not-

---

* Eliot would later call skepticism – "the habit of examining evidence and the capacity for delayed decision" – a sign of religious or cultural development. Although skepticism was "a highly civilised trait," Eliot suggested that when it declined into Pyrrhonism – an extreme skepticism holding all knowledge, including the testimony of the senses, to be uncertain – civilization could die from it. "Where skepticism is strength," Eliot concluded, "pyrrhonism is weakness: for we need not only the strength to defer a decision, but the strength to make one" (*N.T.D.C.,* p. 29).

ing the women drifting by discussing Michelangelo, Prufrock uses their supposedly facile importation of the aesthetic sublime into prosaic surroundings to express his disillusion. The couplet suggests that Prufrock devalues the social self and its performance-oriented consciousness because he experiences social situations as fundamentally critical. He imagines, for instance, the other guests evaluating him with merciless comments on his spindly arms and legs and thinning hair.

Perhaps justifiably, Prufrock fears the evaluations of others. Though he dismisses the "faces" around him, he cannot evade the eyes that peer through their masks. Eyes act as agents of consciousness, and self-consciousness. Eyes hold a terror for Prufrock because strong "I's" back them up, reaching into his private self to discover its fragility and lack of a coherent "I." These are the "I's" that pin him wriggling on the wall and fix him in a catch phrase. More piercingly than sticks and stones, their words dent Prufrock's rock-proof emotional armor. The violent image of his reduction into an insect and impalement for scrutiny reflects the aggression he perceives in these stares and his own sense of helplessness. It also accounts for the tactic he uses to defend himself emotionally against them, which is to dismiss what happens in these shuttered salons as inconsequential, tedious, and formulaic.

By a curious, ambivalent duality, these occasions cause him to suffer not only psychological violence, but excruciating boredom:

> For I have known them all already, known them all –
> Have known the evenings, mornings, afternoons,
> I have measured out my life with coffee spoons;

Prufrock remains more than merely censorious, because he criticizes not only the faults of others, but his own shortcomings as well. Scorning a defunct society, he mercilessly exposes his own anemic penetralia. On one hand, the ambiguity in "measuring" may refer to marking time, in which case the predictability of a life paced by polite coffee ritual states one kind of horror, a social kind. On the other hand, the "measuring out" also describes Prufrock helplessly observing a drop of his inner life disappear down someone else's throat with every vampiric swallow of coffee. With this alarming, almost gruesome image, combining social tedium and personal depletion, Prufrock acknowledges his own ineffectuality. It is one thing to indict others; it is quite another to pronounce a sentence of doom upon oneself.

The conflict – of which he appears to be aware – between Prufrock's remote, unconvincing social self and his megalomaniacal yet naive central self condemns him to boredom and passivity. Able to imagine no more authentic social role than that of the Fool, he concludes with a self-mockery both comic and pathetic:

No! I am not Prince Hamlet, nor was meant to be;
Am an attendant Lord, one that will do
To swell a progress, start a scene or two,
Advise the prince; no doubt, an easy tool,
Deferential, glad to be of use,
Politic, cautious, and meticulous;
Full of high sentence, but a bit obtuse;
At times, indeed, almost ridiculous –
Almost, at times, the Fool.

It seems curious that in the second line of this passage Eliot omitted a second reference to the word "I" where it would ordinarily appear, as if by this indirection to emphasize the self-deprecating center of Prufrock's problem. Yet six of the seven lines following this passage begin with the "I," which, suppressed in social surroundings, springs to life with a vengeance in his fantasy.

The imaginary grandeur surrounding Prufrock's central self only confirms its actual meagerness. Prufrock's fantasy is not unlike the soiree he attends. Although superficially remote from the drawing room, his dream world's chambers allude to its claustrophobia with singing mermaids sailing the surface of a passionate ocean as Prufrock drifts down to the seabed on a voyage to erotic doom. There "human voices" once more become the agents of extinction, this time by drowning. The poem began, "Let us go then, you and I." Despite the subjunctively formal yet congenial voice of a guide who will lead us safely through a lurid, menacing psychological landscape, the progress the tour traces is decline. Prufrock draws "you" – the visitor and follower in the initial pairing of "you and I" – by degrees into his collapse. Only betrayal greets the "us" and "we" of the final stanza, which reveals Prufrock as not quite the suave *cicerone* his initial manner promised. His vision equates imagined depths with life, and life with sleep; he associates human voices and society with wakefulness, and wakefulness with a watery death.

His confusion marks the limits of irony, the weapon Prufrock's central and social selves employ to take potshots at one another. The central self regards with suspicion the social self's role-playing, performance-oriented gestures, undercutting its ability to play a social part with any conviction. By contrast, the social self, always aware how theatrical sincerity appears, derisively deflates the central self's *endimanché*, metaphysical seriousness. From either point of view, the other self looks a bit absurd, and their inhibiting, mutual mockery clinches Prufrock's psychological deadlock. He can neither ignore society nor enjoy it: All he can do is fear it.

His inability to conclude a truce between his two selves, so that each might act in its proper sphere without interference, leaves the impression that even though Prufrock has never done much living, life has nonetheless worn him out. He seems to have all the time in the world, but no idea how to fill it. His exhaustion, the most terrible symptom of all, stares back from the psychic no man's land at the bottom of his character, resonating wearily in languid, insinuating rhythms as he speaks of how they may reconsider a hundred indecisions in an hour or two. Such *conversazione* remains too, too *civile,* yet devoid of *sprezzatura;* time slows down, and capriciously the hours pass, reversing decisions already reached and revisions already completed. Prufrock embodies the dull thing he criticizes; that he knows this truth about himself distinguishes him from the hypocrite. The poem's circularity; repetition of key images, phrases, and sounds; anaphora; irregular rhymes that lazily resound, like a pendulum; its leisurely, iambic irony: These techniques define Prufrock as a prematurely aged specimen. The poem renders the sort of person who, despite his inexperience, recoils from experience because of the logical or moral inconsistencies it seems inevitably to contain. Another sort of person, unaware that sincere and dramatic selves may diverge, consumes experience with an appetite, transacting business and pleasure without reflection. The wise naif is as harmed by experiences he cannot avoid as the innocent campaigner remains unscathed by experiences he fails to understand. Prufrock, drowning in mermaid-infested dreams, dwells among the former group; Sweeney, stirring the water in his bath, occupies a blithe place in the latter.

Perhaps Prufrock should simply find more interesting companions, or at least accept invitations to less predictable parties. Yet having analyzed his own dilemma, Prufrock fails to do anything about it. Eliot may have written the poem to warn himself away from a fate he wished, in his early twenties, to dodge, and in 1962 Eliot acknowledged that Prufrock partly incorporated his own feeling.[1] Pound, trying to persuade Harriet Monroe to print the poem in 1915, made a fundamental point: "'Mr. Prufrock' does not 'go off at the end.' It is a portrait of failure, or of a character which fails, and it would be false art to make it end on a note of triumph."[2]

Elisabeth Schneider's insight pinpoints that failure, arguing that the poem asks whether change is possible and answers that it is not, at least for a figure like Prufrock.[3] Prufrock cannot change because his two selves set up ambushes for one another. Either of these two competing selves could provide a source of regeneration. A role played consistently, and in earnest, would eventually affect the central self, if only by its becoming automatic. And if sincerity extended to control social behavior, not only might Prufrock's complaints about his trivial companions bear some weight, but he might then be able to resist them publicly rather than under his breath. But as things stand, Prufrock neither accepts the game and plays it to win nor recognizes his own unsuitability for it and declines to play at all. Having forestalled either possibility, he can only resume his odd imposture, leaving him open to the destructive criticisms either self all too easily makes: irony (when self-directed, a travesty of social interaction) and fantasy (the indulgence of a detached, uncommitted spirit). These alternatives encourage the self's increasingly painful privacy. Knowing that the self's conception diverges from its presentation to others only accelerates Prufrock's downward spiral. As Eliot wrote in *The Confidential Clerk,* when one's two lives have nothing to do with one another, they become unreal.

This theme, the self-consciousness born of conflicting selves, recurs throughout *Prufrock and Other Observations.* Several other characters seem unusually aware of the gap between sincerity and society. The poems also display a propensity for multiple voices, narrative interruption, and abrupt shifts in point of view. Such devices illustrate the tension arising between central and social selves, creating not only a susceptibility to others but also a corresponding resistance to them. "Conversation Galante," for instance, often cited as the poem most influenced by Laforgue and the French Symbolists, describes characters who, instead of being observed by a critical narrator, observe and comment upon themselves. Here and in Eliot's juvenilia ("On a Portrait," "Nocturne," "Humouresque (after J. Laforgue)," and "Spleen"), Laforgue helped Eliot experiment with ironic, multiperspective commentary by a narrator upon other characters, by characters upon themselves, and by the reader upon the poem.

In *The Symbolist Movement in Literature,* Arthur Symons wrote that reason seemed fragile in moments when consciousness simultaneously expanded and contracted into something wider than the universe and yet too narrow to hold the thought of self. He asked if the sense of identity were about to vanish in such moments, or whether they realized instead a more profound, universal identity.[4] The Symbolist temperament grasps at extremes, adopting the extraordinary as its norm, as when the speaker in "Conversation Galante" mixes the metaphysical and the mundane by calling his companion the "eternal humorist" and "enemy of the absolute." Eliot borrowed something of Laforgue's method, which Symons described as a kind of travesty, incorporating odd and unusual, "non-poetic" words and subtly allusive, factitious, and reflected meanings. Laforgue combined these meanings in a kind of serious play by lampooning sentimentalism, treating trivial matters seriously, and juxtaposing colloquial and high diction.

Eliot's ambivalence, his ironic deflation of metaphysics by applying them to personalities, and his eager self-deprecation owe much to Laforgue. In the middle stanza of "Conversation Galante," for instance, the ambiguous word "inane" echoes both homo duplex selves. Its playful sense, "silly" (a mood of youth), as well as its more serious meaning, "empty" (reflecting a mood of adult disillusion), hit just the Laforguian note as described by Symons.[5] Although the couple's badinage insists, at some level, upon referring to their own predicament, they retreat at once from whatever emotional seriousness they tender, as if to risk sincerity is to risk far too much. In self-defense, they call the little chances they take digressions, insane, or too serious.

While "Conversation Galante" involves verbal doubleness protecting mixed motives, "La Figlia Che Piange" relies on the speaker's divided perspective, his Prufrockian habit of imagining himself and his companion as a scenarist would. (Earlier poems, such as "Nocturne," anticipated this "external" point of view: "Blood looks effective on the moonlit ground.") Especially in the three lines beginning "So" (i.e., "in that fashion"), the speaker conceives a parting scene. He seems altogether too concerned with staging the dramatic requirements of their parting, yet oddly disinterested when it comes to the emotions.

> She turned away, but with the autumn weather
> Compelled my imagination many days,
> Many days and many hours:
> Her hair over her arms and her arms full of flowers.
> And I wonder how they should have been together!
> I should have lost a gesture and a pose.
> Sometimes these cogitations still amaze
> The troubled midnight and the noon's repose.

The syntax and repetition, rhymes both leisurely and surprising, and formal diction – "compelled," "cogitations," "amaze," and especially the subjunctive "should have lost" – reflect the speaker's effort to disengage himself from the scene emotionally by imagining it dramatically, from "outside."

The first stanza – a mise en scène of sorts – appears assuredly directorial until its verbs betray their auteur's ambivalence. "Stand" relaxes into the irresolute "lean"; "clasp" is followed by its opposite, "fling"; and "weave," used four times, inserts a measure of irony into a poem portraying a leave taking and a relationship coming apart. The second stanza discomposes this uneasy tableau, torn between extremes of violent hyperbole – with a soul leaving the body "torn and bruised" – and understatement at once sentimental and cynical – "incomparably light and deft," but also "faithless." Unconcerned with her emotions because confused about his own, he makes something of an emotional poseur. His extravagant, stagy gesture reflects the speaker's emotional parsimony; Eliot writes with an element of irony that eludes the speaker as he sets up his scene and blocks out his emotions. "I should have lost a gesture and a pose." Who is the audience? In what sense, or on whom, should these things have been "lost"?

The speaker's curious comment seems guilty of at best illogic and at worst duplicity. His feelings may simply remain too precious – or too coldblooded – for words to express. It is always possible that the central self's secrets will shrink from exposure to the light of publicity. Or perhaps the speaker's manipulative legerdemain seems a shade too premeditated, too composed, to be quite plausible. If the latter, his attitude toward the scene's emotional interior recapitulates indecision about its exterior. Its gesture and pose leave him to contemplate a parting physically completed, but emotionally unresolved. If his parting shot is "faithless" – dishonest, disloyal, or false – why then do "these cogitations still amaze / The troubled midnight and the noon's repose"? The daydreams and nightmares that worry his waking moments and sleepless nights suggest an ambivalence that distills the scene's ambiguity. Internal dissonance suspends this nervous speaker between roles as reluctant participant and eager spectator, hammy actor and dispassionate critic.

"Portrait of a Lady" likewise presents a man straining to keep his distance while in a woman's presence, yet unable to stop thinking of her once outside it. Despite a similar predicament, however, the murky awkwardness between the man and woman in "Portrait" makes the state of affairs in "La Figlia" seem almost lucid by comparison. Technically, however, "Portrait" remains a more direct and better-organized composition. Instead of having a single character express both "inner" and "outer" perspectives, "Portrait" divides the labor. Here the woman does the talking, the narrator mainly, if not manfully, contributing only a series of well-timed smiles, which he hopes will conceal his private, unspoken responses.

"Portrait of a Lady" proceeds by interruption, with quotations and parentheses sprinkled throughout for ironic punctuation. The homo duplex paradigm, however, defines its basic strategy, with Eliot once more alternating two points of view. Her reticent guest's evaluative *monologue intérieur* counterpoints the lady's diffuse, melancholy speeches. At best he makes only unenthusiastic, unwilling concessions to the occasion. The distancing quotation marks and his scenarism (in which, he says, the scene seems to arrange itself) portray the narrator evading his discomfort in a social situation whose demands he nonetheless senses acutely. The churchy, Gothic atmosphere of winter smoke, fog, and wax candles portend the twinned kinds of communication, things said and left unsaid, that keep him on his guard.

Though both characters feel obliged to maintain the social surface, the lady exploits it, taking advantage of her visitor's passive reluctance to disturb the mannerly peace. We may wonder about their motives and the nature of their association, yet its dynamic seems clear enough: She tenders and assumes intimacy, as he resists and withholds it. The narrator, like Prufrock, responds to external, social demands with an inner sense that he is about to be overwhelmed. His eerie silence in the lady's presence, given his keen awareness of the things unsaid between them, alerts us to his sense of being off balance and mortally ill at ease. And as it begins to beat a drumlike rhythm, the narrator's relentless pulse reminds him of the occasion's dissonance, its oxymoronic "capricious monotone," boring but unpredictable like their conversation, supplying a "false note."

"Portrait of a Lady" also contrasts two settings linked to the two selves. In the lady's shuttered, private drawing room, a forced, leaden smile "falls heavily among the bric-à-brac." Its almost palpable claustrophobia diverges sharply from the social, public world, whose open air the narrator desires like a zone of tranquillity. There he might assume a more breezy personality, having a smoke and discussing "late events" over a beer, keeping to news that is interesting, remote, and, best of all, impersonal. In such a fashion would he try to regain neutral ground, steering their conversation away from the lady's obsessions – friendship, understanding, innocence, and youth – none of which, apparently, she possesses. His choice to withdraw to a park or restaurant reflects how the poem converts public space into a sphere of safety, while treating private domesticity as an arena of danger. Far from regretting the "odds and ends" of life, he welcomes the relief that public spaces might provide in this painful situation.

While the lady all but begs her visitor to squeeze something serious and intimate out of him, he remains impassive, the correcting of watches against the public clocks being about as far as he will venture toward shared experience. We overhear the narrator evaluate this lady as she neurotically twists a long-suffering lilac stalk. With a delicacy so exaggerated it becomes clumsy, she tries to turn his notice to a difficulty she knows he recognizes but about which he pretends innocence. She calls youth cruel and without remorse. But when she accuses youth of smiling at situations it cannot see, the narrator in a moment of exquisite irony smiles both at her and to himself. He enjoys a little private joke at her expense, visibly confirming but inwardly contradicting her analysis of his character. All is not quite as she says. Though he may indeed be cruel, the narrator surely sees the situation, even if he does not quite command it. By the end of the poem, he will also have to grapple with a feeling very like remorse. Although able to preserve his self-possession at this crucial moment, he spends most of his effort keeping himself distant and uncommitted, as the conversation "slips among velleities and carefully caught regrets."

A connoisseur of social awkwardness, Eliot surely meant this phrase's ambiguity to reflect the indeterminacy of this meeting. Their conversation "slips": On the one hand, it moves quietly, even stealthily, touching no sensitive subject. On the other, it permits things to fall, deliberately, yet as if by accident. The conversational gambits that "slip" are then carefully "caught," in at least three senses: first, as one might rescue a piece of the lady's bric-a-brac accidentally nudged off a mantle; second, as in to "catch" a nuance or a subtle meaning; and finally, to be caught oneself, in the sense of being trapped. "Velleities," a crucial word in this circumstance, means "low degree of volition not prompting to action." Like Prufrock, the narrator in "Portrait" finds himself trapped by susceptibility to social demands and by his stubborn refusal to accede to them. He feels superior to this lady, presumably much older than he. Yet she maintains the upper hand, subtly exposing his inadequacy, passivity, and sham aplomb. As he takes his hat to go, he is embarrassed to feel he must make amends to her for what she has said to him. He reminds himself that he is a man of simple pleasures, but reading comics and the sporting page does not insulate him from more complex feelings, elicited by an overheard melody or fragrant hyacinths, which disturb his self-possession.

As maudlin, sentimental, and unsatisfactory as the lady's demands for friendship and intimacy may be, they establish a point; the narrator cannot convincingly argue that a life drinking beer, clockwatching, or reading a newspaper in public offers any advantage over the lady's genteel solitude. Even in public, sentiment, sensuality, and things that "other people" have desired trouble him, so that he can hardly say whether his way or the lady's is right or wrong, better or worse. Spring sunsets resuscitate the lady's "buried life"; in August the weary street piano has the same effect upon the narrator. The pair are not completely different after all, both dreaming of desire.

The attributes of the "mechanical and tired" street piano and of the common, "worn-out" song reach beyond their immediate contexts and frame the poem's emotional texture. Eliot grew up listening to genteel words and rhythms, voices never raised and purged of anger or discomposure, voices whose highly conscious syntax, diction, and tone are freighted with a quality of moral weariness. In these first poems, Eliot renders genteel American diction and rhythm by instinct – an instinct, however, from which he had already distanced himself, as his superb ironies reveal. This accuracy alone marks "Portrait of a Lady" as one of his greatest poems. Eliot's mastery of conversational rhythms and diction captures the soothing, uninflected simplicity of cultivated American speech:

'For everybody said so, all our friends,
They all were sure our feelings would relate
So closely! I myself can hardly understand.
We must leave it now to fate.
You will write, at any rate.
Perhaps it is not too late.
I shall sit here, serving tea to friends.'

The shrinking fourth, fifth, and sixth lines imitate the lady's frail attenuation; she, and the length of the line, at last recover strength only by drawing upon the refined ritual of the tea ceremony. By rhyming four out of five lines, Eliot mimics perfectly the predictability of the lady's life and personality.

Perhaps, too, the muted but relentless rhyme echoes the polite aggression in the lines themselves, which seem to give up on their relationship only to conclude that she nonetheless wants to carry on. Thus one may detect a veiled threat in the last line. She will serve tea to friends; friends will be sure to show up to drink it; not to appear means that friendship has ceased. These lines also state a formal irony, in which the highly wrought, utterly composed rhyming lines comment upon the scene's social and emotional discomposition. As the enjambed second line encourages a reader to hurry past, only to discover its rhyme repeated like the tom-tom or a mechanical street piano, the three lines dwindle to an anticlimax that remains among the most evocative, closely observed moments in all Eliot's verse.

Yet it is during this moment, when rhymes and rhythms realize their greatest plangency, that the lady delivers her last-ditch invitation-cum-threat. The possibility that their relationship might continue after he has gone abroad once more plunges the narrator into the vertigo of self-consciousness. Learning he will go abroad, she asks him to write to her. His response reveals how facile his self-possession is. The emphasized "*this*" implies that until now, the visit has not gone quite as he might have anticipated. Yet when the dreaded moment of his leave taking finally arrives, his fragility reduces him to the lady's level, even if her fragility is of another kind, breakable rather than tractable, brittle not pliable. Though he might have expected she would wish to correspond, he collapses when she asks point blank why friendship failed. Enigmatic smiles seem useless against such a remark, and the effort his insincerity requires catches him unawares. He feels embarrassed, as though having extended a purely social, insincere smile, the mirror accusatorily catches him *in flagrante delicto*. Self-consciousness, snuffing out the brightly burning self-possession that had momentarily lit them both, now overcomes him: "My self-possession gutters; we are really in the dark."

The final two verse paragraphs state the speaker's indecision about

whether to rely on his manners or his inner self. After Herculean efforts
to avoid being put out of countenance, he concludes:

> And I must borrow every changing shape
> To find expression . . . dance, dance
> Like a dancing bear,
> Cry like a parrot, chatter like an ape.
> Let us take the air, in a tobacco trance –

The self that borrows shape to express itself is the social one. Yet none of
the similes, concrete instances of those alternatives, inspires much confidence in such expression. Dancing bear, crying parrot, and chattering
ape suggest comic, circus-like travesty and ventriloquism, masks as inauthentic and transparent as the refrain "Let us take the air, in a tobacco
trance –." That line falls as flat and irresolute here as it had earlier.
Presumably the expedient it recommends – admiring monuments, discussing public events, and the like – would similarly founder. As Eliot
once wrote, "Nothing makes a man more ridiculous really than the fear
of ridicule."[6]

By contrast, the final verse paragraph suggests another resolution,
linked to the pastel, smoky April or August that stirs obscure desire. He
speculates upon her demise and how it would leave him to face his
ambivalence, pen in hand. Instead of questioning his ideas, this time he
asks whether his emotions are right or wrong. Distance of time and place
might offer emotional distance as well, which the speaker could employ
to apprehend what did, or did not, transpire between the two of them.
Perhaps his central self might act upon past events, organizing them even
if social forms could not. But the narrator denies himself this possibility
by once more asking whether he and she really differ so very much. Can
he truly regard himself as her superior in feeling, understanding, or social
accomplishment? If her social self is embarrassingly invasive and her
central self too vulnerable, is his personality any more resilient?

The lady, after all, demanded more of him than he of her. Though her
death would release her from their association, it would force him to
shoulder the not inconsiderable burden of trying either to understand or
to forget it. By exerting a measure of control over his thoughts, her
death might give her what she never gained in life, paradoxically resolving the situation to her advantage. Although her parlor resembled Juliet's
tomb, unlike Juliet no passion led the lady to die for love, and despite the
hopelessness of their relationship, her visitor was no Romeo. Notwithstanding the lady's complacent, guilt-inflicting intimacies and cloying
preciousness – "You will write, at any rate" – can the narrator feel
superior to her? "And should I have the right to smile?"

"Portrait of a Lady" has a somewhat incomplete title, for it paints as clear a portrait of the visitor as it does of the lady. The poem portrays a lady, but also the strain of being something less than a gentleman. Although unwilling to befriend her, he nonetheless feels obligated to maintain the surfaces of friendship. He will not be genuinely amiable, yet cannot appear rude. He feels, approaching her door, as if he "had mounted on my hands and knees." The mask of manners exhausts his inner reserves, until he barely has the physical strength to climb the stairs. Yet he persists, out of duty or to expiate his guilt, as though performing some self-mortifying penance, making on his knees a humiliating pilgrimage to a shrine. It is an impossible situation, and likewise impossible to determine which of the two behaves worse. Who is leading, or misleading, whom? As "Prufrock" does, "Portrait of a Lady" illustrates Eliot's preoccupation with public and private, propriety and intimacy, and how social and central selves may become confused to the point of agony. Both poems concern situations, as Matthew Arnold once phrased it, "in which there is everything to be endured, nothing to be done."[7]

In these long poems, central and social selves seem to be at odds with one another. Both convey a sense that human relations remain unsatisfying and inadequate. Why is Prufrock a failure? Because his two selves cancel one another, so he cannot act, a casualty of self-inflicted irony. Why is the lady in "Portrait" so unsettling? Because she challenges her visitor's definition of the occasion, insists upon converting acquaintance into emotional intimacy, and then with the righteous vigor of those who deem themselves victims, abuses her guest's good manners when he does not respond. Although the visitor wishes to withdraw to the safety of the public world, doubt, emotion, and even the cloak of manners subvert his fragile self-regard. His retreat into propriety and diffidence seems as unsatisfactory as Prufrock's escape into fantasy. Barely able to master the social occasion, he finds he cannot control his own inner self.

These characters find social relations a burden, and their emotions lack form and control. Self-consciousness paralyzes rather than liberates them. Instead of pursuing self-affirmation, the characters grapple with self-doubt, even self-annihilation, bespeaking a weak, inchoate central self. To alienation and psychological disintegration they add pessimism regarding any possible change. They decline to jump in either direction, refusing the consolations of either sincerity or immersion in social role.

Such figures, unable to align their two selves, contrast strongly with Eliot's defense of rhetoric, "'Rhetoric' and Poetic Drama."[8] That essay connects language, drama, and personality, seeks to redeem the word "rhetoric" from signifying any pompous, overdone language, and tries to restore its technical meaning. It urges the complex, self-conscious, dramatic self that Eliot's early poetic characters lack. And as it sets forth the positive context for Eliot's poetic characters, the essay continues the work of reassessing the Romantic and Victorian simple self.

In the nineteenth century, Eliot argues, rhetoric came to bear almost exclusively negative connotations. He objects to employing the word simply to abuse a bad or second-rate style. Complaining of critics who lazily call any fault of Elizabethan or Jacobean verse "rhetorical," Eliot advocates purging rhetoric of its exclusively negative connotations in favor of more neutral or technical ones. Using "rhetoric" simply as a synonym for bad writing tends to obscure the word's positive qualities. "Let us avoid the assumption that rhetoric is a vice of manner," Eliot concludes, "and endeavor to find a rhetoric of substance also, which is right because it issues from what it has to express."

Accepting his own invitation to dissect "rhetoric" and reassemble it critically, Eliot first attacks the conventional tendency to equate poetic with conversational language. He argues that if we reserve the word "rhetorical" for "any convention of writing inappropriately applied," then colloquial poetic language has developed into a negative rhetoric fully as false and mechanical as the poetic diction it replaced. Eliot would redefine rhetoric more neutrally: Language and form must change as substance and intention do, becoming fluid, malleable, and theatrical. Authors adopt masks and personae, becoming verbally insincere (in Wilde's sense) so that they may adequately present their various feelings. This definition implies that writers develop many selves, expressing each in a style distinctive to it. To give the effect of speech, a writer must speak "sincerely" in his own voice or adopt a role and use another voice, fitting language and style to the moment as it varies. Eliot argues that by this adaptation from monotony to variety, Elizabethan drama developed a "progressive refinement in the perception of the variations of feeling, and a progressive elaboration of the means of expressing these variations."

Eliot next makes a logical but crucial point. Language not only reflects the refinement of feeling and intellect, and rhetoric does not merely express how a culture and individuals pass from crude, simple monotony to sophisticated, complex variety. The process may also work in reverse. Complex language calls into being complex states of thought and feeling. Art imitates life, but also affects it. New names, as Eliot's dissertation had argued, enable us to recognize, acknowledge, and perhaps even experience new emotions and thoughts. If Elizabethan drama changed from Kyd and Marlowe's rhetorical bombast to the subtle, dispersed utterance of Shakespeare and Webster, Eliot traced the difference not only to an "improvement in language," but also to a "progressive variation in feeling." He explored the phenomenon on several other occasions.[9]

This theme underpins Eliot's famous review of Grierson's *Metaphysical Lyrics and Poems,* praising this rhetorical complexity and the variety of thought and feeling it reflects and creates. Even when the metaphysical poets wrote in a syntax that was not simple, it represented "a fidelity to thought and feeling. . . . And as this fidelity induces variety of thought and feeling, so it induces variety of music."[10] In "The Metaphysical Poets," Eliot does not follow up his strongest point, which is that rhetorical complexity can *foster* variety of thought and feeling. Instead he argues the less challenging mimetic theory that poets simply try to "find the verbal equivalent for states of mind and feeling."

In "'Rhetoric' and Poetic Drama," however, Eliot traces the finest Elizabethan rhetoric to a positive, role-playing self-consciousness that rhetoric can induce in the mind of a theatrical character or, indeed, of a living person. Shakespeare's finest rhetoric, he argues, occurs when a character "*sees himself* in a dramatic light." Eliot alleged that Jonson's most successful oratory conformed to that formula and became tedious only when a speech was addressed to the audience rather than to the play's other characters. Paradoxically, self-conscious rhetoric makes the distinction between players and audience more rather than less clear. "Bad" rhetoric, overstepping its bounds, directs itself primarily to the audience. True rhetoric, emphasizing the play's boundaries by rigorously observing them, addresses the other characters as the audience observes and, as it were, overhears. When it is otherwise, when a character appeals directly to members of the audience and disregards their position as spectators, Eliot finds that we lose the chance to observe how a character views himself and risk succumbing either to the temptations of our own sentiment or to a "vicious rhetoric."

This is more than a point of decorum. Because these remarks inevitably extend beyond Elizabethan plays, Eliot hastens to explain why this rhetorical self-consciousness affects contemporary drama so little. Trying to appear more "natural" – the word again implies language arbitrarily limited to "conversational" effects – drama instead simply becomes more crude. Paradoxically, lack of artifice narrows its emotional and expressive range and deprives the characters of the "dramatic sense." Eliot, however, exposes a false assumption of modern dramaturgy, which erroneously believes that allowing a character to be consciously dramatic will make it seem less real. Instead, Eliot urges, "in many of those situations in actual life which we enjoy consciously and keenly, we are at times aware of ourselves in this way, and these moments are of very great usefulness to dramatic verse. A very small part of acting is that which takes place on the stage!" Eliot's final sentence alludes to perhaps the most far-reaching implication of the homo duplex paradigm. Role playing occurs not only in drama but in everyday life. In so doing it transforms the world itself into a kind of theater.

Surely the melancholy of the nineties aesthetes, as well as their brilliance, stems partly from this equivalence. Once life becomes situational and personality fluid, reality exists only to be controlled and exploited. Mutable theatricality tends to undercut notions of fixed, absolute order – be they Platonic, Natural, Christian, political, or otherwise – beyond what people's own behavior permits them to construct and believe. It tends furthermore to compromise any self save the one offered to an audience; the more the self seeks solitude, the less reality it discovers. On one hand, *theatrum mundi* contains seeds of pessimism, since we can depend on no final, permanent order or ideal to authorize our conduct. On the other, however, it renders actuality more brilliant and energetic, since without such an orientation, we fall back upon fiction making, evaluating ourselves and others insofar as those fictions convince or divert us.

Eliot's exclamation spotlights the acting, the performing, the "insincerity" in our lives. Not only does he suggest that acting occurs far more frequently in real life than in the theater, but he pays this theory the compliment of asserting that the moments when we are most theatrically aware remain just those moments in which we become most ourselves, and most alive. Illustrating the point by saying that Rostand had this dramatic sense, Eliot wrote that "it is what gives life to Cyrano. It is a sense which is almost a sense of humor (for when anyone is conscious of himself as acting, something like a sense of humor is present)." Prufrock has something approaching this sense of humor about himself. He nonetheless seems convinced of the correctness of his own point of view vis-à-vis that of everyone else, so while others may laugh at him, he cannot laugh at himself. Although he sees that he is at times "almost ridiculous," the acknowledgment falls short of a sense of humor about himself, becoming rather more like self-pity. Prufrock's dramatic self-awareness verges on pathos, since his mock heroics are not simply comic. "Shall I part my hair behind? Do I dare to eat a peach?" Because Prufrock can find no role he cannot ridicule, he has no role he can act out with either conviction or enjoyment. That the characters in "Prufrock" and "Portrait of a Lady" do not "enjoy" their situations is the most telling thing they disclose about their own character. Instead, each seems to manifest more or less severe tensions of role strain, the difficulty in fulfilling role obligations.[11] These characters reveal themselves most notably by their reluctance or inability to find a role that will gratify or enforce their sense of self. Hence they experience discomfort in roles they did not choose but feel they cannot abandon.

If we do not create our own roles, however, they will nonetheless be forced upon us. That paradox exposes a defect of any theory of personal identity or society predicated exclusively upon sincerity. From the point of view of drama or poetry, the most pertinent critique of such sincerity is that it precludes the expression – and perhaps even the formation – of significant emotion, that is, emotion complex enough to remain faithful to a complex reality. That complexity and significance, their formation and expression, remain Eliot's goal all along.

Another passage from "'Rhetoric' and Elizabethan Drama" shifts the center of dramatic gravity away from incommunicable inner emotion toward significant, self-conscious "rhetoric." Because Maeterlinck's characters do not consciously delight in their roles, they are sentimental. Eliot once more attacks a fallacious assumption of modern drama, disputing the notion that by remaining inarticulate, emotions gain intensity. What they gain in intensity, he suggests, they lose in significance. Among his other shortcomings, Prufrock is also a rhetorical failure, sighing, "It is impossible to say just what I mean." The narrator of "Portrait" can likewise imagine no more suitable persona than the street-carnival grotesques of dancing bear, chattering ape, or crying parrot. By negative implication, these speakers suggest that maturity, resilience, and wholeness correspond to rhetorical proficiency and to the adoption of at least one suitable role.

These poetic characters do not realize the alignment of self and role that "'Rhetoric' and Poetic Drama" calls for. Poetic drama, for example, must "take genuine and substantial human emotions, such emotions as observation can confirm, typical emotions, and give them artistic form." Genuine, substantial, observable, and typical: The first two qualities pertain to the central self, but the latter two refer to the social one, and to rhetorical presentation. Admittedly, as in the 1927 essay, "Shakespeare and the Stoicism of Seneca," Eliot's position would later expand from the profoundly secular homo duplex to admit the Christian hierarchy of lower, mortal flesh and higher, immortal spirit. But Eliot formerly emphasized the outward, behavioral, social signs and attacked the not always reliable dictates from within.

Eliot's theory, then, tries to balance central and social selves, while his poetic characters warn against what happens when personality disintegrates. Eliot also tries to show how sincerity and form, emotion and rhetoric fuse in a work of art. Most important, his poetry and criticism illustrate and contradict tendencies they profess to find in the modern world, which either splits the two selves irrevocably or else denies their separate existence to begin with. Homo duplex also complicated Eliot's idea of the poet's role and added to its social content. Instead of restricting his role to seer, mystic, or prophet – heightened states peculiar to the

central self – the poet may also behave less seriously; he may perform
and entertain. By reference to an essentially public, social, and entertain-
ing dimension, from which nineteenth-century values of sincerity had
separated it, Eliot wished to expand the poet's role to that of a music-hall
comedian.[12] His essay "Marie Lloyd" argued a necessary collaboration
between artist and audience.[13] Trying to revive an essentially social function, Eliot's desire to combine comedy with seriousness, and theater
with poetry, is one of the most important themes of his career. It is,
moreover, one that evidently flowed from elements within his personal
character.[14]

The homo duplex theme, indeed, can unlock a casual aside in Eliot's
critical prose. Only years of intelligent effort, an intense moment, or
both could win "great simplicity" for a writer. That victory, Eliot
claimed, "represents one of the most arduous conquests of the human
spirit: the triumph of feeling and thought over the natural sin of language."[15] A phrase like the "natural sin of language" points to how
words (except, paradoxically, through the supervening agency of rhetoric) fall short of fidelity to the innocent, preverbal conceptions of the
central self (or, given that he uses the words "feeling and thought," of
what Eliot might have termed the finite centre). The phrase contains a
homo duplex assumption about the self and language: that words, as a
social medium, betray thoughts and adulterate feelings when called upon
to express them. The inner self feels or thinks, but verbal expression
necessarily changes – if Eliot's metaphor is accepted, stains – those
thoughts or feelings. A word's history – the social inheritance it bears
through long use – limits, defines, and categorizes inchoate feeling into
something connected with and similar to the feelings of every other prior
speaker, or present hearer. (In Eliot's analysis of Bradley, this is how
disparate finite centres come to intend identical reference.) The poet has
diverse ways to overcome the "natural sin of language," but each of
them, save the alternative of silence, requires more, rather than less,
rhetorical skill to make it possible to say just what he means.

Eliot summoned the other half of the homo duplex paradigm when
arguing that Poe, Whitman, and Hawthorne suffered not because their
society lacked an intelligentsia, but from the "defect of society in the
larger sense. . . . Their world was thin; it was not corrupt enough."[16]
Governed emotionally by a Puritan model of a pure, sincere central self,
their social world had remained incompletely complex, insufficiently
reticulated by the tissues and mendacities of manners and mixed motives.
In short, it was not social enough; it was "too innocent." This judgment
implies that the social world – built up of social selves that seem "corrupt" when their partly predictable and partly novel behavior is compared with the central self's innocence in solitude – forms a prerequisite

to literary expression, which must rely not only on the natural sin of language, but also on sin of other sorts. Even though, as we have seen, he was not the first to acknowledge the difficulties posed by a unified, sincere self, Eliot remains one of few writers who have considered how role playing and theatricality might offer American society a way to repair the effects of its innocence.

"The natural sin of language" and a social world "not corrupt enough": These opposite, paradoxical phrases not only suggest how deeply the homo duplex model infused Eliot's early thought, but also reflect his ambivalence toward the choices it enforced. Homo duplex did not pose a simple problem. On the one hand, Eliot acknowledged the central, pristine self and the tragic ease with which language may traduce it. On the other, he affirmed the strain the isolated author bears without a supporting cast of worldly actors politely and insincerely perjuring their nagging, innocent central selves so as to gratify their opportunistic social ones. The paradigm persisted in his thought even after its Christian reconstitution. He defined a person, for instance, as "both an individual and a member." Although a person has a unique, inviolable personality, he also fits into society as one of its members. Eliot argued that if society conceived of itself as simply a sum of individuals, it produced the "chaos of liberal democracy." Like Bradley in "My Station and Its Duties," Eliot urged that someone wholly isolated from the community "is no longer a person." He added that "a man is not himself unless he is a member; and he cannot be a member unless he is also something alone. Man's membership and his solitude must be taken together."

Thus far, Eliot restates the homo duplex theorem in relation to secular society. But between and above the two termini – social and central selves, or "membership and solitude" as he calls them here – Eliot inserts the *tertium quid* of divinity. In the way Bradleyan logic had taught him to do, Eliot superadded a novel factor to the homo duplex equation: the presence of God, which for Eliot seemed not only to confirm the pattern, but to intensify its empirical accuracy and its psychological necessity. Eliot described moments in the life of the soul when a person's awareness of isolation from all other human beings might prove nearly crushing. Eliot pitied a person who was alone without God in such moments and whose only companions were himself, his meanness, and his futility. Individuality was not enough, Eliot argued; neither was membership; and neither were the two together enough, without God. "It is after these moments, alone *with* God and awareness of our worthiness, but for Grace, of nothing but damnation, that we turn with most thankfulness and appreciation to the awareness of our *membership:* for we appreciate and are thankful for nothing fully until we see where it begins and where it ends."[17]

Eliot paid considerable attention to the failed self, a failure the modern world mirrors in its social anomie and innumerable private capitulations to neurosis. The homo duplex model helps explain the dissonance in Eliot's characters and underlies some of his criticism. Eliot's poetic characters, and modern people, often seem alternately overwhelmed by emotion or by the demands of social roles, yet curiously bereft of their not inconsiderable consolations. Modern life having withheld a satisfying arrangement between the two selves, Eliot wrote to diagnose the divisions, and perhaps to heal them.

4

Where Are the Eagles and the Trumpets? American Aesthetes

No State, in the European sense of the word, and indeed barely a specific national name. No sovereign, no court, no personal loyalty, no aristocracy, no church, no clergy, no army, no diplomatic service, no country gentlemen, no palaces, no castles, nor manors, nor old country-houses, nor parsonages, nor thatched cottages, nor ivied ruins; no cathedrals, nor abbeys, nor little Norman churches; no great Universities or public schools – no Oxford, nor Eton, nor Harrow; no literature, no novels, no museums, no pictures, no political society, no sporting class – no Epsom nor Ascot! Some such list as that might be drawn up of the absent things in American life.

Henry James, *Hawthorne*

I must study politics and war that my sons may have liberty to study mathematics and philosophy. My sons ought to study mathematics and philosophy, geography, natural history and naval architecture, navigation, commerce and agriculture, in order to give their children a right to study painting, poetry, music, architecture, statuary, tapestry and porcelain.

John Adams (quoted in James Truslow Adams,
The Adams Family)

INTRODUCTION

On "St. George's Day," 1928, T. S. Eliot wrote the following words in a letter to Herbert Read. His sentence's syntactic shape, a sprawling but deliberate parataxis, reflects the difficulty Eliot felt, even as a small boy, confronting a problematic regional, national, historical, and therefore personal identity.

Some day I want to write an essay about the point of view of an American who wasn't an American, because he was born in the South and went to school in New England as a small boy with a nigger drawl, but who wasn't a southerner in the South because his people were northerners in a border state and looked down on all southerners and Virginians, and who so was never anything anywhere and who therefore felt himself to be more a Frenchman than an American and more an Englishman than a Frenchman and yet felt that the U.S.A. up to a hundred years ago was a family extension. It is almost too difficult even for H. J. who for that matter wasn't an American at all, in that sense.[1]

Evidently Eliot early experienced an element of exile, feeling himself to be "never anything anywhere." He speaks of two categories – time and space – that place people, and especially artists, but does so to point out how they dispersed rather than concentrated his identity. Even the logic seems a bit loose; the makeweight "therefore" is almost a piece of wit. And among other odd distinctions (such as that between Southerners and Virginians), he is using the word "American" in a particular sense, one that excludes, for instance, Henry James. Whether familial, regional, linguistic, historical, or educational, the feeling of dislocation and home-lessness lies behind Eliot's numerous efforts to resolve these ambiguities.

A more familiar passage, itself a strategy of resolution, betrays none of the floppy form or emotional indeterminacy of the one written to Read. In "Tradition and the Individual Talent," Eliot called tradition more than simply unquestioning imitation of the previous generation's successes and something other than coming into a legacy. Obtaining possession of a significant tradition required conscious effort to acquire the historical sense, a sense of the timeless and of the temporal together that forces a writer to feel "that the whole of the literature of Europe from Homer and within it the whole of the literature of his own country has a simultaneous existence and composes a simultaneous order."[2] Though differing for-mally, these two passages reflect the importance Eliot attached to a writer's sense of history: politics, community myth, and, most of all, public time. Some people find themselves peculiarly placed, however, and for them the division between public and private history, between na-tional and individual life, almost vanishes. To Henry Adams, for instance, a presidential grandfather and great-grandfather would not seem remote, historical figures bearing an exclusively public demeanor. Likewise, as they did for Eliot, the convulsions of seventeenth-century New England could retain a certain immediacy in the twentieth if they involved the family's memory as well as the nation's.[3]

By 1928, Eliot had at least officially reoriented himself in time and space, having the previous year become a British subject.[4] He nonetheless felt that "the U.S.A. up to a hundred years ago was a family extension." Few others writing in the twentieth century had the genealogy to make that statement (one who had was Henry Adams). In fewer still would Andrew Jackson's election a century earlier have remained so meaningful, poignantly symbolizing the end of a system and of the ideal that informed it. Defending pre-Jacksonian democracy, Eliot wrote in 1928 that when the notion of electoral suffrage changes from a privilege and duty to a right, democracy shifts from government by a visible oligarchy to government by an invisible one. He did not ridicule the idea of democracy itself, but simply argued that a real democracy always required some limitation by hereditary rights and responsibilities. The United States, he said, had been more or less democratic until 1829, when "Andrew Jackson became President, when the system which is euphemistically known as *la carrière ouverte aux talents,* and more exactly as the Pork Barrel System, became powerful." Instead of asking what would replace a defunct democracy in the modern world, Eliot urged that the proper question would ask how, out of the materials at hand, to build a new structure in which democracy could live.[5]

Space: Only by being born of an old American family in a youthful region of the country could Eliot harbor thoughts arising from divided loyalties, from a sense that the cultural center lay half a continent away. Time: Only by placing a certain construction upon history could the English Civil War, the Salem witch trials, or a presidential election sixty years before one's birth seem to influence one's own life. Yet they appear to have done so: Expatriation remains a crucial fact about Eliot's career, without which it would not have existed in the same form, if at all. Unless we recognize Eliot's emigration and repatriation as crucial life choices and personal assertions, much of what Eliot deemed important and much of his career's significance – and its oddness – will escape our notice.[6] Radically uprooting oneself as Eliot did implies not the insignificance of nationality and history, but quite the opposite. It implies that these things have become burdens, impeding the formation of one's personality and of one's art. Eliot transplanted himself to England as a reaction to another place and another history. *Poems, 1920* addresses some of the ways public history intersected with Eliot's private past, particularly those events in American history that spurred his departure.

Comparing Eliot with other writers who occupied analogous personal, philosophical, social, genealogical, political, and cultural positions helps reveal what Eliot reacted against in American history and culture. One taught him: George Santayana, twice, at Harvard College.[7] One he praised: Henry James, countless times in essays or private letters. One he quoted at a crucial moment: Henry Adams, on whose historical viewpoint Eliot based "Gerontion." Santayana, James, and Adams, all at least a generation older (only Santayana may be called a contemporary, and he was twenty-five years Eliot's senior), interpreted the American public life into which Eliot matured. They offer at least analogies to, and at most direct influences upon, Eliot's view of his nation and its history and his conception of modernism. Educated to revere tradition, these writers defined modernity as what broke with tradition, competed with it, and overthrew it. Literary modernism therefore means little until we understand its reactive aspect.

These writers' social opinions merit attention not merely as literary sources that Eliot would later reference. They also set forth an emotional response elaborated into the aestheticist ideology, a system with its own axioms, rules, and conclusions and with its own distinctive – for the most part adversarial – posture toward American society. As such it is not so anomalous, for instance, to focus on Henry James's travel writing while largely ignoring his fiction. The object is not to find literary sources but typical habits of mind, patterns of reaction, styles of sensibility, and ways of organizing social perception and discourse that influence Eliot's writing. Sometimes Eliot left obvious clues. His reading of *The Education of Henry Adams,* for instance, finds its way into "Burbank with a Baedeker: Bleistein with a Cigar" and "Gerontion." On other occasions, only more general connections are possible, or necessary, to establish. But having described the social views of these three writers just after 1900, we shall have discovered many of the attitudes that inform *Poems, 1920.*

Thus the argument, and the method. A further preliminary step remains, defining "aesthete," or "aestheticism." Though the English nineties set the type most notoriously, it was more various elsewhere in Europe and hardly suits its American exemplars. Americans did not produce an aestheticism empty of or deliberately opposed to moral criteria, as contemporaries construed Wilde, Pater, or Swinburne to have done.[8] American aestheticism did not divorce itself from morality, but instead borrowed its severity and rhetoric. It involved an unstable, unpredictable, and even violent compound of moral and aesthetic, mixing serious and playful motives in a single sensibility. What is right and good is not inevitably beautiful. (Some things are not beautiful, even if you say they are.) Less clearly perhaps, though the aesthetes continually pointed it out, what is wrong and evil is not invariably ugly. But however much the aesthetes might have protested that they had transcended such easy equivalences, they did not simply oppose aesthetic to moral criteria. Instead they drew upon both criteria to argue that artistic form provided an independent source of moral value.[9]

Aestheticism depended upon a certain stance not only toward art, but toward American society. Aesthetes – and their better-heeled camp followers – often used art to stake out their own turf on the social battlefield.[10] If aesthetes found most Americans insufficiently serious about beauty, they themselves had difficulty taking anything seriously except art. (They likewise recoiled, however, from those who took art *too* seriously, as James mercilessly demonstrated in *The American,* whose Unitarian minister Benjamin Babcock spoiled the pleasure of art by insisting upon how instructive it was.) Their social views frequently voiced a complaint against a society that they felt ignored and had no place for them. Perhaps one must exaggerate the importance of one's work in order to do it at all. Correctly perceiving their peripheral social importance, they boldly urged society to place art at the center of experience and to put artists in a position to influence society's decisions.

Their case against American society undoubtedly contained some merit. Although Whistler claimed "there never was an Art-loving nation,"[11] the aesthetes found themselves in a relatively new society, even more recently reconstituted legally, socially, and economically after a civil war. Beneath its superficial consensus, the aesthetes detected currents flowing against them, and in America's perfervid spike-pounding, track-laying, mountain-leveling expansion they could scarcely participate. Whether society was actively hostile or merely indifferent, the estrangement this attitude created between art and life only nourished the aesthetes' social critique. What they regarded as socially immoral or physically ugly caused them to flee to the redoubt of aesthetic perfection. Their loyalty to art and their use of it as a source of moral as well as aesthetic value rendered the American world by contrast still more irremediably ugly.

The aestheticist critique of American life composes a litany of antinomies. Politically, they viewed democracy skeptically, feeling more at home in a hierarchical society and tending to prefer quality to equality. Even though all were devoted to their own careers, they opposed industrialization passionately, sometimes extending this opposition to condemn all entrepreneurial or moneymaking activity. (Although he later became a businessman, Eliot's years working in a large bank left him with an informed skepticism about finance.)[12] Eliot's view, if late in the sequence, was not atypical. The cultural health of Europe, he argued, was not compatible with extremes of either nationalism or internationalism. But those extreme ideas themselves arose from the "relentless pressure of modern industrialism," which had created the problems that the extreme ideas tried to solve. Not the least important effect of industrialism, Eliot concluded, was a kind of mental mechanization that sought "solutions in terms of *engineering,* for problems which are essentially problems of *life.*"[13]

The aesthetes combined high academic achievement with an intellectual, critical temperament surviving their departures from academia, which, to a man, they scorned. That temperament alone placed them outside an economic culture willing to propitiate academic institutions but which could hardly have considered intellectual activity itself anything but eccentric, or worse. Perhaps most important, their pessimism set them apart from a culture officially optimistic, sentimental, and dedicated to progress. Unlike much of American society, at least outside the South, the aesthetes questioned the interpretation of history as progress, argued that too much of the past and present were being sacrificed to the future, and used history to attack contemporary life. Since the past had things of value that the present had forfeited, the aesthetes found it an unfortunate fact that history could not be re-created or relied upon to recur.

It is a measure of their peculiar circumstances that despite Santayana's nonsensical epigram, the aesthetes complained because history *failed* to repeat itself. At no other point does their remoteness from contemporary attitudes so clearly emerge. Most Americans of the time, conceiving evil or suffering in it, feared that history could and would repeat itself. Horrified at what they considered the ugliness and superficiality surrounding them, the aesthetes despaired because it would not. In the thirties, noting "our over-estimation of the importance of our own time," Eliot expressed a typically aestheticist antiprogressivism, saying that the doctrine of progress did little to make the future seem more real, but made the past seem much less real. The doctrine of progress, he claimed, encouraged people to assume that the past had meaning only in the present and to inquire not about what the people of a past age had made of themselves but instead to ask what that age had done for us in the present. Viewing a past age as great in itself, or precious in the eye of God, was an alien notion. Whereas other ages might have been "ego-centric" through ignorance, Eliot called the modern age egocentric through "complacent historical knowledge:" "Everything in the past was a necessary evil – evil in itself, but necessary because it led up to the present. Thus we take ourselves, and our transient affairs, too seriously."[14]

Although they sought admission of their views into the political forum, the aestheticists nonetheless indulged a contempt for politicians and their invertebrate inclination to treat principle with a rigor that public service tended to relax. This attitude expanded to condemn the "active man" generally. Though hardly idle, sometimes working themselves into a state of physical or emotional breakdown, the aesthetes were not dynamic, active, and populist, but static, contemplative, and genteel, however much they would have chafed against the last label. It is true that Eliot, whose parents would not own a copy of *Adventures of Huckleberry Finn* and refused to allow him to read such a book in his boyhood,[15] later defended the Phoenix Theater's decision to perform seventeenth-century plays unexpurgated. (Calling the refusal to expurgate wholly justified, Eliot insisted that hearing the indecencies of Elizabethan and Restoration drama gave him a "sense of relief" and left him a "better and a stronger man.")[16] Yet Eliot frequently deleted provocative or offensive matter from his poetry, as *The Waste Land* manuscripts show. All the aesthetes suffered from this ambivalence, rejecting inadequate genteel literary standards but confronting behavior not conforming to polite canons of taste with genuine disgust.

Yet another paradox in the aesthetes' lives was that all spoke for homogeneity and a common culture, issued jeremiads on the decline of language, and evaluated immigration into America in the most dire terms. Yet they were themselves cosmopolites, participated in an international republic of letters, and three of the four were expatriates for much of their lives. On occasion they could scathingly lampoon parochialism[17] and would have suffered cruelly had circumstances forced them to test their beliefs about the virtues of rootedness and provinciality.

Perhaps most important, the aesthetes reacted to the way religion in the nineteenth and early twentieth centuries had ceased to be a satisfactory object of either faith or reason. Childhood exposure to liberal Protestantism had inoculated them against its innovations. (Eliot and Adams survived a stiff dose of Unitarianism, James's household cultivated a not wholly dissimilar Swedenborgian creed, and even Santayana grew up in Boston regularly attending Unitarian services after early Sunday mass.)[18] They made corresponding claims for art that would have substituted its ideals for those of religion. In conferring value, providing perspective, and offering contact with eternity, art might have seemed at least initially to replace religion. Late in his life, James pushed aestheticism perhaps as far as it could go:

> So far from that of literature being irrelevant to the literary report upon life, and to its being made as interesting as possible, I regard it as relevant in a degree that leaves everything else behind. It is art that *makes* life, makes interest, makes importance, for our consideration and application of these things, and I know of no substitute whatever for the force and beauty of its process.[19]

Of the four, only Eliot, after an extended period of skepticism, took the step necessary to reintegrate art and religion, philosophy and theology, reason and faith.

The following sketches of Santayana, James, and Adams necessarily emphasize particular strands of the aestheticist complex and omit others. Though others have noticed the resemblances between these figures,[20] their similarities to Eliot, their usefulness in analyzing the world he came from, and the comfort he took from their kinship of discontent justify this renewed scrutiny. Its specific interest is in determining a precise context for *Poems, 1920* and a broader one for *The Waste Land*. More generally, the American aesthetes reflected their era; what today may seem strange and even reprobate in Eliot was often only an instance of attitudes widely held among his social class or its literary subset. Finally, the aesthetes' effort to erect in art a substitute for religion proved crucial to Eliot's career, which for a considerable while joined that effort, if ultimately rejecting it.

Besides Eliot, American aestheticism after 1900 touched Pound, Stevens, Van Wyck Brooks, Edmund Wilson, F. Scott Fitzgerald, and an entire modernist generation. (Though it is difficult to mark a clear boundary between these art movements, one way of thinking about the different generations is that while aestheticism worshiped beauty, modernism believed in art.) The influence of aestheticism extended to literary modernism in England through Pound and Eliot, whose experience in post–Civil War America had given them a head start in grasping the swift changes in European life after World War I. To Eliot, those events must have contained a personal irony, for they deprived him yet again of something he had seemed to lose once already: the ideal of a conservative intellectual order, a moral social myth, and a living cultural tradition. By studying these authors, we may glimpse how time and space, public and private may intersect; how history may seem to repeat itself despite particularities of place; how public time influences private experience, and how both affect art; and how the fortunes of art (here, "Anglo-American literary modernism") may themselves turn upon historical accident.

SANTAYANA AND THE CRITIQUE OF GENTILITY

> I smile, of course, and go on drinking tea.

George Santayana's importance to American aestheticism does not come from his formal aesthetics. *The Sense of Beauty,* for instance, treats art not as a repository of quasi-sacred values or transcendent play, but as one of humanity's diverse behavioral expressions, subject to analysis and demystification. One section, "The Authority of Morals Over Aesthetics," seemingly minimizes art's significance. Calling art secondary, derivative of moral occasion, "superficial," "unstable, superadded," and even parasitical hardly suggests the vaporous, hothouse sentiments ordinarily associated with a panting aestheticism.[1]

Santayana does not linger at this theme, however, and soon returns to more familiar territory, discussing how art may console pain and offer shelter from the world's rigors.[2] The likelihood that alienation might awaken a need for aesthetic refuge lurks behind Santayana's claim that social and aesthetic objects estrange people who invest emotion in them:

> If artists and poets are unhappy, it is after all because happiness does not interest them. They cannot seriously pursue it, because its components are not components of beauty, and being in love with beauty, they neglect and despise those unaesthetic social virtues in the operation of which happiness is found. On the other hand those who pursue happiness conceived merely in the abstract and conventional terms, as money,

success, or respectability, often miss that real and fundamental part of happiness which flows from the senses and imagination. This element is what aesthetics supplies to life; for beauty also can be a cause and a factor of happiness. Yet the happiness of loving beauty is either too sensuous to be stable, or else too ultimate, too sacramental, to be accounted happiness by the worldly mind.

The separation of artists from people who live according to conventional criteria of happiness not only leaves artists unfit to live in the world. It also causes their happiness to differ in kind insofar as the criteria of beauty and ugliness are directly linked to social facts and signs. The artist differs from the businessman, whose happiness is money, success, or respectability. The life of the senses and imagination opposes "happiness conceived merely in . . . abstract and conventional terms," and the aesthetic mind contradicts the worldly one. Finally, though he does not say it expressly, Santayana implies an equation between art and beauty antipathetic to "social objects," which while "diffuse," "abstract," and "verbal," are also by implication *ugly*.[3]

Character and Opinion in the United States and Santayana's essay "The Genteel Tradition in American Philosophy" treat these and other volatile themes in the "tone and attitude of a detached observer." "I have no axe to grind," he promises, just before calmly invoking an impending apocalypse. In one way or another, the other three writers make this or a similar disclaimer. James presents himself as the "restless analyst," Adams composes a third-person autobiography, and Eliot theorizes an "impersonal" poetic. Santayana may have indulged the pretense of disinterested objectivity to disarm his readers or to distract them from his discussion's obvious emotional import. In any case, the tone, the attempt at dispassion, and the theme recur:

> Civilisation is perhaps approaching one of those long winters that overtake it from time to time. A flood of barbarism from below may soon level all the fair works of our Christian ancestors, as another flood two thousand years ago levelled those of the ancients. Romantic Christendom – picturesque, passionate, unhappy episode – may be coming to an end. Such a catastrophe would be no reason for despair. Nothing lasts for ever; but the elasticity of life is wonderful, and even if the world lost its memory it could not lose its youth. Under the deluge, and watered by it, seeds of all sorts would survive against the time to come, even if what might eventually spring from them, under the new circumstances, should wear a strange aspect.[4]

"Perhaps," "from time to time," "nothing lasts for ever"; calling the Christian era a "picturesque," "unhappy episode": It makes a risky business to prefer expression of this sort to the less well camouflaged emotional distaste of James, Adams, and Eliot. Santayana's style aside, what remain are the idea of diluvial barbarism and the conclusion that Christianity's value endures in its "fair works," in its material residue rather than in any spiritual or moral elevation.

Having conjured up the specter of the flood, Santayana dispels the threat by pronouncing it fait accompli. In America at least, apocalypse has already won the day, leaving "much forgetfulness, much callow disrespect for what is past or alien."[5] This mild criticism aside, Santayana resumes a more agreeable demeanor:

> May Heaven avert the omen, and make the new world a better world than the old! In the classical and romantic tradition of Europe, love, of which there was very little, was supposed to be kindled by beauty, of which there was a great deal: perhaps moral chemistry may be able to reverse this operation, and in the future and in America it may breed beauty out of love.[6]

Here Santayana obliquely contrasts America and Europe, the Old World and the New, a division to which the past and the future correspond in their turn. And to coincidence of time and space, Santayana significantly adds the categories of art and morality or, to use his terms, beauty and love.

America differs from Europe historically and geographically, of course, but also morally. Specifically, it sees history as a version of its morality; Europeans settled the land more from ideal than material motives. "It is notorious how metaphysical was the passion that drove the Puritans to those shores; they went there in the hope of living more perfectly in the spirit. . . . Americans are eminently prophets; they apply morals to public affairs; they are impatient and enthusiastic."[7] But after three centuries, this fancied metaphysicality, "propheticism," and moral enthusiasm create not grace but awkwardness: a troubling rift between ideal and real, which in everyday life expressed itself in a comic, calculating undertone. "Their humour and shrewdness are sly comments on the shortcomings of some polite convention that everybody accepts tacitly, yet feels to be insecure and contrary to the principles on which life is actually carried on."[8] Santayana here refers to his most famous social critique, American gentility, the "polite convention" that nonetheless departs so markedly from life as it is carried on. This split so infuses the writing of James, Adams, and Eliot that it is often difficult to distinguish the moments when they criticize American gentility most severely from those in which they operate most clearly from its social and philosophical premises. At times they assail the genteel tradition; at other times they retreat to it as a welcome shelter.

Santayana views genteel American culture as ornament and appliqué, trimmings imported from the alien European tradition and tacked onto American life like an incongruous crust:

> What people have respected have been rather scraps of official philoso-
> phy, or entire systems, which they have inherited or imported, as they
> have respected operas and art museums. To be on speaking terms with
> these fine things was a part of social respectability, like having family
> silver. High thoughts must be at hand, like those candlesticks, probably
> candleless, sometimes displayed as a seemly ornament in a room blazing
> with electric light.[9]

Americans, though admirably attentive to "high things," erroneously
revere anachronistic ideas and artifacts out of context. Hence they fail to
be true either to European precedent – the empty candlesticks – or to
their own, technological accomplishments – the blazing electric lights.
Instead of hybrid vigor, this inexpert blending of two traditions makes
falsehood and bad faith matters of conventional observance.

James, Adams, and Eliot assumed Santayana's "cynical view," accepting by choice or necessity the "awful deprivations of disbelieving." Santayana diagnosed this disbelief as a symptom of America's failed philosophical tradition (an idea incorporated into Eliot's thought on the
subject). Having earlier referred to the metaphysical passion animating
the Puritans, Santayana tells how that transplantation yielded not a tradition but an antitradition, in which philosophical systems change regularly, responding, like fashion, less to logic than to mood. "Especially in
America, . . . ideas are abandoned in virtue of a mere change of feeling,
without any new evidence or new arguments. We do not nowadays
refute our predecessors, we pleasantly bid them goodbye. Even if all our
principles are unwittingly traditional we do not like to bow openly to
authority."[10] What characterizes philosophical tradition applies to society as well. The feeling that the stream of tradition had vanished into the
arid sand of practice, leaving only loomings of a new and unfamiliar
world, remained a key emotional problem that aestheticism could as-
suage and one upon which modernism would later insist. Like the other
aestheticist writers, Santayana deemed the Civil War a historical water-
shed. In antebellum society,

> the subtler dangers which we may now see threatening America had not
> yet come in sight – material restlessness was not yet ominous, the
> pressure of business enterprise was not yet out of scale with the old life
> or out of key with the old moral harmonies. A new type of American
> had not appeared – the untrained, pushing, cosmopolitan orphan, cock-
> sure in manner but not too sure in his morality, to whom the old
> Yankee, with his sour integrity, is almost a foreigner.[11]

Santayana summarized how this divorce from tradition jeopardized
society and art, but also scrutinized how the resulting social displacement
affected individual lives, unleashed ascendant historical energies, and en-

gendered unwelcome novelty. Santayana in any case remained quite aware that the strains following the Civil War had existed long before and had developed out of the society's history and settlement. He described Americans as historically and socially uprooted, arguing that because they had failed to arrest that uprooting and actually encouraged it, the country and its people consequently could find no rest. Although "polite America" had kept its Puritan English "household gods" intact and its conscience in touch with the rest of the world, distance and revolutionary prejudice against ancient or foreign things worked against it. Moreover, "inbreeding and anemia" had disconcerted polite America by shifting the ground beneath its feet, forcing it to give way to a "crude but vital America" sprung up from the soil:

> This young America was originally composed of all the prodigals, truants, and adventurous spirits that the colonial families produced. . . . reinforced by the miscellany of Europe arriving later, not in the hope of founding a godly commonwealth, but only of prospering in an untrammeled one. The horde of immigrants eagerly accepts the external arrangements and social spirit of American life, but never hears of its original austere principles, or relegates them to the same willing oblivion as it does the constraints which it has just escaped. . . . We should be seriously deceived if we overlooked for a moment the curious and complex relation between these two Americas.[12]

On no account did the aesthetes, however, so deceive themselves. All had a painful awareness of the two Americas and of how far their separate ideals and ideologies diverged. American aestheticism partly reacted to just this problem: an older, "politer" America confronted a younger, "cruder" one, with all of the attendant religious, ethnic, occupational, and value-oriented conflicts. To be placed in either camp entailed consequences harmful to national (and personal) coherence; history constrains and enfeebles one group, while the other, having rejected gentility and history alike, explodes in a raw, highly suspect energy. Gentility versus crudity, entropy versus frenzy, Prufrock versus Sweeney: Both parties suffer from the antagonism that neatly divides them.

On the one hand, the American striver, innocent of history, hopeful about the future, preselected by a series of temporal and spatial accidents, enacts his national role. Because the lazy, deeply rooted, and fortunate stayed at home, untempted by dissatisfaction or wilder instincts, Santayana called the American

> the most adventurous, or the descendent of the most adventurous, of Europeans. It is in his blood to be socially a radical, though perhaps not intellectually. What has existed in the past, especially in the remote past, seems to him not only not authoritative, but irrelevant, inferior, and outworn. He finds it rather a sorry waste of time to think about the past

at all. But his enthusiasm for the future is profound; he can conceive of
no more decisive way of recommending an opinion or a practice than to
say that it is what everybody is coming to adopt. This expectation of
what he approves, or approval of what he expects, makes up his optimism. It is the necessary faith of the pioneer.[13]

Although perhaps no less purely a creature of imagination than his aestheticist opposite, in most other ways this American contrasts with those
possessing minority manners, interests, and temperaments and for
whom the official version of American society and values offers hardly a
toehold. The pioneer opposes the poet and other "luckless Americans,"
intellectually intrepid yet domesticated socially:

> The luckless American who is born a conservative, or who is drawn to
> poetic subtlety, pious retreats, or gay passions, nevertheless has the
> categorical excellence of work, growth, enterprise, reform, and pros-
> perity dinned into his ears: every door is open in this direction and shut
> in the other; so that he either folds up his heart and withers in a cor-
> ner . . . or else he flies to Oxford or Florence or Montmartre to save his
> soul – or perhaps not to save it.[14]

If America offered only a single salvation – "the gospel of work and
the belief in progress"[15] – then the aesthetes, biting the hand that neglected to feed them, adhered instead to faith in art and the conviction of
decline. Aesthetes discredited action because active people had no use for
art. Yet this antagonism only compounded the aesthetic difficulties a
commercial, underpopulated, unhistorical society posed for those wishing to create a national literature. Santayana, James, and Eliot, finding
the absence of literary ancestors an insurmountable obstacle, and perhaps
so as not to fold up and wither, fled the American vacuum for the
European plenum. They simply found lacking nearly all the elements
they felt necessary to support literary and personal identity. They considered the American people uncultured, uneducated, unmannered, and
uninteresting; the American landscape, unedifying, unromantic, or just
plain ugly; American society, undifferentiated and, in any case, incompletely social; American letters, impotently genteel and feminized;
American democracy, conformist and corrupt, leading nowhere; the
American woman and the American man, hopelessly distant, as was the
American mind from its will, ideals from conduct, public profession
from private practice. (More than one of these condemnations seems
dubious at best, especially the boredom concerning the landscape. Eliot,
however, comparing Turgenev's Russia to James's America and by implication to his own Midwestern origins, once pointed out the supposed
"advantages" of coming from a "large flat country which no one wants
to visit.")[16]

Echoing James's famous negative catalogue of Hawthorne's America, Santayana warned that its "great emptiness," not simply a physical but moral one, still starved its thinkers and artists, withholding the banquet of nourishments other societies set before their artists. Even though emptiness could bring one kind of freedom to the soul and body, it pruned away any "decorative flourishes," leaving the life and mind dry and direct, and their works "stark and pragmatic."

> You will not understand why anybody should make those little sacri-fices to instinct or custom which we call grace. The fine arts will seem to you academic luxuries, fit to amuse the ladies, like Greek and Sanskrit; for while you will perfectly appreciate generosity in men's purposes, you will not admit that the execution of these purposes can be anything but business. Unfortunately the essence of the fine arts is that the execution should be generous too, and delightful in itself; therefore the fine arts will suffer, not so much in their express professional pursuit – for then they become practical tasks and a kind of business – as in that diffused charm which qualifies all human action when men are artists by nature. Elaboration, which is something to accomplish, will be pre-ferred to simplicity, which is something to rest in; manners will suffer somewhat; speech will suffer horribly. [17]

Santayana's analysis subtly but distinctly raises a key aestheticist diffi-culty, the submerged equation of males and business, on one hand, and its opposite, females and art, on the other. The aesthetes experienced this perennial American division of sexual labor as a seemingly bottomless reservoir of anxiety. Its persistence in our time seems to validate their sense that, culturally speaking, the United States remained somehow arrested at the colonial stage. Each resolved the problem differently; in Eliot's case (not unlike that of Wallace Stevens), a full-fledged business career, if in one sense antithetical to literature, in another remained neces-sary for it.

Typical aestheticist reasoning blamed the artist's problems on the soci-ety's flaws. The aestheticist indictment combined crudity of manners and blandness of intellect with a sense of historical rupture and inattention to speech and language. It added up to another aestheticist equation: Artless life and lifeless art drive writers out. The situation created a prophylaxis ensuring that nothing of national literary significance would appear. Given the American voice, language, and newspapers, which "harden" taste and sensibility to ugliness or affectation, Santayana felt he had to look no further to discover what difficulties beset even the enlightened, ambitious artist:

> The artistic idiom is foreign to him; he cannot be simple, he cannot be unconscious, he has no native, unquestioned, inevitable masters. And it is not easy for native masters to spring up; the moral soil is too thin and

shifting, like sand in an hourglass, always on the move; whatever traditions there are, practical men and reformers insist on abandoning; every
house is always being pulled down for rebuilding; nothing can take
root; nothing can be assumed as a common affection, a common pleasure; no refinement of sense, no pause, no passion, no candour, no
enchantment.[18]

If this passage outlines the bleak aestheticist reality, it is important to
remember that the aesthetes did not neglect to state the positive ideal in
whose name they made their criticisms. Aestheticism on one level offers
a strategy devised to overcome personal and social alienation; it positions
art as the organizing, value-conferring component of human personality
and society alike, the sine qua non of humanity and civilization.

A society that conceives of itself formally, where behavior corresponds to artistic criteria and inspires works of art and in which practice
and pleasure fuse, constitutes the aestheticist desideratum:

> In a thoroughly humanized society everything – clothes, speech, man-
> ners, government – is a work of art, being so done as to be a pleasure
> and a stimulus in itself. There seems to be an impression in America that
> art is fed on the history of art, and is what is found in museums. But
> museums are mausoleums, only dead art is there, and only ghosts of
> artists flit about them. The priggish notion that an artist is a person
> undertaking to produce immortal works suffices to show that art has
> become a foreign thing, an *hors-d'oeuvre,* and that it is probably doomed
> to affectation and sterility.[19]

This quotation returns us to our starting place. For aesthetes, not only
must aesthetic quality support the moral emotion to which it is attached,
as Santayana argued in *The Sense of Beauty.* Aesthetic quality, presumably with intent to discipline or elevate, must also invade the social
sphere, must "slip in fitly into the interstices" of *social* life. As the aestheticists threw good manners after bad, they felt American society had
somehow placed them in a false position. Art was only one of the means
they used to shore up a weakening sense of where they belonged.

HENRY JAMES: AN ANALYSIS OF RESTLESSNESS

. . . the exactitude of *The American Scene.* . . .[1]

"The restless analyst": The persona of impersonality, cleverest mask of
all, offered Henry James considerable freedom. Nominally effacing his
own presence to the point of inconsequence, he thereby complimented
the importance of his material as well as his own manipulation of it. But
if for no other reason than that the style reasserted a personality the
persona claimed to subdue, James's ploy did not, could not succeed. The
analyst was, after all, restless. His searching objectivity faltered when it

confronted subjects that most concerned him: the land- and cityscape; aesthetic criteria applied to history, places, manners, and speech; the contrasts between Europe and America; and most emotionally volatile of all, the bases of social order.

These preoccupations do not of themselves convict James of aestheticism, but his evaluation by visual, dramatic, formal, or other artistic criteria sustains that judgment. One of innumerable tableaux in *The American Scene* illustrates James's habit of mind:

> Cape Cod, on this showing, was exactly a pendent, pictured Japanese screen or banner; a delightful little triumph of "impressionism," which, during my short visit at least, never departed, under any provocation, from its type. . . . There was a couchant promontory in particular, half bosky with the evergreen boskage of the elegant kakemono, half bare with the bareness of refined, the *most* refined, New England decoration – a low, hospitable headland projected, as by some water-colourist master of the trick, into a mere brave wash of cobalt.[2]

Whether it be a Cape Cod landscape or a social fact, the most frequent transformation James performs upon any object consists of comparing it to a work of art. It was for James "the human, the social question always dogging the steps of the ancient contemplative person and making him, before each scene, wish really to get *into* the picture, to cross, as it were, the threshold of the frame."[3] Even concerning a social matter, James uses aesthetic vocabulary – "scene," "picture," "frame" – to organize his analysis. The title *The American Scene* itself implies a dramaturgical viewpoint, casting the continent's physique as a stage on which a national drama will unfold. James's scrutiny excludes little: "The appearances of man, the appearances of woman, and of their conjoined life, the general latent spectacle of their arrangements, appurtenances, manners, devices, opened up a different chapter, the leaves of which one could but musingly turn."[4] He will consider not simply the land but social life, too, as a "latent spectacle," a coy oxymoron archly acknowledging James's surreptitious vantage point.

James reverses ordinary categories as a matter of analytical method. Instead of traveling from life to art, James begins with art and measures life against it, specifically inquiring whether life organizes itself on formal principles. If a community or a landscape conforms to a type, composes itself to resemble a work of art, or possesses historical associations, James will likely approve it. But what lacks form contains only ugliness, a logic to which James adhered less for accuracy than for expedience:

> One's philosophy, one's logic might perhaps be muddled, but one clung to them for the convenience of their explanation of so much of the ugliness. The ugliness . . . was the so complete abolition of *forms;* . . .

What "form," meanwhile, *could* there be in the almost sophisticated dinginess of the present destitution? One thoughtfully asked that, though at the cost of being occasionally pulled up by odd glimpses of the underlying existence of a standard. There was the wage-standard . . . the well-nigh awestruck view of the high rate of remuneration open to the most abysmally formless of "hired" men.[5]

James's prose, especially the late style, packs so much matter into even a short passage that it offers a reader the same agreeable frustrations James himself complained of while trying to sort out the abundant impressions his American tour presented. This quotation contains many themes that aggravated James's aestheticism: that the future would likely be uglier than the past; that social life should organize itself formally and be evaluated by its manners; that America, innocent of either physical or social form, remained to that extent uncivilized; and that American society recognized only an economic standard, a national obsession to which James elsewhere assigned the principal blame for nearly all the defects he detected in the sturdy but threadbare social fabric his book endeavors to disentangle.

Like the other aesthetes, James compared the American scene not only with art, but also with Europe, possessing everything America lacked: Europe had form in art, landscape, and society, and it had history. The early *Italian Hours* and the late *American Scene* illustrate these contrasts.[6] Italy, the aestheticist country par excellence, balanced America, a place James considered largely unredeemed by any hint of beauty, history, or association. *Italian Hours* explains why Europe so absorbed James, why it was so necessary to him. *The American Scene* recalls why he left the United States. Taken together, they complement one another, each employing an absent landscape and society to gloss the one before James's view.

As Santayana had done, James drew a nearly absolute antithesis between the means of business and the ways of art. Commerce spoiled landscape; railroads particularly symbolized how technology violated nature and inverted man's relationship to his own products. James compared the old coach roads unfavorably to the great straddling, bellowing railway, the high, heavy, dominant American train that reverses the relation of the parties concerned, suggesting that the country exists for the "cars" which overhang it like a conquering army, and not the cars for the country. These trains penetrated the high valleys and had altered unmistakably the old felicity of proportion.[7] Technology disrupts what James most values, confusing the natural and the built environment and upsetting aesthetic unity, human scale, and civic identity. Furthermore, it erases time; America's historical amnesia remained for James its cardinal sin. Regarding the placing of historic markers, he wrote that European cities had cultivated the form to the greatly quickened interest of street scenery. But he asked, "Is it not verily bitter, for those who feel a poetry in the noted passage, longer or shorter, here and there, of great lost spirits, that the institution, the profit, the glory of any such association is denied in advance to communities tending, as the phrase is, to 'run' preponderantly to the sky-scraper?"[8]

James praised instead communities such as Newport, Rhode Island, and Washington, D.C., which unlike New York did not center around "mere economic convenience." James assumed as an axiom that culture, in the European sense of high art, could not flourish without a leisured audience. The American commercial ethos, however, left this audience desiccated or stillborn. At Newport, for instance,

> the strange sight might be seen of a considerable company of Americans, not gathered at a mere rest-cure, who confessed brazenly to not being in business. . . . cosmopolites, united by three common circumstances, that of their having for the most part more or less lived in Europe, that of their sacrificing openly to the ivory idol whose name is leisure, and that, not least, of a formed critical habit. These things had been felt as making them excrescences on the American surface, where nobody ever criticized, especially after the grand tour, and where the great black ebony god of business was the only one recognized.[9]

The economic ethos not only blots out the past, but cancels any possibility of an ethical, civilized, "cultured" future. Ceaseless urban construction and commercial expansion, and its disregard for the critical spirit or standards of taste, prevent New York City, for instance, from ever achieving anything greater than architectural surrealism. These habits, according to James, abort any possible maturity, order, or tradition. Because it will never age, the great city will never equal the harmonious European monumentality that represents James's urban ideal:

> It is only a question of that unintending and unconvincing expression of New York everywhere, as yet, on the matter of the *maintenance* of a given effect – which comes back to the general insincerity of effects, and truly even (as I have already noted) to the insincerity of the effect of the sky-scrapers themselves. There results from all this . . . that unmistakable New York admission of unattempted, impossible maturity. The new Paris and the new Rome do at least propose, I think, to be old – one of these days.[10]

New York's response to James's accusation, as he phrased it, revealed his sense of the city's futile dynamism: "I build you up but to tear you down."[11]

These tendencies traveled easily, but destructively. James recorded how even in Italy business and technology divorced modern life from tradition, precluding their stable relation. Past and present collide when James pauses at an Italian wayside shrine, sniffs, discovers how it is lit, and pronounces it symbolic. "The odour was that of petroleum; the votive taper was nourished with the essence of Pennsylvania. I confess that I burst out laughing . . . to me the thing served as a symbol of the Italy of the future. There is a horsecar from the Porta del Popolo to the Ponte Molle, and the Tuscan shrines are fed with kerosene."[12] Technological bathos ruins the effect; like ill-conceived decor, confused historical associations "clash." James's response reminds us how indispensable the disparagement of philistinism, bad taste, or (as here) bathetic anachronism was to aestheticist apprehension. Eliot's quatrain poems, for instance, perfect James's aestheticist cringe into modernist black humor.

Italian Hours paints history as a picture to prove the past's evident superiority to the present. Although James concedes that if Renaissance Italy was as "ardently mercantile" as nineteenth-century America, "it loved not its ledgers less, but its frescoes and altar-pieces more."[13] Furthermore, compared with industrial America, James considered even nineteenth-century Italy more civilized, with its picturesque leisure, social forms, and spontaneous theatricality, the Italian's "great desire to please and be pleased."[14] Europe, especially Italy, and particularly Venice, realize for James an aestheticist ideal, blurring barriers between art and social life nearly to the vanishing point. Nowhere else, he maintained,

> do art and life seem so interfused and, as it were, so consanguineous. . . . You don't go into the churches and galleries by way of a change from the streets; you go into them because they offer you an exquisite reproduction of the things that surround you. All Venice was both model and painter, and life was so pictorial that art couldn't help becoming so.[15]

In James's vision of an aestheticist society, art and life illuminate one another, fusing to virtual identity. Form defined the ideal; fine art became lifelike because life was so very artful. Such a society, James argued, maintained a proper regard for its artists, agreed about its social ideals and artistic form, and organized life to include pleasure as well as economic gain.[16] Finally, the ideal society remained free of something James found so debilitating in America, the presence of people who did not share language, religion, or a "common culture."

The American Scene accumulates evidence about the extent to which immigrants punctured James's carefully constructed but ultimately unconvincing persona of detachment. His comments range from the merely highfalutin to an outrage whose emotional and polemical content gives them the character of what would be instantly condemned as racism today.[17] For James, ethnic pluralism jeopardized social order and cultural achievement. He assumed that America should and could produce art equal to that of Europe. He further assumed that American high culture would arise from distinctively American elements in the country's tradition, from shared assumptions about education, morality, and manners, and, most important, from a common language used and preserved self-consciously.[18]

Immigrants offer James another instance of an American incongruity that is at least bathetic indecorum and at worst surrealist horror. As James frets about the future and about the national identity, his account seems so self-consciously disingenuous that one reckons James must have felt his own reasoning to be the only possible civilized response:

> The question settles into a form which makes the intelligible answer further and further recede. "What meaning, in the presence of such impressions, can continue to attach to such a term as the 'American' character? – what type, as the result of such a prodigious amalgam, such a hotch-potch of racial ingredients, is to be conceived as shaping itself?" The challenge to speculation, fed thus by a thousand sources, is so intense as to be, as I say, irritating . . . you find your relief not in the least in any direct satisfaction or solution, but absolutely in that blest general drop of the immediate need of conclusions, or rather in that blest general feeling for the impossibility of them, to which the philosophy of any really fine observation of the American spectacle must reduce itself, and the large intellectual, quite even the large aesthetic, margin supplied by which accompanies the spectator as his one positively complete comfort.[19]

Here James employs aesthetics for palpably anesthetic purposes. Having spoken earlier of being "quickened well-nigh to madness," he as much as admits his failure to come to intellectual or emotional grips with these facts. Responsive to his objective observation, James is also candid enough to admit that these events, emotions, and data surpass his ability to understand or express.

Each of the aestheticist writers perceived that history tended to efface their institutions, values, and culture, whose social influence waned as time elapsed. Their sense of dispossession especially manifested itself in language, and we should not underestimate its importance to James and the social viewpoint he speaks for. Language and literature were – and are – identity conferring, and then as now people felt that the diversity of turn-of-the-century America provoked essential questions of national (and, though they might have admitted it less willingly, personal) identity. James asked questions about the character and meaning of America that still have considerable poignance. Although muffled since 1907, the question has yet to receive any convincing answer. If it lacks a common tongue, culture, or values – Eliot, after his conversion, would have added a common religion to the list – is America a real society? Can it have a national culture?

> One's supreme relation, as one had always put it, was one's relation to one's country – a conception made up so largely of one's countrymen and one's countrywomen. Thus it was as if, all the while, with such a fond tradition of what these products predominantly were, the idea of the country itself underwent something of that profane overhauling through which it appears to suffer the indignity of change. Is not our instinct in this matter, in general, essentially the safe one – that of keeping the idea simple and strong and continuous, so that it shall be perfectly sound? To touch it overmuch, to pull it about, is to put it in peril of weakening; yet on this free assault upon it, this readjustment of it in *their* monstrous, presumptuous interest, the aliens, in New York, seemed perpetually to insist.[20]

James argues, in essence, that to be everything is to be nothing. Here he probes for the idea, if one exists, around which a society (as opposed to a collection of discrete parts only spatially related) organizes itself. The aesthetes wished to distill, concentrate, and develop the national tradition, such as it was. They equated broadening and expanding American society's "idea," by contrast, with dilution and entropy. James recommends keeping the idea simple, homogeneous, and traditional, a conception many of the immigrants, for obvious reasons, would have disputed. America-the-homogeneous, a concept of dubious validity historically, had been doomed from the start, and the country's social history would increasingly become one of cultural and demographic struggle. James prophetically understood this, yet also sensed that America had stacked its historical, social, ethnic, and symbolic deck against his "safe" instinct. Indeed, given American society's diversity, it is possible to argue that indulging James's "safe" instinct might have charted much the riskier course.

From James's point of view, however, the nation's decision to live dangerously left a sour, humiliating sense of dispossession:

> The combination there of their quantity and their quality . . . operates, for the native, as their note of settled possession, something they have nobody to thank for; so that *un*settled possession is what we, on our side, seem reduced to – the implication of which, in its turn, is that, to recover confidence and regain lost ground, we, not they, must make the surrender and accept the orientation. We must go, in other words, *more* than half-way to met them; which is all the difference, for us, between possession and dispossession. This sense of dispossession, to be brief about it, haunted me so, I was to feel, in the New York streets and in

the packed trajectiles to which one clingingly appeals from the streets, just as one tumbles back into the streets in appalled reaction from *them,* that the art of beguiling or duping it became an art to be cultivated – though the fond alternative vision was never long to be obscured, the imagination, exasperated to envy, of the ideal, in the order in question; of the luxury of some such close and sweet and *whole* national consciousness as that of the Switzer and the Scot.[21]

Switzerland, then, illustrates a "close, sweet, and whole national consciousness," despite its cultural, religious, and linguistic heterogeneity. We may only hope James selected this curious example advisedly, that we might refine our sense of his ideal upon it. That having been said, however, the more important feature of this soliloquy remains the elaborate psychological strategy it adopts to outflank the sense of dispossession. Consider James's initial remedial tactic, embodied in his ambiguous use of the word "confidence." Regaining the conviction of the right to personal possession – the first sort of confidence, a belief in one's own rights, goals, and abilities – necessarily involves recovering the sense of social confidentiality, a relation of intimacy and candor with one's fellow citizens, which they reciprocate. But this latter confidence is the very thing that has vanished, given the undeniable diversity that so offends James. His retreat amounts to employing self-deception to evade his innermost reactions. Not to discover one's "supreme relation" in one's fellow citizens, after all, implies a kind of social retreat and a consequent personal alienation or identity crisis. Not to be able to express one's own ideas, to feel that one's emotions have been rendered inauthentic, socially unacceptable, or morally reprehensible is to feel that one part of one's ideal code asks another part to subside, or to lie. Remaining in America thus cruelly requires that one deceive either one's fellow citizens, or oneself.

James faced overwhelming social facts: commercialism; industry and technology; an ethos of activity and motion, tearing down and building up uninformed by plan, value, or aesthetic; immigrants; the leveling aspects of democracy; the decline of previously authoritative values; and indifference or hostility toward accomplished language. To these implacable forces, James made several responses. He substituted values of artistic permanence and form to compete with, to answer the agents of social change and disorder. He also fled to Europe: Miraculously, a change of place permitted a change of value and of style. James responded to dispossession in yet a third way, typical of aesthetes, which necessarily involved the other two: He withdrew into history. In the past, art appeared – to an eye already inclined to believe it – more valuable, permanent, beautiful, and respected than it did in the present. Aestheticist writers used art to tell time and valued art because it rendered history so much more attractive than the present. Even more crucially, history – especially European history – seemed to imply superior social forms as well. The aesthetes did not hesitate to link art and society causally, to claim that the artist's historical status once had greater, even vital, importance. Aesthetes felt that social organization in the past had made great art possible and even provided its inspiration. Society imitated art; art reflected society.

Considering how far their social and emotional foundations had eroded and how considerably their sense of audience had dwindled, it is not difficult to see why aesthetes might elevate the European past into an ideal imaginative matrix. It offered a social, historical, and aesthetic ideal – whose plausibility the artifacts and texts amply supported – they could use to overcome their contemporary loss of prestige and self-respect. These stratagems – escape to Europe, through art, into history – seemed to promise a way out of the social and cultural straitjacket that many American writers and artists felt bound them. James expressed it this way:

> My recovery of impressions . . . may have been judged to involve itself with excursions of memory – memory directed to the antecedent time – reckless almost to extravagance. But I recall them to-day, none the less, for that value in them which ministered, at happy moments, to *an artful evasion of the actual*. There was no escape from the ubiquitous alien into the future, or even into the present; *there was an escape but into the past*.[22]

Throughout his tour, James assailed the absence of tradition, the lack of aesthetic interest, the defiance of history, and America's contemporary profligacy. Such a society seemed neurotically to postpone the time when it might achieve a national consensus, a social ideal, or a high culture, each one of which James presumed necessary to realizing the others. America suffered most plainly by comparison with Europe insofar as it had refused to permit time to leave any mark upon American places. James could lodge the complaint with some justice partly because so much of the country was still so new; others had made the same point.[23] Even so, *The American Scene* again and again reports how willfully America had effaced even the marks of its brief experience, deliberately leaving itself barren of "this seed of the eventual human soul."[24] His praise for the places exempted from this criticism – Salem and Concord, Massachusetts, Philadelphia, and Washington, D.C., among a very few others – reflects the aestheticist reversal of the usual American categories. Most Americans viewed change, innovation, and the future positively, linking these things to "progress." By contrast, to aestheticists the ideas of tradition, settlement, and the past summoned up the positive response. The values they treasured reminded the man in the street of what he wanted to be rid of. The common man trusted the future to punish the past by demolishing or forgetting it. For the aesthete, the past extended an eternal rebuke to the present.

What America withheld, however, Europe offered, fusing art and reality and acknowledging the past's claim upon the present. "What was the secret of the surprising amenity? – to the essence of which one got no nearer than simply by feeling afresh the old story of the deep interfusion of the present with the past." James's inquiry leads him to explain to himself why "Italy is really so much the most beautiful country in the world. . . . Seen thus in great comprehensive iridescent stretches, it is the incomparable wrought *fusion,* fusion of human history and mortal passion with the elements of earth and air, of colour, composition and form, that constitute [Naples's] appeal and give it the supreme heroic grace."[25] In "The Saint's Afternoon and Others," in *Italian Hours,* James invests even the European natural order with a suprahuman capacity to produce superior artistic or social arrangements. He places nature above art or history, elevating it to an aesthetic and moral absolute. Overlooking the Bay of Naples, James has an epiphany:

> The way in which the Italian scene on such occasions as this seems to purify itself to the transcendent and perfect *idea* alone – idea of beauty, of dignity, of comprehensive grace, with all accidents merged, all defects disowned, all experience outlived, and to gather itself up into the mere mute eloquence of what has just incalculably *been,* remains forever the secret and the lesson of the subtlest daughter of History. All one could do, at the heart of the overarching crystal, and in presence of the relegated City, the far-trailing Mount, the grand Sorrentine headland, the islands incomparably stationed and related, was to wonder what may well become of the so many other elements of any poor human and social complexus, what might become of any successfully-working or only struggling and floundering civilisation at all, when high Natural Elegance proceeds to take such exclusive charge and recklessly assume, as it were, *all* the responsibilities.[26]

In Europe, it would seem, Nature conspired with civilization to merge real and ideal. By imperiously snatching control over landscape, Nature assumed power over history and prevented the abuses manifest in America, where human power, denying the past, dominated the land in the name of the future. In Europe, Nature was an artist. In America, it was a beast of burden.

In James we observe the effects on a writer pursuant to his conclusion that American art, society, and history have no place for him. Santayana, perhaps because he was younger than James and Adams, passed his early childhood in Europe, and wrote as a philosopher, could remain somewhat more aloof in his aestheticism, yet he too fled to Europe as soon as he was financially able. James, also favored by a cosmopolitan, intellectual, and philosophical background, and perhaps by having ancestors no more notable than they were, apparently persuaded himself of his own objectivity. But Henry Adams, whose sense of dispossession had a political dimension Santayana's and James's lacked, responded not with detachment or objectivity but with something at times resembling panic. Adams, whose family for three generations had known conspicuous political accomplishment, found the burden of history almost unbearable as he made his own distinctive contribution to American aestheticism.

THE DISPOSSESSION OF HENRY ADAMS

> I have seen the moment of my greatness flicker.

The similarities among Santayana, James, Adams, and Eliot may arise as much from private sources as from the public events of America after the Civil War. Their lives as well as their thought resemble one another in many ways. All had New England connections, however distant; they shared similar religious backgrounds, to an extent; all attended Harvard, if unhappily; three were related, albeit remotely.[1] All four experienced a degree of isolation in childhood, perhaps having something to do with being younger or youngest brothers.[2] Early in *The Education,* for instance, Henry Adams tells how an attack of scarlet fever at age three altered his position in family politics and how a traumatic yet educative convalescence stamped his character:

> Sickness in childhood ought to have a certain value not to be classed under any fitness or unfitness of natural selection; and especially scarlet fever affected boys seriously, both physically and in character, though they might through life puzzle themselves to decide whether it had fitted or unfitted them for success. . . . The habit of doubt; of distrusting his own judgment and of totally rejecting the judgment of the world; the tendency to regard every question as open; the hesitation to act except as a choice of evils; the shirking of responsibility; the love of line, form, quality; the horror of ennui; the passion for companionship and the antipathy to society – all these are well-known qualities of New England character in no way peculiar to individuals but in this instance they seemed to be stimulated by the fever.[3]

This passage includes some garden-variety aestheticism – "the love of line, form, quality" – and a few skeptical vestiges of a moral vocabulary – "the habit of doubt," "a choice of evils," "the shirking of responsibility." Here we need no more than acknowledge these "serious" aspects of the aestheticist emotional complex and reiterate that this complexity distinguishes American aestheticism from any purely "art for art's sake" simplex. A too proudly held moral disillusion; a facile self-mistrust bordering on self-pity; a curiously bold rejection of social judgments (curious because the passage's quasi-Darwinian coordinates address not physical but social fitness); and the attempt, after this confessional litany, to link it to the "New England character": These things point out the complexity of Adams's aestheticism, its imbalance between bruised, unresolved emotions and intellectual detachment, and its blend – very similar to that of Eliot – of aggressive self-assertion and self-protective diffidence.

Of these four writers, Adams had the most politically oriented career. Even more markedly than Eliot – whose grandmother was an Adams – his genealogy and the first century of American national history fused a nation and a family. With a famous revolutionary ancestor (Sam Adams), a presidential great-grandfather and grandfather, and a father who was a congressman and ambassador to the Court of St. James during the Civil War (with Henry acting as his private secretary), Adams may perhaps be excused for feeling that "had he been taken into the confidence of his parents, he would certainly have told them to change nothing as far as concerned him. He would have been astounded by his own luck. Probably no child, born in the year, held better cards than he."[4] Even this hyperbole understates the case, and Adams's autobiography exists less to record his life than to recount how a player with a winning hand, and several good cards up his sleeve, nonetheless contrived to leave the table empty-handed.

Adams traces his fate to historical change, incorporating economics, demographics, morality, war, politics, and science. His idea of the American past (which corresponded to an idea about its future) disqualified him as much from living in the American present as it had Henry James. Both felt overwhelmed by events and sensed an American hostility to their ideas and opinions. If Adams knew he held a good hand, he nonetheless concluded that the social deck was stacked against him or that history had marked the cards in another player's favor.

Adams explained his dispossession partly by feeling his exemplary family and prime asset to be, paradoxically, a handicap. He betrays a sense of generational competition, as if his forebears' successes so heightened his expectations that they began to interfere. (The same was true of his brothers; the record of the fourth Adams generation, though not disreputable, is nonetheless not a pretty one.)[5] His family's prominence bequeathed a legacy of values that, by the time Henry Adams inherited it, had become seriously depleted. Adams's heritage in this way became as much a burden as an advantage: not the hazard of new fortunes, but of old eminence. It demanded the highest achievement, yet he felt it left him without the character, values, or political base with which to gain it. As a child, Adams had suffered little doubt about what the future expected of him:

> It was unusual for boys to sit behind a President grandfather, and to
> read over his head the tablet in memory of a President great-
> grandfather, who had "pledged his life, his fortune, and his sacred
> honor" to secure the independence of his country and so forth. . . . The
> Irish gardener once said to the child: "You'll be thinkin' you'll be
> President too!" The casualty of the remark made so strong an impres-
> sion on his mind that he never forgot it. He could not remember ever to
> have thought on the subject; to him, that there should be a doubt of his
> being President was a new idea. What had been would continue to be.
> He doubted neither about Presidents nor about Churches, and no one
> suggested at that time a doubt whether a system of society which had
> lasted since Adam would outlast one Adams more.[6]

This, then, was Adams's original sin, to assume that "what had been
would continue to be." The sin was actually more like naiveté. This
being America, he unrealistically expected that his ancestors could
grandfather him into position and power, rather than perceiving that he
would have to sweat and jockey for them like everyone else engaged in
the American free-for-all.

As Adams draws the lessons and antilessons ("to secure the independence of his country and so forth") from his life, he frequently casts
himself as a naif, an intellectual Pierrot victimized by the political harle-
quinade. He traced the role to developmental anachronism. "Whatever
was peculiar about him was education, not character, and came to him,
directly or indirectly, as the result of that eighteenth-century inheritance
which he took with his name."[7] Besides a famous name, Adams also
inherited from the eighteenth century a code of values, an attitude toward the world, and a self that boded ill for a nineteenth-century child.
That legacy, beneath its political surface, had a deep structure that was
obstinately moral, and more than moral, Puritan.

> Resistance to something was the law of New England nature; the boy
> looked out on the world with the instinct of resistance; for numberless
> generations his predecessors had viewed the world chiefly as a thing to
> be reformed, filled with evil forces to be abolished, and they saw no
> reason to suppose that they had wholly succeeded in the abolition; the
> duty was unchanged. That duty implied not only resistance to evil, but
> hatred of it. Boys naturally look on all force as an enemy, and generally
> find it so, but the New Englander, whether boy or man, in his long
> struggle with a stingy or hostile universe, had learned also to love the
> pleasure of hating; his joys were few.[8]

The Education amply testifies to just these pleasures, made more negative
and more pungent by postbellum America's lack of interest in reform. At
least in New England, the Civil War had seemed to confirm a reformist
view of the world, but in fact its motives were more mixed than moral.

The War between the States had conflated morality and economics, or to use Adams's terms, the interests of others and self-interest. But it also liberated forces owing nothing to the prewar, moral consensus. As Santayana and James argued (Eliot later endorsed the sentiment), the Civil War encouraged growth, expansion, and commerce, but undermined culture, stability, and morality.

What is more, the war's aftermath drained relative power from New England, leaving it to make the best, or worst, of its eighteenth-century code. Whoever remembered that code found themselves inconvenienced by a singular incapacity for amnesia:

> The stamp of 1848 was almost as indelible as the stamp of 1776, but in the eighteenth or any earlier century, the stamp mattered less because it was standard, and everyone bore it; while men whose lives were to fall in the generation between 1865 and 1900 had, first of all, to get rid of it, and take the stamp that belonged to their time. This was their education. To outsiders, immigrants, adventurers, it was easy, but the old Puritan nature rebelled against change. The reason it gave was forcible. The Puritan thought his thought higher and his moral standards better than those of his successors. So they were. He could not be convinced that moral standards had nothing to do with it, and that utilitarian morality was good enough for him, as it was for the graceless.[9]

Though perhaps only a minority of his class experienced this debilitation, something significant nonetheless occurred. Adams and others adhered to values that confirmed their sense of moral superiority even as it disequipped them for political or economic success. The dissonance also affected Eliot. A prewar moral imagination, linked to New England and Unitarianism, survived to influence his family's, and his own, attitude toward the post–Civil War ethos: morality versus utility, truth versus interest, honesty versus politics, right versus power. The empirical accuracy of these antinomies matters less than how accurately they reflect the way certain dispossessed people viewed their own position in the world. (Although his American origins were few, even Santayana, arriving from Spain at the mean Boston docks, felt a "terrible moral disinheritance," giving him an "emotional and intellectual chill" at bidding goodbye to his Spanish boyhood.[10] He may indeed have shared the emotion with James, Adams, and Eliot, but Santayana's feeling arose because he came to America. Native-born aestheticists, by contrast, experienced disinheritance because they had stayed put.)

Adams candidly admits a predisposition to confusion that predated the Civil War. As he grew up surrounded by violent New England contrasts, a contrary climate fixed his character:

> The chief charm of New England was harshness of contrasts and extremes of sensibility – a cold that froze the blood, and a heat that boiled

> it – so that the pleasure of hating – one's self if no better victim offered
> – was not its rarest amusement. . . . The double exterior nature gave
> life its relative values. Winter and summer, cold and heat, town and
> country, force and freedom, marked two modes of life and thought,
> balanced like lobes of the brain. . . . the bearing of the two seasons . . .
> ran through life, and made the division between its perplexing, war-
> ring, irreconcilable problems, irreducible opposites, with growing em-
> phasis to the last year of study. From earliest childhood the boy was
> accustomed to feel that, for him, life was double.[11]

Here is Adams's own version of homo duplex, of radical ambiguity, of
moral and practical criteria at odds. His suspension between moral and
natural poles, a self-conscious doubt about his identity and purpose, and
his loyalty to antique but superior values bred a need to reconcile these
and similar "opposites or antipathies," leaving him something of an old
man even in youth.

The post–Civil War era, however, belonged to New Men, creatures of
utility, will, and action, who thought about values, and perhaps about
anything, hardly at all. Adams and men like him seemed to know everything about power but how to get some of it. (Reviewing *The Education*,
Eliot called Adams "born to the governing-class tradition without the
inherited power . . . born to exercise governance, not to acquire it.")[12]
So the New Men proceeded to build the railroads, make the fortunes,
and staff the government jobs Adams felt belonged to him:

> Intellect counted for nothing; only the energy counted. The type was
> pre-intellectual, archaic, and would have seemed so even to the cave-
> dwellers. Adam, according to legend, was such a man.
>
> In time one came to recognize the type in other men, with differences
> and variations, as normal; men whose energies were the greater, the less
> they wasted on thought; men who sprang from the soil to power . . .
> for whom action was the highest stimulant – the instinct of fight. Such
> men were forces of nature, energies of the prime, like the *Pteraspis,* but
> they made short work of scholars. They had commanded thousands of
> such and saw no more in them than in others. The fact was certain; it
> crushed argument and intellect at once.[13]

Adam might have been such a man, but not Adams. What James saw in
the landscape, Adams detected in politics: a victory of force and utility
unredeemed by morality, intellect, or art. New politicians – to Adams's
mind, a type that never doubted, seldom questioned, yet often erred –
didn't simply hold power, they gripped it by the throat. Henry Adams
never ceased blaming them for being what they were and blaming himself for not being more like them. James's grandfather had mixed only in
local, Albany politics. His significance for his descendants was to win the
fortune (next to Astor's, the largest in New York State at the time of his

death)[14] that guaranteed their leisure. The political success of Adams's ancestors, by contrast, rendered Henry's shortcomings all the more clear. Scornful of politicians yet obsessed by their misdeeds, *The Education* only partly camouflages Adams's sense that he had been the victim of his ancestors, of the system, and of himself.

James and Adams largely agreed about the "forces" that civil war had released to cloud the American atmosphere. Commercial people, immigrants, and the uneducated masses threatened them both. Each reacted bitterly to feeling alien in a nation they had once called their own. The Civil War years, Adams felt, had caused coal, steam, and iron – the mechanical energies – to dominate the earlier economy of agriculture, handwork, and learning. As a result, he claimed,

> his world was dead. Not a Polish Jew fresh from Warsaw or Cracow – not a furtive Yacoob or Ysaac still reeking of the Ghetto, snarling a weird Yiddish to the officers of the customs – but had a keener instinct, an intenser energy, and a freer hand than he – American of Americans, with Heaven knew how many Puritans and Patriots behind him, and an education that had cost a civil war.[15]

It takes a measure of *chutzpah* for the descendant of power and privilege to consider himself at a disadvantage vis-à-vis those he regards as his social inferiors. But there is more to it than that. His disquiet reveals the conflicted anxiety of the aestheticists' feelings, having it both ways by accusing the immigrant both of social inferiority and of retaining a superior ability to prosper in American society. Striving so irrationally to be low man on the totem pole must surely be one of the strangest manifestations of humanity's competitive instincts. Yet to this temptation James, Eliot, Santayana, and Adams each in their turn unwisely yielded.

Not only had Adams discovered his social displacement, but the country itself required knowledge and energies he lacked, producing a new "type" that had little use for men like Adams. Settling its territories, giving them railroads, and building individual fortunes left American men with little interest in anything else. Such concentration drew men of talent or purpose away from politics and summoned from this agonistic ethos a type wealthy enough for leisure and travel, but quite innocent of what to do with either. Like James, Adams found their "singular limitations" incomprehensible. The certainty that the feeling was mutual undoubtedly emphasized his dismay.[16] Adams criticizes them on the one hand for lacking moral seriousness and on the other for not knowing how to play. When they traveled, for instance, such Bleisteinian tourists did not know what to make of Europe. They surely lacked the aestheticists' pained sense that technological development on the one hand and moral regression on the other had rendered the accumulation of Western civilization obsolete. Here lies the essence, the "problem," of the aestheticist attitude toward history, which is also perhaps transparently an attitude toward the present.

Although Santayana, James, and Eliot use the idea, the absence of cause-and-effect relationships in history aroused Adams's most intense response. He laments his early instruction that history implied progress, especially after the United States had embarked upon its imperial course. With the Civil War having overcome any reluctance to enforce unity militarily, the United States took the step by which it invited comparison with the other two examples of imperial permanence in the West. Adams wrote that Rome, free of economic or actual values, seemed to him a "pure emotion":

> He could not in reason or common sense foresee that it was mechanically piling up conundrum after conundrum in his educational path, which seemed unconnected but that he had got to connect; that seemed insoluble but had got to be somehow solved. . . . Rome was actual; it was England; it was going to be America. Rome could not be fitted into an orderly, middle-class, Bostonian, systematic scheme of evolution. No law of progress applied to it. Not even time-sequences – the last refuge of helpless historians – had value for it.[17]

The rise and fall, in the same city, of an empire and a church teach Adams another disillusioning lesson – that history lacks any interest in morality, permanence, or progress. (It is the *failure* of Imperial Rome and of the Catholic church that impresses Adams.) At the end of his life, Adams despaired of contemporary history and of his own capacity to explain it. It revealed no pattern whatsoever, least of all of the religion that had given it moral criteria and animated its highest culture. The 1904 assassination of a Russian minister stirred Adams's historical pessimism:

> Martyrs, murderers, Caesars, saints and assassins – half in glass and half in telegram; chaos of time, place, morals, forces and motive – gave him vertigo. Had one sat all one's life on the steps of Ara Coeli for this? Was assassination forever to be the last word of Progress? . . . The Virgin herself never looked so winning – so One – as in this scandalous failure of her Grace. To what purpose had she existed, if, after nineteen hundred years, the world was bloodier than when she was born? The stupendous failure of Christianity tortured history.[18]

If juxtapositions of modern events and ancient places struck James as surrealistic, Adams responded by trying to find a design of unity in history. But the only pattern he could find was no pattern: dislocation, irrationality, and (his favorite term) chaos. In this respect, History resembled Nature, and Jehovah. All three contradicted what eighteenth-century, optimistic, Unitarian Boston once promised him. Far from being rational, orderly, and benevolent, he called Nature's attitude toward life "a phantasm, a nightmare, an insanity of force" when reacting to his sister's death in Italy from tetanus caused by an accidental wound:

> For many thousands of years, on these hills and plains, Nature had gone on sabring men and women with the same air of sensual pleasure. . . . the idea that any personal deity could find pleasure or profit in torturing a poor woman, by accident, with a fiendish cruelty known to man only in perverted and insane temperaments, could not be held for a moment. For pure blasphemy, it made pure atheism a comfort. God might be, as the Church said, a Substance, but He could not be a Person.[19]

This Darwinian perception comes from someone able to recall a pre-Darwinian world. Adams felt betrayed by the lack of morality or plan in the physical or metaphysical universe, in the lives of nations, or in his own life. "In essence incoherent and immoral, history had either to be taught as such – or falsified. Adams wanted to do neither."[20]

This confession of intellectual impotence informs one of the most poignant scenes of *The Education*. The century was ending not in peace and progress, but by reviving Adams's memories of the last great cataclysm. The surrealism of the episode – a telegram announces the beginning of the Spanish-American War as Adams meanders amid Egyptian antiquities – affords his self-pity a negative epiphany:

> As they were looking at the sun set across the Nile from Assouan, Spencer Eddy brought them a telegram to announce the sinking of the Maine in Havana Harbor. This was the greatest stride in education since 1865, but what did it teach? One leant on a fragment of column in the great hall at Karnak and watched a jackal creep down the debris of ruin. The jackal's ancestors had surely crept up the same wall when it was building. What was his view about the value of silence? One lay in the sands and watched the expression of the Sphinx.[21]

Keats in his ode might have taken comfort from the nightingale, from the fancy that its song had cheered an ancient mood, from the certainty that the nightingale sang innocent of mortality. In an access of sympathy, the poet might even have dissolved his identity into an idea he conceived he heard embodied in the trilling of the bird. But Adams, picking through the ruins, knows no more of history than the scavenging jackal knew of the temple. History withholds any lesson, any satisfaction of education. Adams and the feral animal resemble one another, yet even their resemblance works to Adams's disadvantage. The jackal does not wonder at the silence as it shambles amid the rubble. Adams, however, invited by history to discern its meaning and translate its garbled syllables, hears nothing. Unable to forget what the jackal has never known, the scholar stares back leaden-eyed, as though it were a looking glass, at a mute, inscrutable Sphinx.

Adams, of course, quite underestimates his ability to interpret history. His pattern was antipattern; history's, that it had none; its lesson, the futility of seeking a lesson in it. History taught Adams that it would deny, to whoever pursued it, the possibility of finding historical laws that might permit prediction. The lesson left him in 1900 facing a world and a future radically new and unfamiliar. Adams, having satisfied himself that the sequences of individuals, society, time, and thought could not withstand scrutiny as historical explanations, "turned at last to the sequence of force; and thus it happened that, after ten years' pursuit, he found himself lying in the Gallery of Machines at the Great Exposition of 1900, his historical neck broken by the sudden irruption of forces totally new."[22] The analysis of force having led to no "larger synthesis," Adams found a smaller, personal one, thus ironically achieving his early goal, "to shape himself to his time."[23] As Yvor Winters has suggested, Adams's historical vector, objective and impersonal, recapitulated private disillusion: "By that path of newest science, one saw no unity ahead – nothing but a dissolving mind." So Adams, manifesting the aestheticist reflex, turned to the past for an ideal of unity "from which he might measure motion down to his own time, without assuming anything as true or untrue, except relation."[24] This relational method comes close to what Eliot took from his study of Bradley, though its literary result, the romantic, concrete, passionate *Mont-Saint-Michel and Chartres*, differs sharply from Eliot's theoretical, abstract dissertation.

Mont-Saint-Michel offers an ideal tacitly opposed to the modern era, representing everything it is not, embodying everything the intervening centuries have lost. Adams's Middle Ages, unified by faith, contradicts each undesirable particular of his restless modern world. He furthermore paints it as an artist's paradise, demanding and even gorging itself on images, edifices, and decorations of the highest quality and beauty. Though the church would hardly countenance such a tenuous approval, Adams's equation nonetheless argues a splendid aestheticism. In Adams's vision, the medieval church exercised power because it commanded belief; we know it commanded belief because the artifacts it inspired survive. In its spectacle, it endures; its illusions make it permanent; only by its theatrical materiality may we conceive of the age's spiritual sincerity:

> For us the poetry is history, and the facts are false. . . . The fact, then as now, was Power, or its equivalent in exchange, but Frenchmen, while struggling for the Power, expressed it in terms of Art. They looked on life as a drama – and on drama as a phase of life – in which the bystanders were bound to assume and accept the regular stage-

> plot. . . . Courteous love was avowedly a form of drama, but not the
> less a force of society. Illusion for illusion, courteous love·. . . was as
> substantial as any other convention; – the balance of trade, the rights of
> man, or the Athanasian Creed. In that sense the illusions alone were
> real; if the Middle Ages had reflected only what was practical, nothing
> would have survived for us.[25]

The last phrase subsides with an ominous undertow, containing a germ
of prophecy about the improbability that modern civilization (which
Adams argued was glued together – however tenuously – by practicality) would survive or pass anything on.

Finally, however, Adams values medieval France not for its truth but
as a historical measuring point, an image of realized unity, a counterpoint
to relativistic, modern chaos. Compared with the Thomistic "Church
Intellectual," Adams dismissed modern systems as variously complex,
chaotic, self-contradictory, and obsolete.

> But beyond all their practical shortcomings is their fragmentary char-
> acter. An economic civilization troubles itself about the universe much
> as a hive of honey-bees troubles about the ocean, only as a region to be
> avoided. The hive of Saint Thomas sheltered God and man, mind and
> matter, the universe and the atom, the one and the multiple, within the
> walls of an harmonious home.[26]

This shimmering, hospitable ideal illustrates the double aestheticist strategy. On one hand, aestheticists tried to negate modern America because
it had no place for them. On the other, as Adams does in *Mont-Saint-
Michel and Chartres,* they erected monuments to another place and time,
the European past. Some were not so thorough as Adams, but on both
sides of the Atlantic, aesthetes carefully located an ideal somewhere else,
and in another time. For Pound and James, and possibly Santayana too, it
was Renaissance Italy; for Eliot, the era of Dante, or perhaps the English
Renaissance before the Civil War and its disastrous "dissociation of sensibility." Adams chose medieval France, with its complementary edifices
of Thomistic theology and Gothic architecture, to supply the intellectual
order and aesthetic beauty modern America lacked. In those structures,
emotion, intellect, society, history, time, and the universe could achieve
harmony, beauty, and, most crucially, unity. Mont-Saint-Michel, in
Medieval France,

> still kept the grand style; it expressed the unity of Church and State,
> God and Man, Peace and War, Life and Death, Good and Bad; it solved
> the whole problem of the universe. . . . One looks back on it all as a
> picture; a symbol of unity; an assertion of God and Man in a bolder,
> stronger, closer union than ever was expressed by other art; and when
> the idea is absorbed, accepted, and perhaps partially understood, one
> may move on.[27]

Gazing at the picture, immersed in the past, the viewer may nevertheless reflect that an elegiac note qualifies his enjoyment, that he must submit to the realities, or unrealities, of the present as best he can. The aesthetes found this submission critically difficult. Their writing sought to engage in a debate about the place that art would have in contemporary life. American society won the debate by declining to take part, proving the aesthetes' point but leaving them alone in the forum.

SOCIETY, HISTORY, AND ART

Aestheticism, as a cultural episode, hardly confined itself to the United States. All over Europe, the temperature and humidity rose, tinging art with an exotic, hothouse blush. French symbolism was perhaps the most extreme case, as Arthur Symons wrote, verging on religion, revolting against exteriority, rhetoric, and a materialistic tradition, endeavoring by means of the symbol to make visible the soul of things. This method, Symons reasoned, gave literature its authentic speech, but by attaining the liberty to speak intimately and solemnly, as formerly only religion had spoken, literature became a kind of religion, with the duties of a sacred ritual.[1] Compared with this priestly, mystical quality of French Symbolism, in Austria art served a more expressly social function. As Carl Schorske relates, the Viennese middle class initially made the arts a vehicle to assimilate into the aristocracy and tried to combine moralism, faith in science, and political liberalism with the traditionally "sensuous, plastic" aesthetic culture of Austrian nobility. As its political fortunes declined, however, the bourgeoisie employed art less as a means of social aspiration and more as a barrier against political disintegration. Though following another historical and social plot, in Austria the aestheticist episode came to resemble the French denouement. Art became a substitute for action; when politics proved futile, art became religious, transformed, Schorske writes, from an ornament to an essence, from an expression to a source of value.[2]

The parallels between Austrian and American aestheticism invite us to notice how the fortunes of a class affect its art. Vienna's aesthetic culture flourished during the ascendancy of its liberal class, but as the metropolitan bourgeoisie lost ground before regional, ethnic, and social pressures, its faith in the moral and legal components of its liberalism likewise subsided. Instead, it looked increasingly to aesthetic culture for values that would confirm identity, a high stronghold – a sanctuary – to which the middle class could retreat to avoid the political tides surging against it. For what the analogy is worth, the place of aestheticism in the decline of an Austrian social class partly resembles the American situation.

English aestheticism seems less obviously linked to a politically discontented social class; its origins, though complex, are well enough known not to require summary here. One analogy, however, remains worth pursuing, the late tendency, most prominently advanced by Walter Pater, to recommend aestheticism as a perceptual strategy. The tactic aimed not to recreate the world in the image of art, but rather to cultivate a personal consciousness receptive to beauty as an antithesis to a prosaic world. Paterian aestheticism advises a perceiver to discard evaluative and even linguistic categories around which conscious life coheres. It advocates exclusive apprehension of particulars and abandonment of the categorical, in favor of "impressions, unstable, flickering, inconsistent, which burn and are extinguished with our consciousness of them."[3]

Without forms through which to organize and filter perception and ideas, however, analytical consciousness and – what is more – the self tend to evaporate. "It is with this movement, with the passage and dissolution of impressions, images, sensations, that analysis leaves off – that continual vanishing away, that strange, perpetual, weaving and unweaving of ourselves."[4] In the original essay, this sentence was followed by a remarkable passage excised by Pater from all later versions of his conclusion to *The Renaissance*. It acknowledges the high price that restricting the conscious mind to pure perception exacts:

> Such thoughts seem desolate at first; at times all the bitterness of life seems concentrated in them. They bring the image of one washed out beyond the bar in a sea at ebb, losing even his personality, as the elements of which he is composed pass into new combinations. Struggling, as he must, to save himself, it is himself that he loses at every moment.[5]

Pater's aesthetic of sympathy humbles, even humiliates, consciousness until it cannot be distinguished from the sense impressions that bombard it. The commitment to see all of reality, to allow what is immediate to pass unmediated, inevitably becomes more than a perceptual strategy, tending to take on morally and socially adversarial implications. "The theory or idea or system which requires of us the sacrifice of any part of this experience, in consideration of some interest into which we cannot enter, or some abstract theory we have not identified with ourselves, or of what is only conventional, has no real claim upon us." Moreover, as Pater's conclusion earlier stated, "failure is to form habits: for, after all, habit is relative to a stereotyped world."[6]

This sort of aestheticism looks very much like a disease that pretends to be a cure. "Habits" and "stereotypes" seem merely invidious synonyms for active mental functioning. The sane mind is the one with structures, able to perceive relevant similarities and evaluate significant differences. Sorting consecutive sense impressions, it deposits them into categories; those same impressions tend to overwhelm an open mind cultivated into vulnerability. The American aesthetes produced their own version of Paterian discomposure, though by a different path. Adams, for instance, called it the "dissolving mind." Eliot, transmuting the image, praised James for a "mind so fine that no idea could violate it."[7]

The American aesthetes reached this point – fine or otherwise – because their moral and social categories failed them, no longer organizing reality but merely condemning it or holding it at arm's length. Allegiance to a set of moral and social categories they could not discard fragmented their perceptions. No such scruple, however, encumbered history. As Eliot perceived, the moral calculus of cultivated, liberal Protestants relied upon ethics without theology. It required altruism – social and moral sympathy – but neglected the strong, resilient self or spirit that must go with it, thus demanding that its adherents give what they did not always have. The regimen might operate satisfactorily given social position, power, and financial resources. But once these things became threatened (after 1828 and more clearly after 1865), they could no longer sustain this moral ideology, leaving its adherents to confront its contradictions more squarely. It must have seemed particularly bitter that Unitarian values, so markedly the agents of progress, should have become among the most conspicuous victims of the forces they had encouraged. *The Waste Land,* American aestheticist poem par excellence, is one result, weaving its recombinant if distinct threads of breakdown, moral jeremiad, and aesthetic reverie.

That poem and Eliot's career extend roots deep into American social history. They particularly reflect an old American pattern in which members of families in decline,* facing issues of problematic deference and status discrepancy, frame a literary response.[8] Art, so to speak, becomes the memory of success that no longer succeeds. Richard Hofstadter's *The Age of Reform from Bryan to F.D.R.* contends that two similar political movements, Populism and Progressivism, resulted from demographic and economic changes after the Civil War. Participants in these movements had not necessarily lost economically because of those events, but they did suffer from political changes.[9] Until shortly after the Civil War, wealth, status, and power spread broadly through American society. In small communities, the locally eminent man of moderate means – a preacher, editor, lawyer, or small merchant or manufacturer – could command deference and exert influence. After the Civil War, however, the economy, the pattern of settlement, and the distribution of power and deference changed. T. S. Eliot, whose father was secretary of

---

* Charlotte and Henry Ware Eliot, Sr., for instance, had seven children, but only two grandchildren and one great-grandchild (Edward Cranch Eliot, *The Family of William Greenleaf Eliot and Abby Adams Eliot of St. Louis, Missouri, 1811–1952,* 4th ed. [by John Greenleaf Eliot] [n.p., 1952]).

a successful local brickmaking company, whose mother was a school-
teacher, and whose grandfather was a notable clergyman, reformer, and
educator, grew up in a family marked by these gradual but unmistakable
developments.[10]

In fact, the Civil War need prove no barrier in tracing the roots of this
group in general, or of Eliot in particular. As Eliot's repeated references
to the Jacksonian deluge remind us, his family's values partly descended
from the culture that had earlier achieved political expression in the
American Whig party.[11] In any event, Hofstadter argues that new
wealth, of national rather than local magnitude, provoked an "upheaval
of status" among these local elites. National fortunes dominated an increasingly centralized economy, and political alignments changed ac-
cordingly. Old, college-educated families, with deep roots in local communities as the owners of family businesses, political leaders, directors of
philanthropic and cultural institutions, and initiators of civic improve-
ments, found themselves with a reduced voice in political and economic
decisions. The new corporations, national in scope, corrupters of legisla-
tures, political bosses and their machines checked their community activities and their personal careers alike. Most poignantly, their own scru-
ples, social prominence, and good reputations hampered them in this
uneven struggle.[12] In other words, their morality compelled them to
abstain from what would enable them to keep political and economic
dominance, offering choices that countenanced only reaction or retreat.
By accident or innocence the people comprising this group, having all
but held the cities and towns in their hands, let the country slip through
their fingers. If some of them harbored apocalyptic thoughts, they did so
with some cause. Their cultural hegemony, formerly a fact of their lives,
no longer existed, and therefore neither did their world.

Hofstadter might be describing Eliot's family and their St. Louis,
scandalized by municipal corruption and election rigging that Lincoln
Steffens exposed in 1902.[13] Hofstadter's conclusion that the clergy probably lost most conspicuously from the "status revolution"[14] confirms
the point, since Eliot descended from many ministers and his mother was
a devoted religious writer. Hofstadter's "displaced social elite" encapsu-
lates Eliot's background: a powerful, educated, locally eminent family,
accustomed to providing leadership and accepting deference, with roots
in the community, of New England stock and culture, philanthropically
and civic minded, and tending to put public duty before private interest.
Elements of such local elites reacted to their displacement politically or
participated, as did the Eliots, in local reform movements.[15]

In "The Progressive Impulse," Hofstadter refers to another characteristic response to sociopolitical upheavals. The suspicion and even hostility that Santayana, Adams, James, and Eliot display toward urban
immigrants is only one of a cluster of Mugwump responses typical of the

educated Yankee classes. Not only did the immense post–Civil War fortunes threaten this class from above, but urban immigrants implicitly denied their cultural values and explicitly challenged established political leadership, their numbers fencing off the Yankees into gilded but politically powerless enclaves, where they brooded about the end of traditional American democracy.[16] As Francis Parkman wrote in 1878, for example, "Two enemies, unknown before, have risen like spirits of darkness on our social and political horizon – an ignorant proletariat and a half-taught plutocracy. Between lie the classes, happily still numerous and strong, in whom rests our salvation."[17] Hofstadter's analysis (suggesting, for example, why Sweeney or Bleistein became objects of Eliot's disapproval) finally sets forth how the responses to the "status revolution" took political (Populism and Progressivism; Mugwumps; reform, nativist, and other movements), social (patriotic, genealogical, and civic associations; philanthropy and social work; patronage of the arts), journalistic (muckrakers like Tarbell or Steffens), and religious (the "social gospel" movement) forms.[18]

As the dubious cliché has it, history may be what is written by the winners. Much of American literature, however, seems to have been written by those whom history subdued. The arts, though they have often wished to do so, cannot escape social and political events, and the unplanned obsolescence of this class provoked a literary response as well: the rise of a genteel literary establishment. Santayana (who named the tradition in his famous 1911 essay), James, Adams, and Eliot all had roots in gentility, and each tore them up, with various results. "The Love Song of J. Alfred Prufrock," for instance, besides being a "serious" or "sincere" poem, also satirizes the overbred, feminized, fragile figures that decorated the genteel literary establishment, moving like shadows through the period's cultural salons. "Prufrock" and other early poems reflect Eliot's effort to distance himself from literary gentility and from the genteel part of his own sensibility. To overcome the role and that part of himself to which it referred, he satirized it, perhaps hoping that publicity might discourage what privacy preserved. "Prufrock" blends satire and sincerity, lyric and lampoon, a finger in someone else's ribs and a knife in one's own, hurt shared and a hair shirt. It deftly mocks an effete social surface, treating comically what undoubtedly seemed "at times almost ridiculous," while probing the musty, anaerobic privacies of a genteel type.

Though Santayana, James, Adams, and Eliot diverged from the genteel literary establishment, they nonetheless reflect its influence, especially on social matters. As John Tomsich explains in *A Genteel Endeavor*, genteel culture reacted to a society economically and demographically mobile, prosperous but uncultivated, by assuming the mission of teaching its members how to behave.[19] Genteel literary ideas about art and national life, through Charles Eliot Norton – its most talented figure and, typically, another of T. S. Eliot's distinguished relatives – greatly influenced subsequent thought. *Mont-Saint-Michel and Chartres, Italian Hours,* and *After Strange Gods,* for instance, reflect Norton's idea that common ideals, in a homogeneous culture, gave great nations great art.[20]

Possibly Eliot's strongest link to the previous generation, this idea surfaces frequently in his social writing, and at surprising moments in purely literary criticism as well.[21] What America seemed to lack – homogeneity, common ideals, and, especially, great art – appeared to exist overseas. The enviable prestige of thought and culture in England, for instance, greatly troubled the genteel writers. Both Santayana and James made this complaint, and if Adams's exposure to English diplomatic chicanery sharpened into Anglophobia, his medievalism more than made up for it. Santayana, James, and Eliot followed this pattern to its extreme, so identifying culture with English or European models that they could no longer remain in America. The genteel writers wanted European art in America. Their modernist offspring determined that if they could not have art in America, they would have art without it.

His review of Van Wyck Brooks's *The Wine of the Puritans* clearly links the twenty-year-old Eliot to the genteel temperament, eerily anticipating ambiguities he spent decades resolving. Written for the *Harvard Advocate* while Eliot was an undergraduate, the review is his first published prose:

> This is a book which probably will chiefly interest one class of Americans (a class, however, of some importance): the Americans retained to their native country by business relations or socialities or by a sense of duty – the last reason implying a real sacrifice – while their hearts are always in Europe. To these, double-dealers with themselves, people of divided allegiance except in times of emotional crisis, Mr. Brooks' treatise will come as a definition of their discontent. But he should find a larger audience than this class alone. The reasons for the failure of American life (at present) – social, political, in education and in art, are surgically exposed; with an unusual acuteness of distinction and refinement of taste; and the more sensitive of us may find ourselves shivering under the operation. For the book is a confession of national weakness; if one take it rightly, a wholesome revelation.[22]

It is easy to see how Brooks's essay – itself a treatment of the themes Adams, James, and Santayana discussed – could elicit these remarks. The conflicted sensibility of which Eliot speaks so knowingly could be traced throughout his own class. Eliot's family betrayed little evidence that their hearts were in Europe, but their values and history were undoubtedly the source of the "sense of duty" that remaining in America satisfied but that simultaneously exacted a "sacrifice." Though he does not name them, those Americans of specifically aestheticist temperament – the leisured cosmopolites James encountered at Newport, for example, or Santayana's solitary, gaunt idealists – seem most likely to have been the "double-dealers" of whom Eliot writes. Though assuming the "failure of American life," Eliot comments that Brooks surgically exposed those reasons with an unusual "refinement of taste," refinement and taste being perhaps the two most important touchstones of genteel values.

The genteel literary establishment, though committed to creating an American culture, nevertheless tended to look to Europe for its standards. Eliot's criteria – "taste" and "refinement" – betray his genteel inheritance. For him, however, genteel culture had failed, and his discussion reveals both his links to the genteel culture and his dissatisfaction with its shortcomings. A few years later, Conrad Aiken, his closest friend at this time, would call Eliot's temperament the "average hyperaesthetic one," suggesting both Eliot's values as a young adult and the extent to which others shared them.[23] It is one reason why so much of American modernism took place abroad. The "sacrifice" must have proved too great and the blandishments of art too strong. Growing up, Eliot had felt himself to be "never anything anywhere"; at age twenty he was analyzing the problem as one of "divided allegiance." Not long after writing this remarkable paragraph, which all but charts the course of his life, Eliot followed his heart – to Europe. There he would extend the sequence, in 1926, by asserting the likelihood that some of the strongest influences upon the thought of the next generation would be those of the "dispossessed artists."[24]

Their hyperconsciousness of English and European social differences also reinforced the genteel writers' tendency to interpret their own position, or lack of it, in aristocratic terms.[25] Arguing with approval that some of the qualities that had typified New England literary society before the Civil War persisted into recent times, Eliot suggested that "precisely this leisure, this dignity, this literary aristocracy, this unique character of a society in which the men of letters were also of the best people, clings to Henry James."[26] Another aside, from Eliot's review of Adams's *The Education,* however, indicates the studied lengths to which such analysis could be taken. Adams, it explains, might not have considered James "educated," though Eliot praises James for having acquired an intelligence superior to that of Adams by successfully incorporating his senses into his erudition. Dwelling on the difficulties imposed by Adams's background, however, and by implication his own, Eliot concluded by excusing Adams, if not condemning James: "Henry James, however, was comparatively parvenu. He did not have the Presidents, the Minister, the Unitarian clergy in force behind him."[27]

By contrast to what they took to be a fully realized, stable European social hierarchy, with a peasantry and aristocracy, genteel thinkers measured (and deprecated) the movement of post–Civil War America toward an urban, technological society as opposed to a village and agricultural one. Eliot consistently criticized urban, industrial civilization; his eventual Christian nostalgia, though acknowledging social change, partly rephrased the genteel sociological critique. Speaking of "its religious organisation," Eliot concluded that Christendom had remained fixed at a simple, fishing and agricultural stage and acknowledged that Christian social forms had adapted imperfectly to modern, material society.[28] The pessimism of James and especially of Adams and Eliot resembles the ideas about history and human nature held by the lesser known, genteel circle. Its members found it difficult to be optimistic about human nature, feared democracy, and espoused values of order, discipline, and tradition. Immersed in cultural confusion, they could not imagine the future with the same attention they devoted to the past.[29] Unable to conceive of institutional alternatives to the age's social and intellectual upheavals – civil service reform could hardly suffice – and likewise unsuccessful at politics or economics, the genteel writers turned, as if obeying some archaic instinct, to culture.[30] Other members of their class made religious, scientific, political, or ideological responses to social instability. The genteel writers, however, like their more famous counterparts, found in culture a source and repository of ideals. For them, art became an extension of politics by other means.

Nineteenth-century American aesthetic culture, however, proved intellectually and theologically unsatisfactory. Unable to free themselves from an anxious but vague agnosticism by reasserting traditional cosmologies or adopting newer ones, they defended traditional values with culture. But culture alone, without an intellectually revived theology, could not prevent those values from seeming anything other than opinions; culture could not adequately justify a morality having a religious origin.[31] This issue illustrates how Eliot both conformed to and departed from the genteel pattern. He devoted considerable early attention to the ideal of culture, especially as it related to social organization. A professionally trained philosopher, Eliot grasped how far culture fell short of forming an adequate foundation for society, morals, or manners. In 1927, he dismissed pure aestheticism, without a theological framework, in the most graphic terms. Referring to I. A. Richards, Eliot wrote, "Poetry 'is capable of saving us,' he says; it is like saying that the wallpaper will save us when the walls have crumbled."[32] Having consigned hell and the risk of an adverse finding on Judgment Day to the theological dustbin, liberal Protestantism forfeited any effective means by which to sanction genteel governance of collective behavior. Having cast off eternal consequences, earthly behavior ceased to admit religious scrutiny. Without infernal stick or heavenly carrot, gentility made what had once been sinful merely vulgar. Later it became fashionable. Today, of course, it is commonplace.

The aestheticist might have argued that the wallpaper performs both ornamental and structural functions. Eliot's reassertion of the difference, his insistence that art cannot accomplish both goals, and his passion for holding up the roof suggest how decisively he had shifted away from aestheticism. After 1927, having officially added religion to his artistic and social interests, Eliot in *After Strange Gods, The Idea of a Christian Society, Notes Towards the Definition of Culture, To Criticize the Critic,* and in many essays tried to fuse culture and social ideals with the cement of theology and faith. Some lines from "Choruses from 'The Rock'" pose the issue:

> Do you need to be told that even such modest attainments
> As you can boast in the way of polite society
> Will hardly survive the Faith to which they owe
> their significance?

Thus Eliot chose to emphasize the religious origin of secular politeness and acknowledge that aesthetic culture had its root in the church. Arriving after the era of literary gentility and willing to profit from Adams's, James's, and Santayana's scrutiny of genteel shortcomings, Eliot could anatomize and thus transcend them.

He could do so because his social origins – Eliot's membership in a kind of relict cultural species – inevitably stained his emotional lenses. *Prufrock and Other Observations* showed Eliot trying, not always with complete conviction or success, to distance himself from gentility. As they illustrated genteel standards being exposed and irritated, *Poems, 1920* revealed, from another point of view, Eliot's proximity to the same phenomena he had formerly satirized. The narrator of "Portrait of a Lady" had "remarked":

> An English countess goes upon the stage.
> A Greek was murdered at a Polish dance,
> Another bank defaulter has confessed.

The three lines neatly summarize the issues troubling the American aestheticist writers: downward social mobility, violent ethnic conflict, and financial dishonesty. Yet if these "late events" had seemed like mere newspaper copy in *Prufrock and Other Observations,* remote items idly noted and promptly forgotten, in *Poems, 1920* they leaped out of the headlines and into the poems. Though both volumes have seriocomic qualities, in terms of social content *Poems, 1920* is far more inclusive and ambitious. On one hand, its poems explore historical disjunction and ridicule gentility and aristocrats for their failures. On the other, they criticize Bleistein, Doris, Rachel, and especially Sweeney, the emblem of the mass man, as the figures to which the modern world gives way. Eliot at this stage deliberately thought in terms of "types," and his change in target produced a sharp change in tone. In *Poems, 1920,* a nineteenth-century aestheticist American sensibility anachronistically confronts the modern world. Out of that collision creeps a poetic of cultural conflict.

5

The Silhouette of Sweeney:
Cultures and Conflict

This town interests me and I see kind adventurous people; Mr. Eliot, the Unitarian minister, is the Saint of the West, and has a sumptuous church, and crowds to hear his really good sermons. But I believe no thinking or even reading man is here in the 95,000 souls. An abstractionist cannot live near the Mississippi River and the Iron Mountain. They have begun the Pacific Rail Road; and the Railroad from St. Anthony's Falls to New Orleans. Such projects cannot consist with much literature.

Emerson, writing to Lidian Emerson
from St. Louis, 1852

When we have fully discovered the scientific laws that govern life, we shall realise that the one person who has more illusions than the dreamer is the man of action. He, indeed, knows neither the origin of his deeds nor their results.

Oscar Wilde, "The Critic as Artist"

Writing to his brother in 1919, Eliot predicted the disapproving litany that greeted his quatrain poems then, and that has done so since. He considered "Burbank" and "Sweeney Among the Nightingales" among the best poems he had written. Calling these two poems "intensely serious," Eliot nonetheless remarked that the ordinary London journalists considered him a wit or satirist, and speculated that Americans would regard him as "merely disgusting."[1] Both responses, one on each side of the Atlantic, miss the point: London dismisses Eliot as a lightweight, while Boston sniffs that its sensibilities have been bruised. "Merely disgusting" strikes just the studied note of victims trying to disguise satirically inflicted wounds. Their verdict insults Eliot's motives as well, pronouncing him insufficiently serious and implying that he intended only to shock. Eliot's phrase reveals something about how he regarded this part of his audience, the genteel readers not dissimilar to

154

some of his poetic characters. It is easy to see how, for instance, "Mr. Apollinax" ritually punctures genteel balloons. And "Portrait of a Lady," for all its adroit tragicomedy of manners, on a simpler level mercilessly impales an overrefined matron besieged by too much leisure behind Boston's bricks and bow windows. Perhaps settling a score, Eliot once called Boston society "quite uncivilized but refined beyond the point of civilization."[2]

Literary modernism, to its coconspirators Pound and Eliot, partly involved demolishing such gentility insofar as it confined contemporary verse. Eliot in particular flouted genteel literary conventions far more frequently than he has been credited with having done. The genteel strictures barred "vulgar slang" from literature, for instance, along with explicit sexual references, disrespectful treatment of Christianity, and unhappy endings.[3] His prim, fastidious reputation notwithstanding, Eliot's early writing infringed each of these taboos in their turn. As he recalled in 1947, the modernists wanted to use not only modern material, but modern words. They attacked not only ossified poetic diction, but also the constrained subject matter of contemporary verse. One of their "tenets" was that before aspiring to poetic elevation, verse should take on the virtues of prose, assimilating its diction to "cultivated contemporary speech." Its imagery and subject matter, moreover, should incorporate objects and topics associated with the lives of modern people. And it should search out "non-poetic" material that stubbornly refused poetic "transmutation," using words that poetry had never used before.[4]

As a preliminary matter, we might note how the adjective "cultivated" qualifies Eliot's dictum about inclusive poetic diction by means of a social criterion redolent of gentility. It also serves as a reminder – if one is needed – that Eliot's modernism was not an excuse for license. "Contemporary speech" would have let virtually anything into modern verse. "Cultivated contemporary speech," by contrast, restricts diction so severely – since Eliot elsewhere argued the scarcity of cultivated people in the modern world – that one may wonder how much new language Eliot's formula would finally have admitted. That having been said, Eliot's poetic pointed two ways. First, modernism tried to discover ideas, imagery, and diction that would allow poetry to incorporate new subjects that traditional methods had resisted. In 1921, Eliot described verse as "always struggling, while remaining verse, to take up to itself more and more of what is prose, to take something more from life and turn it into 'play.'" He traced the failure of contemporary verse to its inability "to draw anything new from life into art."[5]

Second, however, and somewhat at cross-purposes with this ludic motive, Eliot did not use modern idioms or material disinterestedly. He introduced modern particulars to evaluate the tendencies they represented, as judged against inherited criteria. His evaluations reflect the primordial seriousness of his family and their culture, intensified by social experience. Combined with and filtered through American aestheticism, these changing circumstances reveal Eliot importing the modern world into verse not to praise but to expose it. Eliot had grown up hungrily pursuing the ideal in history, art, tradition, morality, and religion until they constituted his emotional as much as his intellectual identity. On one hand, he knew firsthand the ideal cultural values of which he was a product; to them he was loyal by background and, so far as possible, by choice. On the other, he learned the weakness of those values in modern society, and how decisively contemporary life contradicted them. That empirical dissonance forced him to jump off the genteel fence.

Poems, 1920 turned to the particulars to which adherents of traditional liberal values had given ground, recording the negative, often nebulous frustrations these social facts provoked. While politer members of the genteel class, mortally addicted to decorum, suppressed such responses as untoward, Eliot's art upset decorum with corrosive derision. To react passionately to the loss of a religious, social, and historical tradition, and to do so in the name of art and culture, meant merely to say that such things mattered. It meant that Eliot discarded (often to his subsequent embarrassment) the genteel values of toleration and inoffensiveness, disobeying their self-contradictory commandments to avoid behaving offensively oneself but to tolerate behavior that offends.

It also meant that many readers would consider these quatrains odd, disturbing, or difficult. Eliot's critical prose, his workshop criticism explaining and defending his poetic practice, offers some clues about how to evaluate both the form and the matter of this poetry.[6] In analyzing another poet's technique, Eliot often glosses his own. He praises the "high speed" of Marvell's verse, for example, its "succession of concentrated images," and a quality of surprise that, since Homer, had contributed an important poetic effect. Eliot pointed to this last quality several times, relating it to an "inexhaustible and terrible nebula of emotion" surrounding and mingling with our exact, practical passions.[7] This emotional nebula contributes to a Gothic poetry of effect throughout the quatrains, whose language has a "third dimension" and whose "network of tentacular roots" reaches down to the deepest terrors and desires.[8] They aspire to an effect of terror Eliot discerned in Poe and Blake and in genuinely new works of art.[9] In the poems of a contemporary, Jean de Bosschère, Eliot also distinguished a remoteness that his own quatrain poems imitate. De Bosschère, Eliot said, remained an intellectual by refusing to adulterate his poetic emotions with human ones. Instead of refining ordinary human emotion, he aimed at emotions of art. Although the method necessarily limited de Bosschère's audience, Eliot found the effect of "intense frigidity" it sometimes produced "altogether admirable."[10] A similar frigid effect in a section of *In Memoriam* gave Eliot a not unwelcome "shudder."[11]

Eliot's comments on tone and diction also clarify the "poetry of effect" to which *Poems, 1920* aspired. For instance, the presence of Donne and Webster in "Whispers of Immortality" recalls Eliot's approval of the metaphysical school for its "sudden contrast of associations," telescoped images, and simple, elegant language.[12] Nearly all these effects – rapidity, surprise, the emotional nebulae, frigidity, and especially terror – characterize the intense, elevated responses to the most serious moment in art, tragic catharsis. Eliot seems to recommend that poetry aspire only to tragic *effects,* that is to say, terror without the pity and tragedy without the plot. (The plot of "Sweeney Among the Nightingales," for instance, invoking this repertoire of tragic verbal effect, appears to involve little more than a contretemps in a low-rent bar.) Their presence might also suggest another source of Eliot's later religiosity. Christianity could provide the other component of the cathartic formula – an authentically tragic plot, arousing genuine pity to balance the terror, which without credible motive is simply tragedy's cheap thrill – and supply other than merely verbal access to these most serious emotional responses.

Eliot later argued, however, that seriousness did not necessarily depend on purely tragic machinery. Tragedy remained inadequate, he argued, to those experiencing the "full horror of life." When horror and laughter became as horrible and laughable as they could be, they might merge. Only when one laughed, "shuddered," or felt both responses at once from *Oedipus, Hamlet,* or *King Lear* would one perceive that tragic and comic dramatists had the same aim and were equally serious.[13] Eliot's essay on Andrew Marvell confirms the point and may contain the most important clue to the quatrain poems and their characters. Marvell's wit, Eliot said, combined seriousness with levity in an alliance that tended to intensify the seriousness.[14] Eliot once concluded that although a dramatist did not need to "understand" people, he nonetheless had to be "exceptionally aware" of them.[15] He made little effort to "understand" Sweeney, Grishkin, Bleistein, or Burbank, but remained exceptionally aware of their foibles and graceless gestures. Eliot could satirize gentility firsthand, but descending a notch or two on the social scale required a more external approach.

Ben Jonson's method helped him find it. Eliot advised that a less awestruck view of Jonson's learning and a clearer grasp of his rhetoric could lead not only to enjoyment and "instruction in two-dimensional life," but to the awareness of Jonson as "a part of our literary inheritance craving further expression." In that legacy Eliot discerned values – "a brutality, a lack of sentiment, a polished surface, a handling of large bold designs in brilliant colours" – that made Jonson particularly sympathetic to the modern age.[16] The quatrain poems, like Jonsonian drama, tried to be both satirical and "intensely serious" by simplifying the characters they contained.

Neither monomania nor the dominance of a particular humor explained Jonson's simplification. Instead, Eliot wrote, Jonson simplified by reducing detail; by seizing aspects "relevant to the relief of an emotional impulse which remains the same for that character"; and by conforming the character to a particular setting. This "stripping," as Eliot called it, combined with a "flat distortion in the drawing," made Jonson's drama an art of great caricature.[17] In Eliot's own serious caricature, highlighting one or two features of a character while ignoring the others, ridicule coexists with realism. Some people behave so extremely or possess characters so misshapen that caricature may constitute representational fidelity. Mascara cannot conceal the mask: It rather renders the latent patent. Sweeney, Grishkin, and the others find it impossible to alter the fashion of their countenances; having merged with their masks, they remain to that extent less human. The homo simplex that such features betray, and the rigidity and un-self-consciousness that they reflect, resemble those of animals. They are why people visit zoos.

Hence caricature may be at once ridiculous and yet retain a moral point. The quatrain poems shift among all three possibilities of caricature – comic, realistic, moral – as Eliot, from behind his urbane deadpan, stage-manages the jerky, awkward movements of his marionette-like characters. Learned diction, irony, formal syntax and stanzaic arrangement, and bathos distance the poet from the things described. They cause a seriocomic effect at moments condescending or disgusted, yet also make possible the escape valves of buffoonery and burlesque. Sometimes one can all but hear the sticks slap.

As Eliot intimated in 1918, the quatrains' aggressive humor also contains a degree of defensiveness. He argued that the intelligent Englishman, more aware of loneliness than intelligent men elsewhere, had a public, objective wit, a humor representing the instinctive attempt by a sensitive mind "to protect beauty against ugliness and to protect itself against stupidity."[18] The phrase exposes another of Eliot's debts to the aesthetes. Humor protecting beauty against ugliness and sensitivity against stupidity pinpoints the defensive aestheticist ideal that Eliot associated with acquired, high culture. The remark also betrays his sense that social change had placed the ideal at issue, and therefore at risk. The characters in *Poems, 1920* have little sense of art, religion, civility, reason, or kindness – the ideals Eliot's criticism referred to so frequently. The quatrain poems will remain no more than witty, satirical, or "merely disgusting" should a reader forget their essential, if oblique, argument that the modern world has discarded those ideals. Unless a reader can perform the backward inference, distancing himself from these poems by imagining an extrinsic ideal against which to measure the behavior within them, the poems' realistic and moral dimension will not emerge, and their comedy will seem flat and gratuitous.

Warning against modernity by rendering it risible and grotesque was the cryptic device Eliot employed to adapt caricature to moral purposes. The quatrain poems demand double vision, a stereoscopy that must observe how the real and the ideal compete, and how their contest affects Eliot's recoil from any conventionally sincere persona. Doubleness – as well as their "deep discontent and rebelliousness" – moreover explains Eliot's affinity with the Elizabethans. He proposed that John Marston, for instance, wrote so as to say

> something else than appears in the literal actions and characters whom he manipulates. It is possible that what distinguishes poetic drama from prosaic drama is a kind of doubleness in the action, as if it took place on two planes at once. . . . In poetic drama a certain apparent irrelevance may be the symptom of this doubleness; or the drama has an under-pattern less manifest than the theatrical one.[19]

These phrases – "deep discontent and rebelliousness," the distinction between two kinds of dramatic "saying" (between a literal, surface meaning and a deeper one), a similar "doubleness" of incident involving "two planes" of action, an "apparent irrelevance" and an "under-pattern" that suggest another reality, recessive and obscure, yet more real – apply to the tone, figures, and action in the quatrain poems. Having quit the struggle to be humane, their characters think, feel, look, and act like animals. In "Sweeney Among the Nightingales," for instance, recalling his appearance in "Sweeney Erect," the initially simian Sweeney comes to resemble a zebra and then a giraffe. Rachel's paws tear at her food. Further down the urban bestiary, the man in mocha brown is dismissed as a "vertebrate" (the synecdoche apparently flatters him, all things considered), and the predication – "contracts," "concentrates," and "withdraws" – implies his serpentine quality.

Both words in "Sweeney Erect" contain phallic import, but "erect" also suggests the anthropological "homo erectus," an upright primate. As we watch Sweeney yawn and stretch as he awakens, however, clawing at the pillow slip and aspiring only to challenge the confines of the bed frame, the description warns that his superiority remains purely physical and that he is no simian only by virtue of a taxonomical technicality. Elsewhere, a porcine description further diminishes Sweeney's stature, as he "shifts from ham to ham." "Whispers of Immortality" compares Grishkin to a jaguar, while "A Cooking Egg" descends further down the phylogenetic chain of being, from the jungle to feral, scavenging North London "multitudes." In *Poems, 1920,* this comparison of people to animals recurs to the point of mechanism. "Burbank with a Baedeker: Bleistein with a Cigar" reveals its hostile dimensions, high and low. The Princess Volupine – vulpine as well as voluptuous – wears animal skins, an aristocrat indulging a troglodytic totemism: "Money in furs." Here the device also sinks to its notorious nadir, comparing Bleistein to rats and then to protozoans, the lowest life form. The comparison, redolent with anti-Jewish overtones and exposing Eliot's satire and its supposed ideal content to grave criticism, reveals the most unfortunate link between Eliot and the aestheticist writers of the previous generation.

Poems, 1920 implies that the modern world transforms people into animals that exist unaware of the ideal. The disputations of Christian divines produce an enfeebling complication; Origen is "enervate." Exegetes like Origen obscure the Word and disperse its energy, so it can neither elevate the spirit nor restrain the appetites of a modern man like Sweeney, physically clean, perhaps, but morally ignorant. Sweeney bathes while Rome disputes; neither takes any notice of what the other does. The ideal and the actual remain helplessly, hopelessly split, as do the past and the present.

Webster and Donne, whose unified sensibilities comprehended mortality, inspired the intellect and spirit. In "Whispers of Immortality," however, three centuries later Grishkin sinks into carnal knowledge and metaphysical ignorance. Unlike Donne, Grishkin relies upon the flesh exclusively. Her pneumatic bliss would not be the spiritual kind, but rather, since her eye is "underlined for emphasis" and her bust "friendly" and "uncorseted," a mechanically carnal sort. "Pneumatic" exemplifies Eliot's syzygial stereoscopy, using a single word to connote opposed qualities, in this case the medieval spirit and modern flesh. Like Sweeney, Princess Volupine, Bleistein, Doris, Rachel, and other unnamed characters, Grishkin represents a modern "type," who has dispensed with any ideal, spiritual, or divine essence, leaving her alone with the animal remnant. Day to day adventures presumably have the blood pounding in her ears so noisily that she cannot hear what immortality "whispers."

Her behavior does not upset the descriptive, morally nonevaluative "Abstract entities," which conveniently accommodate themselves to her. They "circumambulate" – walk around – her carnal charm, while "our lot" must "crawl," reduced in stature by its metaphysics. Has "our lot" sacrificed earthly living to its metaphysics? Is something quite wrong with those who insist upon keeping metaphysics warm, instead of the flesh, or is their duty a necessary one? Has Grishkin lost her soul to a metaphysic that tells her she lacks one? May "our lot" claim a superior vision, based not on abstractions but upon the fact of death, which, as Emerson said, at least is reality that will not dodge us? Given the portraits of Webster, Donne, and Grishkin, this final argument probably comes closest to Eliot's point. The way he has lined up the antitheses, however, makes morbid metaphysical accuracy cold comfort.

Still it remains consistent with Eliot's belief that classicism demands an allegiance to something outside the self. The spiritual amputees who populate the quatrains will not, or cannot, give any such allegiance. Eliot accused such votaries of the inner voice of refusing to hear any other. Riding ten to a compartment to a football match, he said, they heard it breathe its "eternal message of vanity, fear, and lust."[20] Grishkin's eye is underlined; she resembles a jaguar at the hunt, poised to spring; her "friendly" bust promises "pneumatic bliss." Vanity, fear, and lust: So it is with Grishkin, and with Sweeney, who "knows the female temperament," "tests the razor on his leg" as the epileptic on the bed shrieks, and giggles among the nightingales.

Long after these poems appeared, Eliot commented on the issue they raise, on the animal and spiritual halves that fuse to form that tense thing, human nature. He recalled the "great strain" experienced by the "erect animal to persist in being erect, a physical and still more a moral strain."[21] The view that people have a mixed nature, part animal and part divine, produces these characters' tragicomic aspects. These human beings are funny, the quatrain poems argue, because they behave like animals, and tragic because their innocence of ideality bars them from their full humanity. Instead of submitting to complexity, the tension between animal and ideal, they surrender to simplicity; instead of distancing themselves from animals, they indulge their appetites and so come to resemble animals all the more, effacing their humanity and distinction in the process. Eliot once argued to discredit the idea that violent excitement makes human beings most real. Far from differentiating people from one another, he reasoned, violent physical passions "rather tend to reduce them to the same state."[22] When people abandon the idea of Original Sin, that is to say, their sins cease to be very original.

Eliot's poetic characters forgo another distinctly human faculty. They hardly speak. No conversation interrupts the quatrain poems, whose ominous silence the painstaking persiflage in *Prufrock and Other Observations* only emphasizes. Prufrockian company valued gentility at any price, sacrificing its conversation to preserve a social surface as smooth as a mirror, if as brittle. (In "Rhapsody on a Windy Night," even the street lamp talks too much.) No such self-consciousness troubles Sweeney's world, where only a hysterical, epileptic shriek and Sweeney's simian laughter punctuate events. Even the anonymous "multitudes" weep inaudibly; it is partly their mute, dispirited conformity that renders them so sad.

If "Prufrock" presented civilization evaporating into mere refinement, the quatrains portray crudity condensing into bestiality. Sexual lust, of course, is not the only sort that taints the modern world in the quatrain poems. Avarice corrupts sex and spirituality alike. Greed presumably explains why the Princess Volupine, here vulpine in a second sense, jilts Burbank for Sir Ferdinand. "Sweeney Erect" and "Sweeney Among the Nightingales" take place in brothels. In "A Cooking Egg," money adulterates even heaven, where to gain entry the founder of Imperial Chemical Industries evidently located either a small enough camel or a sufficiently large needle. Cupidity also corrupts the church, having counterfeited its spiritual blessings in favor of institutional self-preservation, living off its dividends, slumbering and enjoying the benefits of compound interest. Money becomes the modern medium for atonement, as acned petitioners seek intercession or absolution "clutching piaculative pence." (It may be significant that Eliot's own background could have led him to these provocative references to the ecclesiastical necessity for and embarrassment about money.)[23]

"Sweeney Among the Nightingales" crystallizes Eliot's themes and method in *Poems, 1920*. A difficult poem, its essential ambiguity nevertheless may not be entirely a flaw; experience presents many such moments, especially among new or strange company. An apocryphal comment seems to reflect Eliot's conscious attempt to render this impenetrability; Matthiessen recorded Eliot's remark that "all he consciously set out to create in 'Sweeney Among the Nightingales' was a sense of foreboding."[24] Most clearly of all the 1920 poems, it relies on a "poetry of effect," with "high speed," "multiplied associations," an "effect of terror," "surprise," the "alliance of levity and seriousness," and "frigidity" causing a "shudder," like the lines from *In Memoriam* caused Eliot. And like Marston, the poem tries to say something other than appears in the literal actions and characters Eliot manipulates. Like the metaphysical poets, he tries to find verbal equivalents for – admittedly obscure – states of mind and feeling.[25] As he often confirmed, Eliot's verse did not come from a purely intellectual source. He disallowed the notion that thoughts were necessarily precise and emotions vague. Instead, Eliot affirmed the existence of precise emotion, whose expression required as great intellectual power as expressing precise thought. "Every precise emotion," he concluded, "tends towards intellectual formulation."[26]

The question, given the poem's shortage of clear plot or expository sequence, is just *what* "something else" or state of mind and feeling underlies the literal action and verbal equivalent. Eliot's background provides a clue to the emotion that "Sweeney Among the Nightingales" seeks to make precise. Simply put, the poem reflects Eliot's predisposition to feel a "sense of foreboding," which makes "Sweeney Among the Nightingales" a vehicle for social fears. Nobody speaks in its inarticulate, threatening world; human relations invite danger and possess sinister profiles. The cruelty, fear, violence, and animal and vegetative imagery label the modern world a jungle. Mute, mostly nameless "vertebrates" with "murderous paws," its people become either predators or prey. Clouding the atmosphere, the adjectives imply menace and scandal: "stormy," "slide," "drift," "veiled," "hushed," "shrunken," "silent," "suspect, thought to be in league," "indistinct," and "dishonoured." The natural ("Death and the Raven drift above") and mythical ("And sang within the bloody wood when Agamemnon cried aloud") references, though their cosmic, tragic overtones render Sweeney's carrying-on trivial by comparison, emphasize a sense of doom.

The atmosphere crackles as if electrically charged. Overheated and overstimulated, the skewed appetites of these frugivores crave food that is unnatural, forced, "hothouse." The characters behave with carefree cruelty, yet they are also bored. When "the person in the Spanish cape" tries to sit on Sweeney's knees, they spread, she slips, he laughs, she yawns.

> The silent man in mocha brown
> Sprawls at the window-sill and gapes

In "The Metropolis and Mental Life," Georg Simmel wrote, "there is perhaps no psychic phenomenon which is so unconditionally reserved to the city as the blasé outlook."[27] Yet as one may gape from astonishment or shock as well as from boredom, the word "gapes" illustrates Eliot's use of a single term to unite opposite meanings, and so reinforce the poem's cloudy atmosphere. Neither is it quite possible to determine whether the silent man "sprawls" because he feels relaxed, awkward, or unnatural. These ambiguities suggest that Eliot judges the characters' behavior to alternate between apathy and violence, with no middle ground. The epigraph ("Alas, I am struck by a mortal blow from within!") implies that Sweeney might become an unsuspecting modern Agamemnon, but also that their lack of a spiritual or intellectual core leaves these characters their own victims.

Their bad manners, so routine as to become trivial, further condemn them. Recalling how coffee and tea rituals became emblems of civility in the *Prufrock* volume suggests that an overturned coffee cup here connotes low-life indecorum and social conflict. Whereas gentility hid behind a benign opacity, rarely permitting sincerity to discompose its social masks, the characters in *Poems, 1920* remain entirely transparent. Their masks reveal, instead of conceal. Since vanity, fear, and lust deform their natures, what seems to be caricature and exaggeration instead becomes mimesis. They and their masks coincide; both character and mask are grotesque, animal, crude. Their angular, unpredictable manners and awkward movements correspond to something schematic and cartoonish in their nature.

Eliot's focus on manners in these and other poems links him closely to Henry James, even if Eliot's outlandish approach incorporated extremities James scarcely hinted at. Both perceived the deterioration of manners as a sign of social as well as personal decay and retained a hyperconsciousness of ethnic, religious, and social differences. Both felt that modern society increasingly tended toward an odd assortment of discrete groups divided by ethnicity, religion, education, and even language, without a shared spiritual ideal or social code. In short, social life created conflict among strangers, instead of cooperation. Civility – an opacity that pretends to transparency – at its root means the regulation of behavior among strangers by a code not only to which all have reference but to which all, more importantly, consent. In an "unsettled" society such as the one in which Eliot felt he had matured, this conflict meant a clash of values, which revealed itself as a clash of manners. It is in this respect that *Poems, 1920* reflects a poetics of *kulturkampf*.

Adams, James, Santayana, and Eliot owed allegiance to traditional culture, manners, and values, regarding the ideals and artifacts associated with them as inarguably superior to alternatives. They sensed nevertheless the encroachment of something they considered inferior and less coherent. The diversity of values in and the abundance of ideas about American social life account for the ethnic and social unease in *The American Scene, The Education of Henry Adams,* and *Poems, 1920.* Eliot shared his predecessors' apocalyptic forebodings, even if he differed from them insofar as he eventually made Christianity the bulwark against a modern deluge rather than the thing it would sweep away. In 1931, he castigated the experiment of trying to create a civilized but non-Christian mentality. Although predicting its ultimate failure, Eliot counseled patience and the necessity of preserving the faith alive so as to "renew and rebuild civilization, and save the World from suicide."[28] All four aestheticist writers conceived of modernity similarly, focusing on the rupture between millennia of classical and Christian culture and the modern world; only Eliot, however, self-consciously moved beyond disillusion to restore communication between modernity and tradition.[29] He initially attempted to do so by means of culture, "Tradition and the Individual Talent" offering the best-known example of that early strategy. Unlike the aestheticists, Eliot later shifted away from culture and toward religion. But until he did so, Eliot appears to have experienced emotions of personal dissonance, social *kulturkampf,* and historical pessimism whose intensity exceeded even the earlier generation's grand aestheticist gestures. Having matured among a group of people whose social fortunes had witnessed descent from what once seemed sublime to a gentility that increasingly appeared ridiculous, Eliot's 1920 poems teem with references to historical pessimism, social bathos, and personal disillusion.

Though often seeming to act primarily as a lightning rod for critical discontent, "Burbank with a Baedeker: Bleistein with a Cigar" reflects Eliot's social experience and the aestheticist sensibility rooted in it. Its malignant anti-Jewish lines stand out so plainly they tend to obscure how likewise negatively the poem treats its other characters. Emblems of genteel ineffectuality and commercial myopia, Burbank and Bleistein embody two ways to travesty the past and its beauty – the bland leading, or misleading, the blind. The dim but pervasive presence of Adams's *Education* reinforces the poem's atmosphere of disapproval.[30] Eliot dislikes the decayed aristocrat, who corrupts the superficial Burbank: "They were together, and he fell." "Defunctive" music accompanies Burbank's collapse, and Hercules, the god of action and strength, deserts him, though the princess stays all night and all the next day.

The third stanza's elevated language, quoting Marston's *Antonio and Mellida* and Horace's "Pallida Mors," implies that the princess might resemble Cleopatra, and Burbank, Antony. But Eliot asserts the resemblance to make the bathetic point that Antony and Cleopatra were more noble, heroic, and interesting than Burbank and Volupine, whose conquests seem by comparison rather puny. Only a "little" bridge transmits Burbank to his "small" hotel; never having risen, he nonetheless "descended," and then "fell." Princess Volupine, too, despite her Jonsonian name, is "meagre," consumptive, and "blue-nailed" (connoting either ill health or execrable taste in cosmetics). She throws Burbank over for another man whose bathetic surname ("Klein" comes as something of a letdown after "Sir Ferdinand," as Eliot snootily urges by his arrangement of the line and stanza break) translates into the English "little."

After the comparison of ancient heroes to modern antiheroes, Eliot's fourth stanza glances forward, as its initial word, "But," signals. The stanza's first line echoes one from Browning's "How It Strikes a Contemporary," a poem full of references to seeing (its central figure, a poet, "watched" and "glanced" and seemed to see both the surface and the heart of everything and everyone) and knowing (various characters "conned," are "conscientious," and take "cognisance"). Quite unlike Browning's all-seeing, all-knowing poet, Bleistein also compares unfavorably with Antony and Cleopatra, and even with Burbank. Although shallow, Burbank packs his compendious if meager Baedeker, which at least shows his minimal interest in understanding what he encounters. He merely attends to culture; new money pretends to it; a decayed aristocracy trades on it. Bleistein, however, tours equipped only with a cigar and knows not what he sees. Here appears a characteristic aestheticist moment, which finds Eliot illiberally making social judgments on cultural grounds. Bleistein does not look at a picture; this is no *ekphrasis*. He views Venice itself: a "perspective" of Canaletto, not one of his canvases. But Bleistein fails to appreciate its beauty or how closely it and Canaletto's paintings – faithfully rendering turbid, glaucous water and mottled, flawed façades as well as Venetian splendor – resemble one another.

In *Italian Hours,* Henry James explains the aestheticist ideal that eludes Bleistein and places this episode in context. The passage suggests the distinctly aestheticist logic Eliot employs by setting the scene in Venice:

> The whole Venetian art-world is so near, so familiar, so much an extension and adjunct of the spreading actual, that it seems almost invidious to say one owes more to one of them than to the other. Nowhere, not even in Holland, where the correspondence between the real aspects and the little polished canvases is so constant and so exquisite, do art and life seem so interfused and, as it were, so consanguineous. All the splendour of light and colour, all the Venetian air and the Venetian history are on the walls and ceilings of the palaces; and all the genius of the masters, all the images and visions they have left upon the canvas, seem to tremble in the sunbeams and dance upon the waves. That is the perpetual interest of the place – that you live in a certain sort of knowledge as in a rosy cloud. You don't go into the churches and galleries by way of a change from the streets; you go into them because they offer you an exquisite reproduction of the things that surround you. All Venice was both model and painter, and life was so pictorial that art couldn't help becoming so. With all diminutions life is pictorial still, and this fact gives an extraordinary freshness to one's perception of the great Venetian works. You judge of them not as a connoisseur, but as a man of the world, and you enjoy them because they are so social and so true.[31]

Although a man of the world and certainly no connoisseur, Bleistein nonetheless fails to notice how pictorial Venice and realistic art converge. Eliot asserts James's epiphany negatively. James says anyone can see how ideal and beautiful Venice is. Eliot implies that one would have to be insensible not to see it and proceeds to illustrate the point:

> But this or such was Bleistein's way:
> A saggy bending of the knees
> And elbows, with the palms turned out

Uncomprehending, Bleistein does not see what the painter found in it. Blind to the aesthetic glories Venice invites him to enjoy, Bleistein responds with the baggy-pants gesture of the vaudevillian, the Philistine, and the tourist: a shrug.

Bleistein's vision is impaired. He sole eye is "lustreless" and "protrusive" (aggressive rather than receptive) and "stares" (instead of "observe," "regard," or "study") "from the protozoic slime." In a not atypical aestheticist misstep, Eliot implies that the inability to appreciate art and beauty constitutes grounds for exclusion from the human species. "Burbank" also operates from the antigenteel premise that it is better to give offense than to receive it. The poem deliberately violates the core genteel values of tolerance and inoffensiveness, perhaps the only aspects of gentility to have survived. But is the poem intentionally impolitic, or simply impolite? The group libel illustrates a danger of the aestheticist temperament, inflating the authority of art in proportion to its unwillingness to admit the claims of moral community or social necessity. To evaluate reality – and humanity – solely in terms of beauty and ugliness invites another kind of blindness, more willful than Bleistein's and with worse consequences. Possibly Eliot did not realize the danger; we read this language with the burden of hindsight, history having changed its meaning, making Eliot's error more pronounced. It nonetheless remains difficult to argue that it is much less flawed by having been written before the crimes that followed. The shortcomings of aestheticism, its harmful effects on intellectual conscience, fairness, and common decency, Eliot later came to acknowledge.[32]

If Burbank, Volupine, or Bleistein – or the gondoleer, for that matter – are to mean anything, a reader must nonetheless accept some of the social presumptions on which "Burbank" rests: the social territory, the before and after of their lives, how and why they visit Venice, what each brings to and expects from the visit, and how their behavior conforms to type. James explained the method:

> The power to guess the unseen from the seen, to trace the implication of things, to judge the whole piece by the pattern, the condition of feeling life, in general, so completely that you are well on your way to knowing any particular corner of it – this cluster of gifts may almost be said to constitute experience, and they occur in country and in town, and in the most differing stages of education.[33]

Eliot paid express tribute to this method by asserting that James's stories subordinated the characters to a relation, a situation, or an atmosphere. Eliot considered the "real hero" in James's stories to be a "social entity of which men and women are constituents." The weight of the cultural baggage required to interpret "Burbank" seems deliberately to discourage many readers, who might likely consider the "social entity" to which the poem's characters contribute as more villain than hero. Behaving as a cultural politician, Eliot both flatters and threatens his audience, who he once estimated, no doubt only half seriously, to number "about three thousand people in London and elsewhere."[34] His method is modern and mandarin, using erudite material without express generalization or transition, causing the cognoscenti little trouble and giving the ignoscenti little reason to expend any. The method implies that social and cultural knowledge force a reader to accept Eliot's conclusion: "The smoky candle end of time declines."

Whether this line winks at that other burning thing, Bleistein's cigar (or makes a terrible pun on Sir Ferdinand's surname), it links this poem's social caricature to Eliot's historical pessimism: The rotting city and its characters symbolize different kinds of decay, physical and cultural. In a fluid social structure (new money rising, old sinking) and a fluid substructure (as rats and tides nibble at the city's foundations), bad manners drive out good, and the water that carried commerce to create the wealth that built the city now undermines it. All these *stranieri* seem oblivious to this process save Burbank, and even he notes its least significant aspect. In a phrase that echoes "the smoky candle end of time declines," Burbank is described as "meditating on Time's ruins." ("Ruin," from the Latin *ruere*, "to fall," describes Burbank's fate while "together" with the princess. Eliot may also refer to a recent event of some symbolic importance. In 1902, the campanile of St. Mark's had collapsed. Its reconstruction, to the original design, was completed in 1912.) Eliot once defined "Baedeker culture" as "only an antiquarian piety towards the works of plastic art of the past."[35] The guidebook having told him that a winged lion symbolized the Venetian Republic, Burbank poses a question whose irrelevance reveals his superficiality:

> Who clipped the lion's wings
> And flea'd his rump and pared his claws?

He learns the fact, but misses its meaning. Burbank's question pertains absolutely, save for its fixated practicality ("Did Venice have a municipal wing clipper? A civic claw parer? Did they keep the lion in a cage?"). Eliot asks how Venice kept itself in working order. How did it keep the piling in repair? How did the island city's culture develop without being chased out by barbarians on shore? How did Venice resist its "money in furs" and develop instead its gemlike architecture and fine art? How did the city preserve a social consensus? (Does "the boatman smile" deferentially or with furtive, resentful knowledge of just how and why the princess will "entertain" Sir Ferdinand?) In short, why did Venice decline? And why does the past seem so much more heroic and beautiful than the present?

Burbank, inquiring about the winged lion's grooming, intended no more than that. Yet the poem considered as a whole asks the same question, incorporating Burbank's mundane particulars while looking far beyond them. Although superficially preoccupied with the antimyth of contemporary decay – the traffic of Philistines and philanderers and particularly the gruesome Volupine – the very negativity of "Burbank" counterpoints the myth of historical Venetian humanism, culture, and good governance.[36] Thus the poem requires not only a Jamesian alertness to social inference, but an aptitude for sensing positive cultural ideals that form the foundation – evidently fairly shaky, like the tenuous Venetian substructure – supporting Eliot's condemnation of contemporary behavior.

The contrast between glorious history and the shabby modern foreground recurs in "A Cooking Egg," though not without considerable variation in its purpose. "A Cooking Egg" at first seems to condemn the idea of an afterlife for rendering the question of earthly desires moot. Precisely because heaven makes these things unnecessary, one had better have them now, a notion Matthiessen suggests when he hears the poem echo Ruskin's response to Rose La Touche's death.[37] The key word is "want," whose double meaning Eliot evokes each time he uses it. Though one may certainly desire Honour and Capital passionately, "to want" in the third and fourth stanzas more likely means "to lack." After the lying together and a bridal reference to Lucretia Borgia, however, the fifth and sixth stanzas shift the meaning of "to want" toward "to desire." Honour, Capital, and Society – traditional objects of earthly acquisition and symbolic of the vanity of mundane desire: Seemingly worth everything on earth, they become valueless in heaven. As the speaker implies by her position as fourth in the series, so it is with Pipit. "I shall not want Pipit in Heaven": though echoing the comforting phrase from the Twenty-third Psalm, this wanting refers exclusively to earthly craving. "I want Pipit now."

Its dramatic situation placing it squarely in the *carpe diem* tradition, "A Cooking Egg" begins just after the speaker has sprung his sexual proposition. The genteel, naive Pipit, chaperoned by images of dead, respectable ancestors, sits upright in shock at the speaker's unwelcome advance. She reminds him that carnal sin will bar his spirit from heaven and that to enjoy eternal togetherness, he and she must chastely practice forbearance on earth. Surprisingly, instead of quoting Matthew 22:30, he answers by accepting these premises but reversing their conclusion. He affirms that his desire for her is purely earthly and thus will surely vanish with the body once they meet again in heaven. He uses the terms of Pipit's own argument to refute it: It is fallacious to reason that earthly sin will prevent carnal enjoyment in heaven, since heaven transfigures the nature of pleasure. Once divested of the body, the soul becomes carnally disinterested. So it is disingenuous to argue against consummation of earthly desire by reference to exclusion from heaven on that basis. No similar consummation can occur there, no matter what on earth Pipit and the speaker decide to do or not to do. Pipit's heaven may be a lovely place, in other words, but none in fact do there embrace.

If its central stanzas implicitly assert the exclusively present tense of carnal desire and the irrelevance of such desire in heaven, the poem concludes on a far less excited note. The penny world behind the screen – a heightened, private dream of desire provoked – dwindles to a mood of desire disappointed and deferred. Instead of a comfortable sitting room, the speaker broods over tea in lonely, grim surroundings. Perhaps what he observes forces him to dwell upon how he resembles the other sad, aimless city dwellers. His ardent argument, his heroic use of intellectual rigor to urge sexual conquest, has failed. He now possesses neither Honour, Capital, Society, nor Pipit. As implied comparisons to his own debacle or as distractions from it, he sees images of decline in history and in his surroundings. Each results in an image of buried life, of energy spent, of historical and emotional entropy. The poem's form seems to recapitulate this diffusion. At the height of his appeal, the speaker combined wit and erudition in rhyming stanzas. But at this low point, bathos and formal irregularity break the pattern. Two "ubi sunt" questions, counterpoised with careful irony, transport the poem from the present to the past and back again. The sequence suggests that any hope of success with Pipit now remains as irretrievably remote as Roman imperial glory. Rhyming "crumpets" with "trumpets" sardonically deflates that line's momentary poetic flight, as the failed speaker returns to a bleak, solitary present.

Then rhyme vanishes from the poem altogether: "A.B.C.'s" does not rhyme with "crumpets," implying that the poem's form crumbles in a way that parallels the speaker's dispersed melancholy. The effect differs from simple bathos: The poem suddenly descends from its brief sublimity, but crash-lands into a depressing mood, not a ridiculous one. Though it earlier soared with insinuating confidence, the poem now spins out of control in a sort of poetic vertigo. Rejection vanquishes desire; contemporary squalor overwhelms images of historic glory. The speaker meant to pose a clear and present amorous danger, but has gone down in the flames of his own ardor. He succumbs to a mood of futility, leaving his poem wanting even the pleasure of rhyme that its form would lead us to desire.

"A Cooking Egg" seems to remember something Eliot wrote two years earlier when reviewing a philosophical treatment of education. There Eliot argued that students should be taught to respect truth, beauty, and goodness for their own sake, instead of for whatever prudential reward those values might bring. Eliot called the "aesthetic activity" no less important than the love either of truth or of knowledge. He then explains that sexuality might offer the only available "escape from a prosaic world" to a boy whose childhood had contained no beauty and who had not acquired a detached curiosity for it. If such was a danger, a greater catastrophe might follow: passing from violent excitement to a "maturity of commonplace." As both a prophylaxis to and a release from these twin horrors, Eliot recommends learning to love with the passions of the spirit, which he alleges to be disinterested, inexhaustible, and permanently satisfying.[38] "A Cooking Egg" renders the thrill of a sexual gambit and its potential for escape from a prosaic world of knitting and faded ancestral portraits. Although excluding a "maturity of commonplace," however, it also convincingly illustrates emotional defeat. Arguably, the positive pole to which "A Cooking Egg" makes no express reference but which it nonetheless embodies is precisely the – Bradleyan? Christian? aestheticist? – ideal of the "detached curiosity for beauty" and the disinterested exercise of spiritual, permanent passions.

This analysis of "A Cooking Egg" implies that when Eliot wrote the quatrain poems he was willing to flout his predisposition to respect religious belief. Indeed, both the profane argument of "A Cooking Egg" and the blunt, if conventional, satire of "The Hippopotamus" (making the customary objection to the way the institutional habits of churches compromise their spiritual mandate) inch fairly close to blasphemy. Could their irreverence have led Eliot years later to attempt their ex post facto defense? In "Baudelaire" he called blasphemy, when not purely verbal but genuine in spirit, a product of partial belief. Such blasphemy, he argued, because it was as impossible to the atheist as it was to the perfect Christian, was a way of affirming belief.[39]

Poems, 1920, however, also contained an express criticism of skepticism in "Gerontion," a portrait of religious disillusion and despair. In "Gerontion," "we would see a sign," but none appears. "After such knowledge, what forgiveness?" None comes forward. What so many characters in the quatrain poems lack, Gerontion possesses in disastrous quantity: He pursues consciousness of history and of self to the furthest extreme. Many critics have observed how Gerontion's mood and problem resemble Prufrock's. Both characters question the worth of thought or action. Both poems end "unhappily," one in dreams, the other in sleep. Both concern time, eternity, and the way they relate to passion.

Bluntly put, they suggest that passion relates to time and eternity unsuccessfully and that passion and metaphysics may be irreconcilable.

"Prufrock" and "Gerontion" also illustrate Eliot's skill in creating a voice and persona. We ordinarily hear private feelings with a sympathetic rather than a critical attitude, taking for granted that sincerity (for some reason associated with vulnerability, crisis, or grief) and the discourse and pose that render it must be taken seriously. Prufrock and Gerontion speak in tones implying accord on fundamental assumptions, yet revealing themselves in a private way, with apparently unreserved candor. It seems as close as poetry comes to reproducing the quality of intimacy between two people – friends, lovers, or family – who feel they may confide in one another.

Caveat lector. The manner also reminds us that the voice extending these privacies belongs to a stranger, warning us to reserve judgment. Prufrock began with the formal "Let us go then, you and I," but ended having enticed the unwary into his collapse: "Till human voices wake us, and we drown." Gerontion plaintively introduces himself, his past, and his home. Suddenly, however, as in "Prufrock," the "I" becomes "us" in the long fourth verse paragraph. Even greater intimacy follows: The archaic sincerity of "I would meet you upon this honestly" may seem abrupt until the speaker proceeds.

> I have lost my sight, smell, hearing, taste, and touch:
> How should I use them for your closer contact?

This qualified confidence, simultaneously disconcerting and authoritative, repelling and compelling, suggests a final similarity between "Prufrock" and "Gerontion." Both share an unstable poetic voice. It is one thing for a poem's speaker to argue a point of view to the reader; it is another for a speaker to argue with himself and to change his mind as he goes along, as Prufrock and Gerontion do. From one vantage point, the ideas held by Prufrock (that the future has nothing to offer) and Gerontion (that the past has no meaning) demand to be rejected, if only because they make sanity, action, and life itself problematical and even impossible, practically speaking. Poetry, to be sure, cannot dispense with truth about life quite so pragmatically. But if history has no meaning, neither has the self, its memories and experiences rendered mere interpretations, subject to continual revision. "Gerontion" appeared at a moment when the historical cataclysm of World War I had brought all these assumptions into question.

Published in 1920, "Gerontion" contains several references to that conflict and its aftermath. The war, inflicting 16 million casualties and widespread political collapse, woke Europe to its vulnerability. Gerontion calls his home a "decayed house," the goat coughs, the woman sneezes, and Gerontion, a "little old man," has lost his five senses. Gerontion eventually labels his nearly insane (or senile) conceits simply "tenants" and drought thoughts. Contemplating a latent confusion that the war accelerated and the peace exposed, Eliot (as Adams had done) measured decline from a medieval ideal to its modern antithesis. Eliot argued that even with its dissensions and filth, Dante's Europe was more united mentally than the modern world could conceive. Eliot did not trace nationalism and its separation of nation from nation to the Treaty of Versailles, but instead asserted that the "process of disintegration which for our generation culminates in that treaty" began shortly after Dante lived.[40]

Indeed, Eliot's background may have predisposed him to see these symptoms of decline. Eliot's St. Louis and Boston youth deposited images like a decaying house – a building as well as a family – other sordid urban imagery, and social pressures from below. His family, in a gesture almost symbolic of its values in response to changing times, retreated by standing still. In St. Louis his grandmother followed her natural desire to stay in the house her husband, Rev. Eliot, had built. Eliot's own father did not want to leave the house he had established close by. Thus the family unwittingly became the victim of the eternal pattern of instability, development, and decline that afflicts American cities. Even after all their friends had moved to fashionable areas farther west, Eliot remembered that he and his family "lived on in a neighborhood which had become shabby to a degree approaching slumminess."[41] This palpable decline received municipal reinforcement when, by the late nineteenth century, Chicago had clearly eclipsed St. Louis, which in the early 1900s felt further humiliated by revelations of big-city political corruption.[42]

Besides the decay of a neighborhood and a city, the history of Eliot's family, his class, and their place in America stained Eliot's sensibility. The victory of Jacksonian democracy over Quincy Adams's federalism still reverberated, tinging American history with a pessimism Eliot related directly to that event, reflected in his proprietary sense that "*our America*" ended with Jackson's election.[43] That victory, and later the Civil War, contradicted a historical pattern whose moral integrity Henry Adams, Eliot, and those of their cultural group had formerly assumed. Their assumption extended at least as far back as the American Whigs, who traced their values and political institutions to English precedent, English historical culture, and their development in the United States. The Whigs discerned in the pattern a divinely inspired historicism that had universal import, authorizing "progress" as improvement in the human condition, more political liberty, increased power over nature, elevated moral standards, and richer quality of life.[44] Adams repudiated nearly all of these values, especially the notion of historical progress. So did Eliot, with a qualification. Arguably, Eliot's return to England may simply reflect the impulse of his cultural group to see itself as an American continuation of English society rather than an abrupt break with it. If this is so, then his transplantation to England reveals the depth of such cultural origins, to which Eliot remained loyal and on which he was prepared to base life decisions. Culture matters, Eliot's life might seem to say, more than nationality.

From this point of view, for instance, a revolutionary war did not upset the historical pattern or discard its associated values; instead, a war of independence confirmed them. A political failure had occurred, but cultural continuity persisted to flourish through the federal period.[45] Thus cultural rupture came not with political independence, but much later. Eliot, in fact, called the real American revolution not the eighteenth-century conflict, but a "consequence of the Civil War." For him, as for James and Adams, the triple engine of industrial plutocracy, breakneck expansion, and immigration issued from that social trauma. Although his family was strongly pro-Union, Eliot more than once expressed regret at the war's unforeseen social consequences.[46]

The sensibility disillusioned in Europe after World War I may have been trained to evoke that response in post–Civil War America. Fought to uphold idealism and preserve a status quo, these wars demolished them both. This paradox, implicit in Santayana's, James's, and Adams's view of society after the American Civil War, generates the emotional and intellectual issue "Gerontion" addresses in Europe after World War I. Battlefield casualties, unscrupulous war profiteers, political collapse, and what Eliot considered a defective peace treaty: Eliot's writing frequently expressed his sense of the injuries World War I inflicted upon traditional Europe. This awareness prompts Gerontion's question, "After such knowledge, what forgiveness?" and the passage on history that follows it.

In 1955, "The Literature of Politics" paraphrased the central paragraph in "Gerontion."[47] Probably as a concession to the occasion, "A Conservative Political Centre Literary Luncheon," Eliot's reconsideration remains inexact. Urging the impossibility of infallible prediction, it solicits assent from personal experience rather than from history. Recognizing the necessity of adapting to what is new and unexpected, it contains a measure of optimism having no equivalent in "Gerontion." In most respects, however, Eliot's paraphrase restates the poem's fourth paragraph. "Unnatural vices are fathered by our heroism" compares to "every reform leads to new abuses"; "Virtues are forced upon us by our impudent crimes" becomes the more polite "Sometimes our most irrational blunders have the most happy results." Even Eliot's connection of political action and blindness (suggesting that we move in dusky light, with failing sight) echoes Gerontion's sightlessness (and perhaps the Platonic allegory of the cave). Even its most bland assertions, that no formula for prediction exists, and that unforeseen consequences arise from our acts, summarize Gerontion's idea about history.

The poem's middle passage expounds that rule of unintended consequences. If action has consequences other than intended ones, while inaction – by negative inference – has predictable consequences, then action, because arbitrary, becomes irrational. This reasoning seems to make inaction not only a rational choice, but the preferred one. The passage does not, however, take the next logical step, which would be to ask whether inactivity had not itself consequences as definite as action. How then does inaction differ from action, especially insofar as the condemnation of action supposes that an action's effect diverges from its cause? To choose to act involves motive, or intent: the desire that an act will produce the result intended. "Gerontion" argues that history intervenes between a cause and its intended result. Inaction, however, also involves motive and intent, insofar as the choice not to act proceeds from a desire to produce no result. More to the point, history as set forth in "Gerontion" would likewise intervene between this inactive cause and effect. Hence action and inaction cannot be distinguished by arguing that the former produces unintended consequences, while the latter does not.

History, in "Gerontion" an *un*designing woman, appeals to vanity, confuses motive, and scrambles connections between cause and effect. To thwart every means of imposing a pattern upon history – to say an action's results cannot be predicted – demoralizes Gerontion. Feeling likewise at the mercy of historical forces, Henry Adams had tried to solve his spiritual and intellectual confusion by interpreting his life as affected by historical events. Adams went further, however, asking history to perform several religious functions. That is, though subject to interpretation, history did actually happen; like religion, it defines what is real and what is not. By a soul or spirit, a religion may also define a person's inner reality, and by abstracting from human behavior through time, history may deduce an entelechy, a consistency of personality and motive – the equivalent of a soul or human nature – from the multiplicity of human activity. Finally, history may suggest goals and attempt to predict the future, thus resembling religious prophecy. Adams's religion of history failed, however, because he could not establish sequence and relation, which undercut the meaning history had initially seemed to offer. Neither could it offer Adams any pattern of consistent human motive or personality. And since no pattern supported a "science of history" – which would in turn have legitimized prophecy – Adams was left lying before the Gallery of Machines at the Great Exposition of 1900, his "historical neck broken."

The same paralysis afflicts Gerontion, who not only personifies history as a woman, but deifies history as a goddess. The sexually suggestive, ambiguous diction ("cunning passages, contrived corridors and issues") further reveals Gerontion's history to be a wily, seductive, unpredictable goddess, bestowing her gifts in an inconsistent, destructive fashion. Thus redefined, history emerges as a divine femme fatale, an object of both profane and holy desire. On one hand, "Gerontion" is part sermon. Consider the "history" paragraph: the hypophoric "After such knowledge, what forgiveness?" followed by a series of anaphoric imperatives ("Think . . .") and descriptions ("gives . . ."). Explication – or, here, the listing – of paradox is a favorite sermonic device, seeking to explain the divine in words. On the other hand, "Gerontion" departs from public utterance; it is also part confession, seeking through words to purge the soul of what separates it from divinity. History thus becomes an object of passion, to be desired, as well as a goddess of power, to be propitiated. History arouses vanity, but also frustrates it, promising tantalizing rewards in order to withhold them.

At least in its central passage, "Gerontion" does speak coherently of history, if only to pronounce history incoherent when judged against moral criteria. The poem asserts a history and humanity at cross-purposes. History never provides a nation or civilization with what it needs, when it needs it. Paradoxically, history has bad timing, giving too late and too soon. More insidiously, history has a perverse sense of audience, is untrustworthy, and plays upon vanity and weakness so as to divorce action from morality:

> Think
> Neither fear nor courage saves us. Unnatural vices
> Are fathered by our heroism. Virtues
> Are forced upon us by our impudent crimes.

The sexual anxiety of "unnatural" vices and "impudent" crimes, which are "fathered" and "forced," suggests a mixture of anger, betrayal, and disgust at the illogic of history, that the things it "propagates" – wisdom, experience, morality, honesty, and even pragmatism – have so little relevance when humanity contemplates them to discover their pattern. Virtue, heroism, courage, ambition, and passion become synonyms for vice, crime, fear, vanity, and confusion. Without pattern or purpose, history careens toward the entropy of "fractured atoms." Gerontion's malaise represents what Eliot in 1917 had called a skeptical, empty generation, "sick with its own knowledge of history."[48]

A collapse of intellectual order thus evokes a collapse of personal volition. Many modernists and aestheticists, their intellectual categories crushed and emptied by contemporary history, avenged its chaos by abandoning it. For Adams, the parallel edifices of Thomistic theology and the Gothic cathedral's stained glass and stone realized medieval perfection. Eliot embodied his intellectual, theological, and historical ideal in Dante's *Divine Comedy*. Yet as Frank Kermode and others have noted, Eliot's historicizing conforms to other aspects of his thought. What characterizes "Prufrock," "Gerontion," and *The Waste Land* – the sense that the mind is at war with itself, split, or dissolving – also pervades Eliot's conclusions about history. Eliot's most famous historical interpretation, the dissociation of sensibility, is significantly a *mental* symptom, occasioned by a war. If seventeenth-century poets "possessed a mechanism of sensibility which could devour any kind of experience," why could that mechanism not "devour" the experience of a civil war, blamed for destroying the sensibility? Kermode has argued that Eliot's theory implicitly paralleled a mid-seventeenth-century Fall of Man, whose soul thereafter became irrevocably divided against itself.[49] Kermode persuasively urges that Eliot converted the era before the English Civil War into an object of historical nostalgia, due mainly to the heroic, colorful, dramatic nature of the Anglican church. Since, as Kermode tells us, the symptoms of the dissociation appear before the mid-seventeenth century, and outside England, the theory reveals less about a time and place in history than it does about Eliot's designs upon it.

But if the dissociation of sensibility responds primarily to Eliot's interpretive needs, what does the theory reveal about them? His statements add a personal, American dimension to the theory, insofar as it may restate nineteenth-century American history as a historical Fall.[50] In its prelapsarian state, Adams's and Eliot's people led and governed. Fought for the best moral reasons (at least from the New England viewpoint), the Civil War unforeseeably released forces that compromised some of their moral premises nearly as much as slavery had. After the Civil War, an articulate segment of those people, morally disillusioned and socially displaced, found themselves living in a society drifting out of focus. Eliot professed this view when he called the American Civil War "certainly the greatest disaster in the whole of American history," from which the United States had not recovered and might never recover. He concluded by criticizing the readiness to assume that the good effects of wars, if any, persist and that time obliterates their ill effects.[51] On another occasion, Eliot stated that reading *I'll Take My Stand* would force a New Englander to admit that the Civil War and its aftermath ruined that region in the same way it ruined the South and, moreover, that New England had been ruined first.[52] Eliot witnessed the moral community to which he had belonged allow itself to be dislodged, in a sense the victim of its own ideals. Neglecting to develop an ideology of conservatism or permanence, having destroyed its Southern counterpart, and lacking the reserves of status, obligation, or attachment to the land it might have relied upon in Europe, it failed to ensure its self-preservation.

Such social experience may influence the range of a poet's imagination, training him to notice certain things and ignore others, and to interpret in a certain way. In Eliot's case, the "accumulated sensations of his first twenty-one years" left an acutely historical, social, pessimistic sensibility. Some of these sensations doubtless originated in his family and its membership in a social group that remembered its own ascendancy and now uneasily contemplated its decline. Others probably originated in a more general, public way. American society by 1900 had tripled its size, filled up much of a continent, fought a civil war, experienced an industrial revolution, and welcomed the largest migration in history, all within three generations. Such developments hardly encourage permanence, traditional culture, or social stability. Eliot nevertheless grew up amid these minority values, whose decline influenced his writing, as for instance, his characteristic imagery of burial and drowning, remnants and waste, as well as his preference for exhausted personae, older than himself.[53]

It also occasioned a long engagement with issues of value, action, life, and meaning. For all his supposed impersonality, Eliot distributed intensely personal obiter dicta throughout his essays, in such moments writing a kind of confessional criticism. One example, "Cyril Tourneur," written in 1930, seems to dismiss the apocalyptic strain in "Gerontion," *The Waste Land,* and "The Hollow Men," all but comparing them to nursery rhymes:

> We are apt to expect of youth only a fragmentary view of life; we incline to see youth as exaggerating the importance of its narrow experience and imagining the world as did Chicken Licken. But occasionally the intensity of the vision of its own ecstasies or horrors, combined with a mastery of word and rhythm, may give to a juvenile work a universality which is beyond the author's knowledge of life to give, and to which mature men and women can respond.

Here Eliot chooses to comment sagely upon "The Love Song of J. Alfred Prufrock," possibly "juvenile" because based on narrow experience, but nonetheless containing an "intensity of vision" and a "mastery of words and rhythm." Without warning, however, Eliot then transforms reminiscence into revelation:

> The cynicism, the loathing and disgust of humanity, expressed consummately in *The Revenger's Tragedy,* are immature in the respect that they exceed the object. Their objective equivalents are characters practising their grossest vices; characters which seem merely to be spectres projected from the poet's inner world of nightmare, some horror be-

yond words. So the play is a document on humanity chiefly because it is a document on one human being, Tourneur; its motive is truly the death motive, for it is the loathing and horror of life itself. To have realized this motive so well is a triumph; for the hatred of life is an important phase – even, if you like, a mystical experience – in life itself.[54]

Eliot expressed these sentiments after acquiring a religious orientation from which to evaluate his earlier life and career, but links to his earlier poems seem evident. He had long been interested in mystical experience and had apparently himself experienced the "loathing and horror of life itself"; his poetry from 1917 to 1925 at moments seems preoccupied with the "death motive." "The Hollow Men," in particular, and parts of *The Waste Land* if not "Gerontion" as well, seem to reflect something like a mystical experience arising from the "hatred of life."

Eliot's remarks point to a process of creation in which Eliot's personal past confronted public history, a confrontation whose initial stages produced an immature cynicism exceeding its object. It nevertheless made possible the conviction in the voice of "Gerontion," allowing Eliot to objectify his own experience of historical decline and to discuss public matters emotively. Nevertheless, we may scarcely regard Gerontion and his ideas as purely autobiographical expression. Like Prufrock, Gerontion and his failure embody a warning. Historical chaos, that is, may cause demoralization, and to conceive of memory and history as Gerontion does may reproduce his withdrawal into psychological and rhetorical disintegration. The poem does not quote Adams accidentally or gratuitously; it portrays a mind dissolving. As his review of *The Education* indicates, Eliot approached its ideas on familiar terms, linking them to Adams's social position, family, the "Boston doubt," and skeptical Unitarianism. Although not destructive, Eliot said, this mental attitude – which was also a cultural inheritance – was nonetheless dissolvent. Where Adams stepped, the ground did not simply give way; it "flew into particles."[55] This skeptical dust, further decomposed, finds its way into Gerontion's "fractured atoms."

But to leave the matter there and identify Gerontion's ideas with those of Eliot leaves a reading of the poem that is both too innocent and too passive. For all their similarities, Eliot also criticized Adams from a point of view outside their shared background, taxing him for "immaturity" insofar as his erudition lacked a "sensuous" component.[56] Eliot's evaluation – one of many voicing this idea – echoes Bradley's distinction between feeling and thought, which "The Metaphysical Poets" would elaborate two years later. Though "notably erudite," Adams failed to incorporate his erudition into his sensibility. Unlike the metaphysical poets, Adams revealed no "direct sensuous apprehension of thought," no "recreation of thought into feeling."[57] "The Metaphysical Poets" argues that this failure, far from being peculiar to Adams, became widespread after the seventeenth century, causing an inability to make sense of diverse ideas or disparate experience. In a unified sensibility, the poet's mind compels heterogeneous material into unity. Furthermore, unlike the ordinary man's chaotic, irregular, fragmentary experience, the poet can amalgamate disparate experience into a new whole.[58]

Gerontion's mind cannot perform this Bradleyan process. He perceives heterogeneous material, but cannot fuse it into categories, or "wholes." To be sure, Gerontion, a former warrior, is a man of action, not a poet. Everyone, however, must to some degree make this relating, unifying effort. There is nothing peculiarly poetic about it. As Eliot wrote earlier, describing Bradleyan, transcendent logic, the soul must unify jarring, incompatible viewpoints by passing to a higher one that shall include them.[59] Though certainly analogous to poetic metaphor, on an ordinary level this process means simply trying to make sense of one's experience.

If the metaphysical poets had a sensibility that could "devour" disparate experience, Gerontion clearly lacks it. Like the victims of the dissociation, Gerontion has "revolted against the ratiocinative, the descriptive"; he thinks and feels "by fits, unbalanced"; he "reflects." Though lucid at times, at others Gerontion simply makes no sense, dispensing with the proprieties of discourse. He violates the first rule of rhetoric: He does not consider his audience. Lines like "rocks, moss, stonecrop, iron, merds" or the section following "In depraved May" observe only the most minimal structures of either intellectual or emotional logic. Perhaps rocks, moss, stonecrop (the popular name for *Sedum,* a genus of succulent perennials or subshrubs of the orpine family), iron, and merds share a connection other than overtones of sterility, coldness, or disgust; it seems impossible to say. Though the assembly seems only a particularly oblique and pointless instance of Eliot's sensitivity to ethnic multiplicity, Silvero, Hakagawa, de Tornquist, and von Kulp might actually communicate in some cognizable ceremony. Yet the speaker, whose emotional state so overwhelms him that it makes ordinary logical, dramatic, and syntactic considerations irrelevant, offers little basis to say for sure.[60] Who are "De Bailhache, Fresca, Mrs. Cammel"? Does the poem tell why, or in what sense, they are "whirled beyond the circuit of the shuddering Bear in fractured atoms"?

That it does not remains a crucial fact about Gerontion, especially once we notice how "Gerontion" and "The Metaphysical Poets," appearing in 1920 and 1921, set forth positive and negative versions of a single set of premises. In each case historical change produces rhetorical decay, a symptom of mental disconnection. In "Gerontion," Eliot portrays a dissociated sensibility through rhetorical breakdown, paralleling World War I's aftermath to the way the English Civil War dissociated the seventeenth century's sensibility. Experience that it cannot "compel into unity" overwhelms Gerontion's mind. It is possible, even likely, that Gerontion expressed Eliot's own disappointment and outrage that Europe had buried so much of its past in a world war, or simply chose to forget it. One does not want to push this speculation too far, however. Eliot is not Gerontion, and recognizing the limits of Adams's view of history, he is not Henry Adams, either.

To think history will conform to one's own expectations, especially if they are moral ones, seems a risky, even futile, enterprise. As the poem ends, a change in Gerontion's attitude seems to acknowledge these limitations:

> What will the spider do,
> Suspend its operations, will the weevil
> Delay?

Clearly not: the spider and weevil, agents of eternal decay – evidently the one thing that *can* be counted on in history – "suspend" their activity under no circumstances, least of all for sentiments such as his. Gerontion's bitter lament changes nothing, and he knows it. The dead end of history may not even be worth bothering with. Eliot himself ultimately elected a religious truth whose divine chronology existed outside secular history's designless sequence.

Eliot's American roots and his uneasy relation to them influenced his social and historical imagination long after the poems that allude, on one level or another, to an "unsettled" society.[61] "Gerontion" forms only a preliminary part of that process, expressing the despair absolute values feel upon discovering their relativity. For Eliot, in other words, modernity implied historical self-consciousness. Unlike the past, modern times can no longer view history as a development of an organizing tradition. Statements to the contrary in "Tradition and the Individual Talent," for instance, reflect that essay's prescriptive ambition, which remains at odds with the descriptive viewpoint Eliot's poetry adopts, expressing his empirical sense of how unfamiliar the modern world seemed compared with what led up to it. Before the modern era, at least for the sake of Eliot's argument, historical consciousness tended to emphasize continuity more than difference between past and present. Eliot's historicism, by contrast, acknowledged the divergence of modernity from history even as it tried, with only intermittent success, to resurrect the resemblances. Eliot could not fuse ancient and modern without the torsions of bathos, incongruity, irony, disillusion, and pessimism. Hence his exultant exposition of Joyce's solution to the problem in *Ulysses,* which Eliot reviewed in 1923.

Joyce's "mythical method," manipulating a "continuous parallel between contemporaneity and antiquity," supplies what Gerontion's disintegrating mind could not. Gerontion had found no link between cause and effect, or past and present; he saw no coherence in human personality or motive. Myth, however, can create these things, implying that people behave in one sense outside time, that on some level their consciousness preserves some consistency – some "identical reference" – despite time's changes. Linking past and present, this consistency posits a more or less finite range of human nature and implies that if behavior falls within that range, so will its consequences. Such an implication to some extent restores cause and effect, all but demolished by Adams's historical cynicism.

Instead of ordering history by time sequences, the mythic method categorizes human personality and behavior into types, which may thus become typical, or even archetypal. Since it is both exterior and interior, the method moves well beyond an art of caricature and its quite different use of types. Mythic typicality nevertheless retains the enormous benefit of implying that these types may be finite in number. It also promises that we may apprehend ourselves and our behavior not only through conventional mythology, but through anthropology, ethnology, psychology, and even – Eliot perhaps giving in too readily to the moment – astrology. The mythic method offers a solution to Gerontion's problems, finding meaning where he can find none and giving shape and significance to the "immense panorama of futility and anarchy which is contemporary history."[62]

To describe contemporary history as "futility and anarchy" reveals the key point of identical reference between Gerontion and Eliot. Yet by comparing contemporary history to a "panorama," Eliot significantly chooses an aestheticist metaphor to describe how the modern world perceives history, as an unending spool of time on which images appear and reappear.[63] Because American history moved in a different direction than Adams, James, Santayana, and Eliot wished, they argued that history had lost its meaning and began seeking ways to make sense of it again. Art was one of these; it may well be that the prime motive behind American aestheticism was to appeal history's verdict in the higher court of art.

Having dispensed with time sequences in favor of psychologically and anthropologically patterned, timeless "types," Eliot concludes that "instead of narrative method, we may now use the mythical method. It is, I seriously believe, a step toward making the modern world possible for art."[64] "Making the modern world possible for art": This phrase makes as good a summary of the aestheticist contribution to literary modernism as we are likely to find. Note how nearly it verges on paradox, apparently saying that the modern world exists as material for art, and how it necessarily implies that the modern world may also *resist* artistic treatment. By negative implication, the statement suggests that art might *fail* to give shape and significance, that modern reality might simply outrun the resources of art. Eliot's tone releases an audible sigh of relief that Joyce's innovation has delayed that vacuum by the skin of its mythological teeth.

The phrase "making the modern world possible for art," then, recollects Eliot's aestheticist loyalty to the idea that the world exists as material for art, and not the other way around. Art is preexistent, valuable in and of itself, timeless and unchanging, and monumental (as in Part I of "Tradition and the Individual Talent"). The phrase further suggests that art redeems time and human life in a quasi-religious way. So does the mythic method, supposing that contemporary behavior confirms ancient types. This is why the method offers both a way of importing the past into the present and a way of remaining resolutely modern – that is to say, aware of the past, as Eliot put it, "in a way and to an extent which the past's awareness of itself cannot show."[65] Historical self-consciousness becomes a distinctly modern trait, as Eliot notes when he defends Samuel Johnson against the charge of "obtuseness." He argued that in Johnson's time a historical sense had not yet appeared. Johnson thus could teach the modern, historically self-conscious era that the only choice was to develop the historical sense further, if only by understanding a critic, such as Johnson, in whom it was not apparent.[66]

The mythic method may rescue the modern world, and the modern mind, from the fetters of historical consciousness. The method gives shape and significance to randomness and gives form to the world and to consciousness, a gift that supports sanity instead of hobbling it. Here historical consciousness and aestheticism converge. Artistic beauty had initially rendered time and materiality purposeless and ugly; without art, time passed unredeemed, and the material world disorganized consciousness. The mythic method, however, reasserts artistic, historical, and conscious form, adding value to art, time, and consciousness, placing these things into a pattern deduced from historical culture, as interpreted by modern methods. The method detectably influences Eliot's later work, such as "Journey of the Magi," "A Song for Simeon," *Murder in the Cathedral,* and to an extent his other plays. In those works Eliot aligns historical eras, showing how emotions, events, and dramatic situations parallel one another. He puts modern words in ancient mouths, and ancient plots on modern ground.[67]

His solution contains an irony. It was the amorphous self that made the world seem so ugly and formless in the first place, dispatching the fragile consciousness to find value in art that it could not locate either within or beyond itself. The mythic method, discovered by means of art, is not a dissolving but a resolving influence. This may have been what it provided Eliot, who four years after reviewing *Ulysses* in these terms committed himself to the traditional Western myth, Christianity. In Eliot's case, aestheticism provided him with an avenue of retreat from an ugly, immoral world and a chaotic self. But it also pointed out the path – Christianity – by which he could redeem the world's ugliness and mortality, and unify himself.

6

Being Between Two Lives: Reading The Waste Land

[Dandyism is] above all a burning need to acquire originality, within the apparent bounds of convention. It is a sort of cult of oneself, which can dispense even with what are commonly called illusions. It is the delight in causing astonishment, and the proud satisfaction of never oneself being astonished.

Charles Baudelaire, "The Painter of Modern Life"

Man is an analogist, and studies relations in all objects.

Emerson, "Nature"

The essential Relativity of all knowledge, thought, or consciousness cannot but show itself in language. If everything that we know is viewed as a transition from something else, every experience must have two sides; and either every name must have a double meaning, or else for every meaning there must be two names.

Alexander Bain, *Logic: Deductive and Inductive*, Book 1, Chapter 1

Though it is rare to find a discussion that does not add to one's understanding of *The Waste Land,* a sense nonetheless persists that something about the poem remains disembodied, out of context, just beyond critical reach. However necessary, the decades of source hunting and literary sleuthing proved to be only an intermediate stage that, far from slowing down the proliferation of interpretation, probably accelerated it. Despite renewed attention to *The Waste Land* recently, asking "How do we read this poem?" remains a legitimate question. Perhaps it is the only question. Yet as if this fundamental inquiry were not difficult enough, the subsidiary problems of linking *The Waste Land* to Eliot's prose criticism and fitting it into his poetic development also remain to be explored.

We perhaps rightly do not know just how to regard *The Waste Land.* It

is not inconceivable that the poem that causes our confusion might deliberately have been designed to create it. The manuscript evidence suggests
that Eliot himself felt differently about it as he went along, changing his
procedure as the poem developed. A change of procedure is a change of
emphasis, and therefore of meaning, which in turn reflects matters in
Eliot's career that happened before and after *The Waste Land*. These
remarks try to shed some light on the rights and responsibilities the
reader may expect, and must accept, upon picking up Eliot's poem.

As is well known, Eliot's earliest poems imitated Laforgue (and other
nineteenth-century French poets) and the Jacobean dramatists. In a 1939
letter, "Eliot parle de l'influence de Laforgue comme d'une 'espèce de
possession par une personnalité plus puissante,' comme d'une possession
démoniaque."[1] Eliot discovered Laforgue in Arthur Symons's *The Symbolist Movement in Literature*, some of whose judgments and language
today seem quaint but which contains many passages reminding us how
deeply the book nourished Eliot's imagination. Eliot felt indebted to
Symons, and acknowledged that by leading him to Laforgue and to the
other French Symbolists, Symons's book had affected his life.[2] The
book's main themes – self-consciousness; the problematic nature of
human identity and a corresponding interest in essence versus exteriority; the Symbolist cultivation of strangeness; the idea of universal analogy and correspondences; the need for masks; the conventionality of
time; the extremes of solipsism, mysticism, and aestheticism – all appear
at some stage of Eliot's work.

Laforgue, however, influenced not only Eliot's poetry, but his personality as well. Symons quotes Gustave Kahn's impression of his friend
Laforgue: "D'allures? . . . fort correctes, de hauts gibus, des cravates
sobres, des vestons anglais, des pardessus clergymans, et de par les néces-
sités, un parapluie immuablement placé sous le bras."[3] Conrad Aiken,
Eliot's best friend during his Harvard years, called him a "singularly
attractive, tall, and rather dapper young man." After a year in Paris, Eliot
returned to Harvard "perceptibly Europeanized: he made a point, for a
while, a conspicuously un-American point, of carrying a cane – was it a
malacca? – a little self-conscious about it, and complaining that its 'nice
conduct' was no such easy matter."[4] Aiken would later render Eliot as

> an extremely controlled, precise, disciplined person – as much so in his
> own life as in his poetry. . . . "Manners" is an obsolete word nowa-
> days, but he had them. . . . Sometimes I've thought Tom might have
> liked to have been an actor. . . . His urge for the theatre was uncon-
> querable. There was some of the actor in Tom and some of the clown,
> too. For all his liturgical appearance (he only lacked a turned-around
> collar, it sometimes seemed) he was capable of real buffoonery.

Eliot, it seems, borrowed more than Laforgue's irony. The diffidence, the manners correct almost to superciliousness, the severe, nearly liturgical costume, the cane (later transformed into his notorious umbrellas, custom-made with outsized handles, with which in the early 1920s Eliot once defended a performance of "Le Sacre du Printemps" from the audience's derision), and the clownish or ironic undertone: All suggest that Laforgue legitimized aspects of Eliot's sensibility and behavior.[5] The borrowing from Laforgue seems to have been a double one – with a serious side (the somber, if dapper, attire, the cane, the manners) tending toward the dandy and a comic side (the buffoonery Aiken mentions, as well as the bathos, ironies, vaudeville quotation, and self-mockery) tending toward the clown. Many memoirs, anecdotes, and poems indicate how Eliot's personality admitted these apparently contradictory impulses: the music hall mixed with metaphysics and intellectual, theological seriousness alternated with jokey, role-playing clownishness.

Both moods influence Eliot's inaugural poem. Written just two or three years after Eliot first read Symons and discovered Laforgue, "The Love Song of J. Alfred Prufrock" culminates a series of Laforguian experiments, a few of which appear in *Poems Written in Early Youth,* others surviving only in manuscript. Prufrock's sartorial punctilio gives his game away; he is the dandy in action:

> My morning coat, my collar mounting firmly to the chin,
> My necktie rich and modest, but asserted by a simple pin –

Though the opposites – "rich" yet "simple," "modest" but also assertive and "mounting firmly" – perfectly express Prufrock's ambivalence, they also reflect his careful, almost fussy self-presentation. However fearsome his inner demons, we should not forget he wears a "morning coat," or cutaway, a coat with tails for formal daytime occasions. Acutely sensitive to his own external appearance, Prufrock defiantly observes the latest fashions in cuffed trousers ("I shall wear the bottoms of my trousers rolled"), broods tonsorially ("Shall I part my hair behind?"), and portentously declares himself on the matter of shore wear ("I shall wear white flannel trousers, and walk upon the beach").

Prufrock's attention to detail seems so correct, so anxiously serious, that it reduces him to a clown. He wears, wearily, a mask. The eternal Footman, despite (or because of) Prufrock's overwrought demeanor, responds with a "snicker." (Even in metaphysical circles, it would seem, good help is hard to find.) And Prufrock calls himself

> Deferential, glad to be of use,
> Politic, cautious, and meticulous;
> Full of high sentence, but a bit obtuse;

> At times, indeed, almost ridiculous –
> Almost, at times, the Fool.

The sad clown, Pierrot, mingles the serious and the comic, the liturgical with the buffoonish. These elements, and even the bald spot in the middle of his hair (both clowns and monks are bald) – suggest that Prufrock's "Fool" descends from Laforgue's "Hamlet" and *L'Imitation de Notre Dame de la lune*.[6]

From nineteenth-century France Eliot also inherited the legacy of the dandy. The dandy relied as much on the sartorial, social, and personal surface as did the clown, but with different motives and dramatic intentions. Instead of comic excess, the dandy emphasized severity, angularity, sobriety, and an almost fierce suppression of instinct. Pierrot's vacant, vulnerable passivity signaled his availability as a victim. By contrast, the dandy devotes himself to aggressive, total control and enselfment almost to superfluity, sharpening his wit and demeanor should he need them to parry a riposte or avenge a slight. By making life a matter of control and by measuring conduct against stylistic norms,[7] the dandy counts upon his mastery of custom and personality to subdue any social matrix and dominate it dramatically. Instead of cultivating his character – the "central self" – and expecting it to conform to abstract, moral criteria, the dandy polishes his manners – the "social self" – evaluating them according to criteria no less elevated and severe, yet concretely gestural. Against morals he pits mores and manners, which he takes quite seriously indeed.

Even in this respect, then, Eliot's attention extends in opposite directions: toward a private self sad, disillusioned, and victimized – a Pierrot – and toward a public self rigorous and polished – a dandy. That Prufrock contains both these qualities is what makes him so convincing a character, as well as one so imbued with pathos. We remark his unshakable conviction about his own shortcomings, while noting his summary dismissal of whoever bores him. Prufrock's complexity explains something about that of his creator and, given these predilections, about Eliot's exile. In America, the dandy cuts an almost revolutionary figure, his disdain of popular acceptance emphasizing those aspects of the gentlemanly ideal that have been most thoroughly discredited socially, culturally, and, perhaps especially, sexually. American culture, as has been remarked, treats dandies and aesthetes even less kindly than do most other countries.[8]

Eliot's interest in dandies descends primarily from Baudelaire, who in moralizing the dandy's role modernized it as well, making it a vehicle with which to rebel against democratic, materialistic mediocrity. As Ellen Moers describes the progression, after Dickens's dandyism of failure and Barbey d'Aurevilly's mode of dissatisfaction, Baudelaire offered a dandyism of despair, detached, irresponsible, self-absorbed, and idle, but also morally critical of contemporary life. Defying respectable society, Baudelaire's dandy reasserted Original Sin, observing and accepting evil in a modern form.[9] Dandy gravity thus exerted a stronger influence upon the young Eliot than did the clownish Pierrot (though that role still held a greater appeal than is commonly assumed).[10] We do not ordinarily think of Eliot as a renegade, but only because the refinement upon which he reneged has so largely disappeared and because his apostasy necessarily remained of a refined, if not always subtle, kind.

"Baudelaire," although a later essay, confirms this view of Eliot's relation to his own pose and his own verse. Either Baudelaire must reject the contemporary world in favor of heaven and hell because he cannot adjust to the actual world, or because he perceives heaven and hell he must reject the world: Both ways of explaining Baudelaire's dualistic, negative metaphysic, Eliot concludes, are tenable.[11] Somewhat trivialized, this reversible formula applies to Prufrock; considerably enlarged, it describes *The Waste Land*. So does Eliot's comment upon how personality relates to artistic form. By their superficial coherence, excellence of form, and perfection of phrasing, Baudelaire's poems might give an appearance of presenting a definite, final state of mind. To Eliot, however, they seemed to have "the *external* but not the *internal* form of classic art. One might even hazard the conjecture that the care for perfection of form, among some of the romantic poets of the nineteenth century, was an effort to support, or to conceal from view, an *inner* disorder."[12] If we substitute "self" (especially the "social self") and "dandies" for "form" and "romantic poets," the substituted formulation makes a concise theory of the dandy, and of the Puritan. His comment, moreover, seems to acknowledge that Eliot's position vis-à-vis his early poetry resembled that of "some of the romantic poets of the nineteenth century." As had many nineteenth-century French Symbolist and "decadent" writers, Eliot created compensatory literary worlds because of a deep dissatisfaction with reality.[13] *The Waste Land* exemplifies this effort, and we overlook its author's critical, negative stance toward contemporary life at the risk of misunderstanding one of the poem's important motives.

"Baudelaire" further suggests that Eliot understood the strategies that the self – and the poet – may use to divert attention from a vulnerable, fragile, or socially unacceptable inner identity and fix it instead upon the external surface. *The Waste Land* itself arguably employs such a strategy. Alternatively, the dandy's intensively developed social self converts what society regards as subsidiary or peripheral into matters of primary importance. What many people view as concessions to social reality – dress, manners, small talk, quotidian politesses of diverse kinds – become for the dandy a kind of weapon.[14] The dandy's expert hypercivility exploits a smooth social surface, his offensive politeness discomfiting those who fail to keep pace. So that they may obscure inner facts, the dandy's external features proliferate. His superficial conformity may become so pronounced that it codifies itself in structured, formalized rebellion; it becomes "impersonal" through exaggerating personality.

This formula contributes to Eliot's emphasis on craft and technique, by which various rhetorical skills shift attention from the poet to his verse. Eliot's doctrine of impersonality thus in one sense implies its opposite upon deciphering his code. He called the bad poet unconscious where he ought to be conscious, and conscious where he ought to be unconscious. These two "errors," as Eliot termed them, tended to make the bad poet "personal," when in fact poetry did not cause a release of emotion or the expression of personality, but permitted instead an escape from them.[15] This famous formulation cancels conventional connections between poetry and sincerity and affirms Eliot's dandiacal poetic motives. Poetry did not explore and reveal the personality and emotions. Instead, it offered a respite from these burdensome aspects of the self. Dandyism, then, supported Eliot's anti-Romanticism, a classical tendency at once serious and stylized almost to mannerism or parody.

The dandy aimed to be himself not by relaxing or unbuttoning, but by tightening and controlling. Conceiving of the self as a gentleman, the dandy subjected it to the perfection of its accessories, resistance to vulgarity, and abomination of instinct, passion, and enthusiasm.[16] Thus to the dandy, certain kinds of freedoms and pleasures remained alien indulgences. In its rigorous dominion over the visible self, recoil from whatever was emotional, instinctual, or animal, and disgust with vulgarity, the dandy's posture did not preclude moralism. Both the dandy and the Puritan were elitist (the one socially, the other spiritually) and jointly condemned what they perceived as "animal." A dandyism capable both of criticizing conventional morals by flouting them and of expressing moral suffering as a way of escaping it may partly explain Eliot's affinities to the French tradition. The English dandy, descended from Brummell, tended to be useless, sensual, and merely foppish. Brummell, in his biographer's words, had every quality to make him "agreeable, amusing and ornamental, but not one that tended, in the most remote degree, to make him useful."[17] In the Victorian era, then, one chose to be either entirely useful or utterly useless, with a no man's land in between. In France, however, Baudelaire launched an alternative, serious dandyism, symbolically clothed – before it became fashionable – in black, the mourning color, admirably suiting (so to speak) a declining age: "Nous célébrons tous quelque enterrement."[18] Laforgue's liturgical costume fit into this line of melancholy, diffident resistance to "ce stupide dix-neuvième siècle," which like Eliot's both proclaimed a badge of class disaffection and masked inner turmoil.[19]

Beyond these personal affinities, Eliot's critics have largely overlooked how Eliot's attraction to nineteenth-century France reached beyond purely literary influence and how that literary choice matched his other early model, the Elizabethans and Jacobeans. Eliot's choice of sources remains neither arbitrary nor fungible and reflects distinct historical preferences. Jacobean and nineteenth-century French literature resembled one another historically and socially. Seventeenth-century English society was unsettled; its aristocracy was inexperienced; its religious establishment was divided; its court and monarchs were suspect economically, morally, and sexually. These schisms caused individual tensions as well, but in social terms the stress of doubleness arose as two social ideologies developed into distinct, competing cultures within a single society, which led finally to war.[20]

The similarities between Jacobean England and nineteenth-century France, though far from being identities, nonetheless seem significant. The primary resemblance consists in the notion of two antagonistic cultures occupying a society undergoing a prolonged shift from one *Weltanschauung* to another. Whereas the social and ideological friction heated up to a civil war and a regicide in seventeenth-century England, nineteenth-century France began at that point. A century after 1789, after assorted monarchies, empires, communes, and republics, there still existed in France, especially among artists and intellectuals, alienation from some of the same forces that in England had been on the ascendancy before 1641.[21]

Eliot's allegiances tethered him to the more traditional, "orthodox" ideology, seemingly doomed to decline along with the social class whose property it was. His literary choices represent his untheoretical but sure grasp of different historical periods undergoing a similar struggle. Eliot's sensitivity to this struggle owed much to what had happened in his own country, and to his own class, after the American Civil War. America, like Jacobean England and postrevolutionary France, underwent a civil war, the assassination of its head of state, and the conversion of its economy from regional, agricultural bases to national, urban, industrial ones. The class loyal to traditional ideology found itself displaced by economically motivated, democratic, less well educated "new men," a displacement producing emotional and ideological responses for which the literature of seventeenth-century England and nineteenth-century France provided rhetorical analogues and historical models. Ideological change and social displacement, and the notion that such developments elicit similar emotional and literary responses, provide the assumption from which to reason that Eliot's social experience affected his choice of literary models.

Such responses and experience reveal a sensibility with peculiar appetites and therefore satisfied by distinct rhetorical preferences. Something of this appears in Eliot's discussion of Andrew Marvell's wit – the "structural decoration of a serious idea," which Eliot found in Gautier, as well as in the *"dandysme"* of Laforgue and Baudelaire.[22] In "The Metaphysical Poets," setting forth a theory that glances forward to *The Waste Land,* Eliot linked the two periods explicitly. Because modern civilization contains "great variety and complexity," Eliot proposed that its poets must therefore be "difficult." They must become more indirect, allusive, and comprehensive, forcing and if necessary dislocating language into their meaning. This produces something resembling the metaphysical poets' conceit and also close to Eliot's nineteenth-century French models. Corbière and Laforgue, Eliot concluded, more closely resembled the school of Donne than did any modern English poet.[23] The Jacobeans and French Symbolists supported Eliot's rhetorical predilection for effects of doubleness, plurisignation, irony, ambiguity, and semantic disarrangement. Moreover, these models strengthened Eliot's preference for Gothic effect, proved that connotation could be cultivated until it surpassed denotation, showed how poetic craft could divert attention from the author's emotions to the verbal surface, and complemented Eliot's use of suggestion and techniques of strangeness. In *The Waste Land* and elsewhere, Eliot also drew upon the fund of historical incident and iconography the Jacobean and especially the Symbolist eras offered.[24]

Eliot ransacked the Jacobeans and Symbolists for rhetorical correlatives to his mental environment. Extremes within the same society appear to engender extremes within individual consciousness: They dissociate the sensibility. In an atmosphere overheated by social friction or violence, poets may prefer vagueness, ambiguity, suggestion, obscurity, allusion, and ellipsis instead of valuing precision, clarity, coherent narrative and syntax, and fixed, paraphrasable content. When formerly shared values must compete against newer ones, what was once absolute becomes merely relative; a temple of thought gives way to the marketplace of ideas. The emotional and intellectual complexity this competition calls forth in turn elicits verbal ambiguity and complexity. Politics, ideology, and the movement of social classes affect consciousness, which in turn influences verbal technique. This equation links nineteenth-century France and seventeenth-century England to Eliot as a post–Civil War American.

"From Poe to Valéry" suggests how social unease seems to hasten the progression from unconscious to self-conscious language, leading ultimately to *la poésie pure.* Eliot's use of ambiguity, however, extended

deeper than the purely verbal or superficial borrowing. For reasons having to do with his cultural inheritance, self-division, and emotional du-
alism, Eliot apparently had to master the techniques of obscurity in order
to write at all. Those contrivances therefore cannot be divorced from the
matter they set forth. A sense that existence is obscure or unknowable
engenders a search for literary devices connoting doubleness or conflict –
ambiguity, paradox, irony, or tension – with which to represent that
ambivalent sense of things. The presence of such elements in Eliot's early
verse, as well as in his early life, suggest that this verbal ambiguity flows
from a more deeply ambiguous sense of experience.

Ambiguity of experience, however, suggests experience unformed,
whereas ambiguity of language signifies that language has maximally
realized its formal properties. This paradox recalls the crux dividing the
moral (or serious) from the rhetorical (or dramatic) perspective. Ambiguity of response toward experience may demonstrate a failure of moral,
evaluative, and conceptual apparatus to account for a reality that outdis-
tances or contradicts it. As intellectual and social structures crumble, so
the structures of consciousness – and art – disperse. Yet ambiguity of
language – using a single word to convey multiple meanings or connotations or attaching several meanings to one word – signifies the *success* of a
verbal address toward the same world. In an ambiguous world, verbal
ambiguity may thus become the most complete mimesis. Eliot's mastery
of these techniques accounts for some of the singular attractions of the
early verse – the images, music, and especially Eliot's voice and rhythms,
which are among the most personal and distinct of all poetry in English.

The Waste Land, however, enlarges verbal and semantic disestablish-
mentarianism to encompass poetic form as a whole. Instead of complicating words and phrases by double reference, it multiplies the refer-
entiality of each phrase, sentence, or paragraph by making it potentially
significant to any other. The fragment, the poem's generic staple, and the
lack of explicit authorial connective tissue dislodge expectations about a
poem's form. On one level, the fragments mimetically render a disconnected reality and criticize its confusion. Portraying a culture and its
Weltanschauung breaking apart, *The Waste Land* posits a moral center and
a remembered order, but insists that the center is no longer shared and
that the order persists only in memory. Our frustrations with the poem's
discontinuous form, as it were, imitate Eliot's with the disorderly world.
Semantic, verbal, and formal disconnection, upsetting expectations
about poetic discourse, also dispatches preconceived ideas about order
applied to the world. There may have been in 1922, and now certainly
are, readers who do not expect much in the way of order in either the
poem or the world. Just as surely, however, Eliot was not one of them.

The Waste Land loses much of its moment if we forget the poetic and social predispositions to order that it deliberately violates and depicts being violated.

This is far from the entire picture, of course. The poem's fragmentary quality raises the question why its separate scenes appear in sequence, in the same poem. "Whispers of Immortality," for instance, though stating the relation between Donne and Webster expressly, leaves the connection between those two poets and Grishkin unstated and implicit. Origen, Sweeney, and similarly disparate characters appear side by side, yet their relation – though felt to be more than merely spatial – is nowhere made explicit. If the poem means to sustain attention, such characters must bear some relation, either of resemblance or of contrast, beyond simply appearing in the same poem. Spatial relation precedes, but also presupposes, intellectual relation.[25] In *The Waste Land,* voices, fragments, multiple genres, and narrative discontinuity reproduce Eliot's sense of a world withholding the aesthetic and moral order he expected it to supply.

Yet the poem's emotional consistency provokes another sort of scrutiny; though stylistically discrete, to have any larger significance its rhetorical units must establish reference beyond themselves. As Eliot had written in his dissertation, "meaning involves relations; at least (we need) the relation of identity through which a universality of function is recognized through a diversity of situation."[26] In Bradleyan terms, the discovery of relations objectifies feeling into thought. In this sentence, Eliot probably refers to the necessity that a word mean the same thing in different semantic circumstances. If it does not, and means something new every time it is used, the word can hardly be said to have a meaning, or indeed, any meaning. Yet words *can,* within limits, acquire meanings in different situations, a property poetic language so clearly exploits. There exist "relations" other than identity; a word also establishes relations with other words through syntax, connotation, metaphor, etymology, and dozens of other ways. The process by which individual words or the rhetorical units of a long poem become meaningful involves their linkage by author and reader to other termini: no meanings but in relations.

Eliot did not write *The Waste Land* to produce a meaningless poem or well-crafted, arty chaos. Arguing how the poem upsets predispositions to poetic order tells only half the story and explains why focusing only on its experimental form, without more, can so easily overstate the case. Its fragmentary, sudden shifts of scene, character, tone, time, and language deliberately forestall the habitual suspension of disbelief and thereby create a state of readiness. It is the first of many acts of aggression the reader will encounter. Yet if we listen for the "under-pattern" Eliot heard in the Jacobeans, *The Waste Land* reveals a web of subcutaneous nerve cells whose synapses fire periodically as we proceed through the poem. Underlying relation counterbalances the poem's epidermal confusion. The diverse methods by which *The Waste Land* builds up this tissue of relatedness, and just what sorts of relations it contains, I shall explore and illustrate in the following pages.

Separate scenes with similar reference, for instance, imply one sort of relation. In "The Burial of the Dead," a speaker says he could not speak; his eyes failed; he knew nothing; he was neither living nor dead. At least on a first reading – and how quickly one loses touch with that experience – a reader cannot yet know that later on, a woman (the hyacinth girl, whose wet hair, now dry, spreads out in fiery points?) asks a man (the same man?) a series of questions to which, out of the usual sequence, he seems already to have responded. Answer first, and ask questions later. In "A Game of Chess," she commands him to speak to her and asks him why he never does. She asks him if he knows, sees, and remembers nothing. And she asks him if he is alive or dead. When similar words or incidents appear in distant scenes, their intentional similarity enables us to recognize a "universality of function" in diverse situations. Answer and question bring two otherwise unlike scenes into relation, forcing the reader to identify what that relation is.[27]

One of the poem's premonitory nerve centers, the visit to Madame Sosostris, predicts several future scenes and illustrates another kind of relation. Here diverse parts begin to relate, not only as a plot, but through thematic and verbal associations the Tarot scene anticipates and later events will recall. Her visitor treats Sosostris skeptically, even patronizingly, noting how she throws a "wicked" pack of cards. Although not uncomplimentary, the American slang sense of "wicked" (meaning excellent, capable, keen)[28] also helps declare the speaker's independence from what he observes. The jaunty, journalistic "Madame Sosostris, famous clairvoyante" and the ironic "known to be the wisest woman in Europe" disclose his facile doubts about her acumen. And by snidely mimicking her slightly flawed English – "Tell her I bring the horoscope myself" – the speaker betrays his own vanity. Neither he – nor the reader – can as yet suspect that each card she interprets taps a spring of meaning that will seep throughout the poem. We shall follow some of these as they surface in later scenes, tying the poem together each time they emerge.

"Belladonna" glances forward to "A Game of Chess." "Bella" denotes "beautiful" but also borrows something from "warlike," as in bellicose. The folk etymology "beautiful lady" appears to have been influenced by the cosmetic use of *Atropa belladonna* to dilate the eye. The plant's opposite properties preserve the ambiguity: Its cosmetic use recalls the sense of "beautiful" in "bella," while its lethal chemistry (it is the deadly nightshade, source of the poisonous crystalline alkaloid, atropine) echoes its "warlike" connotation. "Belladonna" sums up the woman's twofold nature as "A Game of Chess" begins. The opening scene details her boudoir (replete with marble, jewels, colored glass, copper, gold, and colored stone: "the Lady of the Rocks") and her toilette (surrounded by luxurious furnishings, mirrors, and perfumes). Beauty presently changes to belligerence, and as the scene unfolds she metamorphoses into the lady of situations.

In another prolepsis, Sosostris mentions "your card, the drowned Phoenician Sailor" and "the one-eyed merchant," whose associations attach to Eugenides and to Phlebas, reinforced by the clairvoyante's comments on "the wheel" and other cards: "Fear death by water. I see crowds of people, walking round in a ring." The poem will develop each of these references, though at this stage they appear to be only an unreliable clairvoyante's random observations, not to be taken particularly seriously.

The subsequent encounter with Eugenides contains several curiosities of reference and association. One recalls Eliot's father, who before T. S. Eliot's birth spent seven years working at a St. Louis wholesale grocery concern in various capacities. As shipping and receiving clerk, he prepared commercial documents and oversaw the flow of goods. His memoir recorded his dockside visits and knowledge of the boats' names, one of which was *The Sultana,* which it is possible to link both to Eugenides' Turkish origin and to the dried fruit he carries.[29]

Another recalls Bertrand Russell's description of Eliot's graduate school colleague, with whom he once arrived to ask Russell a question. "Eliot is very well-dressed and polished with manners of the finest Etonian type. The other, an unshaven Greek appropriately named Demos, who earns the money for his fees by being a waiter in a restaurant. The two were obviously friends and had on neither side the slightest consciousness of social difference." Also "unshaven," Eugenides speaks "demotic" French.[30]

Finally, employed in Lloyds Bank and perhaps by way of his father's experience, Eliot introduced the commercial shorthand "c.i.f. London" into his poem. Oddly, Eliot's original note incorrectly defined the phrase.[31] "C.i.f." followed by a destination abbreviates "cost, insurance, and freight," terms of a once-common shipping contract for the sale and transport of goods. The quoted price includes not only the goods, but also insurance and freight to the stated destination. Thus the seller performs his contract upon delivering goods to the shipper and tendering documents to the buyer. Even though the goods have not yet arrived at their ultimate destination, title passes to the buyer, who assumes all risks after the goods have been placed on board. "The seller completes his contract when he delivers the merchandise called for to the shipper, pays the freight thereon to the point of destination, and forwards to the buyer bill of lading, invoice, insurance policy, and receipt showing payment of freight."[32]

Though Eugenides, the Smyrna merchant, is cognizable as a modern Phlebas – one of the ancient trading tribe, the Phoenicians – other evidence joins the two. Eugenides quotes a price for a shipment of "currants"; another sort of "current" browses upon Phlebas' skeleton. The link involves more than a simple homonymous pun. Both these Aegeans, Phlebas and Eugenides, pursue waterborne commerce. Himself a sailor, Phlebas turned the wheel and looked to windward, keeping his eye, like the "one-eyed merchant," on "the profit and the loss." So had Eugenides to calculate when quoting a commodity "c.i.f."; although adaptable to other forms of shipping, in practice this contract was used primarily to allocate the risks of long distance, oceanic conveyance, risks Phlebas' demise makes evident.

"Current," moreover, derives etymologically from the same root as "currency," and the two words share a number of overlapping associations. We speak today, for example, of "cash flow" and of an "income stream." As in Eliot's time, goods enter the "stream of commerce," borrowers and corporations "float" loans and bond issues, and in banking the total value of uncollected checks or drafts in transit adds up to the "float." "Water," then as now, means stock issued at below par value or for discounted, nonmonetary, or nonexistent consideration, thus reducing the value of previously issued shares because it diffuses ownership but does not correspondingly increase capital. And for an investor or venture to be "under water" refers to heavy debt or imminent bankruptcy and failure. Eliot's work in the City would have acquainted him with these and similar terms and with the financial facts to which they figuratively alluded. (In the 1870s, two friends induced Henry Ware Eliot, Sr., to invest in a business manufacturing pyroligneous acid for the St. Louis lead industry. After four years' struggle against fire, floods, and an "intemperate" partner, the two friends at short notice abandoned Eliot and the business, which then failed. H. W. Eliot's memoir implies that Rev. Eliot bailed him out.)[33] Phlebas thus turns both his ship's wheel and the wheel of fortune. Even business parlance contains an "undertone" making it a kind of poetry and contributing to the imagery Eliot used to express moral anxiety about commercial culture and his participation in it.

We also speak of "liquid" assets and of liquidity, the relative ease or difficulty of converting assets into "currency," or cash. The related sense, "liquidation," occurs when a bankrupt corporation settles accounts with debtors and creditors and goes out of business. These over-lapping associations between water and commerce, currents and curren-cy, highlight another quality of Eliot's verbal practice throughout *The Waste Land,* his use of Gothic language to supply a subliminal menace of death. A "current" is a distinct flow, stronger, swifter, or of a different temperature, within a larger body of water. Just as liquidating a person leaves a corpse, so liquidating a business terminates a corporation: An-other meaning of "liquidate" is to murder. This double sense makes it possible to associate a corpse and a business corporation. Incorporation creates an economic body enjoying legal rights like those of a person – the ability to buy, sell, contract, borrow, litigate – but also distinct from and superior to those of individuals. The law, that is, endows a corpora-tion not only with limited liability – limiting a shareholder's liability to corporate creditors in bankruptcy to his ownership interest – but with eternal life.

The concluding scene of "The Burial of the Dead" first draws atten-tion to this submerged ambiguity. After visiting Madame Sosostris, the speaker reappears in the London financial district, where a river of com-muters crosses London Bridge and travels down King William Street toward the precinct where the great financial institutions are located: the Bank of England and the Royal Exchange, hard by the Stock Exchange, not far from the Cannon Street Hotel, Upper Thames Street, Moorgate, and other locations the poem names. They reverse the journey after the workday, "at the violet hour," echoing Sosostris's prophetic warning of "the Wheel," and "crowds of people, walking round in a ring."

Recognizing one of the commuters, the speaker hails him:

> 'Stetson!
> 'You who were with me in the ships at Mylae!
> 'That corpse you planted last year in your garden,
> 'Has it begun to sprout? Will it bloom this year?
> 'Or has the sudden frost disturbed its bed?

The "corpse" has several associations.[34] Its overt, if metaphoric, sense concerns a bulb (compare the other plant called belladonna, *Amaryllis belladonna,* the hyacinth girl, and "Lil" in Part II) or the "roots" and "tubers" of the poem's opening lines. The "corpse," however, has been "planted." That garden-variety horticultural verb also has an exotic, "Gothic" meaning. As the facsimile edition shows, the original manu-script of *The Waste Land* contained an opening section full of colloquial American speech (e.g., "boiled to the eyes, blind" and "fly cop," mean-ing, respectively, "drunk" and a "detective"). One of many elements that the revisions nearly effaced was the poetry of slang, but traces of it survive nevertheless. In contemporary American slang the word "plant" was a synonym for burying a corpse or a cache of money.[35] The black-humored locution might accuse Stetson of murder or peculation. More likely the excited apostrophe reflects the speaker's surprise, or dismay, that Stetson (whose presence at Mylae – the first major naval victory of Imperial Rome – suggests that he, too, was once a sailor before succumbing to the horse latitudes of finance and commerce) has declined into a commuter, tending a suburban garden. There he has interred his past, and perhaps also his hope for the future. Having buried himself in his work, his living leaves him one of those whom death has "undone."

The speaker's question, "Or has the sudden frost disturbed its bed?" reprises many of these associations. The horticultural sense of a garden or flower bed extends themes present in "corpse," "planted," "sprout," and "bloom." But the "bed" also shares the mortal, murderous associations of "corpse" and "planted" and the notion that death has undone so many. "Bed," that is, may connote a "final resting place" or being "laid to rest," a cemetery as well as a garden plot. Phlebas' corpse occupies its final resting place in yet a third sense of the word "bed," that of a river- or seabed, a sense relevant to the currents, rivers, and bodies of water throughout *The Waste Land*. A fourth meaning involves the sexual or marital bed, here rendered as "disturbed," as a kind of death.

These associations do not exhaust "Death By Water," another of the poem's nerve centers, extending fibrous relations in many directions. The homonymous "current" and "currants" underscore the Gothic tone: Eugenides' currants were eaten; the current now eats Phlebas. It "picked his bones in whispers," that is, removed bit by bit, as meat from bones, eating sparingly or mincingly, without enthusiasm, as in picking at one's food. The irony is hardly subtle; Eugenides, a seller and consumer of food (he asks the speaker to luncheon), is the unconscious opposite of Phlebas, once engaged in the same business but now himself consumed by the current – and the currency – upon which he formerly floated. Buried at sea, his corpse rises and falls, like the commuters flowing up the hill and down King William Street. Phlebas' fate merges the "crowds of people, walking round in a ring" with "death by water," leaving him to perish, "entering the whirlpool."

These associations point to a theme that further illuminates the poem's mood. In due time we shall explore the theme of aggression in *The Waste Land*. Now it is appropriate to point out how Eliot's disillusion with business, commerce, and money joins with it to frame the theme of spiritual deadness. Eliot's family history supplies one source of this ambivalence. Notwithstanding his father's and grandfather's financial success, Eliot inherited their sense of an irreconcilable antinomy between

God and mammon. "The whole district smells of fish," Sir John Betjeman once observed of the area around St. Magnus the Martyr. Its
dozens of empty churches must constantly have reminded Eliot how
financial prosperity had displaced Christian devotion.

In 1921, reporting a proposal to sell for demolition nineteen City of
London churches, Eliot's renewed attack upon the pachydermatous
"True Church" scarcely concealed his loyalties. Few visitors, he sup-
posed, paid much attention to those empty sanctuaries,

> but they give to the business quarter of London a beauty which its
> hideous banks and commercial houses have not quite defaced. . . . the
> least precious redeems some vulgar street. . . . As the prosperity of
> London has increased, the City Churches have fallen into desuetude. . . .
> The loss of these towers, to meet the eye down a grimy lane, and of these
> empty naves, to receive the solitary visitor at noon from the dust and
> tumult of Lombard Street, will be irreparable and unforgotten.[36]

Aesthetic transport occasioned by religious architecture was not new to
American aestheticists; Adams had written in the same vein. And as we
have observed other American aesthetes do, Eliot's condemnation expresses moral disgust in an aestheticist vocabulary: The banks are "hideous" and "deface" their surroundings, and the streets and lanes are
"vulgar" and "grimy." But the churches have a "beauty" that is "precious" and "redeems" their prosperous surroundings, the final verb connoting the two transformations of the precinct, conversion of securities
and negotiable instruments into cash as well as delivery from sin and its
penalties. His attitude discloses an inherited recoil from mammon
merged with an acquired cultural ideal of beauty, refinement, and repose, the latter appearing as the "inexplicable splendour of Ionian white
and gold." Though it is possible to exaggerate the extent to which Eliot
held commerce to account for spiritual deadness, his thinking at this
stage nonetheless warns against acquisitive, commercial motives in the
most dire terms.

Aside from reiterating that warning, "Death By Water" illustrates
another device Eliot uses to unify the poem's disparate episodes. We have
so far discussed several such devices: puns; predictions; verbal echoes and
repetition; semantic and thematic association; and anchoring separate
episodes geographically. Besides these more or less internal mechanisms,
Eliot incorporates extraneous sources to tie his poem together. For example, *The Waste Land* quotes or echoes lines 388–408 of act I, scene ii, of
The Tempest. As I have observed, several crucial nerve centers of *The
Waste Land* influence later or resolve earlier portions, as if by remote
control. Some parts of the poem – "Death By Water," for one, or the
Tarot scene – are simply more important than others, at least in terms of
interpreting the whole. Eliot's references to *The Tempest*, however, take

the unusual step of locating a governing nerve center *outside* his own poem, in the work of another author.

Eliot's notes make the point several times, most clearly by stating that "the one-eyed merchant, seller of currants, melts into the Phoenician Sailor, and the latter is not wholly distinct from Ferdinand Prince of Naples." Though if not wholly distinct, that is to say, not wholly identical either. In act III, scene iii, for example, Ariel spoke of the "never-surfeited sea," which now leisurely nibbles Phlebas' corpse. In some suggestive lines concerning "Death By Water" and "What the Thunder Said," Alonso cried out for his conscience:

> O, it is monstrous, monstrous!
> Methought the billows spoke and told me of it;
> The winds did sing it to me; and the thunder,
> That deep and dreadful organ pipe, pronounced
> The name of Prosper; it did bass my trespass.
> Therefore my son i' th' ooze is bedded; and
> I'll seek him deeper than e'er plummet sounded
> And with him there lie mudded.

Of course, the difference between Phlebas and Ferdinand is that Alonso misapprehends the state of things. Ferdinand is lost, but not dead; unlike Phlebas, who is both, he does not rest at the bottom of the seabed. When Ferdinand sits on the bank "Weeping again the King my father's wrack," he is mistaken, unlike the speaker in *The Waste Land,* and in due time will learn the facts.

Many other similarities between Eliot's poem and Shakespeare's play exist – water metaphors, the conflict between legitimacy and usurpation, and the theme of metamorphosis, for only a few examples; here simply note how widely Eliot has distributed them. Pluck any reference to *The Tempest,* and like a thread in a blanket, others woven elsewhere into the poem's four corners will twitch in response. This example seems to illustrate the theory in "Tradition and the Individual Talent." Allusion, that is, fits into the existing system of reference and meaning, which supports the contemporary work of art but is also altered by it. As the contemporary work of art forms a terminus of relations tying it to previous works of art, new relations thereby established shift preexisting ones. This Bradleyan premise underpins the method by which allusive literary networks grid *The Waste Land,* building up its own meanings through afferent and efferent pathways of extraneous literary relation to and from Shakespeare as well as Jacobean tragedy, Dante, Baudelaire, and other nineteenth-century French writers. *The Waste Land,* indeed, casts its referential net wide enough to include the Bible, the Upanishads, St. Augustine, and the Buddha, as well as *From Ritual to Romance* and *The Golden Bough.* By alluding to "Dans le Restaurant" and "Burbank with a

Baedeker: Bleistein with a Cigar," Eliot even incorporates his own earlier writing, altering the meaning of earlier poems even as he uses them to create meaning in his latest one.[37]

It is neither possible nor necessary to pursue all these extraneous sources. What details this analysis provides can only illustrate Eliot's rich procedure. The innumerable details and the relations they arrange may nevertheless tend to distract attention from the "substance of the poem." That substance, though not always easy to pin down, sends another kind of pattern running through *The Waste Land* like a current. The theme of aggression emerges in scenes establishing the poem's principal emotional coordinates. It is particularly important because it suggests, by negative implication, the poem's primary positive values.

Emotional aggression pervades the initial scenes of "A Game of Chess." In her luxurious boudoir, a woman endeavors through jewels, perfumes, and other high-style artifice to provoke her taciturn lover. She evidently fails, but because her tricks arise from a genuine need for contact, she takes his reluctance personally. Frightened and frustrated, she becomes angry and then abusive, interrogating him with questions recalling what was said to the hyacinth girl. That moment captured a blinding perception of the force of love. Now, however, the woman fairly screams, while the man keeps silent (at least to her; the reader, significantly, is permitted access to his thoughts). Threatened by being "drowned" – intimations of Phlebas' fate – in her perfume and overwhelmed by her rage, the man is protected by his silence, or so he imagines. In truth, it precipitates the storm of abuse that rains down upon him. The woman, tortured by an agony of love remembered but now attenuated or gone irretrievably bad, wants him to lead, to give her something, to make some sign. Her questions simply state how desperately she wants something – anything – to happen. But nothing does. The marital game of chess produces a stalemate: out of wedlock, deadlock. Despite her threat to embarrass him into intimacy by going out in public *en deshabille,* he is the one who exits the perilous straits of a rocky marriage, fleeing domestic danger into the safety of a public house.

There he overhears a tale of another marriage and observes a different kind of aggression. The woman at her vanity received too little attention; Lil suffers because she receives too much – more, apparently, than she wants or than her health can take. Albert, however, presents little immediate peril compared with the narrator's recollected conversation, in which she had the knives out for Lil. She calls Lil dowdy, telling her to replace her decaying teeth with a store-bought set (anticipating the "carious teeth" in "What the Thunder Said"). She hints at Lil's dishonesty (spending teeth money to purchase pills for an abortion) and calls her selfish, foolish, and immature ("You *are* a proper fool. . . . What you get married for if you don't want children?"). She also pointedly threatens Albert's philandering if Lil does not stop looking "so antique." Miraculously, Lil took most of this sitting down, even inviting her inquisitor to dinner – with Albert – the next Sunday. As the group breaks up at closing time, slightly drunk and slurring their words – "Goonight" – it evidently forgives and forgets such aggression in short order. Despite the brass tacks of birth, marriage, life, and death raised as items of gossip, pub culture dismisses such verbal violence as harmless, refusing to let grudges hold up the eating and drinking for long.

What ensues after the typist arrives home at teatime occupies a position farther along the poem's developing spectrum of desire and aggression. This scene elaborates a minor theme introduced when Eugenides inquired after his companion's luncheon and weekend plans. His sexual query altered the center of gravity of his "business proposition," abruptly shifting the emphasis from the former to the latter word. The young man carbuncular, a "small house agent's clerk," also moves in the business world, if in a petty way. He has grandiose plans and an attitude to match: all the assurance – and, the comparison implies, all the moral acuity – of a war millionaire, if without the enabling fortune. His assurance and "bold" stare, his ego swollen to maximum tumescence, his avidity to overwhelm someone weaker than he suggest his own ultimate fragility. He is all aggression: "flushed and decided," he "assaults" and is "exploring," yet he "gropes," as if blinded, when he leaves. The typist makes no "defence" to his onslaught. Ironically balanced opposites render their interaction: His caresses are "unreproved, if undesired," and his vanity makes a "welcome of indifference." Hardly participating, she treats the episode routinely, as much a part of her daily round as a hurried breakfast, crushing commute, or a half-heard tune on the gramophone.

In "A Game of Chess," a frightened, angry woman had emotionally bullied a taciturn man, probably himself frightened into silence and emotional withdrawal. In "The Fire Sermon," by contrast, the bully is a young man, still adorned in adolescent acne ("carbuncular" also ironically denoting a semiprecious gem), yet vain and aggressively sexual. Though something short of rape, his technique seems mainly to consist of an utter lack of interest in his partner. Consumed by his desire, unassuaged by easy, private conquest in the typist's bedsit, the house agent's clerk, seeking novelty or danger, attempts sex in a "narrow canoe" floating down the Thames.

The venture fails. "Undid" denotes the unfastening of her clothing, recalling the catalogue of her "drying combinations," "stockings, slippers, camisoles, and stays." A related sense connotes her ruin by seduction, while a third echoes, "I had not thought death had undone so many," connoting cosmic, spiritual ruin, leaving the body alive but the soul dead. Referring to the canoe, the original manuscript's inclusion of "perilous" in place of "narrow" bolsters an intuited link between this scene and the typist's combinations "perilously" spread, as well as underscoring the theme of spiritual peril.[38] She then says, "My feet are at Moorgate, and my heart under my feet." Moorgate lies near King William Street, Saint Mary Woolnoth, and the bell's funereal peal. There the speaker met Stetson, who had planted a "corpse" in the ground where the typist's heart now lies. (The Elizabethan idiom "under . . . feet" denotes subjection, ruin, conquest, with a subliminal connotation of burial, as in 1 Corinthians 15: 24–7, quoted in the Anglican service "At the Burial of the Dead": "Then cometh the end, when he shall have delivered up the kingdom to God, even the Father; when he shall have put down all rule and all authority and power. For he must reign, till he hath put all enemies under his feet. The last enemy that shall be destroyed is death. For he hath put all things under his feet.")

This time, however, the canoeing incident also undoes the "young man carbuncular." The inversion, noun before adjective, implies that he is heraldically "rampant," a word deriving from "climbing" and "claw." "Rampant" suggests luxuriant growth, like the vegetation they drift past at the great botanical garden at Kew. More insidiously, it suggests how the young man and his desires – socially climbing and sexually clawing – spread unchecked, barbarically out of control. Does the "event" simply repeat the assault on the divan? Evidently not, given what follows in each case. She earlier seemed to have taken no offense, nor does she now. Yet here, he "wept." If he attempted sex in the canoe and failed, the house agent's clerk (inane enough to conceive the plan, and then unable to bring it off) might well have "wept" from his bruised vanity, or even a pang of guilt that he had "gone too far." He might as well promise a melodramatic "new start."

Expiatory promises after sexual humiliation – thus a "non-event" – also make her response plausible. "I made no comment. What should I resent?" If nothing happened in the canoe except some disrobing, a demoralized woman, victimized on other occasions, might conclude that on this one at least she had not been ill treated. Despite the vague action of these scenes, we do know that this latest disaster occurs on the riverbed, and that the next section, "Death By Water," presents another sailor's corpse, resting on the seabed, who like the loveless lovers "was once handsome and tall as you."

The man and woman in the canoe seem to have been brought face to face with their respective predicaments. Sexual failure has occasioned his spiritual crisis; subsequent sexual access will most likely relieve it. Hers, however, seems a crisis of dispiritedness; she lacks even the resources to "resent," to "connect," or to "expect." Thus matters stand at the end of

"The Fire Sermon," after a series of scenes in which an aggressor victimizes a passive recipient. As if to point out the paradox of this earthly pattern, the same one essentially repeats itself when a divine aggressor "pluckest out" the passive subject. For once, however, the passive character is the beneficiary, instead of the victim, of an active power. Divinity exercising its power on our behalf: Modern people experience that kind of power only rarely, the poem seems to say, perhaps, like the typist, having lost the knowledge that they may hope for grace, or something like it, to be extended. (Under the circumstances, synergism is presumably out of the question.) The moment, however, does not last. "Death By Water" illustrates the cruel fact of human impotence. The predictable accident to which first the spirit (crowds of people, walking round in a ring) and then the body (devoured by the current of time) succumb, mortality undoes us all.

Where, then, does "What the Thunder Said" arrive, if passivity before earthly aggression reflects spiritual weakness, but passivity before divine power makes grace possible? Both themes inform this fifth section, especially insofar as its chapel perilous might offer a forum for resolving the paradox between spiritual passivity and mundane aggression. Indeed, at several moments something does seem about to happen. The initial verse paragraphs allude to the primal Christian act of aggression and passivity, the Crucifixion, out of which the victim perfects divine fortitude. Christ's corporeal death and resurrection into everlasting life make this salvation concrete and available, broadcasting the redemptive Holy Spirit to all willing to receive it. The story makes the fundamental Christian distinction that Christ, once corporeally alive but mortal, through resurrection enjoys everlasting spiritual life. Yet the poem states, "He who was living is now dead." And instead of acknowledging that Christ's example makes resurrection and everlasting life available to all who accept the Holy Spirit, the poem concludes, "We who were living are now dying." Christian believers would have phrased it the opposite way; before Christ, they were physically alive, but spiritually dead. After Christ's great example, their faith ensures that they wax spiritually even as they wane physically.

"What the Thunder Said" alternatively offers the Grail legend as an initiation into spiritual power and a way to penetrate divine mystery. Yet the section seems rather to state the difficulty to be surmounted, and the chances of surmounting it, than to succeed in actually overcoming that obstacle. Weston's theory requires some violent contest in the chapel perilous to effect the initiation. Spiritual adventure must complete itself in physical contest; an enemy must threaten the quester's life.[39] Despite many signs of the before and after of struggle, however, what happens falls short of the spirit- and body-concentrating event of focused, physical conflict. "Dry bones can harm no one." Yet without physical jeopardy, no spiritual victory may result. So while the section exhibits a degree of progression, the absence of anything by which to account for the change deprives it of the force it is surely meant to possess. Instead of a resolution, "What the Thunder Said" seems to bring about only an ending. Michael Levenson justly perceives that of the themes mentioned in the introductory note to "What the Thunder Said," Eliot attends only to "*incipient* phenomena ('journey,' 'approach,' 'decay') the stages that precede realization. He employs . . . 'three themes' in this section of the poem, but none of the three achieves dramatic resolution; they remain, indeed, poised in 'continuous parallel.' The result is a particular dramatic inconclusiveness. Parallels multiply, but they do not meet."[40]

To be sure, in fine-tuning the climactic cosmic theater, Eliot cranks up some splendid poetic machinery:

> Then a damp gust
> Bringing rain
>
> Ganga was sunken, and the limp leaves
> Waited for rain, while the black clouds
> Gathered far distant, over Himavant.
> The jungle crouched, humped in silence.
> Then spoke the thunder.

These lines, the fulcrum of the poem's energy and a moment of maximum compression – literally the calm before the storm – develop a pattern of vowels and consonants to express the nervous tension they contain. The *u* vowel predominates: "sunken," "jungle," "crouched," "clouds," "humped," and "thunder." Like the bed of the river Ganga, the *u* lies open to the sky, ready to receive water and meaning, yet with upright sides to collect and retain them. By contrast, the *m* and *n* consonants, often adjacent to the *u* vowel, also pervade the passage: "damp," "Bringing rain," "sunken," "limp," "Himavant," "jungle," "humped," "silence," "Then," and "thunder." The *m* and especially the *n*, "humped" like the sacred mountain "Himavant," add weight to a word's volume. Closed to the sky and positioned like a dome or arch, they resemble structures that protect, support, and shelter. The *u* collects and conserves, like a cup; its opposite, the *n* – a *u* inverted – protects and shelters, like a cap.

Both responses are appropriate to the coming storm. The onomatopoeic "DA," resembling a clap of thunder, and "shantih," the soft susurrus of a life-giving rainshower: these marvelous devices give pleasure with every reading. If ever one wished to suspend disbelief, this is the moment. Once translated from exotic Sanskrit to plain English, however, the very ordinariness of "give, sympathize, control" suggests how little has happened, despite the superb *deus ex natura*. The components of a Gangetic peace that passeth all understanding – detached from the Westonian and Frazerian apparatus and the poetic business – turn out to be familiar Unitarian imperatives, the Sunday school virtues. They pretty much require the Unitarian procedure, as well: not the drama, blood, and thunder of sudden conversion, but years of conscious self-direction.* The poem's grand finale, pretending to be something that makes the soul cohere, turns out to be merely the assertion that it does – or that it could.[41]

At the time, Eliot wrote that "in art there should be interpenetration and metamorphosis."[42] *The Waste Land* contains quantities of the former, but a certain absence of the latter quality raises questions. It is not that these ethical prescriptions are irrelevant, or wrong, or even that they do not fit in this poem. They do: giving to and sympathizing with others, and controlling oneself, prescribe fitting responses to the various incidents of aggression the poem contains. And the modern world contains innumerable people who could profit from them. (One hastens to point out that not many – like Eugenides, the young man carbuncular, or Lil's beery persecutor – will be the sort to read *The Waste Land,* much less heed its precepts.) The difficulty is rather that given the exotic machinery framing these imperatives, a measure of incongruity accompanies their appearance, not so bad as bathos but something of a letdown nevertheless. It is as if the author could not bring himself to set forth such familiar propositions without extraordinary labor. Given their similarity to his ancestral formulas, perhaps for Eliot to profess them required something like this toil and trouble.

The antinomies in the "give, sympathize, control" paragraphs – by far the poem's most obscure – reflect Eliot's personal difficulty, and, I think, an American difficulty. "Surrender" and "prudence," "given" and "retract," "daring" and "obedient," the prison of the isolated self and the calm, carefree responsiveness of intimacy: these ambivalences reflect a self unformed, afraid of the step that will force the identity's precarious possibilities to closure, yet desperate to take it. Americans tend to resist the notion that anything other than a knowing, voluntary choice may bind them individually. This idea, inherited from Protestantism and rationalism and reinforced by Romanticism, seems established in Ameri-

---

* Compare Rev. William G. Eliot, *Discourses on the Doctrines of Christianity* (Boston, American Unitarian Assoc., 1881), pp. 128–9: "We do not believe in an instantaneous and miraculous change, by virtue of which he who is at one moment totally depraved can become in the next one of God's saints. . . . We have greater confidence in the change which comes through the quietness of thought. It may promise less at first, but will accomplish more in the end. It may be accompanied with less of the rapture of religious triumph, but it is more likely to bring us to that peace which passeth all understanding."

can common wisdom, on one hand, and in law and public policy, on the other. It was the motive behind Unitarianism, as we have seen, refusing to admit either the imputed guilt of Adam's sin or the sudden gift of God's grace, leaving the matter of salvation or damnation to the individual's own resources.

In a modern, secular context, the idea tends to dissolve the claims upon us of the past, of our ancestors, of our birth, of our bodies, of even our own seemingly irrevocable commitments. Shading off into antinomianism, criminality, laissez faire, or an anarchic unwillingness to plan, it challenges the right and reach of law, legislation, and decisions taken by society. Many Americans routinely take pleasure in dismissing facts they did not influence or decisions in which they took no part as unjust impositions, satanic conspiracies, or simply matters of grand irrelevance. American identity itself, in this context, becomes a subject of conscious, individual choice to come, and to stay. What is voluntarily chosen, however, may be relinquished, as Eliot's life suggests. Voluntarily choosing to be involuntarily bound, he chose, or thought he chose, to live in a society where one's life was more a fact and less a choice. But the very possibility of making that choice implies that the un-self-conscious fact of living no longer survived to be recovered. Painfully mixing erotic death by burial or drowning with an excruciating labor of rebirth, *The Waste Land* may be read as a poem about the costs of choosing identity, of consciously altering something originally formed unconsciously. It struggles with the question of choice in general, asking how much may be left to the conscious mind, how strong are the claims of ancestral, parental, and national bonds, how much of the life and self one has must be given up to get the life and self one wants.

The poem's final lines further undercut the likelihood that coherence for the soul – or of the world outside – can pretend to be anything more than temporary. The conclusion quotes, inter alia, *"Le Prince d'Aquitaine à la tour abolie." Abolie* – literally, "ruined" or "downed" – seems close to the heart of the matter. In 1921, at work on the poem, Eliot diagnosed his own problem with nerves as an "aboulie and emotional derangement which has been a lifelong affliction."[43] A single vowel separates the physical ruin of *"abolie"* from the emotional ruin of "aboulie," a loss of the ability to exercise willpower and make decisions. The quotation, in which is buried Eliot's self-diagnosis, does not place much confidence in the regenerative power of the ideal so symmetrically proposed a few lines earlier.

"These fragments I have shored against my ruins" seems to confirm the difficulty of spiritual change. No metamorphosis – no miracles – without faith. The very familiarity of this line makes it easy to overlook its implied paradox: Ordinarily ruins result in fragments, instead of fragments protecting against ruin. "Fragments," on one hand, refer to the poem's discrete parts, and perhaps to its allusive cultural diversity. On the other, it suggests that "give, sympathize, control" are fragments of a larger – presumably Christian and orthodox – system, an ethic without the glue of faith, Incarnation, and dogma that will incorporate them into a complete, spiritually reconstituting system. Even though they fall short of that completion, these ethical imperatives nonetheless refer and aspire to it. Indeed, inasmuch as they *do* argue against disillusion, they perform that positive function, despite remaining necessarily negative because, as yet, incomplete. They do not simply call a solution impossible. If anything, they – indeed the entire poem – point toward the solution's ultimate necessity. That a solution is postponed does not subtract from the necessity of persisting to seek one.

Perhaps it is the better part of poetic candor to suggest an ideal and acknowledge its practical insufficiency, rather than to propose that no ideal is possible. The poem's ultimate indeterminacy, that is, hardly seems a particularly grave flaw. Indeed, remembering its indeterminacy helps blunt the interpretive implements that constrain the poem as they force it into one of various schematic cubbyholes. Though *The Waste Land,* and especially the notes, seemingly welcome that kind of hermeneutic shoehorning, the more of these interpretative schema the poem can bear, the more one tends to mistrust any one of them, whether Christian, Hindu, anthropological, mythological, or otherwise. One can make an ambiguity precise by insisting upon one of its terms and dismissing the others. But Eliot wrote ambiguously because he wished to say many things, not because he wished to say only one.

Even the "single-protagonist theory," though welcome because of its procedural focus, does not quite hang together. The poem, to be sure, contains enough consistency of incident, tone, and voice to encourage the notion that a single narrator sees, experiences, speaks, and acts. It is one sort of "relation" to which the poem may plausibly give rise. But a good deal of *The Waste Land* contradicts the protagonist's existence; Levenson's example of Eugenides and the narrator in "The Fire Sermon" is only one embarrassment of this theory. No fictional being could encompass all the poem's variation and still remain sufficiently unified to cohere into something cognizable as a protagonist.[44]

The process of collating the poem's diversity contributes something necessary and interesting to understanding *The Waste Land.* To establish relations among the poem's various parts requires a critical vantage point that commands these diverse elements. To state the proposition in reverse, readers must immerse themselves in the poem's particulars *a priori* so as to discover and create relations between them *a posteriori*. By attaining greater knowledge about the poem's incidents and characters, the reader rises to a prospect from which to view them in more detail and greater breadth. Thus the poem's transcendent, synthetic method: glimpse the ideal by establishing relations. (To paraphrase Emerson's "Circles," discovering relations is a new influx of divinity into the mind. "Hence the thrill that attends it.") Although essentially passive and intellectual, this procedure and the related ethic of give, sympathize, and control make it possible for the poem to incorporate the reader into its activity. Whether one calls it the author or some dramatized, foreshortened, or inflected version of him, the poem's controlling consciousness shares with the reader the task of infusing relations into an inert, lifeless text. He invites the reader to adopt his own, supervening perspective, all-knowing, all-seeing, and all-relating, *the perspective of the maker*.

The Waste Land, then, superficially disjointed, remains fundamentally capable of revealing relations part to part, and part to whole. Yet unless we apply the term to something so odd and partial as to fall into a category sui generis, the poem withholds a protagonist. Among other problems, the vital element of Christian accession or consistency with the Grail legend is missing. The Hindu excursion to the Ganges, moreover, turns out to have ventured not far from the Unitarian River Charles. Ultimately the theatrical and poetical rendering, the ambitious procedure of superficial fragmentation concealing relational unity, and the ubiquitous sense of an independent moral, emotional, and intellectual center carry the poem; not the action or substantive incident, much of whose core remains indefinite. This indefiniteness, I reiterate, is not necessarily a flaw. The chief use of a poem's meaning, Eliot argued, may be only to divert the reader's mind while the poem proceeds to do its work. Some poets, however, "become impatient of this 'meaning' which seems superfluous, and perceive possibilities of intensity through its elimination."[45]

The poem illustrates how the aesthetic difficulty – unifying the poetic fragments – and the psychological and spiritual crux – unifying the self and the soul – compose a single problem. It is nevertheless not unreasonable to conclude that although art can render and organize the fragments, art without faith cannot alone fuse the fragments into the peace which passeth understanding. An extra-artistic, extra-aesthetic thing, faith is what *The Waste Land* points and aspires to, but cannot itself create. As Eliot concluded after his religious conversion:

> Nothing in this world or the next is a substitute for anything else; and if you find that you must do without something, such as religious faith or philosophic belief, then you must just do without it. I can persuade myself, I find, that some of the things that I can hope to get are better worth having than some of the things I cannot get; or I may hope to alter myself so as to want different things; but I cannot persuade myself

that it is the same desires that are satisfied, or that I have in effect the same thing under a different name.[46]

Is it unreasonable to suppose that Eliot could not have written these two sentences until he had completed *The Waste Land* and exhausted its particular possibilities? Only two years before, literary tradition had thrived in a prose garden beneath the filtered, aesthetic shade of *The Sacred Wood;* there the trees flourished, and the gods lived. In *The Waste Land* of contemporary poetry, however, something afflicts the power of art; the gods have fled and the trees have withered, leaving a barren emotional landscape not unlike what Eliot would later call the "well-lighted desert of atheism."[47] In Eliot's career, *The Waste Land* establishes the limit of art, and hence a boundary of his aestheticism. The poem seems to show that even though they may function in similar ways (as I have argued elsewhere), philosophy, art, and religion are not simply different names for the same thing. Though *The Waste Land* may illustrate the effect and desideratum of faith, it cannot by itself supply the cause or the fact of faith. It catches Eliot at the middle point of his long transit from cynic to visionary: In "Preludes," "the worlds revolve like ancient women gathering fuel in vacant lots," while "Burnt Norton" begins "at the still point of the turning world." *The Waste Land,* however, only sets forth what must be done, acknowledges that it should be done, and shows how it might be done. But it does not do it. Yet.

The dandy – at least the *dandysme moral* of Baudelaire and Laforgue – gave a literary embodiment to Eliot's earliest skepticism, which progressed into disillusion before metamorphosing into religious vision. The dandy and the visionary form a curious collection of similarities and differences. Both, for instance, aspire to superiority, mastery, and power, the difference being the realm over which they seek to obtain dominion. The dandy moves in a social arena, applying his wit's sharp blade to trim any rough edges it encounters. The visionary moves at the level of metaphysics, the spirit, and the supernatural, grasping layers of truth and reality beyond everyday consciousness. Whereas the dandy emphasizes personality, impersonality – if not objectivity – distinguishes the visionary.

If *The Waste Land* finds Eliot at midpoint in his journey from skeptical dandyism to religious vision, formally speaking the poem occupies the middle ground between Eliot's early use of personae and dramatic monologue and his late recourse to a first-person, lyric poetic voice. Departing from a technique that typified Eliot's early poetry, *The Waste Land* contains no central, named persona – no Prufrock, no Gerontion – even though at times named characters, such as Tiresias, appear to speak. It merges aspects of both: containing a multitude of voices and characters, yet retaining the recognizable presence of its author. *The Waste Land* portrays Eliot's singular interests and emotions, yet filters them through diverse characters, incidents, and allusions quite distinguishable from him. Presenting dramatized personae as well as Eliot's identifiable lyric voice, *The Waste Land* probably remains something sui generis, profitably (though incompletely) analyzed from either point of view, because containing both of them. What needs to be said – perhaps all that can be said – is that the voice in *The Waste Land* belongs to the poem's author, from whom the voice is partly distinct but with whom it is also partly identical. We may not want it both ways, but that is the way we have it. Ambiguities concerning the author's distance from and presence in his poem constitute perhaps the most difficult "relation" that *The Waste Land* requires the reader, with all possible delicacy, to adjust.

The Waste Land mediates the polarities of Eliot's poetic journey in yet another sense. Tiresias, that is, remains the poem's "most important personage" not simply because he "unites all the rest" or because he joins sexual opposites, male and female. Cynicism and vision also meet in Tiresias. His disillusion arises from seeing too much. Although physically blinded, even "at the violet hour," Tiresias "can see." He need not even look; having "perceived the scene" and having been condemned to await the expected guest, he has not only "foretold" but has "foresuffered" all enacted there, before it even happened. "What Tiresias *sees*" – Eliot's emphasis – "is the substance of the poem." Yet he sees only a more inclusive version of the waste land than the typist and clerk; it cannot yet be called "vision." Despite his vantage point, no more than a typist, a house agent's clerk, and their predictable carryings-on fill his view; only repetition, sameness, and lack of progression reward his superior acuity. Thus his point of view only feeds his cynicism; he has the means to see, but not yet the power of vision.

For Eliot, vision did not simply reach above and beyond; it also extended below and beneath. In literary terms, this inclusiveness involved contacting that "inexhaustible and terrible nebula of emotion which surrounds all our exact and practical passions and mingles with them" or using words having a "network of tentacular roots reaching down to the deepest terrors and desires." It also involves qualities Eliot found in Elizabethan dramatists: a pattern, or "undertone, of the personal emotion, the personal drama and struggle," and a dimension distinct from the literal actions and characters, "a kind of doubleness in the action, as if it took place on two planes at once."[48] Likewise, it involves a wide-ranging emotional inclusiveness, uniting extremes of upper and lower, inner and outer, width and depth. Comparing the characters of Shakespeare and Jonson, Eliot suggested that Falstaff represented the satisfaction of feelings not only more numerous, but more complicated. Calling Falstaff the offspring of feelings deeper and less apprehensible, although not necessarily more intense or strong, than Jonson's, Eliot concluded that Shakespeare's creation did not differ because of the distinction between feeling and thought, or because of Shakespeare's superior perception or insight. Eliot accounted for the difference by pointing to Shakespeare's "susceptibility to a greater range of emotion, and emotion deeper and more obscure."[49]

An upper and lower, a visible surface and an undertone or underpattern, a superficial fragmentation concealing a network of relations uniting disparate parts, and an emotional breadth: These aspects of *The Waste Land* construct an incipient visionary architecture. This must be why the notes exist. Eliot added them so readers would not miss the framework that held the poem's detailed façade in place. (Of course, besides telling readers how to treat the poem, these analogues, allusions, and attributions that link it to external sources must also have reassured the author of its objectivity, that it was not wholly personal. They act as a kind of control to Eliot's poetic experiment.)

Reading *The Waste Land* requires scrutiny of this double structure. Beneath the poem's detailed, shifting surfaces, the reader must discover the relational filigree the fragments conceal. Eliot addressed one of the crucial problems this architecture poses, the task of deciding whether a voice, self, or center ties it together. Speaking of Pound's "peculiarity of expressing oneself through historical masks," Eliot implied how a reader might distill – or "collate" – the author's presence in *The Waste Land*. Pound, Eliot wrote, imposed upon himself the restless condition of changing his mask continually, which in turn required readers to shift their ground. Eliot called Pound more himself and more at ease behind one of his masks than when speaking in his own person. "He must hide to reveal himself. But if we collate all these disguises we find not a mere collection of green-room properties, but Mr. Pound."[50] Masks and poetic surfaces, that is, both conceal and reveal the poet and the meaning beneath and behind.

Two years before *The Waste Land,* Eliot thus suggests a way of placing, or replacing, the poet in his poem. Many years later, writing of St. John Perse's *Anabasis,* Eliot set forth the other, more impersonal demand upon the reader, perhaps recollecting his own long poem:

> Any obscurity of the poem, on first readings, is due to the suppression of "links in the chain," of explanatory and connecting matter, and not to incoherence, or to the love of cryptogram. The justification of such abbreviation of method is that the sequence of images coincides and concentrates into one intense impression of barbaric civilization. The reader has to allow the images to fall into his memory successively without questioning the reasonableness of each at the moment; so that, at the end, a total effect is produced.

> Such selection of a sequence of images and ideas has nothing chaotic
> about it. There is a logic of the imagination as well as a logic of con-
> cepts.[51]

Such a method may tax a reader's intellectual and aesthetic faith, but it
emphasizes two points about the author and his reader. First, the images
and their sequence do succumb to conscious – even "logical" – control;
they are neither random, arbitrary, nor the indulgent gamesmanship of
difficulty for its own sake. Second, a reader must maintain an ambivalent, two-pronged attitude toward such writing, combining passive
receptivity (allowing images to fall into memory "without questioning"
their reasonableness) and active analysis (constantly collating the disguises and synthesizing the relations). Any obscurity, that is, should
progressively dissipate after the "first readings." Rereadings, by coincidence and concentration of the images, should create an impression described by the word to which Eliot increasingly attached the highest
poetic value as he progressed toward vision: The impression should be
"intense."

The Waste Land ultimately arrives at a relationship to the reader that
posits a controlling consciousness aware of all the poem's parts, yet also
aware, like the reader, that its parts know nothing of one another. The reader
must assume the point of view, or adopt the assumptions, of the poet
vis-à-vis his creation, becoming necessarily more aware than the characters within it. Like such characters, the poem's parts have no awareness
of other parts. The poet, however, has placed those parts in relation,
which relation gives the parts a meaning intelligible to – and in a sense
cocreated by – a reader, even though the relations a reader draws between the parts will not invariably match those of the poet. Hence,
though on one level it allows the poet to withhold his personality, suppressing the "links in the chain" means that on the interpretative, func-
tional level the reader and poet converge almost to identity. Unlike the
people in the poem, the author and reader can apprehend all the fragments and discern their relation to one another. And knowing that we
may imitate the poet's superior, more inclusive consciousness makes us
resemble not only the poet in relation to his poem, but also Eliot's poetic
heroes in relation to their surroundings. Such cocreative reading demands a vision that can incorporate above and below, surface and depth,
disorder and "relations." Eliot defined the poet's essential advantage as
not that of having "a beautiful world with which to deal: it is to be able
to see beneath both beauty and ugliness; to see the boredom, and the
horror, and the glory."[52]

We may thus approximate the inclusive consciousness of the poet and
visionary, able to join the opposites of beauty and ugliness, sublimity
and practicality. The dandy poet Baudelaire spread before Eliot the pos-

sibility of extracting high beauty – "intensity" – from the meanest, most "sordid" surroundings. And not only was this beauty composed out of metropolitan imagery, but it was to be presented in a double aspect: both literally – "as it is" – and as something else, as part of an inclusive poetic vision. Baudelaire, Eliot wrote, did not create for others a mode of expression simply by using sordid, metropolitan imagery or images of common life. Instead, by presenting such imagery as it was, while causing it at the same time to represent something more than itself, Baudelaire elevated it to the *"first intensity."*[53] Throughout his early poetry, Eliot had endeavored to capture what had formerly been considered "the impossible, the sterile, the intractably unpoetic." When writing *The Waste Land,* he thought in visionary terms, with an inclusive poetic unity. The five-line stanza beginning "I am the Resurrection and the Life," almost formulaically gathered the opposites of spirit and flesh, mortal and eternal life, fixity and flux, man and woman, suffering and aggression. All these themes appear in *The Waste Land,* yet what is remarkable about this visionary fragment from the facsimile is that Eliot could not fit it into the poem with which it was in many ways so consistent.

It might have pointed in the direction he wished to move but could not yet do so in his poetry. Eliot's progress toward vision transpired only in stages, pursuant to models set forth by the dandies, skeptics, and cynics. Baudelaire, for instance, left Eliot

> a precedent for the poetical possibilities . . . of the more sordid aspects of the modern metropolis, of the possibility of fusion between the sordidly realistic and the phantasmagoric, the possibility of the juxtaposition of the matter-of-fact and the fantastic. From him, as from Laforgue, I learned that the sort of material that I had, the sort of experience that an adolescent had had, in an industrial city in America, could be the material for poetry.[54]

Needless to say, this "precedent" influenced a major poem that intended to represent the sort of experience an adult had in a financial city in England. Eliot carefully phrased this lesson in terms of balanced doubleness – the "fusion" and "juxtaposition" of opposites, the "realistic" and "matter-of-fact" versus the "phantasmagoric" and "fantastic." The quotation also outlines how Eliot approached and defended himself against the sordid, urban reality by seeing it as material for art.

The city – evil, ugly, fascinating – captured Eliot's early awareness. He ransacked St. Louis, Boston, Paris, and London, retrieving images of a decaying, implicitly corrupt civilization. This search, however, set in motion a process that transfigured Eliot's poetry a second time, requiring a new literary model with a different sort of visionary precedent. As the Jacobeans and nineteenth-century French poets had satisfied Eliot's early poetic needs, so Dante ultimately guided his developing awareness of visionary poetry:

> The great poet should not only perceive and distinguish more clearly than other men, the colours or sounds within the range of ordinary vision or hearing; he should perceive vibrations beyond the range of ordinary men, and be able to make men see and hear more at each end than they could ever see without his help. . . . The Divine Comedy expresses everything in the way of emotion, between depravity's despair and the beatific vision, that man is capable of experiencing.[55]

What had once been ambiguities, precisely distinguished subtleties, and hardheaded ironies in Eliot's vocabulary have now become something new, and mystical. Now the poet not only sees more clearly what ordinary people see. He sees beyond ordinary things: He sees "vibrations." No word could more suitably distinguish Eliot at the close of his poetic career from his earliest attitude. Had Eliot encountered this notion of the poet's task in his late twenties, it is almost pleasant to imagine the firestorm of disdain such an indefinite, indefinable word as "vibrations" would have touched off. Yet three decades later, he could seriously and un-self-consciously propose it as an indicium of the poet's uniqueness. It was not the only one, of course, for simply seeing better, and seeing more, do not alone make a poet. The poet must return to earth, into society, using the language of his fellow human beings. Though his visionary self remains isolated, the poet must retain his social personality, expressing what he sees in a social – even democratic – medium. Without language, or an audience, the visionary act remains, from the poet's point of view, incomplete. The seer must also be a sayer. Dante constantly reminded Eliot of the poet's

> obligation to explore, to find words for the inarticulate, to capture those feelings which people can hardly even feel, because they have no words for them; and at the same time, a reminder that the explorer beyond the frontiers of ordinary consciousness will only be able to return and report to his fellow-citizens, if he has all the time a firm grasp upon the realities with which they are already acquainted.[56]

Each step along Eliot's journey from cynicism to vision involved a poetic hero, whose very flaws implied a heroic estimate of the poet's role, of his special abilities, and of his ethic. Eliot's introduction to *Adventures of Huckleberry Finn* sums up the values of these poetic heroes. Published in 1950, well after his major poems and criticism, this essay reflects an interesting engagement with a fellow Missourian. The essay is late in two senses; it is among Eliot's last major literary essays, and because Eliot's parents kept Twain's novel from him as a child, he apparently did not read it until middle age. Eliot's comparison of Tom and

Huck nevertheless illuminates values that informed his poetry from its very beginning. It seems a particularly sweet irony that Eliot found the moral, ethical, and perceptual qualities of his visionary poetic hero distilled in a quintessentially American figure, Huck Finn.

Unlike Tom, whom Eliot calls "wholly a social being" with "imagination," Huck "has, instead, vision. He sees the real world; and he does not judge it – he allows it to judge itself. . . . Huck Finn is alone. . . . The fact that he has a father only emphasizes his loneliness; and he views his father with a terrifying detachment. . . . He is the impassive observer." Penetrating vision; nonjudgmental observation of a world that will convict itself; aloneness and loneliness; and a terrifying detachment: All these qualities set the stage for Eliot's central statement about Huck, which states Eliot's conclusions about his own poetry. "Huck is passive and impassive, apparently always the victim of events; and yet, in his acceptance of his world and of what it does to him and others, he is more powerful than his world, because he is more *aware* than any other person in it."[57]

The key figures in Eliot's early poetry – the speaker in "Preludes," Prufrock, Gerontion, Tiresias – all share this quality; all are somehow more "aware" than any other person they come into contact with. It would furthermore appear by analogy that the same analysis fixes Eliot vis-à-vis his poetic creations; the author is likewise more completely "aware" than his characters, even when they reflect aspects of his own moods, interests, and problems. Perhaps most crucially, passivity and victimization, instead of the products of powerlessness, become the means to power inasmuch as they permit a superior awareness, a more capacious, inclusive consciousness. The observer's detached passivity may subtract from his ability to act, but it adds to his ability to see, and thus to know. Hence even if knowledge is not necessarily power in the world, his superior awareness gives the poetic hero the power to prevail over it. Cynicism, by merely seeing through things, at first sees only disillusion. But having pierced the negative, the ugly, the compromised, seeing through may ultimately lead to insight, to understanding, to vision. The cynic feels he sees too much, too clearly; the visionary wants to see all he possibly can, as intensely as he can.

These values characterize not only Eliot's principal characters, and not only Eliot in relation to his own poems. They also describe Eliot's ideal reader. Given its unusual form, of no poem is this more true than *The Waste Land*. The poem's demands – collating the masks; establishing the relations part to part and part to whole; staying receptive to stylistic shifts and verbal nuance; and remaining detached throughout that process, lest the adoption of a final point of view obscure some relation or bar it from penetrating the consciousness – require the suspension of judgment and preservation of detachment, the *impersonality* and *surrender,* that become critical values not only in reading poetry, but in relation to life.

The Waste Land, then, and our relationship to it, reproduce consciousness, which boils down to the juxtapositions and fusions we arrange between things that have no relation other than that which we give them. Eliot's – and our, once we read and understand the poem – command of reality remains so much more complete than that of its scenes and characters that we and Eliot exist both privileged and burdened by the knowledge. This superior, if painful, consciousness – which includes as an axiom the awareness of how unconsciously most people behave – explains one of Eliot's characteristic emotions: arrogance mitigated by frustration, distance combined with sympathy, and acute regret that this knowledge, such as it is, compensates for the loss of innocence so meagerly. His characters – from "Preludes" forward – inhabit a more limited, less complete, and less conscious universe than Eliot, who appears at various moments to regard their omissions as both unforgivable and tragic.

Nowhere, however, does the method bear greater import than in *The Waste Land,* where a feeling of the dispiriting unreality of things coexists with a kind of voyeurism: observing people who are unaware of any scrutiny heightens the sense of real life while emphasizing the observer's detachment and inability to intervene. *The Waste Land,* then, lies beyond, but also within. It is finally a damaged or partial consciousness that has rendered the world and the self such deadly, boring, and futile places to be. By being an artifact and an allegory of self-consciousness (at equally a personal, aesthetic, historical, and social level), *The Waste Land* epitomizes its author's uniqueness, and his dilemma. Eliot's self-consciousness condemns the self to paralysis, but also may present it with irrevocable, privileged vision. Its ambiguities invite ambivalence, yet also characterize our modern consciousness and our historical time. They preserve Eliot as the characteristic poet of our age, with its curious spiritual demoralization amid material and erotic plenty, its tendency toward credulous emotion and overwrought intellect, and the loneliness of individuals stranded among its crowds. Eliot wrote with a deep doubt of progress insofar as the complexity of human endeavors outruns our capacity to comprehend and perhaps even to exist with them. Are we fated – or doomed – to discover if our self-consciousness can survive our creations? Eliot once wrote hypothetically that advanced, extreme self-consciousness, whether of language – as in the poetry of Valéry – or of indefinitely elaborated scientific, political, and social machinery, might produce a strain against the human nerves, and mind would rebel, producing an "irresistible revulsion of humanity and a readiness to accept the most primitive hardships rather than carry any longer the burden of modern civilization."[58] Has such a point been reached; does it approach; or has it already been surpassed?

Afterword

The first of some remaining matters I should like to discuss concerns a regret. The scope of my remarks provided no suitable occasion to explore, in any systematic way, the tone of iconoclasm, malicious humor, and arch complicity that is so prominent in Eliot's early verse but that nearly vanishes after 1927 (though reappearing at unexpected moments in the drama, such as when the four knights address the audience late in *Murder in the Cathedral*). Part of Eliot's humor had to do with addressing one audience while rebuffing another. Eliot was a crafty cultural politician, and nowhere more clearly than in his early tendency to clothe himself in the style of the buffoon, the joker, the snake in the grass. Though on occasion it got him into trouble, this vein is useful and corrective, and it is Eliot at his most alive. Its disappearance reduced his poetry's breadth, and I wish he had persisted in it a little longer. There is not enough of it around. Although understanding the seriousness is often necessary for understanding the comedy, the opposite is true as well. To overlook Eliot's satire, derision, and a certain vaudeville quality is to miss the ballast of his gravity, pessimism, and intellectual passion. It is to neglect also the clues that most reveal him as a bizarre "late product," a genuine exotic.

I confess it is this sense of the ridiculous that struck me when I first read Eliot, long ago by now. It is, however, a qualified ridiculousness, never far from self-mockery. (Even Eliot's sometime devotion to convention scarcely conceals a note of parody.) It includes a whole arsenal of techniques and effects, from refined irony to absurdist slapstick and camp. Only later, through the process critic after critic has remarked (often with a degree of bemusement or even irritation that poetry – *poetry!* – could so insidiously overtake one's sensibility), did his "serious" aspects begin first to complicate and then to dominate my view of Eliot. "I do not know for certain how much of my own mind he invented" – Empson's high if ambivalent praise shows how dangerous exposure to Eliot's early work can be. Perhaps it is the business of poems to be dangerous.

Eliot's exclusion of humor from his later verse, however, robbed it of some of its danger, and thus of part of its power. That a line like "I have measured out my life with coffee spoons" is at least partly ludicrous makes its terror all the more pressing. That the same poet could express exhaustion and disillusion so terribly and yet at the same time ridicule them so utterly still seems a new thing to me, and a valuable thing. My own treatment of Eliot perhaps errs in favor of the former element – the sources of his disillusion and exhaustion, anger and defiance – and I regret therefore that my remarks too seldom hint at the fun in Eliot's early poems. (Its absence from Eliot's late poems deprives them of a dimension that, given the philosophical and spiritual breakthroughs they implicitly claim, one would have hoped to find.) It is worth making the effort to remember how the comedy countervails the gravity, not only for enjoyment's sake, but for the sake of a complete understanding of Eliot and his writing. Neither Eliot's comedy nor his seriousness need always prevail. Hot and cold, tragic and comic, upright and rebellious, pitiful and playful: The presence of complementary opposites welcomed me into Eliot's poetic universe. Their equipoise, present in images and rhythms as well as in Eliot's tone, addresses something submerged and inarticulable in the sensibility, but necessary to it and of its essence.

We nevertheless can hardly expect a poet to continue to compose to our specifications; his first duty is to conform to his own. For Eliot, this came to mean a commitment to Christianity, of whose nature and qualities I have spoken perhaps too frequently and too speculatively. I can only assert that his commitment altered something essential, even if in other respects Eliot's thought and basic world view remained almost weirdly consistent from first to last. (Compare, for instance, the first three lines of "Burnt Norton" with *Knowledge and Experience in the Philosophy of F. H. Bradley*, pp. 54–5, speaking of past and future as ideal constructions, not true in any actual sense but simply by virtue of their relations to other ideas. "The present of ideal construction, the present of meaning and not simply of psychical or physical process, is really a span which includes my present ideas of past and future.") The later poetry confirms the extent to which Eliot combined, in his early work, highly flexible erudition and command of verbal nuance with an imagination operating within a set of relatively inelastic categories. Satire and humor may vanish from Eliot's later poetry, and the irony change its character, but doubleness – one theme throughout my remarks – does not. It simply becomes more abstract and philosophical, that is to say, more self-conscious – another key motif in my discussions.

It is curious that, on one hand, Eliot's poetic and metaphysics were so inclusive – seeking to incorporate diversities, even to the point of including and reconciling opposites. Yet on the other hand, his social perceptions were so exclusive – so dependent on the class model, so uneasy about social mobility and the ambiguity of change. His theology and poetry absorbed contraries with ambitious appetite, yet his social attitudes tended to resist and refuse, holding unpleasant realities at bay. Yet perhaps it is no paradox at all to watch Eliot's heroic efforts using words to unite remote aesthetic, metaphysical, and semantic disparities, while noting his unwillingness to make the psychological or intellectual effort necessary to stop his quarrel with social ones. If it is a paradox, it is not an uncommon one. A dissonant self, and an imagination under strain, may welcome the risks and pains of art, yet refuse to venture very far into social strain and dissonance.

In these respects, too, I have speculated upon the appeal that Christianity, and especially the Incarnation, may have exerted upon Eliot insofar as it could give him a means of reconciling doubleness of diverse kinds. Such reconciliation proceeds by means of a terrestrial ideal and a divine personage who represents a productive ambiguity, analogous to the way words in poems can represent productive ambiguity, clutching opposites to themselves and holding them in balance and suspension. (I have elsewhere dwelled upon Eliot's attitude toward art. Eliot decisively warned us away from linking him to smoke-and-surplices Catholicism. But perhaps in this single respect – insofar as the Incarnation rhymes so closely with Eliot's preconversion poetic – his Christianity was that of an aesthete.) Christianity evidently assisted Eliot's long effort to reconcile extremes of moral knowledge and mortal existence and to defuse his debilitating sense of radical ambiguity in the world and in consciousness. Self, time, society, nation, history, reality, memory, experience: If these things have a double nature, they have an indefinite one. When Eliot's interests seem remote and even ultramundane at times, herein lie both the precipitating and the mitigating circumstances.

Before he applied religion to them, however, Eliot faced these problems with words, intellectual and poetic. He is among the most purely rhetorical of poets, a characterization my remarks on ambiguity not only do not contradict but reinforce. In this way his rhetoric becomes a function of his sincerity, necessary to express it, necessary to release him from its limitations and yet dramatize his obsession with it. Through doubleness of language, through its maximal employment, through making words work hard, and by making them "incarnations," Eliot's distressed imagination found self-knowledge and relief. Further inquiries therefore might do well to ask again how Christianity met the needs aestheticism had once addressed, taking over poetry's place and giving satisfactions it could not. His religion, that is to say, ultimately affected his imagination, his writing, and all the other categories that his life comprised. It gave Eliot the great relation, and the grand poetic, he had always sought.

Notes

When a quotation from Eliot's major poems or essays or from accessible works by other standard authors is not cited in a note, the text will provide a source. Occasionally the source for two or more brief quotations will appear in the next numbered note. After the first citation, later notes in the same chapter give only author, short title, and page. Citations provide specific acknowledgment of permissions to quote. The notes abbreviate the following book titles:

BOOKS BY T. S. ELIOT

A.S.G.	*After Strange Gods: A Primer of Modern Heresy* (New York: Harcourt Brace, 1934)
C.P.P.	*The Complete Poems and Plays of T. S. Eliot* (London, Faber & Faber, 1969)
F.L.A.	*For Lancelot Andrewes: Essays on Style and Order* (Garden City, N.Y., Doubleday, Doran, 1929)
I.C.S.	*The Idea of a Christian Society* (New York, Harcourt Brace, 1940)
K.E.P.	*Knowledge and Experience in the Philosophy of F. H. Bradley* (New York, Farrar, Straus, 1964)
N.T.D.C.	*Notes Towards the Definition of Culture* (London, Faber & Faber, 1962)
O.P.P.	*On Poetry and Poets* (London, Faber & Faber, 1957)
S.E.	*Selected Essays*, 3d ed. (London, Faber & Faber, 1951)
S.W.	*The Sacred Wood: Essays on Poetry and Criticism* (London, Methuen, 1960)
T.C.C.	*To Criticize the Critic and Other Writings* (London, Faber & Faber, 1978)
U.P.U.C.	*The Use of Poetry and the Use of Criticism: Studies in the Relation of Criticism to Poetry in England* (London, Faber & Faber, 1964)

BOOKS BY OTHER AUTHORS

A.R.	F. H. Bradley, *Appearance and Reality: A Metaphysical Essay*, 2d ed. (Oxford, Oxford Univ. Press, 1897)

223

C.O.U.S.   George Santayana, *Character and Opinion in the United States* (New York, Norton, 1967)

E.E.Y.   Lyndall Gordon, *Eliot's Early Years* (New York, Oxford Univ. Press, 1978)

E.H.A.   Henry Adams, *The Education of Henry Adams: An Autobiography* (Boston, Houghton Mifflin, 1946)

I.H.   Henry James, *Italian Hours* (New York, Grove Press, 1979)

N.S.F.B.   Herbert Howarth, *Notes on Some Figures Behind T. S. Eliot* (Boston, Houghton Mifflin, 1964)

P.T.   Philip Greven, *The Protestant Temperament: Patterns of Child-Rearing, Religious Experience, and the Self in Early America* (New York, Knopf, 1977)

T.A.S.   Henry James, *The American Scene* (Bloomington, Indiana Univ. Press, 1968)

U.C.   Daniel Walker Howe, *The Unitarian Conscience: Harvard Moral Philosophy, 1805–1861* (Cambridge, Mass., Harvard Univ. Press, 1970)

W.G.E.   Charlotte C. Eliot, *William Greenleaf Eliot: Minister, Educator, Philanthropist* (Boston, Houghton, Mifflin, 1904)

1. THE SOULS OF THE DEVOUT

Family, Nation, and Religion

1. *N.T.D.C.*, p. 43.
2. T. S. Eliot, "A Romantic Patrician," *Athenaeum*, May 2, 1919, pp. 266–7.
3. Biographical information has been derived from *N.S.F.B.*; *W.G.E.*; and John J. Soldo, "The American Foreground of T. S. Eliot," *New England Quarterly*, September 1972, pp. 355–72.
4. T. S. Eliot, "American Literature and the American Language," *T.C.C.*, p. 44.
5. *W.G.E.*, pp. xv, 14–15. Rev. Eliot's values might be called typically Unitarian, though the life patterns and achievements of his contemporaries offer few analogies to his unusual errand into the wilderness. One Unitarian contemporary, however, also left auspicious Boston surroundings to minister to a wide open, frontier city. Thomas Starr King arrived in 1860 to take a post at the First Unitarian Church of San Francisco, which "offered the only Unitarian pulpit west of St. Louis" (Kevin Starr, *Americans and the California Dream: 1850–1915* [New York, Oxford Univ. Press, 1973], p. 97). That St. Louis pulpit belonged to Rev. William Greenleaf Eliot. Though King lived in California less than four years before his premature death at age thirty-nine, his high-minded energy and accomplishments paralleled those of Rev. Eliot in St. Louis and similarly impressed the state's citizens (see Starr, *Americans and the California Dream*, pp. 97–105). Significantly, Rev. Eliot's eldest son, Thomas Lamb Eliot (T. S. Eliot's uncle), followed very much in his father's footsteps to another remote western city, establishing a Unitarian church in Portland, Oregon, imitating his father's example in numerous

other ways, and achieving similar local reputation and influence (see *N.S.F.B.*, pp. 14–18).

6. *Letters of Ralph Waldo Emerson,* ed. Ralph L. Rusk (New York, Columbia Univ. Press, 1939), vol. 4, p. 338. For Rev. Eliot's life and achievements, see *W.G.E.; N.S.F.B.,* chap. 1; *E.E.Y.,* chap. 1; and "The Eliot Family and St. Louis," an appendix prepared by the Department of English, Washington Univ., to T. S. Eliot, *American Literature and the American Language* (St. Louis, Mo., Washington Univ., 1953), pp. 33–7.

7. *W.G.E.,* pp. 124–5.

8. *E.H.A.,* p. 34.

9. T. S. Eliot, "A Sceptical Patrician," *Athenaeum,* April 23, 1919, pp. 361–2.

10. Donald Meyer, "The Dissolution of Calvinism," in *Paths of American Thought,* ed. Arthur M. Schlesinger, Jr., and Morton White (Boston, Houghton Mifflin, 1963), pp. 82–3.

11. *W.G.E.,* pp. 13–18, records that Channing had been the pastor of Rev. Eliot's parents and grandparents and that Rev. Eliot was "strongly influenced by [Channing] in his early religious views," attended Channing's Federal Street Church while attending Harvard Divinity School, and was ordained there in 1834.

12. F. O. Matthiessen, *American Renaissance: Art and Expression in the Age of Emerson and Whitman* (New York, Oxford Univ. Press, 1968), p. 446. See also Quentin Anderson, *The Imperial Self: An Essay in American Literary and Cultural History* (New York, Knopf, 1971), pp. 11–12.

13. T. S. Eliot, "[A Review of] Mens Creatrix," *International Journal of Ethics,* July 1917, pp. 542–3.

14. T. S. Eliot, "[A Review of] Religion and Philosophy," *International Journal of Ethics,* July 1917, p. 543.

15. William E. Channing, "Unitarian Christianity: Discourse at the Ordination of the Rev. Jared Sparks," in *The Works of William E. Channing* (Boston, American Unitarian Assoc., 1867), vol. 3, p. 90.

16. See ibid., pp. 69–73.

17. Ibid., pp. 74–5.

18. *U.C.:* on spirit triumphing over matter, p. 41; on perfectability, p. 6; and on ethics and common sense philosophy, pp. 7, 56, 100–9, 120.

19. Channing, "Unitarian Christianity," p. 93.

20. Lyman Abbott, *The Evolution of Christianity* (New York, Outlook, 1925), pp. 254–5.

21. T. S. Eliot, "[Review of] Son of Woman: The Story of D. H. Lawrence," *Criterion,* July 1931, p. 771.

22. T. S. Eliot, "[Review of] Conscience and Christ," *International Journal of Ethics,* October 1916, p. 112.

23. A. D. Moody, *Thomas Stearns Eliot, Poet* (Cambridge Univ. Press, 1979), pp. 41–9, reproduces Eliot's "Syllabus of a Course of Six Lectures on Modern French Literature." For Eliot, "humanitarianism" persisted as a favorite target, linked to religious liberalism and Unitarianism. Comparing Protestantism, the Roman church, and assorted "*disjecta membra*" in America, Eliot

criticized several consequences created by religion without humanism. Among them was "liberal uplift," which led him to characterize liberalism in religion as a "form of bigotry," committed presumably by the "cultivated divines of the most radical wing of Unitarianism" (T. S. Eliot, "Religion Without Humanism," in *Humanism and America: Essays on the Outlook of Modern Civilisation,* ed. Norman Foerster [New York: Farrar & Rinehart, 1930], pp. 107–8).

24. See, e.g., Peter Gregg Slater, *Children in the New England Mind in Death and in Life* (Hamden, Conn., Archon Books, 1977), examining the issue of infant depravity and damnation in New England and relating the progression from seventeenth-century Calvinist innate depravity to Enlightenment *tabula rasa* and finally to nineteenth-century Romantic notions of the child's innate goodness: devilish sinfulness, to impressionable plasticity, to cherubic innocence (see, e.g., p. 50).

This change in the view of children mirrored New England culture's rejection of the idea of Original Sin. Similarly, the Calvinistic angry God of justice gave way to the liberal benevolent God of mercy. The view of Christ's nature also changed, as Matthiessen has described, from essentially divine to qualitatively human. It is not clear what Eliot specifically wished to revive in the complex of doctrines centering around Original Sin, and it is likely that at least initially he used the concept to attack the Unitarian, liberal, and Romantic formulations of his upbringing. Surely Eliot did not wish to reimpose Calvinist notions such as imputed guilt, though he was aware of the infant damnation controversy. See T. S. Eliot, untitled chapter, in *Revelation,* ed. John Baillie and Hugh Martin (New York, Macmillan, 1937), p. 38.

Slater's discussion clarifies that the Romanticism for which Eliot so frequently expressed distaste had its American roots in liberal, Unitarian theological innovations. Eliot's literary criticism, though superficially secular, thus drew on religious doctrine as he experienced it personally in youth.

25. *A.S.G.,* pp. 45–6.
26. Eliot's September 13, 1939, letter to Eleanor Hinkley, in Nevill Coghill's introduction to *The Family Reunion* (London, Faber & Faber, 1969), p. 44.
27. T. S. Eliot, "Catholicism and International Order," *Essays Ancient and Modern* (New York, Harcourt Brace, 1936), p. 131.
28. *W.G.E.,* pp. 13–28.
29. *U.C.,* pp. 140–1. See also Paul Goodman, "Ethics and Enterprise: The Values of a Boston Elite, 1800–1860," *American Quarterly,* Fall 1966, pp. 437–51.
30. *W.G.E.,* p. 35.
31. *U.C.,* p. 135.
32. Two points on belletrism. First, as Part I of Channing's "Unitarian Christianity" points out, Unitarianism depended upon the interpretation of the word. Howe states that no other American denomination devoted so much of its effort and its confidence to literary activity and belles-lettres (ibid., p. 174). Second, the number of Eliot's ancestors and relatives who published poetry and prose is surely significant. Even if his writing did not conform

substantively, Eliot's poetic vocation nonetheless followed a family tradition.

33. Ibid., p. 183.
34. Ibid., p. 147.
35. Ibid., p. 128.
36. Edmund S. Morgan, *The Puritan Family: Religion and Domestic Relations in Seventeenth-Century New England* (New York, Harper & Row, 1966), especially the chapter "Puritan Tribalism."
37. *I.C.S.*, pp. 28, 30.
38. T. S. Eliot, "A Commentary," *Criterion*, July 1933, p. 645.
39. *I.C.S.*, pp. 27–8.
40. Ibid., p. 43; see also p. 34.
41. Ibid., p. 15.
42. *N.T.D.C.*, p. 48.
43. Ibid., p. 48; see also Eliot's comment in Leslie Paul, "A Conversation with T. S. Eliot," *Kenyon Review*, Winter 1964–5, p. 17, that evil in a class society occurs when privilege exists without duty and responsibility. Evil in a classless society, by contrast, occurs by equalizing responsibility through the whole population, making everyone equally irresponsible.
44. *I.C.S.*, p. 65.
45. Ibid., p. 4.
46. Ibid., pp. 13–14.
47. *N.S.F.B.*, p. 88. For convenience, I have quoted Howarth's summary of President Eliot's seven points in "The Religion of the Future," from Charles William Eliot, *The Durable Satisfactions of Life* (New York, Crowell, 1910). For an account of President Eliot's life, personality, and educational reforms, see Hugh Hawkins, *Between Harvard and America: The Educational Leadership of Charles W. Eliot* (New York, Oxford Univ. Press, 1972).
48. See "Modern Education and the Classics," *S.E.*, p. 512, where Eliot proposed that no one could become truly educated unless he had studied a subject that did not interest him, since part of education involved learning how to interest ourselves in subjects for which we have no aptitude. See also T. S. Eliot, "The Christian Conception of Education," *Malvern, 1941: The Life of the Church and the Order of Society* (London, Longmans Green, 1941), p. 203–4, discussing the shortcomings of President Eliot's view that one subject was as good as another for producing educated people, criticizing the notion that eighteen-year-old students were competent to decide upon their university courses, and linking President Eliot's views to "that optimistic faith in the natural goodness of the human will . . . which perhaps a sounder theology might have corrected."
49. *N.T.D.C.*, p. 26; see also p. 84.
50. *I.C.S.*, p. 41.
51. "Second Thoughts About Humanism," *S.E.*, p. 487. Eliot's debt to Irving Babbitt cannot be underestimated. Babbitt's *Literature and the American College* (Boston, Houghton Mifflin, 1908) prefigures many prominent themes: Eliot's suspicion of progress; his critique of President Eliot's educational

reforms; his statements on the desirability of a moral and intellectual consensus to unify society and discipline the individual; his conclusions about the necessity of cultivating moral habit and sensibility; his prescription that the modern world required principles of restraint; his condemnation of the tendency of specialized, secular thought to seek extremes instead of to balance opposites; his preference for breadth and restrained wisdom instead of specialization and enthusiasm; his advice to revive classical learning for the modern world; his conception that a literary work's significance lies not in novelty but in its relation to antecedent literature; and that true modernity does not repudiate the past, but rather extends and builds upon it. On the shortcomings of humanism, however, as propounded by Babbitt and others, Eliot was explicit. See, e.g., "Religion Without Humanism," in *Humanism and America,* ed. Foerster, pp. 105–12, esp. p. 110; and "The Humanism of Irving Babbitt," pp. 471–80, and "Second Thoughts About Humanism," *S.E.,* pp. 481–91.

52. Van Wyck Brooks, *The Confident Years: 1885–1915* (New York, Dutton, 1952), pp. 597–8: "Was it not the key to Eliot's tradition that he not only rejected the tradition but that he *reversed* the tradition of the world he had grown up in, or, rather, the strand of tradition that America represented? . . . Eliot's peculiar antipathies, moreover, were such special idols of the American mind as Milton, beloved of the forbears, and Savonarola, the old Italian Cromwellian Puritan, the culture-hero of the Yankees who tried to restore the liberties of the Florentine people." See also D. S. Savage, *The Personal Principle* (1944), excerpted in *T. S. Eliot: A Selected Critique,* ed. Leonard Unger (New York, Rinehart, 1948), p. 155: "Eliot is concerned to emphasize all those cultural values which have been left out of account in the American idea of civilization, which appear as mere excrescences upon the surface of American life."

53. T. S. Eliot, "The Lesson of Baudelaire," *Tyro,* Spring 1921, p. 4.

54. "Niccolo Machiavelli," *F.L.A.,* pp. 50, 53.

55. Ibid., p. 57.

56. T. S. Eliot, "Israfel," *Nation and Athenaeum,* May 21, 1927, p. 219.

57. *W.G.E.,* p. 152.

58. T. S. Eliot, "Catholicism and International Order," *Essays Ancient and Modern,* p. 133.

59. *A.S.G.,* pp. 15–16.

60. Ibid., p. 21. Since Eliot came from St. Louis and had six years earlier relinquished American citizenship, only his family and its past gave him any warrant to call himself a "Yankee." To Southerners the word presumably meant a Union soldier or a Northerner. To New Englanders, it means a distinct, historical elite. To most other Americans, it refers to anyone from New England, when it does not designate a ballplayer. Only in the last case, in noncompetitive surroundings, is the word a neutral term.

61. T. S. Eliot, "A Commentary," *Criterion,* April 1938, p. 482; see also *I'll Take My Stand: The South and the Agrarian Tradition* (Baton Rouge, Louisiana State Univ. Press, 1980), pp. 53 and 170–1, and Eliot's discussion of how it pertains to New England's decline, to the "interest and urbanity" that Amer-

ican history had until 1829, and to the destruction of the upper classes by
"unrestrained industrialism," in "A Commentary," *Criterion*, April 1931,
pp. 483–5. On Josiah Royce, see, e.g., "Provincialism," *Race Questions,
Provincialism, and Other American Problems* (New York, Macmillan, 1908).

62. T. S. Eliot, "Syllabus of a Course of Six Lectures on Modern French Literature" (1916), in Moody, *Thomas Stearns Eliot, Poet*, p. 44. But see T. S.
Eliot, "Catholicism and International Order," *Essays Ancient and Modern*, p.
135, acknowledging his brief announcement of religious, political, and literary faith that had become "too easily quotable" and that may have given the
impression that all three were inextricable and equally important. See also
A.S.G., pp. 29–30, calling the announcement more illuminative of Eliot's
own mind than of the external world, and dismissing it as a "dramatic
posture."

63. "The Function of Criticism," *S.E.*, pp. 26–7.

64. T. S. Eliot, "Preface," Edgar Ansel Mowrer, *This American World* (London,
Faber & Gwyer, 1928), p. xiv. Three decades later, at the centenary of the St.
Louis girls' school his grandfather founded, Eliot recanted this tale, explaining that he thought he heard it from his father and had told it in good faith.
When his sisters and brother heard it, however, they responded with "cries
of derision," sending letters stating that "grandma had never shot a wild
turkey." Eliot responded, "I'm sorry she didn't" (T. S. Eliot, "Address,"
From Mary to You: Centennial, 1859–1959 [St. Louis, Mo., Mary Institute,
1959], p. 135). Eliot's memory, however, was not so far off the mark. His
father's unpublished biography, describing the rough, unsettled state of the
land around his parents' (T. S. Eliot's grandparents') house, mentions the
area's sparse population, the neighborhood's wild turkeys and deer, and the
frequent visits of not always amiable Indians. If Eliot's grandmother did not
shoot turkeys for dinner, she nonetheless once confronted an Indian, in paint
and feathers, who appeared in her kitchen as she prepared the midday meal.
She fled with her baby for a neighbor's help, only to return later to find
nothing missing except a bright red ribbon the Indian had plucked from her
hair (H. W. Eliot, "A Brief Autobiography," [William Greenleaf Eliot Papers, University Archives, Washington Univ. Libraries, Saint Louis, Mo.,
n.d.], pp. 1–2).

65. *U.C.*, pp. 220–1.

66. Henry James, *English Hours* (New York, Oxford Univ. Press, 1981), p. 97.

67. *N.T.D.C.*, pp. 43–4.

68. Soldo, "The American Foreground of T. S. Eliot," p. 355, and Grover
Smith, *T. S. Eliot's Poetry and Plays: A Study in Sources and Meaning*, 2d ed.
(Chicago, Univ. of Chicago Press, 1974), p. 268.

Self

1. Talcott Parsons, "Mental Illness and 'Spiritual Malaise': The Role of the
Psychiatrist and the Minister of Religion," *Social Structure and Personality*
(New York, Free Press, 1964), p. 302.

2. T. S. Eliot, "Popular Theologians: Mr. Wells, Mr. Belloc and Mr. Murry,"
Criterion, May 1927, p. 256.

3. "The Function of Criticism," *S.E.*, p. 26.
4. Tradition: ibid., p. 24; history: "Tradition and the Individual Talent," *S.E.*, p. 17; religion: "Lancelot Andrewes," *F.L.A.*, pp. 21–2; politics: "Niccolo Machiavelli," *F.L.A.*, p. 49; dogmatic religion: T. S. Eliot, "Religion without Humanism," in *Humanism and America,* ed. Foerster, p. 110; and on *Le Serpent:* T. S. Eliot, "A Brief Introduction to the Method of Paul Valéry," in Paul Valéry, *Le Serpent* (London, Cobden-Sanderson, 1924), p. 14.
5. "Tradition and the Individual Talent," *S.E.*, p. 21.
6. T. S. Eliot, "[Review of] Son of Woman," *Criterion,* July 1931, p. 771.
7. T. S. Eliot, *A Sermon Preached in Magdalene College Chapel* (Cambridge Univ. Press, 1948), p. 5.
8. T. S. Eliot, Introduction to Charlotte Eliot, *Savonarola: A Dramatic Poem* (London, Cobden-Sanderson, 1926), pp. ix–x.
9. T. S. Eliot, Introduction to Djuna Barnes, *Nightwood* (New York, New Directions, 1946), p. xv.
10. Harford W. H. Powel, Jr., "Notes on the Life of T. S. Eliot: 1888–1910," Master's thesis, Brown Univ., 1954, alludes to this and to numerous other themes of Eliot's upbringing. See, e.g., p. 30: "All we can say conscientiously is that Eliot's parents maintained a 'hands off' policy (which they would as Unitarians), while keeping the world of reality on the other side of the door." Compare generally Alice Miller, *Prisoners of Childhood,* trans. Ruth Ward (New York, Basic Books, 1981).
11. *P.T.:* on extended family ties and awareness of social differentia, pp. 151–3; the great chain of being, p. 195; moderate habits, p. 214; and the parish model, pp. 258–9.
12. William G. Eliot, *Discourses on the Doctrines of Christianity* (Boston, American Unitarian Assoc., 1881), p. 132.
13. Ibid., p. 133. Eliot criticized the "verbalism" of liberal sermons since Schleiermacher – a theologian admired in the Eliot family – by comparing their language to that used by medieval theologians or by seventeenth-century preachers. The terms of the comparison – two eras of which Eliot approved – suggest its autobiographical context, since Rev. Eliot's discourse self-consciously incorporates such "verbalism," redefining traditional theological terms in a way that T. S. Eliot labeled "corruption." For him, the comparison revealed that words had changed their meanings, losing what had been definite and gaining what was indefinite ("The Perfect Critic," *Athenaeum,* July 23, 1920, p. 103).
14. *P.T.*, p. 198.
15. Ibid., p. 206.
16. William G. Eliot, *Discourses on the Doctrines of Christianity*, pp. 134–5.
17. *P.T.*, p. 206.
18. William G. Eliot, *Discourses on the Doctrines of Christianity*, p. 136.
19. See pp. 7–8, and the chapters "The Unity of God" and "Argument from History" in ibid.
20. "Philip Massinger," *S.E.*, p. 213. See also the critique of "Liberalism" along these lines in *I.C.S.*, pp. 10–14, and of "nihilism" in Leslie Paul, "A Conversation with T. S. Eliot," *Kenyon Review,* Winter 1964–5, p. 14.

21. T. S. Eliot, Introduction to Barnes, *Nightwood*, p. xiii.
22. See D. H. Meyer, *The Instructed Conscience: The Shaping of the American National Ethic* (Philadelphia, Univ. of Pennsylvania Press, 1974); *U.C.*, p. 2, regarding "Moral Philosophy"; and John Murray Cuddihy, *No Offense: Civil Religion and Protestant Taste* (New York, Seabury, 1978).
23. "The 'Pensées' of Pascal," *S.E.*, p. 413.
24. Ibid.
25. William G. Eliot, *Discourses on the Doctrines of Christianity*, pp. 7–8.
26. "Dante," *S.E.*, p. 262.
27. William G. Eliot, *The Discipline of Sorrow*, 5th ed. (Boston, Walker, Wise, 1863), pp. 100–1.
28. William G. Eliot, *Early Religious Education Considered as the Divinely Appointed Way to the Regenerate Life* (Boston, Crosby, Nichols, 1855), pp. 122–3.
29. T. S. Eliot, "A Note on Poetry and Belief," *The Enemy*, January 1927, p. 16, and "The 'Pensées' of Pascal," *S.E.*, p. 411.
30. "The 'Pensées' of Pascal," *S.E.*, p. 407. For an additional suggestion of Eliot's religious motives, see T. S. Eliot, *Religious Drama: Mediaeval and Modern* (New York, House of Books, 1954), n.p., which he introduced by stating that the theater satisfies a human desire to achieve greater dignity and significance than people can do in either private or public life. "There is a very profound kind of boredom which is an essential moment in the religious life, the boredom with all living in so far as it has no religious meaning."
31. William G. Eliot, *Early Religious Education*, p. 37.
32. Ibid., p. 13.
33. T. S. Eliot's November 6, 1921, letter to Richard Aldington, quoted in Valerie Eliot, "Introduction," *The Waste Land: A Facsimile and Transcript of the Original Drafts Including the Annotations of Ezra Pound* (New York, Harcourt Brace Jovanovich, 1971), p. xxii.
34. Harford W. H. Powel, Jr., "Notes on the Life of T. S. Eliot," p. 28; regrettably, Powel's footnote refers to an unrelated source. See also pp. 4, 30.
35. Valerie Eliot quotes T. S. Eliot in "Note," T. S. Eliot, *Poems Written in Early Youth* (New York, Farrar, Straus & Giroux, 1967), pp. v–vi.
36. T. S. Eliot's letter to Paul Elmer More, quoted by John D. Margolis, *T. S. Eliot's Intellectual Development, 1922–1939* (Chicago, Univ. of Chicago Press, 1972), pp. 144–5. Sections IX and X of More's "Marginalia" are particularly significant in light of Eliot's remarks.
37. See George Bornstein, *Transformations of Romanticism in Yeats, Eliot, and Stevens* (Chicago, Univ. of Chicago Press, 1976), tracing Eliot's critical conclusions to temperament and personal experience. Eliot's later essays often recall poetic discovery as a sequence of intense revelations. See, e.g., "Note to Chapter I: On the Development of Taste in Poetry," *U.P.U.C.*, pp. 32–6.
38. T. S. Eliot, "A Sceptical Patrician," *Athenaeum*, May 23, 1919, p. 362.
39. "To Criticize the Critic," *T.C.C.*, p. 22.
40. T. S. Eliot, "Reflections on Contemporary Poetry," *Egoist*, July 1919, p. 39; reprinted by permission of Mrs. Valerie Eliot and Faber & Faber Ltd. Compare Gregory Jay, *T. S. Eliot and the Poetics of Literary History* (Baton Rouge,

Louisiana State Univ. Press, 1983), pp. 73–9, on this crucial passage, whose juicy substance Eliot repeated elsewhere, if never so revealingly. See, e.g., Eliot's preface to Harry Crosby, *Transit of Venus; Poems* (Paris, Black Sun, 1931), pp. iv–v, arguing that poets use different routes to arrive at originality, some by "progressive imitation." Eliot was dissatisfied with the word "imitation," however, as applied to poets who had some substantive talent. For them, he explained, progressive imitation involved "a finding of themselves by a progressive absorption in, and absorption of, and rejection (but never a total rejection) of other writers."

41. The phrase is borrowed from Richard L. Bushman, "Jonathan Edwards and Puritan Consciousness," in *Puritan New England: Essays on Religion, Society, and Culture,* ed. Alden T. Vaughan and Francis J. Bremer (New York, St. Martin's, 1977), p. 359.

42. See, e.g., "What Dante Means to Me," *T.C.C.,* pp. 126–7, where after quoting two lines of verse summing up Baudelaire's significance for him, Eliot concluded, "I knew what *that* meant, because I had lived it before I knew that I wanted to turn it into verse on my own account."

43. Unlike Laforgue – the undoubted source of Eliot's poetic quickening – Bradley was alive when Eliot first encountered his influence, but the process appears to have been more or less the same. On the diligent few, Bradley's writings "perform that mysterious and complete operation which transmutes not one department of thought only, but the whole intellectual and emotional tone of their being" (T. S. Eliot, "A Commentary," *Criterion,* October 1924, p. 2).

44. T. S. Eliot, "Christianity and Communism," *Listener,* March 16, 1932, p. 383. "The 'Pensées' of Pascal," *S.E.,* p. 405, contains the same phrase: "a temporary crystallization of the mind."

45. In Eliot's mind, "crystallisation" seems to have linked both the religious and the poetic moment and to have suggested some essential similarity. See, e.g., T. S. Eliot, introduction to Ezra Pound, *Selected Poems* (London, Faber & Gwyer, 1928), p. xviii, where Eliot argues a dual progress for the poet, who must diligently experiment and attend to technique while patiently accumulating experience against the occasion, once in five or ten years, in which his experience forms a new whole and finds appropriate expression. He warned, however, that "if a poet were content to attempt nothing less than always his best, if he insisted on waiting for these unpredictable crystallizations, he would not be ready for them when they came." See also p. xx, where Eliot wrote of the same two lines, plotted on a graph, in discussing a poet's work: first, continuous effort in technical excellence, and second, accumulation and digestion of experience. A "masterpiece" occurs when the two lines converge "at a high peak," when "an accumulation of experience has crystallized to form material of art, and years of work in technique have prepared an adequate medium; and something results in which medium and material, form and content, are indistinguishable." See also Eliot's June 1, 1919, letter to Lytton Strachey referring to the "crystallisation" of a well-written work, in Michael Holroyd, *Lytton Strachey: A Critical Biography* (London, Heinemann, 1968), vol. 2, p. 364.

2. *DIVISIONS AND PRECISIONS: AMBIVALENCE AND AMBIGUITY*

"Preludes"

1. Compare Eliot's definition of "wit," distinguishing it from erudition (which sometimes stifled it) and from cynicism, even though the "tender-minded" might confuse the toughness of wit with cynicism. Wit, instead, involves a "recognition, implicit in the expression of every experience, of other kinds of experience which are possible." ("Andrew Marvell," *S.E.*, p. 303).
2. "Dante," *S.E.*, p. 238.
3. "Dante," *S.W.*, p. 169.
4. "Reflections on *Vers Libre*," *T.C.C.*, pp. 185–6.
5. See Sigurd Burckhardt, "Notes on the Theory of Intrinsic Interpretation," in *Critical Theory Since Plato,* ed. Hazard Adams (New York, Harcourt Brace Jovanovich, 1971), p. 1205: "Interpretation, then, would mean the attempt to know the law of a poem *solely from the poem itself,* on the necessary assumption of the infallibility of the poem."
6. George Williamson, *A Reader's Guide to T. S. Eliot: A Poem-By-Poem Analysis* (New York, Octagon, 1974), p. 79; and John Nicholson, "Musical Form and 'Preludes,' " in *T. S. Eliot: A Symposium for His Seventieth Birthday,* ed. Neville Braybrooke (Plainview, N.Y., Books for Libraries Press, 1968), p. 110.
7. Ezra Pound, "T. S. Eliot," *Literary Essays of Ezra Pound* (New York, New Directions, 1968), p. 419.
8. *E.E.Y.*, pp. 4, 32. See also "The Eliot Family and St. Louis," an appendix prepared by the Department of English, Washington Univ., to T. S. Eliot, *American Literature and the American Language* (St. Louis, Mo., Washington Univ., 1953).
9. William Greenleaf Eliot, *A Practical Discussion of the Great Social Question of the Day* (New York, Hewitt, 1879).
10. See T. S. Eliot's Preface to Charles-Louis Philippe, *Bubu of Montparnasse,* trans. Laurence Vail (New York, Avalon, 1945), pp. 10–11.
11. Louis Simpson, *Three on the Tower: The Lives and Works of Ezra Pound, T. S. Eliot, and William Carlos Williams* (New York, Morrow, 1975), p. 108.

Bradley

1. T. S. Eliot to Lytton Strachey, quoted in Michael Holroyd, *Lytton Strachey: A Critical Biography* (London, Heinemann, 1968), vol. 2, pp. 364–5.
2. Even this decision has a family dimension. In 1916, Eliot's mother wrote Bertrand Russell about her son's choice of career: "I have absolute faith in his Philosophy but not in the vers libres" (see *The Autobiography of Bertrand Russell* [London, Allen & Unwin, 1968], vol. 2, p. 59). That Eliot left the field his mother "believed in" and took up the one she did not does not contradict the construction I have placed upon Eliot's early life.
3. "Francis Herbert Bradley," *S.E.*, p. 446.
4. *K.E.P.*, p. 10.

5. *A.R.*, pp. 406–7.
6. F. H. Bradley, *Essays on Truth and Reality* (Oxford, Oxford Univ. Press, 1914), p. 188.
7. *A.R.*, p. 408.
8. Ibid., p. 213.
9. For Bradley's description of this process, see ibid., pp. 140–1.
10. "The Metaphysical Poets," *S.E.*, p. 286. For another reference to dissociation that appears to rely on Bradley's scheme, see the final paragraph, referring to Joyce and Woolf, of T. S. Eliot, "London Letter," *Dial*, July 1921, pp. 216–17.
11. "The Metaphysical Poets," *S.E.*, p. 288.
12. *K.E.P.*, p. 31.
13. Ibid., p. 112.
14. Ibid., p. 136.
15. Ibid., p. 136; reprinted by permission of Faber & Faber Ltd. See also pp. 137–8.
16. Ibid., p. 89; reprinted by permission of Faber & Faber Ltd.
17. Ibid., p. 91; reprinted by permission of Faber & Faber Ltd. Compare Eliot's ideal literary object, whose construction seems to derive from a process of relation and objectification resembling that which produces Bradleyan "thought." The new work of art modifies the "ideal order" that existing works of art compose and that is complete before the new work of art. For order to persist after the new work of art, "the *whole* existing order must be, if ever so slightly, altered; and so the relations, proportions, values of each work of art toward the whole are readjusted" ("Tradition and the Individual Talent," *S.E.*, p. 15).
18. *K.E.P.*, p. 19; reprinted by permission of Faber & Faber Ltd.
19. Ibid., p. 168; reprinted by permission of Faber & Faber Ltd.
20. Ibid., pp. 147–8, on the unification of incompatible worlds and passage from discordant viewpoints to a single, higher, inclusive viewpoint.
21. Ibid., p. 91; reprinted by permission of Faber & Faber Ltd. See also pp. 144–5.
22. Ibid., p. 91; reprinted by permission of Faber & Faber Ltd.
23. Ibid., p. 146; reprinted by permission of Faber & Faber Ltd.
24. Ibid., p. 91; reprinted by permission of Faber & Faber Ltd. See also pp. 36–7, 44.
25. Ibid., pp. 24–5; reprinted by permission of Faber and Faber Ltd.
26. Ibid., p. 104; reprinted by permission of Faber & Faber Ltd.
27. Ibid., p. 132; reprinted by permission of Faber & Faber Ltd.
28. Ibid., pp. 132–3; reprinted by permission of Faber & Faber Ltd.
29. So, for that matter, does poetry. As Eliot wrote in "The Metaphysical Poets," echoing this theory of language, those poets tried to find the "verbal equivalent for states of mind and feeling" (*S.E.*, p. 289). In drama, sequence of incident and action performs the same function. Though not strictly verbal, the "objective correlative" shares a good deal with Eliot's discussion of Bradleyan philosophy. Without translating feelings or emotions into objectified thought, the two cannot be distinguished, cannot be made into an

"it," independent from the self, which will evoke that emotion in an audience, as Eliot implies in his discussion of Hamlet's feelings of disgust that,
although occasioned by his mother, exceed her (see "Hamlet," *S.E.*, pp.
145–6).

30. *K.E.P.*, p. 46; reprinted by permission of Faber & Faber Ltd.
31. Ibid., p. 133; reprinted by permission of Faber & Faber Ltd.
32. Ibid., p. 134; reprinted by permission of Faber & Faber Ltd.
33. Ibid., p. 133; "Leibniz' Monads and Bradley's Finite Centres," *K.E.P.*, p. 205;
reprinted by permission of Faber & Faber Ltd.
34. See Robert Langbaum, "New Modes of Characterization in 'The Waste
Land,'" in *Eliot in His Time: Essays on the Occasion of the Fiftieth Anniversary of
"The Waste Land,"* ed. A. Walton Litz (Princeton, N.J., Princeton Univ.
Press, 1972), pp. 119–25; and Simpson, *Three on the Tower*, p. 108. On this
point and on Eliot and Bradley in general, I must also acknowledge Richard
Wollheim, "Eliot and F. H. Bradley: An Account," in *Eliot in Perspective: A
Symposium*, ed. Graham Martin (London, Macmillan Press, 1970); George
Whiteside, "T. S. Eliot's Dissertation," *ELH*, 34 (1967): pp. 400–24; G.
Watts Cunningham, *The Idealistic Argument in Recent British and American
Philosophy* (New York, Century, 1933); and Anne Bolgan, *What the Thunder
Really Said: A Retrospective Essay on the Making of "The Waste Land"* (Mont-
real, McGill-Queen's Univ. Press, 1973), esp. chap. 6. See also J. Hillis
Miller, *Poets of Reality: Six Twentieth-Century Writers* (Cambridge, Mass.,
Harvard Univ. Press, 1965), pp. 131–89; Sanford Schwartz, *The Matrix of
Modernism: Pound, Eliot, and Early Twentieth-Century Thought* (Princeton,
N.J., Princeton Univ. Press, 1985); Michael H. Levenson, *A Genealogy of
Modernism: A Study of English Literary Doctrine, 1908–1922* (Cambridge
Univ. Press, 1984); and Walter Benn Michaels, "Philosophy in Kinkanja:
Eliot's Pragmatism," *Glyph* (Baltimore, Md., Johns Hopkins Univ. Press,
1981), vol. 8, pp. 170–202.
35. T. S. Eliot, "The Influence of Landscape upon the Poet," *Daedalus*, Spring
1960, p. 421.
36. T. S. Eliot, "Turgenev," *Egoist*, December 1917, p. 167.

Relation, Poetry, and Incarnation

1. For an account of how nineteenth-century "moral philosophy" courses had
urged such ideals, see D. H. Meyer, *The Instructed Conscience: The Shaping of
the American National Ethic* (Philadelphia, Univ. of Pennsylvania Press, 1972).
2. Kristian Smidt confirms this response, though suggesting in addition a Mar-
ian referent, in *Poetry and Belief in the Work of T. S. Eliot* (London, Routledge
& Kegan Paul, 1961), p. 137.
3. See Edward W. Tayler, *Milton's Poetry: Its Development in Time* (Pittsburgh,
Pa., Duquesne Univ. Press, 1979), p. 102, and his discussion of *chronos* and
kairos (p. 17). Tayler's preface, introduction, and conclusion bear on my
discussion of Eliot.
4. Christ the mediator – *der Mittler* – occupies the middle, ambiguous position
between heaven and earth: the *Gottmensch*. As Hegel had it, Christ was the

"union of the most tremendous opposites . . . a frightful combination . . . which absolutely contradicts the understanding." Mark C. Taylor quotes Hegel in *Journeys to Selfhood: Hegel and Kierkegaard* (Berkeley and Los Angeles, Univ. of California Press, 1980), pp. 106–7. Taylor helps determine some of the philosophical elements of Eliot's Christianity, especially insofar as Eliot partakes both of Hegel's "both/and" and Kierkegaard's "either/or." F. H. Bradley dismissed religion but stated that "the religious consciousness rests on the felt unity of unreduced opposites; and either to combine these consistently, or upon the other hand to transform them is impossible for religion" (*A.R.*, p. 392). Though Hegel and Bradley did not necessarily lead Eliot to this notion of Christ, Eliot's conversion appears to have incorporated their notions of the "Absolute" as an all-encompassing reconciliation of opposites.

5. Taylor, *Journeys to Selfhood*, p. 118.
6. Pain and pleasure coincide in images of spiritual/corporeal violence in "La Figlia Che Piange," "Rhapsody on a Windy Night," and "The Death of Saint Narcissus." Most graphically, "The Love Song of St. Sebastian" contains not only Bradleyan language and viewpoint, but a bizarre antiphonal section with self-flagellation and murder.
7. Compare the remarks of a contemporary psychologist who proposed the following theory of laughter, which seems quite close to what occurs in "Preludes": "We, being but imperfectly adapted to the world . . . and therefore necessarily surrounded by the depressing spectacle of suffering, of disorder and of incongruities, and *sympathy* being inwrought in the very bases of our constitution, have been endowed by beneficent Nature with the impulse to laugh at what is displeasing and painful in order that the automatically determined movements of laughter may disperse our attention, may prevent us attending to the displeasing spectacle and, by their stimulating effects, may counteract its depressing influence" (William McDougall, "The Theory of Laughter," *Nature*, February 5, 1903, pp. 318–19).
8. Compare T. S. Eliot, "Rudyard Kipling," *A Choice of Kipling's Verse* (New York, Scribners, 1943), p. 23 (containing the quoted sentence), with "Rudyard Kipling," *O.P.P.*, p. 242 (deleting it).
9. *K.E.P.*, p. 18. See also pp. 21–2.
10. Ibid., p. 163.
11. Bonamy Dobrée's "T. S. Eliot: A Personal Reminiscence," in *T. S. Eliot: The Man and His Work*, ed. Allen Tate (London, Chatto & Windus, 1967), p. 75, quotes T. S. Eliot's November 12, 1927, letter.
12. *K.E.P.*, pp. 147–8. See also note 33 to this section.
13. Ibid., p. 148; reprinted by permission of Faber & Faber Ltd.
14. Ibid., p. 202; reprinted by permission of Faber & Faber Ltd.
15. T. S. Eliot, review of Clive Bell's *Civilization*, *Criterion*, September 1928, p. 164. See also, e.g., "Second Thoughts About Humanism," *S.E.*, p. 488, defining a "Heretic" as someone "who seizes upon a truth and pushes it to the point at which it becomes a falsehood." Compare "The 'Pensées' of Pascal," *S.E.*, p. 413, on the doctrine of grace, which ended in a mystery perceivable but indecipherable, even though many theologians had tried to

solve the problem: "Like any doctrine a slight excess or deviation to one side or the other will precipitate a heresy."

16. "Three Reformers," *Times Literary Supplement*, November 8, 1928, p. 818, unsigned review attributed to Eliot in Donald Gallup, *T. S. Eliot: A Bibliography* (London, Faber & Faber, 1969), p. 221. See also *A.S.G.*, pp. 25–6, generously defining the essential element of any "important heresy" as not simply its error, but its partial correctness. "The more interesting heretics," Eliot wrote, perceived some part of the truth with exceptional acuteness. "So far as we are able to redress the balance, effect the compensation, ourselves, we may find such authors of the greatest value. If we value them as they value themselves we shall go astray."

17. T. S. Eliot, untitled chapter in *Revelation*, ed. John Baillie and Hugh Martin (New York, Macmillan, 1937), pp. 35–7.

18. T. S. Eliot, Introduction to Josef Pieper, *Leisure: The Basis of Culture*, trans. Alexander Dru (New York, Pantheon, 1964), p. xiv. See Bruce Kuklick, *The Rise of American Philosophy: Cambridge, Massachusetts, 1860–1930* (New Haven, Conn., Yale Univ. Press, 1977), describing, inter alia, the professionalization of philosophy at Harvard following the "divorce" of which Eliot speaks.

19. T. S. Eliot, untitled chapter in *Revelation*, ed. Baillie and Martin, pp. 12–13.

20. T. S. Eliot, *A Sermon Preached in Magdalene College Chapel* (Cambridge Univ. Press, 1948), p. 5.

21. "Dante," *S.W.*, p. 169.

22. "The 'Pensées' of Pascal," *S.E.*, p. 408.

23. T. S. Eliot, "The Modern Dilemma," *Christian Register*, October 19, 1933, p. 676.

24. T. S. Eliot, untitled chapter in *Revelation*, ed. Baillie and Martin, pp. 1–2.

25. T. S. Eliot, "Poetry and Propaganda," *Bookman*, February 1930, pp. 601–2.

26. William Empson, *Seven Types of Ambiguity* (New York, New Directions, 1966), p. 192.

27. I. A. Richards, *Principles of Literary Criticism*, 2d ed. (London, Routledge & Kegan Paul, 1926), p. 250.

28. H. W. Fowler, *A Dictionary of Modern English Usage*, 2d ed., rev. Ernest Gowers (New York, Oxford Univ. Press, 1965), p. 305.

29. Henry James, *The Art of the Novel: Critical Prefaces* (New York, Scribners, 1934), p. 222. J. Hillis Miller, *Poets of Reality: Six Twentieth-Century Writers* (Cambridge, Mass., Harvard Univ. Press, 1966), p. 154, applies a comparable theory of irony to Eliot's early poetry, calling it the only successful fusion, yet one that recognizes separateness even while bringing things together. The ironic unity emerging from the clash of fragments "affirms the ideal and at the same time admits the unattainability of the ideal. The images in such poems have that powerful suggestiveness which Eliot wants, but the pervading emotions are distaste for a sordid reality and poignant longing for the lost ideal."

30. See Sigmund Freud, "The Antithetical Sense of Primal Words," *Character and Culture* (New York, Collier Books, 1963); Empson's exploration of this

notion in *Seven Types of Ambiguity*, pp. 192–7, which provides several analogues to my discussion; and Tayler, *Milton's Poetry*.

31. The name given to Jesus – the "Christ" – may contain a verbal irony: The spiritually pure receives a name that reflects the grime applied to Him during anointment. Otherwise, however, the Gospels' ironies are not of the purely verbal sort. As ironies of event and occasion, they join opposites to make a moral or otherwise serious point: Jesus is lowly instead of well born; He is betrayed by a kiss, ordinarily signifying love and trust; a spiritual benefactor, advising people to abandon their treasure to follow Him, Christ is nonetheless crucified between two "malefactors" and thieves; and Pilate releases Barabbas, a murderer, but permits the killing of a god who can give eternal life. The extent to which this pattern pervades the Gospel stories has been overlooked, presumably because of their familiarity. It was undoubtedly not always so, and it is important to reflect on how these episodes constitute a daring, aggressive sensibility. To be unaware of Christianity's strangeness is to miss its point, as Eliot implied when pointing out that innovation in religious drama shocked pious people in the twentieth century, even though in medieval religious drama shepherds could acceptably joke and play pranks. Eliot regretted that neither levity nor unusual seriousness were suitable to modern times, which would not tolerate anything in the nature of a "shock." "We are apt to forget that the original biblical events which in the biblical narrative we treat with such familiarity, are in themselves, if we regard them with fresh eyes, profoundly shocking" (T. S. Eliot, *Religious Drama: Mediaeval and Modern* [New York, House of Books, 1954], n.p.).

32. Peter Sterry, *A Discourse of the Freedom of the Will* (London, Starkey, 1675), p. 179.

33. Compare Bolgan, *What the Thunder Really Said,* p. 116, to the effect that Bradley's and Bosanquet's triadic logic asserted that where two terms or termini – self and world, or husband and wife – existed, so did the relation between them. This becomes a way of understanding; without a husband, there can be no wife, nor a knower without something known. Without the "whole" of the relation, neither term or "side" can be defined solely in terms of the other. "Thus one cannot hope to understand what it is to be a husband merely by probing one's wife. To understand either, both 'sides' of the relationship must be referred to and seen within the context of 'the whole' which in relation (and only in relation) they can 'unite to form' and which thus provides the 'third side' essential to their intelligibility as terms."

See also Johannes Fabricius, *The Unconscious and Mr. Eliot: A Study in Expressionism* (Copenhagen, Nyt Nordisk Forlag Arnold Busck, 1967), esp. "The Conjunction of Opposites in T. S. Eliot's Criticism," pp. 131–40. Despite questionable evidence and method, Anthony L. Jonson's conclusions in *Sign and Structure in the Poetry of T. S. Eliot* (Pisa, Editrice Tecnico Scientifica, 1976), especially as schematized on p. 2, support the conception of poetry as addressing and mediating Eliot's divided consciousness. Kristian Smidt's discussion of the "via media" in *Poetry and Belief in the Work of T. S. Eliot,* pp. 231–3, interprets these ideas in a religious context.

34. Edward Lobb, *T. S. Eliot and the Romantic Critical Tradition* (London, Rout-

ledge & Kegan Paul, 1981), pp. 53–4, quotes Eliot's Clark Lectures on irony
as an expression of suffering and summarizes the analogy between the word
in language and the Christian *logos,* as well as similar analogies Eliot drew
between religion and poetry. Lobb quotes Eliot's incarnational view of the
poetic image clothing the abstract in the flesh on p. 24.

35. T. S. Eliot, "The Aims of Poetic Drama," *Adam International Review,*
   November 1949, p. 12; reprinted by permission of Mrs. Valerie Eliot and
   Faber & Faber Ltd.

36. The quoted passages suggest how incarnation helped Eliot define the sort of
   Christianity to which he could adhere, which his 1928 pronouncement called
   "anglo-catholic." Another of its elements, "royalism," also borrowed from
   the concept. After arguing that the *Action Française* represented a nationalism
   that turned inward rather than seeking foreign aggression, Eliot called not
   nationalism but royalism the "vital dogma." He defined royalism not as state
   worship or state sovereignty, but as the "reintroduction of the idea of loyalty
   to a King, who *incarnates* the idea of the Nation" (emphasis added) ("Mr.
   Barnes and Mr. Rowse," *Criterion,* July 1929, pp. 689–90).
   As to what the nature of royalist incarnation might be, see Eliot's "A
   Commentary," *Criterion,* October 1931, p. 71, which quoted Rev. Charles
   Smyth's "admirable essay" on *The State and Freedom, Christendom,* June 1931:
   "'The Royal Supremacy is not Erastian in its implications, because the King
   is a *persona mixta,* something less than a priest, but something more than a
   layman; he is both a secular and an ecclesiastical person; and it is the
   orthodox theory of the Church of England that it is his office to administer
   the State through his secular officers, and the Church through his spiritual
   officers (not excluding laymen, for they also are *viri ecclesiastici,*
   churchmen).'" Thus if we can infer Eliot's view from his approving quotation of Smyth, as Christ unites God and man, Word and flesh, the king by
   this definition unites nation and citizen, and church and state.
   Whatever the intrinsic value of these ideas, they indicate the conceptual
   attraction and usefulness incarnation had for Eliot. He would later refer to
   culture as "incarnate" in nations (Preface to *Dark Side of the Moon* [New
   York, Scribners, 1947], p. x) and ask whether a people's culture and religion
   were not different aspects of a single thing: "the culture being, essentially,
   the incarnation, so to speak, of a religion in a particular people" (T. S. Eliot,
   "Cultural Forces in Human Order," in *The Prospect for Christendom: Essays in
   Social Reconstruction,* ed. Maurice B. Reckitt [London, Faber & Faber, 1945],
   p. 63). As he explained in *N.T.D.C.,* p. 33, it was error to see religion and
   culture as distinct, separate things connected by a relation, and error to
   identify culture and religion. The concept of incarnation provided a way out
   of these two erroneous alternatives. "I spoke at one point of the culture of a
   people as an *incarnation* of its religion . . . I cannot think of any other [term]
   which would convey so well the intention to avoid *relation* on the one hand
   and *identification* on the other."

37. T. S. Eliot, Preface to Harry Crosby, *Transit of Venus: Poems* (Paris, Black
   Sun Press, 1931), pp. viii–ix; reprinted by permission of Mrs. Valerie Eliot
   and Faber & Faber Ltd. Compare "Dante," *S.E.,* p. 268: Dante's "power of

establishing relations between beauty of the most diverse sorts . . . is the utmost power of the poet." See also Gregory Jay, *T. S. Eliot and the Poetics of Literary History* (Baton Rouge, Louisiana Univ. Press, 1983), p. 155, linking Eliot's attraction to Catholicism to the "transcendental poetics" of its theology. "In contrast to the iconoclasm of Hebrew, Protestant, and Puritan theories of the sign, Catholicism reunites the letter and the spirit, signifier and signified, nature and culture, human and divine in the dogmas of the Incarnation, Passion, and Resurrection."

38. My discussion must acknowledge John Murray Cuddihy's *No Offense: Civil Religion and Protestant Taste* (New York, Seabury, 1978), chap. 8; Tayler's *Milton's Poetry: Its Development in Time;* and Mircea Eliade's *The Sacred and the Profane: The Nature of Religion,* trans. Willard R. Trask (New York, Harcourt Brace, 1959).

39. John D. Margolis quotes Eliot's 1928 letter in *T. S. Eliot's Intellectual Development, 1922–39* (Chicago, Univ. of Chicago Press, 1972), p. 142.

3. A GESTURE AND A POSE: HOMO DUPLEX

Self-Divisions

1. On "auto-machia," see Sacvan Bercovitch, *The Puritan Origins of the American Self* (New Haven, Conn., Yale Univ. Press, 1975), pp. 18–19. On "mastery," see Allen Tate, "Emily Dickinson," *Essays of Four Decades* (Chicago, Swallow Press, 1959), p. 287.

2. T. S. Eliot, "A Commentary," *Criterion,* April 1933, p. 469.

3. Socrates and his opponents may have argued mainly about truth and morality in politics and rhetoric, but their positions presupposed private, psychological values as well. The Platonic "discovery of the soul" and the grand tradition of inquiry it inaugurated, as well as the Socratics' competing conception of psychological and political maturity, set forth educational, psychological, political, and metaphysical points of view of remarkable resilience. See, e.g., Eric A. Havelock, *A Preface to Plato* (Cambridge, Mass., Harvard Univ. Press, 1963), pp. 197–201; Zevedei Barbu, *Problems of Historical Psychology* (New York, Grove, 1960), pp. 80–1 (on self-consciousness) and pp. 73–4, 129 (on homo duplex); and, on Greek education, H. I. Marrou, *A History of Education in Antiquity,* trans. George Lamb (Madison, Univ. of Wisconsin Press, 1982).

4. See George Herbert Mead, *Mind, Self and Society from the Standpoint of a Social Behaviorist* (Chicago, Univ. of Chicago Press, 1934), p. 135, and Erving Goffman, *The Presentation of Self in Everyday Life* (Garden City, N.Y., Doubleday, 1959), esp. the chapters "Performances" and "The Arts of Impression Management."

5. See Eric A. Havelock, *The Liberal Temper in Greek Politics* (New Haven, Conn., Yale Univ. Press, 1957), and idem, *A Preface to Plato.*

6. Richard A. Lanham, *The Motives of Eloquence: Literary Rhetoric in the Renaissance* (New Haven, Conn., Yale Univ. Press, 1976), p. 36.

7. Alphonse Daudet, *Notes on Life* (Boston, Little, Brown, 1900), p. 427.

8. See Richard Sennett, *The Fall of Public Man: On the Social Psychology of Capitalism* (New York, Vintage, 1978).

9. See Masao Miyoshi, *The Divided Self: A Perspective on the Literature of the Victorians* (New York, New York Univ. Press, 1969).

10. See, e.g., Wyndham Lewis, "T. S. Eliot, the Pseudo-Believer," *Men Without Art* (New York, Russell & Russell, 1964), and Louis Menand, *Discovering Modernism: T. S. Eliot and His Context* (New York, Oxford Univ. Press, 1987).

11. F. H. Bradley, *Ethical Studies* (Oxford, Oxford Univ. Press, 1927), pp. 173–4.

12. *K.E.P.*, pp. 142–3; reprinted by permission of Faber & Faber Ltd. See also Eliot's discussion of "identity in diversity" and the ideal nature of the "real" on p. 144, and of the mind's simultaneously "absolute and derived" nature on pp. 145–6. On the half-object, see also Sanford Schwartz, *The Matrix of Modernism: Pound, Eliot, and Early Twentieth-Century Thought* (Princeton, N.J., Princeton Univ. Press, 1985), pp. 183–7.

13. Oscar Wilde, *The Picture of Dorian Gray* (London, Penguin, 1949), pp. 158–9.

14. Oscar Wilde, "The Critic as Artist," *The Portable Oscar Wilde*, ed. Richard Aldington (New York, Penguin, 1977), p. 125.

15. Oscar Wilde, *An Ideal Husband, Plays* (London, Penguin, 1974), p. 158.

16. In "The Two Temples," after a play, "Starting to their feet, the enraptured thousands sound their responses, deafeningly; unmistakably sincere. Right from the undoubted heart. I have no duplicate in my memory of this. In earnestness of response, this second temple stands unmatched. And hath mere mimicry done this? What is it then to act a part? But now the music surges up again, and borne by that rolling billow, I, and all the gladdened crowd, are harmoniously attended to the street." See also Michael Paul Rogin, *Subversive Genealogy: The Politics and Art of Herman Melville* (New York, Knopf, 1983), pp. 232–5.

17. Henry Adams, "Buddha and Brahma," *Yale Review*, October 1914, p. 88; his February 14, 1862, letter to Charles Francis Adams, Jr., appears in *The Letters of Henry Adams, Volume 1: 1858–1868*, ed. J. C. Levenson, Ernest Samuels, Charles Vandersee, and Viola Hopkins Winner (Cambridge, Mass., Harvard Univ. Press, 1982), p. 282.

18. *K.E.P.*, p. 23.

19. Contemporary treatments of personality problems include Morton Prince, *The Dissociation of a Personality: A Biographical Study in Abnormal Psychology* (New York, Longmans, Green, 1906); Ralph Adams Cram, *The Decadent, Being the Gospel of Inaction* (Boston, 1893); George M. Beard, *American Nervousness* (New York, Putnam, 1881); Henry Childs Merwin, "On Being Civilized Too Much," *Atlantic*, June 1897; George Harvey, "Cynicism and Decadence," *North American Review*, June 7, 1907, p. 350; and Ethel Dench Puffer, "The Loss of Personality," *Atlantic*, February 1900. Michael G. Kenney, *The Passion of Ansel Bourne: Multiple Personality in American Culture* (Washington, D.C., Smithsonian Institution Press, 1986), studies several

cases of multiple personality in the ninteenth and early twentieth centuries – including Miss Beauchamp – as a sociocultural "idiom of distress." See also Karl Miller, *Doubles: Studies in Literary History* (New York, Oxford Univ. Press, 1985). T. J. Jackson Lears's aptly titled *No Place of Grace: Antimodernism and the Transformation of American Culture, 1880–1920* (New York, Pantheon, 1981) provides a background to these tendencies and, by implication, to Eliot's responses.

20. William James, *The Principles of Psychology* (New York, Dover, 1950), vol. 1, pp. 293–4.

21. James, *The Principles of Psychology,* pp. 296–9.

Prufrock and Other Observations

1. Interviewed in *Grantite Review,* 24, no. 3, 1962, p. 17, Eliot said of Prufrock: "It was partly a dramatic creation of a man of about 40 I should say, and partly an expression of feeling of my own through this dim imaginary figure." Eliot continued by noting his sense that those dramatic characters who seemed to be living creations had something of their author in them not unlike Yeats's antimask, the opposite of the author as he is. Compare T. S. Eliot, "London Letter," *Dial,* August 1922, p. 331, on Dostoevsky's gift for facing and studying his own weaknesses. By "utilizing" his weaknesses, Eliot argued, Dostoevsky transformed them from individual defects into the "entrance to a genuine and personal universe."

2. Ezra Pound's January 31, 1915, letter to Harriet Monroe, *The Letters of Ezra Pound, 1907–1941,* ed. D. D. Paige (London, Faber & Faber, 1951), p. 50.

3. Elisabeth Schneider, *T. S. Eliot: The Pattern in the Carpet* (Berkeley and Los Angeles, Univ. of California Press, 1975), p. 24.

4. Arthur Symons, *The Symbolist Movement in Literature* (New York, Dutton, 1958), p. 14.

5. Ibid., pp. 56–62.

6. T. S. Eliot, "Christianity and Communism," *Listener,* March 16, 1932, p. 383.

7. Matthew Arnold, "Preface to First Edition of *Poems* (1853)," *Poetry and Criticism of Matthew Arnold,* ed. A. Dwight Culler (Boston, Houghton Mifflin, 1961), p. 204.

8. "'Rhetoric' and Poetic Drama," *S.E.,* p. 37.

9. See "The Social Function of Poetry," *O.P.P.,* p. 21, on how the ability to express and to feel any but the crudest emotions will degenerate under pressure of material change unless a few writers exist who combine an "exceptional sensibility with an exceptional power over words." See also "Charleston, Hey! Hey!" *Nation and Athenaeum,* January 29, 1927, p. 595, in which Eliot wondered whether the modern mechanical complication of life tended to simplify sensibility rather than the reverse.

10. "The Metaphysical Poets," *S.E.,* p. 285.

11. William J. Goode, "A Theory of Role Strain," *American Sociological Review,* August 1960, p. 483.

12. "Introduction," *U.P.U.C.,* p. 32.

13. "Marie Lloyd," *S.E.*, p. 458.
14. Eliot's sister, Ada Sheffield, was recorded in the 1930s as being "both interested and concerned about Tom's 'Way of contemplation', which she was imagining might divorce him from 'human' relationships and drive him into a shadow-world of 'dramatism', into increasing tendencies of outward 'acting' and inward 'mysticism'. She saw two forces pulling apart, yet compensations of each other" (Frank Morley, "A Few Recollections of Eliot," in *T. S. Eliot: The Man and His Work*, ed. Allen Tate [London, Chatto & Windus, 1967] p. 110).
15. T. S. Eliot, "The Post-Georgians," *Athenaeum*, April 11, 1919, p. 171.
16. T. S. Eliot, "American Literature," *Athenaeum*, April 25, 1919, p. 237.
17. T. S. Eliot, "Literature and the Modern World," *American Prefaces*, November 1935, p. 20. On the *tertium quid* elements of this passage, see note 33, Chapter 2, "Relation, Poetry, and Incarnation."

4. WHERE ARE THE EAGLES AND THE TRUMPETS? AMERICAN AESTHETES

Introduction

1. Sir Herbert Read, "T. S. E. – A Memoir," in *T. S. Eliot: The Man and His Work*, ed. Allen Tate (London, Chatto & Windus, 1967), p. 15. Eliot polished these sentiments in his preface to Edgar Ansel Mowrer, *This American World* (London, Faber & Gwyer, 1928), pp. xiii–xiv. Calling himself a descendant of pioneers, he nonetheless observed that his family tended to cling to places and associations as long as possible. That family tendency toward traditions and loyalties, and particularly its tendency to guard "jealously its connexions with New England," gave him a background different from that of Europeans and many other Americans. Only later did Eliot perceive that he had always been a New Englander in Missouri, which he called the "South West," and a Southwesterner in New England, losing his Southern accent without ever acquiring the Boston one. Eliot compared himself to a school friend whose family had lived in the same house in a New England seaport for two hundred and fifty years. Eliot's grandmother, he said, had shot her own wild turkeys for dinner, while that of his friend had collected Chinese pottery brought home on clipper ships. He concluded that it was easier for him, the grandson of pioneers, to move eastward than it would have been for his friend to migrate in any direction.
2. "Tradition and the Individual Talent," *S.E.*, p. 14.
3. Eliot's ancestors participated in the Salem witch trials. Pound wrote that William Carlos Williams "has not in the ancestral endocrines the arid curse of our nation. None of his immediate forebears burnt witches in Salem." Eliot exercised his editorial privilege in a footnote: "Note: We didn't burn them, we hanged them. T. S. E." (*Literary Essays of Ezra Pound* [New York, New Directions, 1968], p. 391; see also *E.E.Y.*, pp. 10, 71n, and *N.S.F.B.*, pp. 6–7).
4. *E.E.Y.*, p. 130.
5. T. S. Eliot, "The Literature of Fascism," *Criterion*, December 1928, p. 287.

6. Although by and large Eliot's critics have not examined this aspect of his career, see Alan Holder, *Three Voyagers in Search of Europe: A Study of Henry James, Ezra Pound, and T. S. Eliot* (Philadelphia, Univ. of Pennsylvania Press, 1966).

7. Eliot took Santayana's courses, "History of Modern Philosophy" and "Ideals of Society, Religion, Art and Science in Their Historical Development," while an undergraduate. Santayana had left, however, by the time Eliot returned to Harvard as a graduate student. Though some dispute exists about the extent of Santayana's influence on Eliot, it seems to have lingered well past Santayana's 1912 departure for Europe. James Houghton Woods recruited Eliot and Bertrand Russell to teach in the Harvard Philosophy Department, but failed when World War I intervened. Woods, "bitterly disappointed," after the war again wanted to offer Eliot a position. Ralph Barton Perry and George Herbert Palmer, however, though granting Eliot's genius, overruled Woods. "Perry believed Eliot was a 'sort of attenuated Santayana,' too 'rare and overrefined'; Palmer that a 'certain softness of moral fibre' had allowed a 'weak aestheticism' to turn Eliot's head" (Bruce Kuklick, *The Rise of American Philosophy; Cambridge, Massachusetts, 1860–1930* [New Haven, Conn., Yale Univ. Press, 1977], p. 410; see also *N.S.F.B.*, pp. 84–5).

8. See, e.g., Algernon Swinburne, from *William Blake* (1868), Chapter 2, quoted in *The Aesthetes: A Sourcebook*, ed. Ian Small (London, Routledge & Kegan Paul, 1979), pp. 3–7. See, e.g., p. 6: "Let us have done with all abject and ludicrous pretence of coupling the two in harness or grafting the one on the other's stock: let us hear no more of the moral mission of earnest art." Though they might have professed abhorrence of the more notorious British aesthetes of the eighties and nineties, Americans nonetheless knew the English aesthetic movement's origins in Ruskin, Arnold, and William Morris, who made the social and moral content of their aestheticism clear. See, generally, Jonathan Freedman, "An Aestheticism of Our Own: American Writers and the Aesthetic Movement," in *In Pursuit of Beauty: Americans and the Aesthetic Movement* (New York, Metropolitan Museum of Art/Rizzoli, 1986), esp. p. 393, concerning how the British fin de siècle gave contemporary American writers "a form of rooted rootlessness, the security of a shared insecurity, a sense of alienation that was also a confirmation of community with those similarly alienated."

9. The similar origins of figures prominent in religion and art betray these endeavors as critical counterweights to American democracy and further suggest the quite traditional social sources of "modernism." As opposed to the leveling, egalitarian, nondiscriminatory impulse that dominates American popular ideology and self-conception, religion and art tend toward hierarchies of value that support moral and aesthetic – and frequently social – discrimination. This similarity, for instance, suggests why the biographies of American artists often reveal religious relations and ancestors, why American aestheticism made its case by employing rhetoric borrowed from moral vocabularies and analogizing its own episodes of aesthetic sublimity to those of religious beatitude, and why American aesthetes seemed to pass so easily between two such otherwise dissimilar, even contradictory value systems.

Shared social origins, and the employment of hierarchical value systems to reject mass morality and popular taste, facilitate this superficially difficult but fairly commonplace translation.

10. In 1885, an English observer captured the phenomenon perceptively, claiming that especially in new countries, people felt the need for social distinction based on something other than birth and wealth.

> In America, accordingly, where modern instincts find their freest field, we have before our eyes the process of the gradual distribution of the old prerogatives of birth amongst wealth, culture, and the proletariat. In Europe a class privileged by birth used to supply at once the rulers and the ideals of other men. In America the *rule* has passed to the multitude; largely swayed in subordinate matters by organised wealth, but in the last resort supreme. The *ideal* of the new community at first was Wealth; but, as its best literature and its best society plainly show, that ideal is shifting in the direction of Culture. The younger cities, the coarser classes, still bow down undisguisedly to the god Dollar; but when this Philistine deity is rejected as shaming his worshippers, aesthetic Culture seems somehow the only Power ready to install itself in the vacant shrine." (F. H. Myers, "Rossetti and the Religion of Beauty," in *The Aesthetes: A Sourcebook,* ed. Ian Small [London, Routledge & Kegan Paul, 1979], pp. 198–9)

11. James McNeill Whistler, "The Ten O'clock," in *Victorians on Literature and Art,* ed. Robert L. Peters (New York, Appleton-Century-Crofts, 1961), p. 143.

12. After serving his "apprenticeship" in the City, trying to master the "classics" on the subject, and receiving his superiors' approval on articles he had written on foreign exchange, Eliot reported that he was never convinced that either the authorities he relied upon or the expert public reading his articles understood economics any better than he did – which was "not at all." Perhaps making the Weberian (or Calvinist) allusion, he concluded that some "gracious natures" made money instinctively, "as the bee makes honey." Others conscientiously carried out the details of the elaborate financial machine. But nobody knew how the machine came to be or what it meant ultimately to accomplish. The bank's other employees, Eliot said, differed from him "chiefly in their unquestioning loyalty to it" (T. S. Eliot, "A Commentary," *Criterion,* January 1931, p. 310).

13. T. S. Eliot, "The Man of Letters and the Future of Europe," *Horizon,* December 1944, p. 386. Someone who had deposed industrial, technological, and entrepreneurial values from their American preeminence would necessarily feel more at home in England, whose culture had performed a similar adjustment. See Martin J. Wiener, *English Culture and the Decline of the Industrial Spirit, 1850–1980* (Cambridge Univ. Press, 1981).

14. T. S. Eliot, "A Commentary," *Criterion,* October 1932, p. 75.

15. T. S. Eliot, Introduction to Mark Twain, *The Adventures of Huckleberry Finn* (London, Cresset Press, 1950), p. vii.

16. T. S. Eliot, "London Letter," *Dial,* May 1921, p. 687.

17. See, e.g., Eliot's reference to the Manchester school politics of the *Daily News* and the *Star,* which "gives a strong aroma of the Ebenezer Temperance Association to their views on art" (T. S. Eliot, "London Letter," *Dial,* May 1921, p. 686).

18. On Santayana's exposure to Unitarianism, see *Persons and Places: The Background of My Life* (New York, Scribners, 1944), pp. 164–5; and James Ballowe, "Introduction," *George Santayana's America: Essays on Literature and Culture*, ed. James Ballowe (Urbana, Univ. of Illinois Press, 1967), pp. 8–10.
19. Letter of Henry James to H. G. Wells, July 10, 1915, *Henry James Letters, Vol. 4, 1895–1916*, ed. Leon Edel (Cambridge, Mass., Harvard Univ. Press, 1984), p. 770.
20. See Dixon Wecter, "The Harvard Exiles," *Virginia Quarterly Review*, April 1934, pp. 244–57; and Martin Green, "The Boston Aesthetes," *The Problem of Boston: Some Readings in Cultural History* (New York, Norton, 1967).

Santayana and the Critique of Gentility

1. George Santayana, *The Sense of Beauty: Being the Outline of Aesthetic Theory* (New York, Dover, 1955), p. 135.
2. Ibid., pp. 135–6.
3. Ibid., pp. 41–2.
4. *C.O.U.S.*, pp. i–iii.
5. Ibid., p. iii.
6. Ibid., p. iv.
7. Ibid., pp. 4–5.
8. Ibid., pp. 5–6.
9. Ibid., p. 6.
10. Ibid., p. 9.
11. Ibid., p. 14.
12. Ibid., pp. 140–1.
13. Ibid., p. 169.
14. Ibid., p. 170.
15. Ibid., p. 211.
16. T. S. Eliot, "Henry James I: In Memory," in *The Shock of Recognition: The Development of Literature in the United States Recorded by the Men Who Made It*, ed. Edmund Wilson (New York, Doubleday, 1943), p. 857.
17. *C.O.U.S.*, pp. 173–4.
18. George Santayana, "Marginal Notes on Civilization in the United States," *George Santayana's America*, p. 168.
19. Ibid., pp. 170–1.

Henry James: An Analysis of Restlessness

1. T. S. Eliot, "Henry James II: The Hawthorne Aspect," in *The Shock of Recognition*, ed. Wilson, p. 864.
2. *T.A.S.*, p. 34.
3. Ibid., p. 35.
4. Ibid., p. 22.
5. Ibid., p. 24–5.
6. *Italian Hours* collects essays written mostly in the 1870s, with revisions and additional material from 1909. *The American Scene*, published in 1907, records James's American tour during 1904–5.
7. *T.A.S.*, p. 27.

8. Ibid., p. 92.
9. Ibid., p. 222.
10. Ibid., p. 111.
11. Ibid., p. 112. James discovered that his boyhood home had been pulled down and replaced: "The effect for me . . . was of having been amputated of half my history" (ibid., p. 91).
12. *I.H.,* pp. 113–14.
13. Ibid., p. 112.
14. Ibid., p. 17.
15. Ibid., p. 19. See the discussion of this passage and Eliot's "Burbank," in Chapter 5, note 30.
16. Ibid., p. 75.
17. Compare Leon Edel's unconvincing introduction to *T.A.S.,* pp. xvi–xix.
18. On the last point, see Henry James, *The Question of Our Speech: The Lesson of Balzac: Two Lectures* (Boston, Houghton Mifflin, 1905), pp. 10–12.
19. *T.A.S.,* p. 121.
20. Ibid., pp. 85–6.
21. Ibid., p. 86.
22. Ibid., p. 87; emphasis added.
23. See, for instance, Rufus Choate's Jamesian description of the American newness, just before the Civil War:

> Consider how new is this America of yours! Some there are yet alive who saw this infant rocked in the cradle. . . . Some now alive saw the deep broad trench first excavated, the stone drawn from the mountain-side, the mortar mingled, the Cyclopean foundation laid, the tears, the anthems, the thanksgiving of the dedication day. That unknown, therefore magnified, therefore magnificent original; that august tradition of a mixed human and Divine; that hidden fountain; the long, half-hidden flow glancing uncertain and infrequent through the opening of the old forest, spreading out, at last, after leagues, after centuries, into the clear daylight of history; the authoritative prescription; the legend, the fable, the tones of uncertain harps, the acquiescence of generations, rising on a long line to life as to a gift, – where for us are they? On all this architecture of utility and reason, where has time laid a finger? What angularity has it rounded; what stone has it covered with moss; on what salient or what pendant coigne of vantage has it built its nest; on what deformity has its moonlight and twilight fallen?" (Rufus Choate, "American Nationality: An Oration Delivered in Boston on the Eighty-Second Anniversary of American Independence, July 5, 1858," *Addresses and Orations,* 6th ed. [Boston, Little, Brown, 1891], pp. 501–2)

24. *I.H.,* p. 308.
25. Ibid., pp. 354, 362.
26. Ibid., p. 359.

The Dispossession of Henry Adams

1. Adams was related both to Eliot and, through the Sturgises, to Santayana. See Ernest Samuels, *Henry Adams: The Middle Years* (Cambridge, Mass., Harvard Univ. Press, 1958), p. 7.
2. William and Henry James reveal how talented brothers may allocate energy, intellectual substance, and personal style. See Leon Edel, *Henry James: The Conquest of London: 1870–1881* (New York, Avon, 1978), p. 137. William's

career, however, commenced only after a prolonged personal struggle; his first choice, at age nineteen, was to become a painter. See Howard M. Feinstein, *Becoming William James* (Ithaca, N.Y., Cornell Univ. Press, 1984).

3. *E.H.A.*, p. 6. Ernst Scheyer, "Adams the Aesthete," *The Circle of Henry Adams: Art & Artists* (Detroit, Mich., Wayne State Univ. Press, 1970), summarizes the aestheticist themes in Adams's writing and relates them to his background.

4. *E.H.A.*, p. 4.

5. See Henry Cabot Lodge, "Memorial Address," quoted in Earl N. Harbert, *The Force So Much Closer Home: Henry Adams and the Adams Family* (New York, New York Univ. Press, 1977), p. 144. See also Paul C. Nagel, *Descent From Glory: Four Generations of the John Adams Family* (New York, Oxford Univ. Press, 1983), chaps. 15-17.

6. *E.H.A.*, pp. 15-16.

7. Ibid., p. 7.

8. Ibid.

9. Ibid., pp. 25-6.

10. George Santayana, *Persons and Places* (New York, Scribners, 1944), p. 9.

11. *E.H.A.*, pp. 7-9.

12. T. S. Eliot, "A Sceptical Patrician," *Athenaeum,* May 23, 1919, p. 361.

13. *E.H.A.*, p. 265.

14. F. O. Matthiessen, *The James Family: A Group Biography* (New York, Vintage, 1974), p. 4.

15. *E.H.A.*, p. 238.

16. See, for instance, Adams's analysis of the "restless, pushing, energetic, ingenious" American of New York or Chicago, and of another American, typical of political Washington, D.C., "patient, helpless, pathetically dependent on his wife and daughters." Despite their differences, Adams condemns both types for being unintellectual and bored (ibid., pp. 297-8).

17. Ibid., pp. 90-1.

18. Ibid., pp. 471-2.

19. Ibid., pp. 288-9.

20. Ibid., p. 301.

21. Ibid., p. 360.

22. Ibid., p. 382.

23. Ibid., p. 269.

24. Ibid., pp. 434-5. See Yvor Winters, *In Defense of Reason* (Chicago, Swallow Press, n.d.), p. 411.

25. Henry Adams, *Mont-Saint-Michel and Chartres* (Boston, Houghton Mifflin, 1904), p. 226.

26. Ibid., p. 350.

27. Ibid., pp. 44-5.

Society, History, and Art

1. Arthur Symons, *The Symbolist Movement in Literature* (New York, Dutton, 1958), p. 5.

2. Carl Schorske, *Fin-de-Siècle Vienna: Politics and Culture* (New York, Knopf, 1980), pp. 8–10.
3. Walter Pater, *The Renaissance: Studies in Art and Poetry,* ed. Donald L. Hill (Berkeley and Los Angeles, Univ. of California Press, 1980), p. 187.
4. Ibid., p. 188.
5. Ibid., p. 273.
6. Ibid., p. 189.
7. T. S. Eliot, "Henry James I: In Memory," in *The Shock of Recognition,* ed. Wilson, p. 856.
8. The feeling survives; see Joan Didion, "[Review of John Cheever's] Falconer," in *New York Times Book Review,* March 6, 1977, p. 1. Nor is the phenomenon limited to the period after the Civil War; see Michael Paul Rogin, *Subversive Genealogy: The Politics and Art of Herman Melville* (New York, Knopf, 1983).

Many issues Santayana, James, Adams, and Eliot discuss appear in Cooper's *The American Democrat,* published a decade after Jackson's election. See also Quentin Anderson's theory of "cultural shrinkage" during this period, in *The Imperial Self: An Essay in American Literary and Cultural History* (New York, Knopf, 1971), pp. 14–16, 60. On "status discrepancy," originally a concept of Max Weber, see N. J. Demerath III, *Social Class in American Protestantism* (Chicago, Rand McNally, 1965), p. 128. Though the term usually involves people who must adjust a high economic status to a low educational, religious, or social one, here the terms of that discrepancy are reversed. Social mobility may propel people down as well as up; here the gap opens between a high social, educational, and religious status and a low (either relatively or absolutely) economic or political one. That much of American literature was composed by writers whose families observed this decline has far-reaching implications for its official canon.
9. Richard Hofstadter, *The Age of Reform from Bryan to F.D.R.* (New York, Vintage, 1955), p. 135. See generally Gabriel Pearson, "Eliot: An American Use of Symbolism," in *Eliot in Perspective: A Symposium,* ed. Graham Martin (New York, Humanities Press, 1970). For a valuable counterpoint to Hofstadter's theory, see Gabriel Kolko's "Brahmins and Business, 1870–1914: A Hypothesis on the Social Basis of Success in American History," in *The Critical Spirit; Essays in Honor of Herbert Marcuse,* ed. Kurt Wolff and Barrington Moore, Jr. (Boston, Beacon Press, 1967).
10. Hofstadter, *The Age of Reform,* pp. 135–6.
11. See Daniel Walker Howe, *The Political Culture of the American Whigs* (Chicago, Univ. of Chicago Press, 1979). The Whigs' New England homeland voted Whig in large majorities and tended to be members of New England Protestant sects such as Congregationalist, Unitarian, and "New School" Presbyterian (pp. 5, 13); they respected custom, status, social deference, and traditions, as opposed to Jacksonian egalitarianism (pp. 31, 82); they valued self-discipline and social uniformity (p. 20); and they emphasized public responsibility, education, and moral reform, as opposed to Jacksonian loyalty to political party, the spoils system, or equalization of opportunity. Significantly, Howe traces the genteel literary tradition to the Whigs (p. 211).

12. Hofstadter, *The Age of Reform*, p. 137.
13. See "Well-Near the Center of Our National Demesne," in *N.S.F.B.*, esp. pp. 42–51; *E.E.Y.*, pp. 1–19; and James's praise of the subtle pleasures of arriving, after New York, in Philadelphia and inferentially describing St. Louis when Eliot lived there: "Philadelphia, incontestably then, was the American city of the large type, that didn't *bristle* – just as I was afterwards to recognize in St. Louis the nearest approach to companionship with her in this respect; and to recognize in Chicago, I may parenthetically add, the most complete divergence" (*T.A.S.*, pp. 274–5).
14. Hofstadter, *The Age of Reform*, p. 150.
15. *N.S.F.B.*, p. 43.
16. Hofstadter, *The Age of Reform*, pp. 177–8.
17. Francis Parkman, "The Failure of Universal Suffrage," *North American Review*, July–August 1878, p. 4.
18. In *Anti-Intellectualism in American Life* (New York, Vintage, 1963), Hofstadter treats themes Santayana, James, and Adams discuss: the feminization of culture as a result of expansionism and big business (p. 50); the disestablishment of patrician leadership (pp. 50–1, 158); and the connection between the dispossessed elite and reformism (p. 174). Crucially, Hofstadter sees that "in the Gilded Age, to be unselfish suggested not purity but a lack of self" (p. 186). See also Frederic Cople Jaher, *Doubters and Dissenters: Cataclysmic Thought in America, 1885–1918* (New York, Free Press, 1964); and Alan Trachtenberg, "The Politics of Culture," *The Incorporation of America: Culture and Society in the Gilded Age* (New York, Hill & Wang, 1982).
19. John Tomsich, *A Genteel Endeavor: American Culture and Politics in the Gilded Age* (Stanford, Calif., Stanford Univ. Press, 1971), p. 24.
20. Ibid., p. 57.
21. See *U.P.U.C.*, pp. 51–2 and 152–3, and *T.C.C.*, p. 189.
22. T. S. Eliot, untitled review of Van Wyck Brooks's *The Wine of the Puritans*, *Harvard Advocate*, vol. 82, May 7, 1909, p. 80; reprinted by permission of Mrs. Valerie Eliot and Faber & Faber Ltd.
23. Conrad Aiken, "Varieties of Realism: Wilfrid Wilson Gibson, William Aspenwall Bradley, T. S. Eliot," *Scepticisms: Notes on Contemporary Poetry* (New York, Knopf, 1919), pp. 203–5.
24. T. S. Eliot, "A Commentary," *New Criterion*, June 1926, p. 420.
25. See Tomsich, *A Genteel Endeavor*, p. 77, regarding "an aristocracy manqué." Chapter 1 noted the New England, Unitarian preference for social hierarchy, which figures in Eliot's self-declaration as a "royalist in politics," and his interest in Maurras and the *Action Française;* see also *N.S.F.B.*, pp. 175–8, and Bernard Bergonzi, *T. S. Eliot* (New York, Collier, 1972), pp. 115–19.
26. T. S. Eliot, "Henry James II. The Hawthorne Aspect," in *The Shock of Recognition*, ed. Wilson, p. 860.
27. T. S. Eliot, "A Sceptical Patrician," *Athenaeum*, May 23, 1919, p. 362.
28. *I.C.S.*, p. 30.
29. Tomsich, *A Genteel Endeavor*, p. 96.
30. Ibid., p. 112; see also p. 187, on failed genteel institutional alternatives. T. J. Jackson Lears's *No Place of Grace: Antimodernism and the Transformation of*

American Culture, 1880–1920 (New York, Pantheon, 1981) expands Hofstadter's theses into cultural areas; see also *In Pursuit of Beauty: Americans and the Aesthetic Movement* (New York, Metropolitan Museum of Art/Rizzoli, 1986). Stowe Persons's *The Decline of American Gentility* (New York, Columbia Univ. Press, 1973) explores the genteel movement's sociology, whose "mass theory" pervades Eliot's poetry (e.g., Sweeney) and social criticism. Patrick Brantlinger's *Bread and Circuses: Theories of Mass Culture as Social Decay* (Ithaca, N.Y., Cornell Univ. Press, 1983), fits Eliot's suspicions of mass culture into the European tradition.

31. Tomsich, *A Genteel Endeavor,* p. 193. See also Roger B. Stein, "Artifact as Ideology: The Aesthetic Movement in Its American Cultural Context," in *In Pursuit of Beauty,* p. 23, on how the aesthetic movement addressed the period's "absence of a spiritual center" and "offered 'art' as a counterbalance to materialism, though its adequacy as a religious remedy was in doubt."

32. T. S. Eliot, "Literature, Science, and Dogma," *Dial,* March 1927, p. 243.

5. THE SILHOUETTE OF SWEENEY: CULTURES AND CONFLICT

1. *The Waste Land: A Facsimile and Transcript of the Original Drafts,* ed. Valerie Eliot (New York, Harcourt Brace Jovanovich, 1971), quotes T. S. Eliot's February 15, 1920, letter on p. xviii.

2. T. S. Eliot, "Henry James: The Hawthorne Aspect," in *The Shock of Recognition: The Development of Literature in the United States by the Men Who Made It,* ed. Edmund Wilson (Garden City, N.Y.: Doubleday, Doran, 1943), p. 860.

3. John Tomsich, *A Genteel Endeavor: American Culture and Politics in the Gilded Age* (Stanford, Calif., Stanford Univ. Press, 1971), p. 122.

4. "Milton II," *O.P.P.,* p. 160.

5. T. S. Eliot, "Prose and Verse," *Chapbook,* April 1921, p. 9.

6. See T. S. Eliot, "To Criticize the Critic," *T.C.C.,* p. 16, describing his earlier criticism as implicitly defending the poetry he and his friends wrote.

7. See "Andrew Marvell," *S.E.,* pp. 295, 300; for other references to the effect of surprise, see "Andrew Marvell," p. 301; "John Dryden," p. 308; and "Dante," p. 247, all in *S.E.*

8. "Ben Jonson," *S.E.,* p. 155.

9. See "The Metaphysical Poets," p. 284, and "William Blake," p. 317, both in *S.E.;* and Eliot's discussion of the "attractive terror" of a new work of art in "Contemporanea," *Egoist,* June–July 1918, p. 84.

10. T. S. Eliot, "Reflections on Contemporary Poetry," *Egoist,* October 1917, p. 133.

11. *"In Memoriam,"* *S.E.,* p. 333.

12. "The Metaphysical Poets," *S.E.,* pp. 283, 285.

13. T. S. Eliot, "Shakespearian Criticism I. From Dryden to Coleridge," in *A Companion to Shakespeare Studies,* ed. Harley Granville-Barker and G. B. Harrison (New York, Macmillan, 1940), pp. 295–6.

14. "Andrew Marvell," *S.E.,* p. 296.

15. "Philip Massinger," *S.E.,* p. 212.

16. "Ben Jonson," *S.E.*, p. 159.

17. Ibid. See also "Christopher Marlowe," *S.E.*, p. 125, where Eliot states that Marlowe's "intense and serious" poetry achieves its effects by methods resembling those of caricature.

18. T. S. Eliot, "Tarr," *Egoist*, September 1918, p. 105.

19. "John Marston," *S.E.*, p. 229.

20. "The Function of Criticism," *S.E.*, pp. 27–8.

21. T. S. Eliot, "Literature and the Modern World," *American Prefaces*, November 1935, p. 21. See also Eliot's argument that the criticism Irving Babbitt lodged against humanitarianism could be brought with equal justice against Babbitt's own humanism. The humanitarian, wrote Eliot, suppressed the properly human, leaving the animal, while the humanist has suppressed the divine, leaving a "human element which may quickly descend again to the animal from which he has sought to raise it" (T. S. Eliot, "The Humanism of Irving Babbitt," *S.E.*, p. 473).

22. *A.S.G.*, pp. 59–60.

23. T. S. Eliot's father's memoir, for instance, recalled Rev. William Greenleaf Eliot's practice of dispatching his young sons to parishioners' homes and businesses to collect annual subscriptions, so that messy business would not have to be transacted each Sunday morning (Henry Ware Eliot, Sr., "A Brief Autobiography" [William Greenleaf Eliot Papers, University Archives, Washington Univ. Libraries, St. Louis, Mo., n.d.], p. 18). Could the "Mr. Eliot" in "Mr. Eliot's Sunday Morning Service" refer to the reverend grandfather, faithfully conducting Sunday morning services, as well as to his skeptical grandson?

24. F. O. Matthiessen, *The Achievement of T. S. Eliot: An Essay on the Nature of Poetry*, 3d ed. (New York, Oxford Univ. Press, 1958), p. 129.

25. "The Metaphysical Poets," *S.E.*, p. 289.

26. "Shakespeare and the Stoicism of Seneca," *S.E.*, p. 135.

27. Georg Simmel, "The Metropolis and Mental Life," in *On Individuality and Social Forms*, ed. Donald N. Levine (Chicago, Univ. of Chicago Press, 1971), p. 329.

28. "Thoughts After Lambeth," *S.E.*, p. 387. See also Eliot's "The Modern Dilemma," *Christian Register*, October 19, 1933, p. 675, a lecture on this theme to a Unitarian, American audience; and compare the similar apocalyptic mode of the other aestheticists in *C.O.U.S.*, p. iii; *T.A.S.*, pp. 381–2; and *E.H.A.*, pp. 471–2.

29. See Lucy McDiarmid, *Saving Civilization: Yeats, Eliot, and Auden Between the Wars* (Cambridge Univ. Press, 1984).

30. "Burbank," first published in *Art and Letters*, Summer 1919, echoes some phrases in Eliot's review of *The Education*, which had appeared shortly before as "A Sceptical Patrician" in *Athenaeum*, May 23, 1919, p. 362. Similarities are underlined. After calling Adams immature and assigning that immaturity to Adams's failure to unite his senses with his intellect, Eliot states that nothing indicated that Adams's senses bore flowers or fruit: "He remains little Paul Dombey *asking questions.*" Eliot then compared Adams with James, both of whom left descriptions of how they landed at Liverpool "and

descend[ed] at the same hotel." Eliot's review then quotes Adams and James; during the latter's excerpt, one sentence reads, "This doom of inordinate exposure to appearances, aspects, images, every *protrusive* item almost."
31. James, *I.H.,* p. 19.
32. "Culture, after all, is not enough, even though nothing is enough without culture" ("Second Thoughts About Humanism," *S.E.,* p. 487). Though culture still retains primary value, at least Eliot has, by 1929, retreated from the extreme of making it *the* basic evaluative criterion, against which all else is measured. Excluding beauty and art from life and consciousness renders civilization impossible. But neither is it possible to base one's claim to civilization solely on feelings for beauty or the production – and especially the consumption – of art. Although in one direction a sine qua non of civilization – an uncivilized society can produce art, but can we call a society that produces no art completely civilized? – art is only one such value among many others. Isolated and detached as they tended to be from the ordinary life of their societies, aestheticists at times forgot this common sense. That may only confirm the pertinence of their diagnosis, which was in large part a protest. A healthier, more civilized society, however, would not have allowed aesthetic values to become so peripheral and precarious – so much the talismanic property of an elite minority – that to pursue them required exaggerating those values to the point of disfigurement, transforming what was simply a professional rationale into a social and philosophical absolute.

See also Eliot's discussion on the social requirements that give rise to "periods of great art (and in that very restricted sense, great civilization)." Any narrow adherence to one set of values, Eliot wrote, tended to be a "menace." "If your values are religious, then you may say that it is better that a million bodies should burn rather than one soul; if they are aesthetic, you may say that it is better that a million lives should be lost rather than one cathedral; if your values are humanitarian, that it is better that art and religion should perish rather than one man die of hunger" ("A Commentary," *Criterion,* July 1932, pp. 681–2).
33. This passage from Henry James is quoted in Matthiessen, *The Achievement of T. S. Eliot,* p. 55.
34. On the Jamesian social entity, T. S. Eliot, "Henry James: In Memory," in *The Shock of Recognition,* ed. Wilson, p. 856. On the three-thousand-member audience, "Ben Jonson," *S.E.,* p. 159.
35. T. S. Eliot, "Cultural Forces in the Human Order," in *The Prospect for Christendom: Essays in Social Reconstruction,* ed. Maurice B. Reckitt (London, Faber & Faber, 1945), p. 58.
36. James S. Grubb's "When Myths Lose Power: Four Decades of Venetian Historiography," *Journal of Modern History,* March 1986, pp. 43–94, outlines the myth (a free, independent city, geographically unconnected to mainland Italy; a civic-minded, wise, stable patriciate, attentive to the common good; a mixed, harmonious polity living in a just, tolerant, pious republic) and the antimyth (venal, brutal, or tyrannical government; duplicitous, corrupt justice; a contentious and divided populace; economic decline; and moral decadence) as presented in historical writing about Venice. Eliot writes mostly

from the latter antimyth, but in such a way as to invoke the positive myth; as Grubb points out, this procedure is hardly a novel one. This traditional ambivalence persists, for example, in two recent historical studies: Edward Muir, *Civil Ritual in Renaissance Venice* (Princeton, N.J., Princeton Univ. Press, 1981) and Donald E. Queller, *The Venetian Patriciate: Reality Versus Myth* (Urbana, Univ. of Illinois Press, 1986).

37. Matthiessen, *The Achievement of T. S. Eliot,* p. 92.
38. T. S. Eliot, [Review of A. Clutton Brock's *The Ultimate Belief,*] *International Journal of Ethics,* October 1916, p. 127.
39. "Baudelaire," *S.E.,* p. 421.
40. "Dante," *S.E.,* p. 240.
41. T. S. Eliot, "The Influence of Landscape Upon the Poet," *Daedalus,* Spring 1960, pp. 421–2. Compare two hostile critics: In "Review of *Burnt Norton, East Coker,* and *The Dry Salvages,*" in *The Collected Essays, Journalism and Letters of George Orwell,* vol. 2, ed. Sonia Orwell and Ian Angus (London, Penguin, 1970), p. 275, George Orwell called Eliot's poems the "last gasp of a cultural tradition," which spoke only to a *rentier* class able to criticize and feel but unable to act, work, fight, or reproduce themselves. And in *Faith, Reason and Civilization,* excerpted in *T. S. Eliot: A Selected Critique,* ed. Leonard Unger (New York, Rinehart, 1948), p. 37, Harold Laski alleged that Eliot's poetry showed a society approaching "the end of a culture as surely as in the days when Claudian celebrated in his epic the last great triumph of Roman poetry." Eliot felt something similar in attitudes toward his religion, claiming that the situation of belief in the modern world was closer to that of the late Roman Empire than to any other period, especially in its psychological mysticism. Untitled chapter in *Revelation,* ed. John Baillie and Hugh Martin (New York, Macmillan, 1937), p. 27.
42. See *N.S.F.B.,* pp. 41–5, and Bernard Bergonzi, *T. S. Eliot* (New York, Collier, 1972), p. 3.
43. Stephen Spender, "Remembering Eliot," in *T. S. Eliot: The Man and His Work,* ed. Tate, p. 56.
44. Daniel Walker Howe, *The Political Culture of the American Whigs* (Chicago, Univ. of Chicago Press, 1979), p. 73.
45. Ibid., pp. 70–1; Howe's chapter "The Whig Interpretation of History" sets forth the historical myth, the positive pole essential to understanding Adams's and Eliot's disillusion with contemporary American history.
46. *N.T.D.C.,* p. 45.
47. "The Literature of Politics," *T.C.C.,* p. 140.
48. T. S. Eliot, [Review of Georges Sorel's *Reflections on Violence,*] *Monist,* July 1917, pp. 478–9.
49. Frank Kermode, *Romantic Image* (London, Fontana, 1971), p. 156.
50. The sensibility that viewed the American Civil War as the occasion of America's fall from grace subsequently observed the same thing in English history. There is even some reason for doing so. The decades preceding the English Civil War were the ones during which the Puritans settled New England so as to escape English religious conflict. That tension swelled immigration –

including some of Eliot's ancestors – to the American colonies, initially with Puritans to New England and later with (numerically fewer) royalists to the South. It has been argued that these distinct migrations to different regions preserved tensions in the New World that resulted, two centuries later, in the English Civil War having to be refought in North America. See, e.g., William R. Taylor, *Cavalier and Yankee: The Old South and American National Character* (New York, Braziller, 1961). This view was evidently a commonplace of the antebellum Southern self-conception; see Anne Norton, *Alternative Americas: A Reading of Antebellum Political Culture* (Chicago, Univ. of Chicago Press, 1986), p. 257 and passim.

51. *A.S.G.,* p. 16.
52. T. S. Eliot, "A Commentary," *Criterion,* April 1931, p. 484. See also Edmund Wilson's description of how the post–Civil War world affected his father's generation, in *A Piece of My Mind: Reflections at Sixty* (New York, Farrar, Straus, & Cudahy, 1956), pp. 212–14.
53. Prufrock, Gerontion, and Tiresias range from prematurely aged to ancient. The poet who asked, "Why should the aged eagle stretch its wings?" was under forty when the line first appeared in *Commerce,* Spring 1928, p. 622.
54. "Cyril Tourneur," *S.E.,* pp. 189–90; reprinted by permission of Faber & Faber Ltd.
55. T. S. Eliot, "A Sceptical Patrician," *Athenaeum,* May 23, 1919, pp. 361–2.
56. Ibid., p. 362.
57. "The Metaphysical Poets," *S.E.,* p. 286.
58. Ibid., pp. 283, 287.
59. *K.E.P.,* pp. 147–8.
60. See Elisabeth W. Schneider's excellent chapter "The Widening Gyre," in *T. S. Eliot: The Figure in the Carpet* (Berkeley and Los Angeles, Univ. of California Press, 1975), esp. pp. 51–8, one of few attempts to address the shortcomings of "Gerontion." Compare James Longenbach, *Modernist Poetics of History: Pound, Eliot, and the Sense of the Past* (Princeton, N.J., Princeton Univ. Press, 1987), pp. 189–94.
61. Eliot referred to the "damage of a lifetime," of "having been born into an unsettled society" (*A.S.G.,* p. 27). He undoubtedly had in mind the multitude of values competing in an America only superficially recovered from civil conflict. An unsettled society could take other forms, both more literal and more subliminal. Eliot once reminisced about growing up in St. Louis, whose outskirts then touched on Forest Park, where the Olive St. streetcar line had its terminus and which was to Eliot, "as a child, the beginning of the Wild West" (T. S. Eliot, "American Literature and the American Language, *T.C.C.,* p. 44). Eliot's comment on the English Civil War applies to – and doubtless arose from – the aftermath of the American one: "The Civil War is not ended: I question whether any serious civil war ever does end" ("Milton II," *O.P.P.,* p. 148).
62. T. S. Eliot, "Ulysses, Order, and Myth," *Dial,* November 1923, p. 483.
63. The panorama was a popular form of visual art in nineteenth-century America, linking landscape, history painting, spectacle, and documentary in a kind

of performance art, a forerunner of the moving picture. See Barbara Novak, *Nature and Culture: American Landscape and Painting, 1825–1875* (London, Thames & Hudson, 1980), pp. 19–26.

64. T. S. Eliot, "Ulysses, Order, and Myth," *Dial*, November 1923, p. 483.
65. "Tradition and the Individual Talent," *S.E.*, p. 16.
66. "Johnson as Critic and Poet," *O.P.P.*, p. 168.
67. "A Song for Simeon" and "Journey of the Magi," Christian poems using the mythical method, contain characters whose pivotal lives extend before, during, and after the birth and life of Christ. They face a new world, Christ's birth, life, death, resurrection, and dispensation having ruptured time as they know it, cutting them off from a more limited, pre-Christian consciousness. Numerous parallels exist between their sort of realization and that of modern times. One suggests that the twentieth century, having divorced itself as absolutely from its past, may resemble the time just after Christ's appearance and disappearance more nearly than any other. Another suggests that the modern era, like the ancient world at the time of Christ, may face radical religious change and a new – perhaps apocalyptic – dispensation. And as the Christian era began in the desert, so has the modern world prepared the ground for rebirth by destroying it – its cities become the waste land, a spiritual, technological, ecological desert. Eliot establishes an emotional kinship between these poems and the modern world: The exhaustion, the wish to die of Simeon and the Magi resemble that of Gerontion. Each pines for the old order, yet knows it has vanished forever, supplanted irrevocably by something radically new. The difference, of course, is that the new order saved the Magi and Simeon so decisively that they could wish for death, as it were, in good faith. Modern man knows a radically new, unfamiliar world, but the Magi and Simeon's faith, and its compensations, tend to elude him.

6. BEING BETWEEN TWO LIVES: READING THE WASTE LAND

1. See T. S. Eliot's Introduction to Ezra Pound, *Selected Poems* (London, Faber & Gwyer, 1928), p. viii, and E. J. H. Greene, "Jules Laforgue et T. S. Eliot," *Revue de Littérature Comparée,* July–September 1948, p. 365, quoting Eliot's October 18, 1939, letter.
2. T. S. Eliot, "[A Review of] *Baudelaire and the Symbolists: Five Essays.* By Peter Quennell," *Criterion*, January 1930, p. 357.
3. Arthur Symons, *The Symbolist Movement in Literature* (New York, Dutton, 1958), p. 56.
4. Conrad Aiken, "King Bolo and Others," in *T. S. Eliot: A Symposium*, ed. Richard March and Tambimuttu (Freeport, N.Y., Books for Libraries Press, 1968), pp. 20–1.
5. Conrad Aiken, "T. S. Eliot," *Life*, January 15, 1965, p. 92. Harford Powel, in "Notes on the Life of T. S. Eliot, 1888–1910," Master of Arts Thesis, Brown Univ., 1954, p. 42, confirms that Eliot "was something of a dandy in dress" at Harvard. According to a classmate, however, when Eliot attended Smith Academy, "he was always in need of a haircut" and was "rather careless about his clothes and linen" (p. 72). Eliot recorded his attempts to

restrain his neighbors with his umbrella at a performance by Sokalova in "A Commentary," *Criterion,* October 1924, p. 5.

6. *"L'Imitation de Notre Dame de la Lune* includes forty-one poems, of which twenty-three deal with Pierrot and his ideas" (Martin Green, *Children of the Sun: A Narrative of "Decadence" in England after 1918* [New York, Basic Books, 1976], pp. 32–3). See also Warren Ramsey, *Jules Laforgue and the Ironic Inheritance* (New York, Oxford Univ. Press, 1953), pp. 140–6, and Robert F. Storey, *Pierrot: A Critical History of a Mask* (Princeton, N.J., Princeton Univ. Press, 1978).

7. Hugh Kenner, *A Homemade World: The American Modernist Writers* (New York, Morrow, 1975), p. 114.

8. Green, *Children of the Sun,* p. 94. Dandyism, aestheticism, and Symbolism nonetheless affected Pound, Faulkner, and Stevens considerably. See Kenner, *A Homemade World,* on Hemingway, esp. p. 152, and on Faulkner, pp. 195–8; and Daniel Fuchs, *The Comic Spirit of Wallace Stevens* (Durham, N.C., Duke Univ. Press, 1963), pp. 3–30.

9. Ellen Moers, *The Dandy: Brummell to Beerbohm* (Lincoln, Univ. of Nebraska Press, 1960), p. 283. Something about dandyism prefers the aftermath of a war. Parisian, distinctly Anglophile French dandyism began the year after Waterloo with Brummell's flight in disgrace to Calais. Perhaps the most widespread English dandyism (in a culture with an extraordinarily long tradition of it) transpired during the 1920s and 1930s as Green's *Children of the Sun* explores so imaginatively and thoroughly. That era observed a milder manifestation in America, presumably because the United States suffered less during World War I but also because of its deep-seated cultural reservations – understating the matter considerably – about dandy phenomena. Nonetheless, Eustace Tilley (complete with pince-nez, high collar, and top hat), the most famous symbol of American literary dandyism, appeared in 1925, when the *New Yorker* commenced publication. As Stanford M. Lyman and Marvin B. Scott discuss in *The Drama of Social Reality* (New York, Oxford Univ. Press, 1975), pp. 141–6, America created its own, less derivative dandyism after the Civil War, when ex-Confederate soldiers and their sons spread dandyism through the American West as dispossessed but well-dressed *banditti.* The South still supplies America's best literary dandies, such as Tom Wolfe: "I used to solve writer's blocks by going out and getting clothes made, you could use up a lot of time that way" (Peter York, "Tom, Tom, the Farmer's Son," *Style Wars* [London, Sidgwick & Jackson, 1983], p. 225). Social strains – which included, in America at least, an unpopular war – in the late 1960s and early 1970s produced yet another phase of Anglo-American dandyism. Its most dazzling and talented figure was David Bowie, whose life and personae pursue many patterns described here almost note for note.

10. "Mrs. Scratton had me to tea again, and . . . she told me of a summer twilight in the Roman theater at Verona when, sitting between Pound and young Eliot, she had been startled and had said to Eliot, 'Why, you're rouged!' at which he had drawn from his pocket a woman's compact and shown it smiling. I felt the musing lady understood this to have been neither androgyny nor histrionics but something more exceptional and strange" (Robert

Fitzgerald, "The Third Kind of Knowledge," *Atlantic,* June 1980, p. 80). Then there is the incident of the pale green face powder; see John Pearson, *Facades: Edith, Osbert, and Sacheverell Sitwell* (London, Macmillan, 1978), p. 239, and Pearson's references to Virginia Woolf's diary, p. 240. Whatever was going on at Verona, Eliot's writing otherwise cocks an eye at the tradition of the dandy, of Pierrot, of aesthetes, "decadents," and Symbolists, in whose lives a degree of sexual experimentalism or ambivalence frequently surfaces. Farther down the road, conversion to Christianity, particularly the more Catholic varieties (Eliot, by becoming an "anglo-catholic," winks at this tradition even as he places himself within it) seems to go with the territory.

11. "Baudelaire," *S.E.,* p. 423.
12. Ibid., pp. 423–4; emphasis added.
13. Jean Pierrot, *The Decadent Imagination, 1880–1900,* trans. Derek Coltman (Chicago, Univ. of Chicago Press, 1981), p. 45.
14. Examine the defiant sneer and indolent posture in Whistler's portrait of Count Robert de Montesquiou, whose vestigial cane has so withered that it has surrendered any value as either weapon or support. Montesquiou relied on his personality instead. Whistler directs the viewer's attention to the formal surface not only of his aristocratic subject, but of his portrait, which achieves the formally impossible – painting a man wearing a black suit on a black background. See also Philippe Jullian's *Prince of Aesthetes: Count Robert de Montesquiou, 1855–1921* (New York, Viking Press, 1967).
15. "Tradition and the Individual Talent," *S.E.,* p. 21. A passage from "Virgil and the Christian World," *O.P.P.,* pp. 122–3, reflects Eliot's awareness of the way rhetorical craft may transfer attention from the poet to his verse and shows Eliot reacting to the reaction to *The Waste Land.* A poet, Eliot explained, may think his poem expresses only his private experience, with the poetry providing a "means of talking about himself without giving himself away." Readers, however, may regard the same poem as expressing their own secret feelings and a generation's despair or exultation. Eliot's announcement of his classicism, royalism, and Anglo-Catholicism, for instance, doubtless surprised or angered many readers who had interpreted *The Waste Land* as an instrument with which to reject the past by asserting its irrelevance to the new world of the present day. Though their outrage proves it was not, their misreading should have been obvious well before Eliot's retrograde avowal. Such readers had reversed the terms of the poem's evaluation, which indicts the present by dramatizing its disregard of the past.
16. Moers, *The Dandy,* p. 18.
17. Ibid., p. 254, quoting Captain William Jesse's 1844 biography.
18. Ibid., p. 272.
19. See ibid., pp. 122–4, and Roger Shattuck, "How Poetry Got Its Teeth: Paris, 1857 and After," *Western Review,* Winter 1959, p. 179.
20. See Lawrence Stone, *The Crisis of the Aristocracy, 1558–1641* (New York, Oxford Univ. Press, 1965), p. 502, on how "Court" and "Country" came to mean political, psychological, and moral opposites.
21. See Theodore Zeldin, ed., *Conflicts in French Society: Anticlericalism, Education, and Morals in the Nineteenth Century,* (London, Allen & Unwin, 1970).

Consider also Edward Lucie-Smith, *Symbolist Art* (New York, Praeger, 1972), p. 54, linking snobbery, dandyism, and decadence to a series of refusals to participate in some event or acknowledge an individual and generalizing about the negative Symbolist emotional climate. Symbolism, Lucie-Smith writes, was a way of saying no to contemporary moralism, rationalism, and the "crass materialism" of the 1880s; of protesting the oppressive doctrines of naturalism; and of reacting to the defeat of France in the Franco-Prussian War and to the ensuing civil strife of the Commune.

22. "Andrew Marvell," *S.E.,* p. 296.
23. "The Metaphysical Poets," *S.E.,* pp. 289–90. In "Andrew Marvell," pp. 292–3, Eliot again links Donne with Baudelaire and Laforgue, apparently calling Donne as much a dandy as either French poet. Donne, like Baudelaire or Laforgue, invented an "attitude," which Eliot defines as a system of morals or of feeling. Eliot wrote that Donne's "curious personal point of view," appearing at one time, could appear at another time as the "precise concentration of a kind of feeling diffused in the air about him. Donne and his shroud, the shroud and his motive for wearing it, are inseparable, but they are not the same thing."
24. See Philippe Jullian's *Dreamers of Decadence: Symbolist Painters of the 1890's* (New York, Praeger, 1971), and *The Symbolists* (New York, Dutton, 1977); Lucie-Smith's *Symbolist Art;* Robert L. Delevoy's *Symbolists and Symbolism* (New York, Skira Rizzoli, 1978); James L. Kugel, *The Techniques of Strangeness in Symbolist Poetry* (New Haven, Conn., Yale Univ. Press, 1971); and Pierrot, *The Decadent Imagination.* Less helpful is Henry Peyre, *What Is Symbolism?* trans. Emmett Parker (University, Univ. of Alabama Press, 1980). See also a rare treatment of how Symbolist art influenced Americans, Charles C. Eldredge, *American Imagination and Symbolist Painting* (New York, New York Univ. Grey Art Gallery and Study Center, 1979); and Bram Dijkstra, *Idols of Perversity: Fantasies of Feminine Evil in Fin-de-Siècle Culture* (New York, Oxford Univ. Press, 1986), arguing that the modernist painters' formal experiments obscured their fidelity to the previous generation's imagery. Eliot's formally innovative poetry likewise incorporates much Symbolist iconography virtually unchanged.
25. Joseph Frank's "Spatial Form in Modern Literature," *The Widening Gyre: Crisis and Mastery in Modern Literature* (Bloomington, Indiana Univ. Press, 1968), remains an important discussion of these ideas, although his comments on Eliot sometimes falter. A better discussion is "Dialectical Form," Chapter 3 of Anne C. Bolgan's *What the Thunder Really Said: A Retrospective Essay on the Making of "The Waste Land"* (Montreal, McGill–Queen's Univ. Press, 1973). Significantly, her chapter analogizes modern literature with the cinema – a twentieth-century permutation on the ancient relation between poetry and the visual arts. Johannes Fabricius, in *The Unconscious and Mr. Eliot* (Copenhagen, Nyt Nordisk Forlag Arnold Busck, 1967), pp. 30–46, also discusses montage, *The Waste Land,* and the "third thing." *The Diary of Virginia Woolf,* ed. Anne Olivier Bell (London, Hogarth Press, 1978), vol. 2, pp. 67–8, records: "I taxed him with willfully concealing his transitions. [Eliot] said that explanation is unnecessary. If you put it in, you dilute the

facts. You should feel these without explanation." Charles Feidelson's *Symbolism and American Literature* (Chicago, Univ. of Chicago Press, 1953), pp. 49–76, also bears on these issues. Eliot's writing illustrates Feidelson's conclusion that "mid-nineteenth-century America was a proving ground for the issues to which the method of modern literature is an answer" (pp. 75–6). Feidelson's remarks are crucial to understanding that however far Eliot extended his search to European sources, the origins of his dualistic, divided sensibility remained in the American tradition. See especially "Toward Melville: Some Versions of Emerson."

26. *K.E.P.*, p. 100.

27. Compare the echoes between lines 19–30 and 331–58, for instance, or between lines 99–103 and 203–6.

28. Harold Wentworth and Stuart Berg Flexner, *The Dictionary of American Slang,* 2d ed. (New York, Crowell, 1975), p. 579.

29. *N.S.F.B.*, p. 19.

30. See Bertrand Russell's March 27, 1914, letter to Ottoline Morrell, quoted in *Ottoline: The Early Memoirs of Lady Ottoline Morrell,* ed. Robert Gathorne-Hardy (London, Faber & Faber, 1963), p. 257; but see further information of Raphael Demos, who took his degree in 1916, later becoming a professor at Harvard, in *The Autobiography of Bertrand Russell, 1872–1914* (London, Allen & Unwin, 1967), p. 212.

31. *The Waste Land: A Facsimile and Transcript,* ed. Valerie Eliot (New York, Harcourt Brace Jovanovich, 1971), p. 147.

32. *Seaver v. Lindsay Light Co.* (1922) 135 N.E. 329, 330; see also *C. Groom, Ltd. v. Barber* (1914) 1 K.B. 316, 323–4; *Tregelles v. Sewell* (1862) 158 E.R. 600, 604; and *Smith Co. v. Moscahlades* (1920) 183 N.Y.S. 500, 503.

33. Eliot began in the Foreign and Colonial Department of Lloyds Bank, prosaically tabulating balance sheets of foreign banks to show their relative annual performance but seeking to learn "something about the science of money." He was later promoted to settling the bank's prewar German claims and debts, more sophisticated work involving international law and the peace treaties. He ultimately represented the bank in provincial industrial centers, edited a daily sheet of commercial and financial extracts from the foreign press, and wrote a monthly article on foreign currency exchange for *Lloyds Bank Economic Review*. Eliot recalled spending his time at the bank dealing with "sight drafts, acceptances, bills of lading, and such mysteries, and eventually writing articles on the movement of foreign exchanges for the bank magazine" (*On Poetry* [An Address . . . on the Occasion of the Twenty-fifth Anniversary of Concord Academy] [Concord Academy, Mass., 1947], p. 7). See also *The Waste Land: A Facsimile and Transcript,* pp. xi–xii, xviii, xx, and xxviii; Donald Gallup, *T. S. Eliot: A Bibliography* (London, Faber & Faber, 1969), p. 363; and Michael Holroyd, *Lytton Strachey: A Critical Biography* (New York, Holt, Rinehart & Winston, 1968), vol. 2, p. 365.

    For the story of Henry Ware Eliot's business problems, see his "Brief Autobiography" (William Greenleaf Eliot Papers, Washington Univ. Libraries, Saint Louis, Mo., n.d.), p. 57 and appended autograph of Henry W.

Eliot, Sr., on the last unnumbered page of "The Reminiscences of a Simpleton."

34. Two related senses of "corpse" might be mentioned: the literary corpus, the body of an author's work; and the corpus of a trust, the principal or trust *res,* from which the beneficiary receives the income. Having inherited only the beneficial interest in his father's estate in 1919, Eliot felt the effects of this division of a financial corpus into legal and equitable title. His siblings received their share outright, but because Eliot's father disapproved of his residence in England, the principal of Eliot's legacy reverted to his family upon his death, leaving his wife, should he have predeceased her, without the income. This was another reason Eliot cited for staying at the bank, bound to the wheel of commerce (*The Waste Land: A Facsimile and Transcript,* pp. xxvii–xxviii).

35. Wentworth and Flexner, *The Dictionary of American Slang,* p. 395: Plant: "To bury, as a corpse; to bury or cache an object, goods, or money. Since 1860." On Eliot's "Gothic" language in *The Waste Land,* see Michael H. Levenson, *A Genealogy of Modernism: A Study of English Literary Doctrine, 1908–1922* (Cambridge Univ. Press, 1986), p. 174.

36. T. S. Eliot, "London Letter," *Dial,* May 1921, pp. 690–1; reprinted by permission of Mrs. Valerie Eliot and Faber & Faber Ltd. By 1928, Eliot was even lamenting the loss of "good," "grave," and "agreeable" bank buildings in this quarter and their replacement by "grander," "expensive and smart" ones. See "City, City," in "A Commentary," *Criterion,* December 1928, pp. 189–90. Betjeman's observation occurs in John Betjeman, *The City of London Churches* (London, Pitkin Pictorials, 1969), p. 22.

37. "Death By Water" not only renders the final paragraph of "Dans le Restaurant," it also makes some submerged allusions to "Burbank with a Baedeker: Bleistein with a Cigar." A fragment not included in *The Waste Land,* "Dirge" embeds the deceased Bleistein in a Gothic parody of Ariel's song from *The Tempest.* See *The Waste Land: A Facsimile and Transcript,* p. 121. "Burbank," after some "defunctive music undersea," placed Bleistein – like Phlebas – in the "protozoic slime." "Dirge" deposits him "full fathom five." "Those are pearls that were his eyes" in *The Tempest* and *The Waste Land;* in "Burbank," combining Eugenides' single eye and ironically comparing the live Bleistein to the pearls in the dead Phlebas' eyes, Bleistein singly stares with a "lustreless protrusive eye."

38. *The Waste Land: A Facsimile and Transcript,* pp. 50–1.

39. See Chapter 13, "The Perilous Chapel," in Jessie L. Weston, *From Ritual to Romance* (New York, Anchor, 1957), pp. 175–88.

40. Levenson, *A Genealogy of Modernism,* p. 200.

41. Eliot wrote that Bradley's Absolute responded only to an imaginary demand of thought and satisfied only an imaginary demand of feeling. Though it pretended to make finite centres cohere, in the end it turned out to be merely the assertion that they do. "This assertion," Eliot concluded, "is only true so far as we here and now find it to be so" ("Leibniz' Monads and Bradley's Finite Centres," *K.E.P.,* p. 202).

42. T. S. Eliot, "London Letter," *Dial*, September 1921, p. 453.

43. See T. S. Eliot's November 6, 1921, letter to Richard Aldington from Lausanne, Switzerland, where Eliot was undergoing psychological treatment from Dr. Roger Vittoz, quoted in *The Waste Land: A Facsimile and Transcript*, p. xxii.

44. On the "single-protagonist theory," see Robert Langbaum, "New Modes of Characterization in *The Waste Land*," in *Eliot in His Time: Essays on the Occasion of the Fiftieth Anniversary of "The Waste Land,"* ed. A. Walton Litz (Princeton, N.J., Princeton Univ. Press, 1973); Stanley Sultan, *Ulysses, "The Waste Land," and Modernism: A Jubilee Study* (Port Washington, N.Y., Kennikat Press, 1977); and Calvin Bedient, *He Do the Police in Different Voices: "The Waste Land" and Its Protagonist* (Chicago, Univ. of Chicago Press, 1986). But see Levenson, *A Genealogy of Modernism*, pp. 186–93.

45. "Conclusion," *U.P.U.C.*, p. 151.

46. "Matthew Arnold," *U.P.U.C.*, pp. 113–14; reprinted by permission of Faber & Faber Ltd.

47. *N.T.D.C.*, p. 72.

48. "Nebula": "Andrew Marvell," *S.E.*, p. 300; "tentacular roots": "Ben Jonson," *S.E.*, p. 155; "undertone": "John Ford," *S.E.*, p. 203; "doubleness": "John Marston," *S.E.*, p. 229.

49. "Ben Jonson," *S.E.*, p. 158.

50. T. S. Eliot, "The Method of Mr. Pound," *Athenaeum*, October 24, 1919, p. 1065.

51. T. S. Eliot, Preface to St.-John Perse, *Anabasis* (New York, Harcourt Brace, 1949), p. 10; reprinted by permission of Faber & Faber Ltd. Compare *K.E.P.*, p. 75, disagreeing that a great poet's ideas were arbitrary. By contrast, in "really great imaginative work," logical necessity bound up the connections, and any apparent irrelevance stemmed from the poet's use of terms with "more or other than their normal meaning, and to those who do not thoroughly penetrate their significance the relation between the aesthetic expansion and the objects expressed is not visible."

52. *U.P.U.C.*, p. 106.

53. "Baudelaire," *S.E.*, p. 426.

54. "What Dante Means To Me," *T.C.C.*, p. 126; reprinted by permission of Faber & Faber Ltd. Symons's *The Symbolist Movement in Literature*, p. 59, further suggests what the French tradition gave Eliot's earliest work. Even through his disdain for the world, Symons wrote, Laforgue retained a heightened consciousness of daily life, seeing "*l'Inconscient* in every gesture," but unable to see it without these gestures. Compare T. S. Eliot, "Eeldrop and Appleplex," *Little Review*, May 1917, p. 8, describing Eeldrop – Eliot's persona in the story – as "a sceptic, with a taste for mysticism."

55. "What Dante Means to Me," *T.C.C.*, p. 134; reprinted by permission of Faber & Faber Ltd.

56. Ibid.; reprinted by permission of Faber & Faber Ltd.

57. T. S. Eliot, Introduction to Samuel L. Clemens, *The Adventures of Huckleberry Finn* (London, Cresset Press, 1950), pp. viii–x; reprinted by permission of Faber & Faber Ltd.

58. "From Poe to Valéry," *T.C.C.*, p. 42.

Index

Adams, Henry, 4, 88, 111, 112, 116, 118, 119, 120, 133, 134–44, 146, 147, 148, 149, 150, 151, 152, 164, 173, 174, 175, 177, 179–81, 182, 200, 247 n.1, 248 nn. 3 and 16, 250 n.18, 252–3 n.30, 254 n.45
  Education of Henry Adams, The, 4, 113, 134–42, 164, 165, 179
  Mont-Saint-Michel and Chartres, 142–4, 149
Adams, James Truslow, 110
Adams, John, 110
Adams, John Quincy, 173
Adams, Samuel, 135
aestheticism, vii, 21, 22, 27, 28, 33, 38, 42, 66, 69, 71, 74, 105, 113–17, 128, 134–5, 139–40, 144–6, 148–53, 158, 160, 164–5, 167, 171, 176, 182–3, 184, 186, 200, 210–11, 215, 221–2, 244 nn.7, 8, and 9, 245 n.10, 248 n.3, 251 n.31, 252 n.28, 253 n.32, 255–6 n.63, 256–7 nn.5, 8, and 10
Aiken, Conrad, 150, 186–7
Alger, Horatio, Jr., 25
ambiguity, 29, 37, 38, 44, 60, 75, 92, 96, 97, 99, 111, 131, 162, 176, 192–3, 195, 198, 209, 212, 216, 218, 221, 235–6 n.4
"literary" (Empson's seventh

type), 40, 59–60, 68–9, 71, 72–3, 160, 163, 221
  philosophical, 8, 45, 51, 55, 76
  psychological, 22, 45, 58, 76, 162
ambivalence, viii, 30, 45, 58–60, 69, 71, 76, 95, 116, 187, 192, 207–8, 218, 257–8 n.10
American culture and society, vii–viii, 5, 22, 28, 70, 74, 76, 83, 99, 108, 110, 112–17, 144–53, 173–4, 177–8, 182, 188, 191, 207–8, 217, 226 n.24, 235 n.1, 244 nn.8 and 9, 245 nn.10 and 13, 247 n.23, 249 nn.8 and 11, 251 n.31, 254–5 n.50, 257 nn. 8 and 9, 259–60 n.25; *see also* aestheticism; United States, Eliot's views on history, society, and culture
Anderson, Quentin, 249 n.8
Andrewes, Lancelot, 23
Anglo-Catholicism, 5, 19–20, 27, 229 n.62, 239 n.36, 257–8 n.10, 258 n.15
Aristotle, 64, 69, 70, 73, 157
Arnold, Matthew, 102
Augustine of Hippo, St., 201

Babbitt, Irving, 16, 17, 227–8 n.51, 252 n.21

263

102, 170, 182, 187, 192, 193,
199, 203, 216, 220, 237 n.29, 238
n.31, 238–9 n.34

Jackson, Andrew, 111–12, 147, 173,
249 nn.8 and 11
James, Henry, 21, 68–9, 110, 111,
112, 113, 116, 118, 119, 120,
122, 123, 124–34, 135, 137, 139,
140, 143, 146, 147, 148, 149,
150, 151, 152, 164, 167, 169,
174, 182, 247 n.11, 247–8 n.2,
250 n.18, 252–3 n.30
American Scene, The, 124, 125, 126,
128, 132, 164, 250 n.13
Italian Hours, 126, 128, 133, 149,
166
James, William, 77, 89–91, 247–8 n.2
Jarrell, Randall, vii
Jay, Gregory, 240 n.37
Johnson, Anthony L., 238 n.33
Johnson, Samuel, 183
Jonson, Ben, 104, 157–8, 212–13
Joyce, James, 182–4, 234 n.10

Kahn, Gustave, 186
Keats, John, 141
Kermode, Frank, 177
Kolko, Gabriel, 249 n.9
Kuklick, Bruce, 237 n.18, 244 n.7
Kyd, Thomas, 103

Laforgue, Jules, 33–4, 46, 95, 186–8,
190, 192, 211, 215, 232 n.43, 259
n.23, 262 n.54
L'Imitation de Notre Dame de la lune,
188, 257 n.6
language and meaning, Eliot's views
on, 26, 54–7, 73, 102–7, 155,
192, 194, 210, 212, 216, 221, 230
n.13, 234 n.29, 238–9 n.34, 242
n.9, 262 n.51
Laski, Harold, 254 n.41
Levenson, Michael H., 206, 209
Lewis, Wyndham, 36
Lobb, Edward, 238–9 n.34
Lucie-Smith, Edward, 258–9 n.21

Machiavelli, Niccolo, 18, 23
Maeterlinck, Count Maurice, 106
Marlowe, Christopher, 103
Marston, John, 159, 162
Antonio and Mellida, 165
Marvell, Andrew, 40, 156, 157, 192
Matthiessen, F. O., 5, 162, 169, 226
n.24
McDougall, William, 236 n.7
Melville, Herman, 84–6, 241 n.16
Miller, J. Hillis, 237 n.29
Milton, John, 18, 33
modernism, 78–9, 112–13, 117, 120,
128, 149, 150, 155, 164, 176,
181, 183, 244 n.9, 259 n.24
Moers, Ellen, 188–9
Monroe, Harriet, 94
Montesquiou, Count Robert de, 258
n.14
moral views of T. S. Eliot, 8–9, 12,
18, 28, 42–3, 59, 66, 156, 158–9,
160, 161, 189, 200, 217, 221, 259
n.23
More, Paul Elmer, 33, 74, 231 n.36
Myers, F. H., 245 n.10

New England, vii, 1, 2–3, 12, 18–19,
110, 111, 125, 134–5, 136, 137,
150, 177, 226 n.24, 228 nn.60
and 61, 243 n.1, 250 n.25
Nietzsche, Friedrich, 28, 76
Norton, Charles Eliot, 149

opposites and unity of opposites, ix,
9, 17, 32, 38, 40, 42, 43–4, 53,
58–60, 63, 64–5, 68–70, 71–3,
74, 75, 76–7, 108, 160, 161, 163,
187, 203, 207, 212, 214, 215,
220–1, 233 n.1, 235–6 n.4, 238
nn.31 and 33, 239 n.36, 239–40
n.37; *see also* philosophy, poetry,
and Christianity, continuities
among
Original Sin, 6–9, 19–20, 26, 161,
189, 226 n.24; *see also* Eliot, Rev.
William Greenleaf
Orwell, George, 254 n.41